The Unadorned Thread of Yoga

THE *YOGA-SŪTRA OF PATAÑJALI* IN ENGLISH

A Compilation of English Translations
of Śri Patañjali's Exposition on the Yoga Darśana

by
Salvatore Zambito

Foreword by
Swami Veda Bhāratī

The Yoga-Sūtras Institute Press
Poulsbo, Washington

Cover design by Heart of Art Design (www.heartofartdesign.com)

Published by
The Yoga-Sūtras Institute Press

Printed in the United States of America

For information contact:
The Yoga-Sūtras Institute Press
P.O. Box 964
Sequim, WA 98382
Yoga-Sūtras Institute website: www.yogasutras.net

Libaray of Congress Cataloging-in-Publication Data

Zambito, Salvatore, 1949-
The Unadorned Thread of Yoga: The Yoga-Sūtra of Patañjali in English / Salvatore Zambito
Bibliography
ISBN: 0-9787676-0-8
1. Yoga. 2. Yoga Sutras. 3. Patañjali
Txu1-340-966 2007

First Edition

ACKNOWLEDGEMENTS

The author wishes to thank the following publishers and copyright holders for their permission to reprint their translations of *The Yoga-Sūtra of Patañjali.*

Abhyasa Ashram: For sūtra translations from *YOGA SUTRAS OF PATANJALI: THE 196 SUTRAS BY PATANJALI,* by Swami Jnaneshvara Bharati. Published by Abhyasa Ashram, Ft. Walton Beach, FL. Copyright 2004 by Swami Jnaneshvara Bharati. Used by permission of Swami Jnaneshvara Bharati.

American Sanskrit Institute: For sūtra translations from *The Yoga Sutra Workbook: The Certainty of Freedom* by Vyaas Houston. Published by the American Sanskrit Institute, Brick, NJ. Copyright 1995 by Vyaas Houston.

Arya, Pandit Usharbudh: For sūtra translations from *Yogasutras: Padartha and Bhavartha.* Unpublished manuscript. Copyright 1974 by Usharbudh Arya, Ph.D./Swami Veda Bhāratī. Used by personal permission.

Inner Traditions International: For sūtra translations from *The Yoga-Sūtra of Patañjali, A New Translation and Commentary* by Feuerstein, Georg. Published by Inner Traditions International, Rochester, VT, 05767. Copyright 1979, 1989 by Georg Feuerstein. To order call 1-800-246-8648.

Integral Yoga Publications: For sūtra translations excerpted from THE YOGA SUTRAS OF PATANJALI. Translation and commentary by Shri Swami Satchidananda. Copyright 1978, 1984, 1990 by Satchidananda Ashram—Yogaville, by permission of Satchidananda Ashram—Yogaville, VA.

Lucis Publishing Co.: For sūtra translations from *The Light Of The Soul, Its Science and Effect* by Bailey, Alice A. Copyright 1955 by Lucis Publishing Co.. pp.3-6; 115-118; 237-241; 373-375. No part of this book may be reprinted except by permission of the holder of copyright, Lucis Trust, New York, NY.

Ramakrishna-Vivekananda Center: For sūtra translations from RAJA YOGA by Swami Vivekananda as published by the Ramakrishna-Vivekananda Center of New York. U.S. Copyright 1955 by Swami Nikhilananda, trustee of the estate of Swami Vivekananda.

Random House, Inc.: From THE YOGA SUTRAS OF PATANJALI by Patanjali, translated by Alistair Shearer, Copyright 1982 by Alistair Shearer. Used by permission of Bell Tower, a division of Random House, Inc., New York, NY.

Theosophical Publishing House: For sūtra translations from *The Science of Yoga*, translation and commentary by I.K. Taimni. Copyright 1961 by Theosophical Publishing House, Wheaton, IL.

Vedanta Press: For sūtra translations excerpted from *How to Know God: The Yoga Aphorisms of Patanjali* by Swami Prabhavanada and Christopher Isherwood. Published by the Vedanta Press, Hollywood, CA 90068-3996. Copyright 1996 by Vedanta Press.

For ordering information please see Appendix III.

CONTENTS

FOREWORD

The Unadorned Thread of Yoga is an important and long overdue endeavour. It fulfils a major need for the serious Anglophone students of yoga as it provides them the opportunity to see the variety of possible interpretations of each Yoga sūtra side-by-side on a single page. It is an unprecedented guide to understanding the subtle variety of possible interpretations.

In recent decades many people in the West have begun the study of Yoga and it is becoming ever more popular. Almost every other issue of Time Magazine mentions Yoga or relaxation or meditation or breathing. This was not the case thirty years ago. But where this Yoga has come from—that it has emerged from enormous, complex, ancient traditions—remains, for the most part, unknown. Few know the depth and the extent of Yoga and that where this much has come from there are yet enormous treasures waiting to be revealed.

The Yoga-Sūtra of Patañjali is the basic text of Yoga theory and practice. Gradually, students are being drawn, irresistibly, to it. At present, many people can do all kinds of twists and poses, but without the essential spiritual awareness. This form of yoga has proved beneficial and helpful, otherwise it would not have become so popular.

However, the true foundation of Yoga is to be found in the *Yoga-Sūtras of Patañjali.*

The dates of the great sage, Patañjali, cannot be ascertained. From the point of view of modern western scholarship it could be a text composed around 4th century A.D. The Indian tradition places it in the far away antiquity of the age of the Ṛṣis[1]. Regardless, Patañjali's 196 statements completely and competently summarize the entire theoretical and applied fields of Yoga.

As Salvatore shows us in this volume, a surprising number of scholarly, as well as saintly, figures have produced English translations of Patanjali's *Sūtra*—over thirty have been collected by Salvatore and twelve are presented here. Yet more may come into light! This does not include the translations in other European and Asian languages.

Why so many translations? Several significant difficulties present themselves when we try to present the *Yoga-Sūtras* to Western students in their language(s).

The first difficulty I will address is rather large.

Yoga has dimensions at the transcendental level, immanent cosmic level, and individual level. To be fully understood, every term in Yoga has to be seen simultaneously at all of these levels. Comprehension depends on the gradation of consciousness and awareness that the exponent and the student bring to the study. The masters advise never to read Yoga texts and Yoga terminologies at just one level. Strive to be

---

[1] The Indian concept of cyclical time views the history of the current cycle of this planet to be close to two billion years and all human history is conceived to be on that scale. In that time scale the age of the Ṛshis ended 5106 years ago (as of 2006 C.E.).

aware of the totality of levels, all in one. A seeker's interpretation and understanding of the definitions is at the level of consciousness s/he has reached. Otherwise, one can write a book to define a single word and yet will never reach completion.

Translating philosophical terminologies between all languages, even modern ones, evades precision. Freud, translated into English, is different from the original German. For example, there is no single word for *mind* in German. *Geist* can be mind, soul, or ghost, as in *Holy Ghost*. However, Freud didn't use *geist*, as it was not equivalent. He used *bewusst/onbewusst—known/unknown*, or that of which one is aware or that of which one is not aware. This is translated into English as *conscious/unconscious*. Translating from Sanskrit to modern languages is far more complex.

The language that we use today is for convenience in modern life. When one communicates only in the present-day language one suffers a great disadvantage in trying to absorb the *Yoga-Sūtra*. One misses whole ranges and connections of subtleties and depths. One has not read the *Yoga Sūtras* if one has not read it in the original Sanskrit and even then much is missed if one (A) does not have access into the methods of unveiling the subtleties of Sanskrit, and (B) has not the personal experience of the practices prescribed in the text.

Most modern languages are mono-lateral. They are confined in their ability to convey dimensions, and therefore cannot accurately explain philosophy, which, by its nature spans many dimensions simultaneously. Sanskrit is a multi-lateral language. That is to say that Sanskrit can precisely convey, through vocabulary and grammatical tools, concepts that embrace dimensions beyond the three (plus time) that confine modern Western language. While some languages like classical Greek, classical Hebrew and Arabic have sophisticated linguistic tools, Sanskrit is unique in the way it expresses philosophy in the completeness of multi-lateral experience. Such experiential philosophy requires this multi-lateral language.

An example of this dimensional confusion surfaces when people ask such questions as: "Swami, are the chakras located in front or are they back in the spine?" As though, in the energy realm, there is a front and a back! There isn't. "Well, they've got to be somewhere (!)" students protest. *Somewhere*—that's a concept of space. Does consciousness have a relevance to spaces? The question is irrelevant. It doesn't apply, the way the principles of Euclid and Newton don't apply to quantum physics. However, the students' minds, conditioned by the assumptions in the structure of their modern language, struggle to grasp this multi-laterality—nay, the transcendental non-laterality.

The reality of chakra "physics" can be conveyed in Sanskrit, but not in modern Western languages. Here, poetry is not similitude but itself the reality. In a certain sense, we might say that Sanskrit has a meta-grammatical, multi-dimensional, trans-lateral "quantum" structure available to it.

Because they address this quantum aspect, the sūtras have their own science in construction. There is a whole different science for interpreting sūtras and only those who are raised in the tradition of Sanskrit grammar and Sanskrit logic can know these rules fully.

Without knowing those rules one cannot translate any sūtra text with full precision. The result is the large number of translations with varying degrees of approximate accuracy. These translations are useful within their limits, but let us not deceive ourselves in thinking that we are receiving the complete picture (A) from any one translation, or (B) even by combining all the available translations together. They are all accurate; they are all short of the fullness of the original.

A further complication presents itself in that all usage of language is imagination! It is *vikalpa*, the second vṛtti—by which words exist, but realities don't (YS. I.9). It is the most sinister vṛtti, the vikalpa—words exist, but realities don't exist that relate to those words; hence, the illusion called language.

An example I often give is this: an astronaut believes in God and before lift-off, he stands, looks up at the sky, and prays to God for success and a safe journey. He sees up there a Moon, his destination. His space ship takes off and he arrives at the Moon. He stands there on the Moon. He comes out of his spaceship; stands on the surface of the Moon and wishes to thank God for having given him thus far a safe journey. He stands and looks up and what does he see up there, from the Moon? The Earth! Up there from the Moon. Shall he pray: "Thy will be done on the Moon as it is on Earth above!"

What happened? Did we turn the universe upside-down? In this form of vikalpa confusion, we still take this up and down so seriously even though we realize that it is so relative that in a larger sense they do not exist at all. Even after hearing this, we continue to do the same. The orientation to which we have been conditioned by language does not change easily.

Students sometimes ask: "Am I ready to teach such-and-such a meditation? What level of meditation am I ready to teach?"

This is another vikalpa confusion: one needs to understand that a technique is only a boat—a boat is not the river. People who have only the boat—the technique—may have memorized the words of the technique, but this does not mean that they are launched in the stream of consciousness and flowing. The meditation guide must be absorbed in the flowing stream of consciousness.

Numerous examples of this kind of vikalpa can be given—where words exist and realities don't match.

So, in Yoga, we go to those prime realities, which exist. We directly enter prime reality through practice. This is related to the quantum element discussed earlier.

Another part of the challenge in sūtra translation lies in the fact, as suggested above, that the sūtras are guides to practice, not treatises of philosophical hypotheses or speculations. There are two kinds of commentators in Sanskrit traditions: those who are scholars and those who are practitioners. Practitioners are few. Scholars are many.

The great sages who composed—rather, received the revelation of—the sūtra texts, in the state of samādhi, were masters of practices. These yogis penetrated through all their koshas, the casings, of which our personalities are constituted. What they saw and experienced, methodically, became the technique. The sūtras then became the laboratory notes of the Masters passing on the techniques and insights.

Often, those who are translating have no idea how or where the material under consideration connects to what practices. Translations from dictionaries and grammatical tables amount to guesswork. The practices are central to the sūtras if one can read them. One can read the sūtras, in this sense, through the direct perception that is attained through practice alone. The practices lead to this direct immersion into the experience of the quantum dimension, the prime reality of the yogin.

All this being said, there is no desire to discourage a student's exploration of the *Yoga-Sūtra* linguistically. On the contrary! Simply stated, one has to start somewhere and that, necessarily, is in one's own language. If that language is English, *The Unadorned Thread of Yoga* will be of immense help.

Salvatore has a grasp of the aforementioned difficulties. *The Unadorned Thread* presents each sūtra on two pages. The text analysis portion on the left will convey roots, prefixes, and suffixes in a manner that will make greater depth of understanding available for English-speaking students. The comparison portion, on the right, will illustrate the rich variety of interpretation and give a hint of the frustration that attends to translating the *Yoga-Sūtra*.

One suggestion to the reader: the way one superimposes one picture upon another, superimpose all thirty-plus translations one upon the other. Let that composite picture tickle your intellectual curiosity and spiritual aspiration. It is the composite meaning that will give you a multi-lateral dimension. Here we give one example as a first exercise. Read all twelve translations of the first sūtra, each separately. Now let us read them as a composite (still incomplete) exposition:

> Now at this auspicious moment of transition,
> with Prayers for divine blessings,
> commences the exposition of and instruction in the discipline and final teaching
> of the sacred art of yoga, the Science of Union,
> following the past Tradition.

As a translator's understanding grows s/he may translate the same sūtra differently at a later period in life. The translation by Arya[2] presented herein is an early one. Perhaps a future edition of *The Unadorned Thread* will include later translations for such comparative purpose. We promise that in the next edition of Arya's work the translation will be different, a little more complete, but still not perfect.

---

[2] Usharbudh Arya is Swami Veda Bhāratī's pre-renunciate name.

In time, as the student absorbs the Sūtra in English, s/he will probably reach a point where the inadequacies of English will be felt. I am certain Salvatore would join me in encouraging Yoga students to begin the practice of Sanskrit. Yes—Sanskrit is a spiritual practice. In fact it may be regarded more as a spiritual practice than a language per se.

Until that day, however, *The Unadorned Thread of Yoga* will serve well in making the *Yoga-Sūtra* available to English speakers in the most comprehensive manner possible.

For rendering a very special tool for the understanding of the *Yoga-Sūtras*, *The Unadorned Thread of Yoga* has my enthusiastic endorsement.

May Patañjali's spirit descend into your mind and lift you
to the heights of Supreme Solitude (kaivalya)[3].

Swami Veda Bharati
Swami Rama Sadhaka Grama
Rishikesh In the Foothills of the Himalayas

On Fifth Night of the Dark Fortnight of the Lunar Chaitra Month
Of the Year named Vilambi 5107 of Kali Era,
Year 1972949107 of the Current Creation Era Known as Varaha-kalpa.

---

[3] The full meaning of *kaivalya*, the goal enunciated in the YS, is Solitude, the *puruṣa* (Consciousness Principle) becoming solo with no further interest in such lowly products of *prakṛti* (material principle) as mind.

PREFACE: BIOGRAPHY OF A BOOK

One evening in the fall of 1981, after I concluded the meditation class I was conducting, one of my students remained to ask a question. I didn't need to frame an original reply because five short statements in the ancient Yoga text, *The Yoga-Sūtra of Patañjali*, addressed her point directly. Instead of presenting just one version of these *sūtras*, I made a comprehensive presentation by showing her how several different translators from various schools of thought and historical periods—each with a different command of Sanskrit and English—had interpreted the sūtras, each contributing a unique insight. After about an hour she stated emphatically, "You really ought to have all these translations side-by-side under one cover. Then you could compare them without spreading all these books all over the floor. It would be invaluable." *The Unadorned Thread* was conceived in that moment. The idea was an obvious one and a logical unfoldment in my already long and devoted relationship with Yoga.

My fascination with Yoga began one evening in 1954 when I was seven years old. My favorite television program, *Science Fiction Theater*, was ending, and behind the slowly ascending letters of the final credits were scenes of dramatic scientific experiments in progress. One of them commanded my rapt attention: a small, dark-skinned man in strange shorts was sitting with his legs intertwined, each foot resting on the opposite thigh. He was wired up to an array of important-looking instruments. Seated in this position, he had somehow isolated and flexed the abdominal muscle that runs between the lower ribs and the pubic bone. The muscles on the sides had been pulled upward and inward toward his back, making the central muscle very prominent. This alone was remarkable, but then he started rolling them all from side to side!

That night I agreed to take my bath with uncharacteristic enthusiasm. I found I could braid my legs like the little guy on TV, but I couldn't flex my abdominals in that position. However, when I got on my knees, *voilá*—success! I could even roll them a little.

That evening was my introduction to Hatha Yoga, through the *Udyanna Bandha* and *Nauli Kriya* (the exercises I had imitated).

The interest stayed with me and I did what research I could through high school, but finding information on Yoga theory and practice in the early 1960s presented a much more challenging literature search than it does now.

When I was nineteen a friend invited me to a class taught by Margaret Yeoman at the Sivananda Yoga Center in Chicago. When we were all gathered in the studio she instructed us to lie down and immediately established an atmosphere of quiet by suggesting that we leave our cares outside the door for next hour, and for that time allow ourselves to be just with ourselves. She then guided us, clearly and unhurriedly, though a series of movements and relaxations.

When the session ended, my body sat up, but all "I-ness" had stopped. All mental operations had gently, effortlessly, and undramatically ceased. In their place was a silence, a direct "knowing-ness" with no sense of separations. It was a state of peace that passed even the need to understand it. I have never been able to describe what happened because this state of consciousness is too simple to express in English—no subject, no predicate. The concept doesn't even exist in English. The words of an old Zen Roshi capture the experience: "The bottom dropped out of my bucket."

Margaret came over, gracefully squatted in front of me, and said, "You have clearly been a yogi for many lifetimes. You are always welcome here and you are never to let lack of money keep you from coming. You can perform Karma Yoga in exchange for classes." She was very sensitive, for at that moment in my life I was a penniless, unemployed hippie.

That was my start.

I attended classes at least once and usually twice a day and learned that a Karma Yogi is a person devoted to spiritual service, generally of the most mundane and practical sort. When almost a year had passed, Margaret said the time had come for me to begin teaching. I was vehemently reluctant. When I told her that the only thing I had in abundance was ignorance, she readily agreed. "However," she continued, "this sense of ignorance will only grow as you learn more. It is important that you responsibly share what little you have as you go along." With her guidance, I began to teach. I loved it.

Another year passed, and in spite of the challenges in my personal practice of postures, breathing, teaching, and caring for the studio, I found myself feeling stuck. I was frustrated because I felt that nothing was happening. Margaret was not concerned at all. She said that fluctuations in practice are to be expected, and besides, "*Things happening* is not the point of Yoga." A real understanding of this was to elude me for years.

That summer I had an opportunity to spend half a day with Peter Max, an artist who had a high public profile in the 1960s. I also knew him to be an experienced Yogi who had brought his guru, Swami Satchidananda, to America and had helped him establish the Integral Yoga Center in New York. When we had a few minutes alone, I told him about my feeling of stuckness. He thought for a moment and asked, "Do you meditate?"

I had to answer "No."

"That may be what's changing for you. I'd say you've probably taken Hatha about as far as you can for now. Have you ever heard of *The Yoga-Sūtra of Patañjali*?"

Again I had to say "No," but on hearing the title I felt a quivering movement deep in my body.

"Everything you need to know about meditation is in that book. I'll send you a copy."

Three weeks later, true to his word, I received my first copy of the *Yoga-Sūtra*. It was *How to Know God* by Swami Prabhavananda, and my relationship with the *Sūtra* began. I read it in two days. I found it somewhat interesting, but dry and abstract, and couldn't quite relate to it. However, I *knew* it was important and resolved to master it.

In 1969, another friend opened a door for me by introducing me to the Theosophical Society. Under the guidance of Michael Kaprilian at Theosophical Society meetings, I again entered the peaceful stillness that I had experienced in my first Hatha Yoga class. I discovered that the peace that confounds all communication is meditation. I found that it was a repeatable experience, though, at that point, not a predictable outcome. Mr. Kaprilian gradually brought me to a preliminary understanding that the point of meditation is the practice itself rather than a drive for a desired state of consciousness.

At the Theosophical Society I came across several more volumes of the *Yoga-Sūtra*, some with significant variations in translation. More interpretations of Patañjali's work moved into my library. The *Sūtra* continued to intrigue me, but still, something indefinable was lacking.

Then I found *The Light of the Soul*, Alice A. Bailey's contribution to the *Yoga-Sūtra* collection. This book had the missing key, but it was in neither the translation nor the commentary. The transforming element, oddly enough, was the format of the book itself. At the beginning of each chapter, the sūtras were presented in continuous, or running, translation without the interruptions of commentary. Suddenly, I "got" the *Yoga-Sūtra*. The continuity flowing through the sūtras, the "thread" braiding the sūtras together from beginning to end, was clearly apparent. When read in context, the sūtras, individually and in full text, shimmered.

Since that time about seventy-five percent of my reading in the *Yoga-Sūtra* has been without commentary, allowing the sūtras to speak for themselves. Reading the *Sūtra* is meditative in itself and aids the unfoldment of intuition. Although it is composed of 196 statements, the *Yoga-Sūtra* is a single organism, and as such it must also be grasped as a whole unit without the distraction of commentary. My experience has been that while informed opinion (commentary) can be useful, even illuminating, it is more helpful for providing definition, elaboration, and suggesting emphasis than for primary understanding.

Over the years I worked with many meditation groups, sometimes as student, sometimes as teacher, eventually retiring to solitary meditation practice in 1975 with the companionship and direction of the *Yoga-Sūtra* and the *Bhagavad-Gita* (also without commentary). In 1981, Dr. Usharbudh Arya drew me out and I took initiation in his spiritual lineage. For about two years I taught meditation under his direction, preparing students for initiation by him or Swami Rama. The idea for this book surfaced in that period. Then I retired to solitary study and practice once again.

After years of collecting the *Sūtra*, I had quite a library of books with the same title. Because of complexities in Sanskrit and the fact that certain concepts in the Vedic civilization do not exist in Western civilization (hence we have no vocabulary for them), a wide variety of authorities have produced over thirty translations in English since the late 19th Century. Translations can vary so greatly at times as to almost seem like different books.

The Unadorned Thread of Yoga provides a comprehensive and readily accessible handbook for study in the essential text of Yoga, in English, by utilizing this diversity in a compendium of translations. The rationale for these variances will be discussed in the sub-chapter, *Why So Many Translations of the Same Book?* and explored further in *Why So Many Translations of the Same Book? (Cont.).*

The circumstances for this compilation to emerge had been slowly arranging themselves and in September 1990, several important pieces fell together. First, after many years without adding to my collection, I acquired a number of significant new contributions to the *Yoga-Sūtra* opus. Second, the computer hardware and word processing software to format columns in a convenient and straightforward way came on the market and to me. Third, and more than I had ventured to ask for, was Gila May. Not only did she provide the software for the project, she gave the book its initial format and entered ten of the *Sūtra* translations. Her experience of publishing a small newspaper for years enabled her to complete that portion of the project in about a month.

The Unadorned Thread of Yoga has been produced primarily with meditators in mind. Particularly, it is a tool for Western Yogis and Yoginis who are being drawn to meditation or are adding meditation to their primarily physical Hatha Yoga practice. It will also be an invaluable resource for scholars of Yoga, the *Yoga-Sūtras*, and Indian studies. *The Unadorned Thread of Yoga* proposes to present an expanded view of this ancient system of personal discipline that integrates physical, psychological, and spiritual practices.

The Unadorned Thread of Yoga assumes that the reader has familiarity with Yoga tradition and history. If readers find this interesting, more comprehensive treatments can be found in *Yoga: the Technology of Ecstasy* by Georg Feuerstein, *A History of Yoga* by Vivian Worthington, or *Patañjali's Paradigm* by Salvatore Zambito (unpublished manuscript as of February, 2006).

The title of this book, *The Unadorned Thread of Yoga*, is a lyrical translation of the word *sūtra* as it applies to a book. A sūtra is a short statement that embodies a significant concept. A sūtra is also a book of these compiled statements. The cultural translation for the term, sūtra, as applied to a book is: *a single thread unadorned by a single bead.*

May the readers and students of this work enter this simplicity.

Twenty-four years after "spreading all these books all over the floor," this stage of completion is before you. Enjoy!

Be sure to visit the Yoga-Sūtras Institute website: www.yogasutras.net

ACKNOWLEDGEMENTS

The near-universal acknowledgement of the debt that authors owe to those who have supported them approaches cliché. However, the universality of the credit is given because of the truth. *The Unadorned Thread of Yoga* is the outcome of years of research. The generosity of so many people in their contributions to it continues to amaze me.

Peter Max, the great American artist, will have my endless gratitude for introducing me to the *Yoga-Sūtra* and gifting me with my first translation. The Chicago Theosophical Society, under the able guidance of Michael Kaprilian, decisively deepened my experience by introducing me to meditation and several translations of the *Sūtra*. Sw. Veda Bhāratī (formerly Dr. Usharbudh Arya) gives those blessed with his presence, the example of a man embodying the *Yoga-Sūtra*. Osho took the drama out of the meditative life and rendered it immediate, deep, flowing, easy—and playful.

My thanks to so many whose enthusiasm for this project is unflagging after 20 years. Thanks to friends who found and passed along translations I had never heard of—especially Vibhāvan. Because of them I now have a large library of books with the same title. Thank you Pat, for introducing me to the T.S. and A.A.B. Thank you Yolanda, for giving me the idea for this book. Thank you Tracy, for kick-starting me into action on this work one afternoon by the lake in McCall, Idaho. Thank you Gila, for keyboarding the first ten translations in the manuscript. Thank you Vyaas Houston, for teaching me Sanskrit—it couldn't have been easy. Thank you Patty Hammerle, for the detailed proofreading of the Sanskrit. Thank you Nisanga, for two decades of breathless cheerleading and reorganizing your life to create a great cover. Thank you Anila, for years of laughter, support, and exploring the mystery with me. Your eagle-eyed editing has opened my eyes to some interesting aspects of the *vṛttis* of my *citta*.

Thank you Garrison Keillor for the phrase, "Still seeking the answers to life's persistent questions." You have captured the essence of the quest in so few words.

Special thanks to the authors and publishers who have made their works available for this compilation.

How can I ever thank my wife, Rebecca? Her support—tangible, spiritual, and apparently infinite—has made this book possible. At times of near despair, her belief in *The Unadorned Thread*, and in me, far exceeded my own. I touch her feet.

INTRODUCTION

What is The Yoga-Sūtra of Patañjali?

The *Yoga-Sūtra of Patañjali* is the central text, the core of practical theory and guiding instruction of all Yoga disciplines and traditions. As such, it defines and delineates the technical, metapsychological, and meditative premises that underlie all of the traditions of the philosophical and practical fields of Yoga. It was composed at least fifteen hundred years ago by the great sage, Patañjali, who was also a renowned master of the Sanskrit language. The *Yoga-Sūtra* is one of humanity's most impressive treatises on consciousness and transcendent psychology. It presents the hypothesis that a transcendent level of consciousness is available to humans and offers a comprehensive technique base to help us access it. Patañjali compiled, condensed, edited and synthesized thousands of years of preexistent material in the field of Yoga. With his own substantial and original contributions, the *Sūtra* effectively superseded all previous technical works.

For the student who chooses to delve more deeply in yoga disciplines, *The Yoga-Sūtra of Patañjali* is the key to unlocking the secrets of this ancient art and science.

Why So Many Translations of The Same Book?

The first translations of the Indian philosophical treatises into European languages appeared in the mid-1800s when Westerners began to show real interest in the world-view of the Indians. This was particularly the case with Madame Blavatsky, Col. Henry Steel Olcott, and the Theosophical Society. In the late 1800s the Theosophical Society published the first translation of the *Yoga-Sūtra of Patañjali* in any European language. Since then at least thirty English versions of the *Yoga-Sūtra* have been produced.

Until recently, the number of people interested in the *Yoga-Sūtra* has not been large. However, this group has been a steady and reliable one that publishers have served for over a hundred years. The *Sūtra* simply offers unique insights and guidance unattainable elsewhere, and all these translations together have made Patañjali's work accessible to an expanding core of committed students.

The challenge of producing any translation can be quite daunting and presents dilemmas well known to linguists and anthropologists. Factors of language and culture permit wide variations of interpretation among legitimate translations of the same work. Regardless of the source and target languages involved, a single statement can usually be translated in a number of correct ways. This is certainly the case with the *Yoga-Sūtra of Patañjali*. Given the complexities of the Sanskrit language and the technical terminology of the yogic concepts, the possibilities are significantly amplified. In fact, its translations can vary so greatly at times as to almost seem like different books.

To give the simplest example, readers may notice that some terms may be quite spelled differently by the translators. This an example of variance from regions and periods. Naturally, defining conceptual variations is far more complex.

In the process of addressing the difficulties, I don't want to exaggerate them. The range of diversity in valid interpretations of the *Yoga-Sūtra* is not so much a reflection on the competence of the translators as it is the outcome of shadings in their linguistic skills, cross-cultural comprehension, direction or focus of interest and, most important, their personal understanding of consciousness processes emerging from experience in meditation.

Therefore, the elements that create the apparent discrepancies are actually potential sources of enrichment. Certainly, this has been my emphasis and my intent in providing a comprehensive compendium of translations. By comparing, contrasting, and integrating the approaches of the various interpretive translations, the reader enjoys the benefit of a much wider range of understanding than any single one of them could give.

While this volume limits itself to examining the sūtras themselves, the volumes from which they are drawn generally have commentary that explains and expands on the concepts and topics presented in each sūtra. A serious student of yoga and the *Yoga-Sūtra of Patañjali* would do well to acquire a library of *Sūtra* translations and commentaries. The versions used in this work have been selected for their quality and range of interpretation. They all would provide an excellent foundation for years of study and reflection.

Sanskrit Alphabet and Pronounciation Guide

अ	आ	इ	ई	उ	ऊ
*a*llow	f*a*ther	*i*t	pol*i*ce	t*o*	r*u*de
	ए	ऐ	ओ	औ	
	pr*e*y	*ai*sle	n*o*	*sau*rkraut	
ऋ	ॠ	ऌ	अं		अः
		reve*lr*y	am; an		*ho*nor

क	ख	ग	घ	ङ
*k*id	wor*kh*orse	*g*o	do*gh*ouse	si*ng*
च	छ	ज	झ	ञ
*ch*ur*ch*	chur*chh*ill	*j*ar	lod*ge*house	piñata
ट	ठ	ड	ढ	ण
*t*ough	an*th*ill	*d*ough	a*dh*ere	u*n*der
त	थ	द	ध	न
wa*t*er	po*th*ouse	*d*oll	God*h*ouse	*n*o
प	फ	ब	भ	म
*p*aper	u*ph*ill	*b*ut	a*bh*or	*m*ud

य	र	ल	व
*y*es	*r*um	*l*ug	*v*ector
श	ष	स	ह
*sh*awl	*sh*un	*s*un	*h*ot

क्ष

ksa

PART I

The Unadorned Thread of Yoga

The Yoga-Sūtra of Patañjali:

Comparison of Translations in English

with

The Sūtras in Sanskrit;

Transliteration in the Roman Alphabet with Diacritical Markings

and

English Definitions

SAMĀDHI PĀDAḤ

Arya	Samādhi-pāda: The Chapter on Samādhi
Bailey	Book I: The Problem of Union
Dvivedi	Section I
Feuerstein	Chapter One: Samādhi Pāda
Houston	Now, The Chapter on Samādhi
Jnaneshvara	Concentration
Prabhavananda	Yoga and Its Aims
Purohit	Illumination
Satchidananda	Book I: Samadhi Pada: Portion on Contemplation
Shearer	The Settled Mind
Taimni	Samādhi Pāda
Vivekananda	Concentration: Its Spiritual Uses

Now, The Chapter on Samādhi

॥ अथ समाधिपादः ॥

atha samādhi-pādaḥ

अथ	atha	Now
समाधि -	samādhi-	samādhi
पादः	pādaḥ	chapter, part

अथ योगानुशासनम् ॥ १ ॥

atha yogānuśāsanam

अथ	atha	Now/Herewith (at this auspicious moment: at this point of transition)
योग - *√युज् yuj: lit.: to yoke; to unite/dissolve; samādhi*	yoga-	(of) yoga; samādhi; union; integration; blending

अनुशासनम्	anuśāsanam		
अनु -	anu-	within/following; here: as a tradition	transmission; instruction, etc. within the (ancient) tradition
शासनम् *√शास् śās: to instruct*	śāsanam	transmission; instruction; teaching; discipline; imparting discipline	

ARYA

I.1 Now, at this point of transition from previous involvements, teaching (or imparting) the discipline of yoga (begins).

BAILEY

I.1 AUM. The following instruction concerneth the Science of Union.

DVIVEDI

I.1 Now, an exposition of *Yoga* (is to be made).

FEUERSTEIN

I.1 Now [commences] the exposition of Yoga.

HOUSTON

I.1 Now, the instruction of yoga.

JNANESHVARA

I.1 Now, after having done prior preparation through life and other practices, the study and practice of Yoga begins.

PRABHAVANANDA

I.1 This is the beginning of instruction in Yoga.

PUROHIT

I.1 Now we begin the exposition of yōga.

SATCHIDANANDA

I.1 Now, the exposition of Yoga is being made.

SHEARER

I.1 And now the teaching on yoga begins.

TAIMNI

I.1 Now, an exposition of *Yoga* (is to be made).

VIVEKANANDA

I.1 Now Yoga is explained.

I.2

योगश्चित्तवृत्तिनिरोधः ॥ २ ॥

yogaś citta-vṛtti-nirodaḥ

योगः	yogaḥ	yoga (is)
√युज् yuj: lit.: to yoke; to dissolve/unite; samādhi		
चित्त -	citta-	energy field called mind
√चित् cit: to perceive/be bright		in all aspects; mind-field; field of consciousness; consciousness; mind-stuff
वृत्ति -	vṛtti-	(mind-field) states;
√वृत् vṛt: to whirl		states/operations/functionings; activities/fluctuations/ oscillations/waves/ modifications/definitions in the energy field called mind
निरोधः	nirodhaḥ	cessation; dissolution;
नि - ni-: under + √रुध् rudh: to restrict or suppress		disappearance; restraint; suppression; control; restriction; inhibition; annihilation; process of ending

ARYA

I.2 Yoga is the cessation of the waves (arising in) (or) activities of the mind-stuff.

BAILEY

I.2 This Union (or Yoga) is achieved through the subjugation of the psychic nature, and restraint of the citta (or mind).

DVIVEDI

I.2 *Yoga* is the suppression of the transformations of the thinking principle.

FEUERSTEIN

I.2 Yoga is the restriction of the fluctuations of consciousness.

HOUSTON

I.2 Yoga is the *nirodha* (process of ending) of the *vṛtti* (definitions) of *citta* (the field of consciousness).

JNANESHVARA

I.2 Yoga is the control (nirodhah, regulation, channeling, mastery, integration, coordination, stilling, quieting, setting aside) of the modifications (gross and subtle thought patterns) of the mind field.

PRABHAVANANDA

I.2 Yoga is the control of thought-waves in the mind.

PUROHIT

I.2 Yōga is controlling the activities of mind(chitta).

SATCHIDANANDA

I.2 The restraint of the modifications of the mind-stuff is Yoga.

SHEARER

I.2 Yoga is the settling of the mind into silence.

TAIMNI

I.2 *Yoga* is the inhibition of the modifications of the mind.

VIVEKANANDA

I.2 Yoga is restraining the mind-stuff (Chitta) from taking various forms (vrittis).

I.3

तदा द्रष्टुः स्वरूपेऽवस्थानम् ॥ ३ ॥

tadā draṣṭuḥ sva-rūpe 'vasthānam

तदा	tadā	then
द्रष्टुः	draṣṭuḥ	[*of*] Puruṣa; Seer's; Witness';
√दृश् dṛś: to see		of the Seer/Witness

स्वरूपे	svarūpe		
स्व -	sva-	[*in*] own	[*in*] (His) own
रूपे	rūpe	[*in*] nature; essence; form; essential or fundamental nature or form	essential or fundamental nature or form

अवस्थानम्	ava-sthānam	abides; established; stabilized;
अव - ava-: away, off, down + √स्था sthā: to stand		settled; remaining; being in a state; appearing; dwelling; resting; radiating

ARYA

I.3 Then (upon the cessation of the mental activities) the seer (self, the spirit) rests in his own true nature.

BAILEY

I.3 When this has been accomplished, the Yogi knows himself as he is in reality.

DVIVEDI

I.3 Then the seer abides in himself.

FEUERSTEIN

I.3 Then the seer [i.e. the Self] abides in [its] essence.

HOUSTON

I.3 Then, the abidance of (I) the seer (*draṣṭṛ*) in (my) own nature (*svarūpa*).

JNANESHVARA

I.3 Then the Seer abides in Itself, resting in its own True Nature, which is called Self-realization.

PRABHAVANANDA

I.3 Then man abides in his real nature.

PUROHIT

I.3 When mind is controlled, Self stays in His native condition.

SATCHIDANANDA

1.3 Then the Seer [Self] abides in His own Nature.

SHEARER

I.3 When the mind has settled, we are established in our essential nature, which is unbounded consciousness.

TAIMNI

I.3 Then the Seer is established in his own essential and fundamental nature.

VIVEKANANDA

I.3 At that time (the time of concentration) the Seer (Purusha) rests in His own (unmodified) state.

I.4

वृत्तिसारूप्यमितरत्र ॥ ४ ॥

vṛtti-sārūpyam itaratra

वृत्ति -	vṛtti-	(with) mind-field states;
√वृत् vṛt: to whirl		states/operations/functionings; activities/fluctuations/ oscillations/waves/ modifications/definitions in the energy-field called mind
सारूप्यम्	sārūpyam	identification with form or nature;
सा - sā-: with; this + रूप rūpa: form, etc.		similarity; conformity; assimilation; assumes the form or appearance of
इतरत्र	itaratra	at other times; in other states; elsewhere; otherwise

ARYA

I.4 At other times (when the is seer is not in his own true nature because the mental waves have not ceased), the seer (falsely experiences himself) as having assimilated and identified with the mental activity (or with the objects of the mental activity).

BAILEY

I.4 Up till now the inner man has identified himself with his forms and with their active modifications.

DVIVEDI

I.4 But otherwise (he) becomes assimilated with transformations.

FEUERSTEIN

I.4 At other times [there is] conformity [of the Self] with the fluctuations [of consciousness].

HOUSTON

I.4 Otherwise, there is conformity to *vṛtti*-definitions.

JNANESHVARA

I.4 At other times, when one is not in Self-realization, the Seer appears to take on the form of the modifications of the mind field, taking on the identity of those thought patterns.

PRABHAVANANDA

I.4 At other times, when he is not in the state of yoga, man remains identified with the thought-waves in the mind.

PUROHIT

I.4 Otherwise He conforms to the nature of mind's activities.

SATCHIDANANDA

I.4 At other times [the Self appears to] assume the forms of the mental modifications.

SHEARER

I.4 Our essential nature is usually overshadowed by the activity of the mind.

TAIMNI

I.4 In other states there is assimilation (of the Seer) with the modifications (of the mind).

VIVEKANANDA

I.4 At other times (when not concentration) the Seer is identified with the modifications.

I.5

वृत्तयः पञ्चतय्यः क्लिष्टाक्लिष्टाः ॥ ५ ॥

vṛttayaḥ pañcatayyaḥ kliṣṭākliṣṭāḥ

वृत्तयः	vṛttayaḥ	the vṛttis (are):
√वृत् vṛt: to whirl		mental states/operations/ functionings; activities of the mind-field; fluctuations/oscillations/ waves in the energy-field called mind
पञ्चतय्यः	pañcatayyaḥ	fivefold (and of two kinds)
पञ्च pañca: five		
क्लिष्ट -	kliṣṭa-	imbued w/kleśas:
√क्लिश् kliś: to be troubled		obstructed/afflicted; painful/impure
अक्लिष्टाः	a-kliṣṭāḥ	not imbued w/kleśas:
अ - a-: un-/non-/not/without; connoting absence +		not obstructed/afflicted;
√क्लिश् kliś: to be troubled		not painful/impure

ARYA

I.5 The vṛttis (are) fivefold (and of two kinds): impure and painful, (and) not impure and not painful.

BAILEY

I.5 The mind states are five, and are subject to pleasure or pain; they are painful or not-painful.

DVIVEDI

I.5 The transformations are fivefold, and painful or not-painful.

FEUERSTEIN

I.5 The fluctuations are fivefold; afflicted or non-afflicted.

HOUSTON

I.5 *Vṛtti*-definitions (of the field) are five-fold. They are either *kliṣṭa*-obstructing (causing pain) or *akliṣṭa*-non-obstructing (not causing pain).

JNANESHVARA

I.5 Those gross and subtle thought patterns (vrittis) fall into five varieties, of which some are colored (klishta) and others are uncolored (aklishta).

PRABHAVANANDA

I.5 There are five kinds of thought-waves—some painful, others not painful.

PUROHIT

I.5 The activities are five-fold; some painful, others pleasurable.

SATCHIDANANDA

I.5 There are five kinds of mental modifications which are either painful or painless.

SHEARER

I.5 There are five types of mental activity. They may or may not cause suffering.

TAIMNI

I.5 The modifications of the mind are five-fold and are painful or not-painful.

VIVEKANANDA

I.5 There are five classes of modifications, [some] painful and [others] not painful.

I.6

प्रमाणविपर्ययविकल्पनिद्रास्मृतयः ॥ ६ ॥

pramāṇa-viparyaya-vikalpa-nidrā-smṛtayaḥ

प्रमाण -	pramāṇa-	right knowledge (based on)
प्र - pra-: ultimate; complete + √मा mā: measure		valid proofs, valid cognition, and valid evaluation; valid means of learning
विपर्यय -	viparyaya-	lit.: reversed movement or direction:
वि - vi-: apart, separate from, reverse to +		erroneous or wrong knowledge;
परि - pari-: all around, about +		perversive/false cognition;
√इ i: to go		misconception; misperception
विकल्प -	vikalpa-	concept; conceptual;
वि - vi-: apart, separate from, reverse to +		conceptualization; abstraction;
√क्लृप् kḷp: to be fit/serve		a verbal construct or conception; imaginary cognition; fancy; linguistic or verbal delusion
निद्रा -	nidrā-	sleep; deep or dreamless sleep
नि - ni-: in, into, downward motion, great +		
√द्रा drai: to sleep		
स्मृतयः	smṛtayaḥ	memory
√स्मृ smṛ: to remember		

ARYA

I.6 Valid proof,
false cognition,
linguistic misconception,
sleep (and) memory:
these are the five activities
of the mind.

BAILEY

I.6 These modifications
(activities) are:
correct knowledge,
incorrect knowledge,
fancy, passivity (sleep) and
memory.

DVIVEDI

I.6 (They are)
Right knowledge,
wrong knowledge,
fancy,
sleep and
memory.

FEUERSTEIN

I.6 [The five types of
fluctuations are:]
valid-cognition,
misconception,
conceptualization,
sleep and memory.

HOUSTON

I.6 They are:
evaluation,
misperception,
conceptualization,
sleep, and
memory.

JNANESHVARA

I.6 The five varieties of thought
patterns to witness are:
1) knowing correctly (pramana),
2) incorrect knowing (viparyaya),
3) fantasy or imagination
(vikalpa), 4) the object of voidness that is deep sleep (nidra), and
5) recollection or memory
(smriti).

PRABHAVANANDA

I.6 These five kinds of thought-
waves are: right knowledge,
wrong knowledge, verbal
delusion, sleep and memory.

PUROHIT

I.6 They are:
experience,
perversion,
delusion,
sleep,
recollection.

SATCHIDANANDA

I.6 They are
right knowledge,
misconception,
verbal delusion, sleep
and memory.

SHEARER

I.6 These five
are: understanding,
misunderstanding,
imagination,
sleep and memory.

TAIMNI

I.6 (They are)
right knowledge,
wrong knowledge,
fancy, sleep and
memory.

VIVEKANANDA

I.6 [These are]
right knowledge,
indiscrimination,
verbal delusion,
sleep and memory.

I.7

प्रत्यक्षानुमानागमाः प्रमाणानि ॥ ७ ॥

pratyakṣānumānāgamāḥ pramāṇāni

प्रत्यक्ष -	pratyakṣa-	direct perception/cognition
प्रति - prati-: towards + अक्ष akṣa: eye		
अनुमान -	anumāna-	(from) inference and logical processes
अनु - anu-: following, after, behind + √मा mā: to measure		
आगमाः	āgamāḥ	(textual, scriptural, inspired, revealed) authority or testimony; revelations
आ - ā-: from all sides, all around + √गम् gam: to go		
प्रमाणानि	pramāṇāni	valid cognitions; valid proofs; tested and attested facts and sources of right knowledge; valid means of learning and evaluation
प्र - pra-: ultimate; complete + √मा mā: measure		

ARYA

I.7 Direct perception, inference, and authority are the (three kinds of) valid proof.

BAILEY

I.7 The basis of correct knowledge is correct perception, correct deduction and correct witness (or accurate evidence).

DVIVEDI

I.7 Right knowledge (is) direct cognition or inference or testimony.

FEUERSTEIN

I.7 Valid-cognition [is based on] perception, inference and testimony.

HOUSTON

I.7 *Pramāṇa*-valid means of evaluation are:
direct perception,
inference, and
testimony.

JNANESHVARA

I.7 Of these five, there are three ways of gaining correct knowledge (pramana):
1) perception, 2) inference, and 3) testimony or verbal communication from others who have knowledge.

PRABHAVANANDA

I.7 The right kinds of knowledge are: direct perception, inference and spiritual testimony.

PUROHIT

I.7 Experience comes from perception, inference, evidence.

SATCHIDANANDA

I.7 The sources
of right knowledge are
direct perception,
inference and
spiritual testimony.

SHEARER

I.7 Understanding is
correct knowledge based
on direct perception,
inference or reliable
testimony of others.

TAIMNI

I.7 (Facts of)
right knowledge
(are based on)
direct cognition,
inference or
testimony.

VIVEKANANDA

I.7 Direct perception,
inference, and
competent evidence
constitute right knowledge or
proof.

I.8

विपर्ययो मिथ्याज्ञानमतद्रूपप्रतिष्ठम् ॥ ८ ॥

viparyayo mithyā-jñānam a-tad-rūpa-pratiṣṭham

विपर्ययः	viparyayaḥ	erroneous or wrong knowledge;
वि - vi-: reverse to; also - apart, separate +		perversive/false cognition;
परि - pari-: all around, about +		misconception; misperception
√इ i: to go		

मिथ्याज्ञानम् mithyājñānam

मिथ्या -	mithyā-	mistaken/erroneous;	mistaken or false idea
√मिथ् mith: to conflict with		false/illusory	
ज्ञानम्	jñānam	knowledge; concept; idea;	
√ज्ञा jñā: to know		insight; awareness; observation; ordinary knowledge based on sense perception and reasoning	

अतद्रूप -	a-tad-rūpa-	not in nature or form of that (object)

अ - a-: un-/non-/not/without + तद् tat-: that; this + रूप rūpa: form, etc

प्रतिष्ठम्	pratiṣṭham	established; based (on)
प्रति - prati-: towards, in direction of + √स्था sthā: to stand		steadfast; (with) foundation; occupying; possessing

ARYA

I.8 The wrong knowledge without a basis in the nature of its objects is termed false cognition.

BAILEY

I.8 Incorrect knowledge is based upon perception of the form and not upon the state of being.

DVIVEDI

I.8 Wrong knowledge is false conception of a thing whose real form does not correspond to that conception.

FEUERSTEIN

I.8 Misconception is erroneous knowledge not based on the [actual] appearance of that [which is underlying the object].

HOUSTON

I.8 *Viparyaya*-misperception is mistaken knowledge, founded on an appearance which is not that.

JNANESHVARA

I.8 Incorrect knowledge or illusion (viparyaya) is false knowledge formed by perceiving a thing as being other than what it really is.

PRABHAVANANDA

I.8 Wrong knowledge is knowledge which is false and not based upon the true nature of its object.

PUROHIT

I.8 Perversion is an idea of an object, not conforming to its nature.

SATCHIDANANDA

I.8 Misconception occurs when knowledge of something is not based on its true form.

SHEARER

I.8 Misunderstanding is the delusion that stems from a false impression of reality.

TAIMNI

I.8 Wrong knowledge is a false conception of a thing whose real form does not correspond to such a mistaken conception.

VIVEKANANDA

I.8 Indiscrimination is false knowledge not based on the real nature [of an object].

I.9

शब्दज्ञानानुपाती वस्तुशून्यो विकल्पः ॥ ९॥

śabda-jñānānupātī vastu-śūnyo vikalpaḥ

शब्दज्ञानानुपाती	śabdajñānānupātī		
शब्द् -	śabda-	word; sound	knowledge based
शब्द् śabd: sound			on words;
ज्ञान -	jñāna-	knowledge;	emerging only
√ज्ञा jñā: to know		concept; idea, etc.	from words;
अनुपाती	anupātī	arises/following/	dependent only
अनु - anu-: following, after, behind +		relying/	upon verbal
√पत् pat: to fall		dependent upon	construction/
			conception

वस्तुशून्यो	vastuśūnyo		
वस्तु -	vastu-	real object; reality;	devoid of
√वस् vas: to remain		substance	substance
शून्यः	śūnyaḥ	devoid; empty	or
√श्वि śvi: to swell			objective reality

विकल्पः	vikalpaḥ	concept; conceptual;
वि - vi-: apart, separate from, reverse to +		conceptualization; abstraction;
√क्लृप् kḷp: to be fit/serve		a verbal construct or conception;
		imaginary cognition; fancy;
		linguistic or verbal delusion

ARYA

I.9 (The knowledge) that follows only a verbal conception but is devoid of a real object is termed linguistic misconception.

BAILEY

I.9 Fancy rests upon images which have no real existence.

DVIVEDI

I.9 Fancy is the notion called into being by mere words, having nothing to answer to it in reality.

FEUERSTEIN

I.9 Conceptualization is without [perceivable] object, following [entirely] verbal knowledge.

HOUSTON

I.9 *Vikalpa*-conceptualization is without an (actual) object–relying upon concept in language.

JNANESHVARA

I.9 Fantasy or imagination (vikalpa) is a thought pattern that has verbal expression and knowledge, but for which there is no such object or reality in existence.

PRABHAVANANDA

I.9 Verbal delusion arises when words do not correspond to reality.

PUROHIT

I.9 Delusion is an idea conveyed by words, without any reality.

SATCHIDANANDA

I.9 An image that arises on hearing mere words without any reality [as its basis] is verbal delusion.

SHEARER

I.9 Imagination is thought based on an image conjured up by words, and is without substance.

TAIMNI

I.9 An image conjured up by words without any substance behind it is fancy.

VIVEKANANDA

I.9 Verbal delusion follows from words having no [corresponding] reality.

I.10

अभावप्रत्ययालम्बना वृत्तिर्निद्रा ॥ १० ॥

abhāva-pratyayālambanā vṛttir nidrā

अभाव -	abhāva-	absence; negation;
अ - a-: un-/non-/not/without + √भू bhū: to be		nothingness; non-occurrence; absence; removal; disappearance
प्रत्यय -	pratyaya-	content of mind-field;
प्रति - prati-: towards, in direction of + √इ i: to go		presented-idea; cognition principle; cognition; causal/awareness principle; *immediate arising thought directed to an object—Houston*
आलम्बना	ālambanā	dependent on; supported by;
आ - ā-: near to, from all sides + √लम्ब् lamb: to rest on; to hang		leaning on; having as a base/ foundation
वृत्तिः	vṛttiḥ	mental operation; activity; state;
√वृत् vṛt: to whirl		modification
निद्रा	nidra	sleep
नि - ni-: in, into, downward motion, great + √द्रा drai: to sleep		

ARYA

I.10 The mental state whose basis is an awareness of absence (negation) (is called) sleep. OR: The mental wave resorting to the causal principle of negation (is called) sleep.

BAILEY

I.10 Passivity (sleep) is based upon the quiescent state of the vrittis (or upon the non-perception of the senses).

DVIVEDI

I.10 That transformation which has nothingness for its basis is sleep.

FEUERSTEIN

I.10 Sleep is a fluctuation founded on the presented-idea of the non-occurrence [of other contents of consciousness].

HOUSTON

I.10 *Nidrā*-sleep is a *vṛtti* depending on a *pratyayas*-the immediate arising thought towards non-wakefulness.

JNANESHVARA

I.10 Dreamless sleep (nidra) is the subtle thought pattern which has as its object an inertia, blankness, absence, or negation of the other thought patterns (vrittis).

PRABHAVANANDA

I.10 Sleep is a wave of thought about nothingness.

PUROHIT

I.10 Sleep is a condition, which depends on the cessation of perception.

SATCHIDANANDA

I.10 That mental modification supported by cognition of nothingness is sleep.

SHEARER

I.10 Sleep is the mental activity which has as its content the sense of nothingness.

TAIMNI

I.10 That modification of the mind which is based on the absence of any content in it is sleep.

VIVEKANANDA

I.10 Sleep is a vritti which embraces the feeling of voidness.

I.11

अनुभूतविषयासम्प्रमोषः स्मृतिः ॥ ११ ॥

anubhūta-viṣayāsampramoṣaḥ smṛtiḥ

अनुभूत -	anu-bhūta-	experienced
अनु - anu-: following, after, behind + √भू bhū: to be		
विषय -	viṣaya-	objects (of sensory experience);
√विष् viṣ: to be active + - अय - aya-: going		field object domain; subject/subject-matter; content; object of sensory experience; realm; scope; matters of enjoyment or experience
असम्प्रमोषः	a-sampramoṣaḥ	lit.: non-theft: not being stolen;
अ - a-: un-/non-/not/without +		not being lost; not allowed to escape;
-सम् sam-: fully, completely +		not forgotten
-प्र - -pra-: away, onward, forward +		
√मुष् muṣ: to steal		
स्मृतिः	smṛtiḥ	memory; remembrance
√स्मृ smṛ: to remember		

ARYA

I.11 When the subject of an experience is not lost, (its wave is termed) memory.

BAILEY

I.11 Memory is the holding on to that which has been known.

DVIVEDI

I.11 Memory is the not-allowing a thing cognised to escape.

FEUERSTEIN

I.11 Remembering is the non-deprivation of the experienced object.

HOUSTON

I.11 *Smṛti*-(the act of) memory is the non-escaping of *viṣay*-experienced objects.

JNANESHVARA

I.11 Recollection or memory (smriti) is mental modification caused by the inner reproducing of a previous impression of an object, but without adding any other characteristics from other sources.

PRABHAVANANDA

I.11 Memory is when perceived objects are not forgotten, but come back to consciousness.

PUROHIT

I.11 Recollection is the calling up of past experience.

SATCHIDANANDA

I.11 When a mental modification of an object previously experienced and not forgotten comes back to consciousness, that is memory.

SHEARER

I.11 And memory is the returning to the mind of past experience.

TAIMNI

I.11 Memory is not allowing an object which has been experienced to escape.

VIVEKANANDA

I.11 Memory arises when [the vrittis of] perceived objects do not slip away [and through impressions come back to consciousness].

I.12

अभ्यासवैराग्याभ्यां तन्निरोधः ॥ १२ ॥

abhyāsa-vairāgyābhyāṃ tan-nirodhaḥ

अभ्यास -	abhyāsa-	[*with/by means of*] (persistent)
अभि - abhi-: to, towards, into +		personal application/practice (and)
√आस् ās: to apply oneself ***OR*** *to sit*		
वैराग्याभ्यां	vairāgyābhyāṃ	[*with/by means of*] dispassion/
वै - vai-: dis- + √रज् raj: be attracted/excited		non-attachment; [*due to*] absence of desire or aversion; [*by*] detachment
तद् -	tad-	(of) those (vṛtti-)
निरोधः	nirodhaḥ	cessation; dissolution;
नि - ni-: under + √रुध् rudh: to restrict or suppress		disappearance; restraint; suppression; control; restriction; inhibition; annihilation; process of ending (occurs)

ARYA

I.12 The cessation of those (vṛttis occurs) through practice and dispassion.

BAILEY

I.12 The control of these modifications of the internal organ, the mind, is to be brought about through tireless endeavor and through non-attachment.

DVIVEDI

I.12 Its suppression is secured by application and non-attachment.

FEUERSTEIN

I.12 The restriction of these [fluctuations] [is achieved] through practice and dispassion.

HOUSTON

I.12 The *nirodha*-ending of those (*vṛtti*) occurs by *abhyāsa*-practice and *vairāgya*-non-attachment.

JNANESHVARA

I.12 These thought patterns (vrittis) are mastered (nirodhah, regulated, coordinated, controlled, stilled, quieted) through practice (abhyasa) and non-attachment (vairagya).

PRABHAVANANDA

I.12 They are controlled by means of practice and non-attachment.

PUROHIT

I.12 Control the activities by practice and detachment.

SATCHIDANANDA

I.12 These mental modifications are restrained by practice and non-attachment.

SHEARER

I.12 These five types of mental activity are settled through the practice of yoga and the freedom it bestows.

TAIMNI

I.12 Their suppression (is brought about) by persistent practice and non-attachment.

VIVEKANANDA

I.12 These [vrittis] are controlled by practice and non-attachment.

I.13

तत्र स्थितौ यत्नोऽभ्यासः ॥ १३ ॥

tatra sthitau yatno'bhyāsaḥ

तत्र	tatra	of these; there; (here: between those two [practice and dispassion])
स्थितौ *√स्था sthā: to stand*	sthitau	[*upon/as regards*] stilling; steadiness; being firmly established; grounded; settling/stabilizing/coming to rest (of the mind-field)
यत्नः *√यत् yat: to marshal*	yatnaḥ	endeavor; effort; exertion; vigilance
अभ्यास - *अभि - abhi-: to, towards, into +* *√आस् ās: to apply oneself **OR** to sit*	abhyāsa	(persistent) personal application/practice

ARYA

I.13 Between those two (practice and dispassion), the endeavor to make the mind settle down (is called) practice.

BAILEY

I.13 Tireless endeavor is the constant effort to restrain the modifications of the mind.

DVIVEDI

I.13 Application is the effort toward the state.

FEUERSTEIN

I.13 Practice is the exertion [in gaining] stability in that [state of restriction].

HOUSTON

I.13 *Abhyāsa*-practice is vigilance in retaining there. (as I, the seer abiding in my own nature, seeing. 1.3)

JNANESHVARA

I.13 Practice (abhyasa) means choosing, applying the effort, and doing those actions that bring a stable and tranquil state (sthitau).

PRABHAVANANDA

I.13 Practice is the repeated effort to follow the disciplines which give permament control of the thought-waves of the mind.

PUROHIT

I.13 Practice is effort towards concentration.

SATCHIDANANDA

I.13 Of these two, effort toward steadiness of mind is practice.

SHEARER

I.13 The practice of yoga is the commitment to become established in the state of freedom.

TAIMNI

I.13 *Abhyāsa* is the effort for being firmly established in that state (of *Citta-Vṛtti-Nirodha*).

VIVEKANANDA

I.13 Continuous struggle to keep them (the vrittis) perfectly restrained is practice.

I.14

स तु दीर्घकालनैरन्तर्यसत्कारासेवितो दृढभूमिः ॥ १४ ॥

sa tu dīrgha-kāla-nairantarya-satkārāsevito dṛḍha-bhūmiḥ

सः	saḥ	that; this (practice)
तु	tu	however; but; moreover
दीर्घकाल	dīrgha-kāla	
दीर्घ -	dīrgha-	long } (for) a
काल -	kāla-	time } long time
√कल् kāl: to count, impel		
नैरन्तर्य -	nairantarya-	without interval; without
नैर - nair: without + अन्तर् - antar: between		interruption; unbroken continuity
य - ya-: non-between-ness		
सत्कार -	satkāra-	reverence; devotion; respect;
सत् - sat: right + √कृ kṛ: to do		adoration; sincerity; earnestness; positive attitude and intent
आसेवितः	ā-sevitaḥ	pursued; practiced; cultivated;
आ - ā-: near, all around + √सेव् sev: to resort to		maintained in assiduous and complete observance
दृढभूमिः	dṛḍha-bhūmiḥ	
दृढ	dṛḍha-	established; firm } (becomes) firm
√दृंह् dṛṃh: to fasten		} of ground;
भूमिः	bhūmiḥ	ground; plane } established at
√भू bhū: to become		} (higher) plane

ARYA

I.14 That (practice), however, (becomes) firm of ground (only when) pursued for a long time, without an interval, and with positive feeling.

BAILEY

I.14 When the object to be gained is sufficiently valued, and the efforts towards its attainment are persistently followed without intermission, then steadiness of the mind (restraint of the vrittis) is secured.

DVIVEDI

I.14 It becomes a position of firmness, being practiced for a long time, without intermission, and perfect devotion.

FEUERSTEIN

I.14 But this [practice] is firmly grounded [only after it has been] cultivated properly and for a long time uninterruptedly.

HOUSTON

I.14 Moreover, that *abhyāsa*-practice has firm ground when attended to for a long time, without interruption, and with devotion to the truth.

JNANESHVARA

I.14 When that practice is done for a long time, without a break, and with sincere devotion, then the practice becomes a firmly rooted, stable and solid foundation.

PRABHAVANANDA

I.14 Practice becomes firmly grounded when it has been cultivated for a long time, uninterruptedly with earnest devotion.

PUROHIT

I.14 Long unremitting sincere practice develops into habit.

SATCHIDANANDA

I.14 Practice becomes firmly grounded when well attended for a long time, without break and in all earnestness.

SHEARER

I.14 The practice of yoga will be firmly rooted when it is maintained consistently and with dedication over a long period.

TAIMNI

I.14 It (*Abhyāsa*) becomes firmly grounded on being continued for a long time, without interruption and with reverent devotion.

VIVEKANANDA

I.14 It becomes firmly grounded by long constant efforts with great love [for the end to be attained].

I.15

दृष्टानुश्रविकविषयवितृष्णस्य वशीकारसंज्ञा वैराग्यम् ॥१५॥

dṛṣṭānuśravika-viṣaya-vitṛṣṇasya vaśīkāra-saṃjñā vairāgyam

दृष्ट -	dṛṣṭa-	seen/perceived/experienced
√दृश् *dṛś: to see*		(with the senses)
अनुश्रविक -	anuśravika-	heard of, revealed, promised in
अनु - *anu-: following* + √श्रु *śru: to hear/learn*		a tradition or scripture
विषय -	viṣaya-	objects (of sensory experience);
√विष् - *viṣ: to be active* + अय - *aya-: going*		field object domain; subject/subject-matter; content; object of sensory experience; realm; scope; matters of enjoyment or experience
वितृष्णस्य	vitṛṣṇasya	[*of*] one who has lost
वि - *vi-: apart, separate from* + √तृष् *tṛṣ: to be thirsty*		craving/thirst (for) [indicates negative possessive]
वशीकार -	vaśīkāra-	mastery; power;
वश् - *vaś: to will* + √कृ *kṛ: to make*		bringing under complete control
संज्ञा	saṃjñā	full knowledge; consciousness;
सम् - *sam-: greatly, fully, completely* + √ज्ञा *jñā: to know*		term; definition; name
वैराग्यम्	vairāgyam	dispassion; detachment;
वै - *vai-: dis-* + √रज् *raj: be attracted/excited*		non-attachment

ARYA

I.15 The mastery (established by) one who has lost craving for (interest in) all matters (objects) experienced (through senses) and those spoken of in the traditions (such as heaven, celestial fragrances and music) is called dispassion.

BAILEY

I.15 Non-attachment is freedom from longing for all objects of desire, either earthly or traditional, either here or hereafter.

DVIVEDI

I.15 The consciousness of having mastered (every desire) in the case of one who does not thirst for objects perceptible or spiritual, is non-attachment.

FEUERSTEIN

I.15 Dispassion is the knowledge-of-mastery of [that *yogin* who is] without thirst for seen [i.e. earthly] and revealed objects.

HOUSTON

I.15 *Vairāgya*-non-attachment is full knowledge (declaration) of (one's own-the seer's) mastery (on the part of one who is) not clinging to *viṣaya*-objects, (already) experienced or described by others.

JNANESHVARA

I.15 When the mind loses desire even for objects seen or described in a tradition or in scriptures, it acquires a state of utter (vashikara) desirelessness that is called non-attachment (vairagya).

PRABHAVANANDA

I.15 Non-attachment is self-mastery; it is freedom from desire for what is seen or heard.

PUROHIT

I.15 Detachment is the deliberate renunciation of desire for objects seen or heard.

SATCHIDANANDA

I.15 The consciousness of self-mastery in one who is free from craving for objects seen or heard about is non-attachment.

SHEARER

I.15 Freedom is that triumphant state of consciousness that is beyond the influence of desire. The mind ceases to thirst for anything it has seen or heard of; even what is promised in the scriptures.

TAIMNI

I.15 The consciousness of perfect mastery (of desires) in the case of one who has ceased to crave for objects, seen or unseen, is *Vairāgya*.

VIVEKANANDA

I.15 The subjugation of the thirst for objects seen or heard of is nonattachment.

I.16

तत्परं पुरुषख्यातेर्गुणवैतृष्ण्यम् ॥ १६ ॥

tat paraṃ puruṣa-khyāter guṇa-vaitṛṣṇyam

तत्	tat	that; this (dispassion) (is)
परं	paraṃ	transcendent; ultimate; supreme
पुरुष -	Puruṣa-	(*as regards/by or for*] the Conscious Being; the Witness; the Presence; the Indweller; the Imperishable One
ख्यातेः √ख्या *khyā: to be known*	khyāteḥ	[*through*] discernment (of Puruṣa); [*through*] vision (of Puruṣa); [*due to*] identity (with Puruṣa); [*due to*] realization (of Puruṣa)

गुणवैतृष्ण्यम्	guṇavaitṛṣṇyam		
गुण - गुण *guṇa: strand*	guṇa-	(for) the attributes of matter (prakṛti): sattva, rajas, tamas; primary-constituents of Nature	freedom from the least craving for the guṇas
वैतृष्ण्यम् वि - *vi-: apart, separate from* + √तृष् *tṛṣ: to be thirsty*	vaitṛṣṇyam	state of being free from all craving; desireless	

ARYA

I.16 That Dispassion is of the higher kind (when it is) the freedom from all craving for the attributes of Matter, through the realisation of Conscious Being.

BAILEY

I.16 The consummation of this non-attachment results in an exact knowledge of the spiritual man when liberated from the qualities or gunas.

DVIVEDI

I.16 That is highest, wherein, from being the *Puruśa*, there is entire cessation of any, the least, desire for the *Guṇas*.

FEUERSTEIN

I.16 The superior [form] of this [dispassion] is the non-thirsting for the primary-constituents [of Nature] [which results] from the vision of the Self.

HOUSTON

I.16 The higher (*vairāgya*-non-attachment) is the non-clinging to the *guṇas* (primary forces of creation) due to identity with *puruṣa*-the self.

JNANESHVARA

I.16 Indifference to the subtlest elements, constituent principles, or qualities themselves (gunas), achieved through a knowledge of the nature of pure consciousness (purusha), is called supreme non-attachment (paravairagya).

PRABHAVANANDA

I.16 When, through knowledge of the Atman, one ceases to desire any manifestation of Nature, then that is the highest kind of non-attachment.

PUROHIT

I.16 The highest form of detachment is the automatic renunciation of the three qualities, the result of Self-experience.

SATCHIDANANDA

I.16 When there is non-thirst for even the gunas (constituents of Nature) due to realization of the Purusha (true Self), that is supreme non-attachment.

SHEARER

I.16 And supreme freedom is that complete liberation from the world of change that comes from knowing the unbounded self.

TAIMNI

I.16 That is the highest *Vairāgya* in which, on account of the awareness of the *Puruṣa*, there is cessation of the least desire for the *Guṇas*.

VIVEKANANDA

I.16 That is extreme non-attachment which gives up even the thirst for the gunas, and which comes from the knowledge of [the real nature of] the Purusha.

I.17

वितर्कविचारानन्दास्मितारूपानुगमात् सम्प्रज्ञातः ॥ १७ ॥

vitarka-vicārānandāsmitā-rūpānugamāt samprajñātaḥ

[samādhi with the following four progressive states]

वितर्क -	vitarka-	(samādhi with) gross thought: reasoning;
वि - vi- particular, distinct, intensity +		cogitation w/sense perception
√तर्क् tark: to reflect		
विचार -	vicāra-	(samādhi with) subtle thought: reflecting
वि - vi-: particular, distinct, intensity + √चर् car: to move, progressive movement		
आनन्द -	ānanda-	(samādhi with) ecstasy; rapture; bliss; joy;
आ - ā-: near to, from all sides + √नन्द् nand: to be happy		rejoicing
अस्मिता -	asmitā-	(samādhi with) "I-am-ness"; pure ego;
अस्मि asmi-: I am + -ता tā: -ness		sense of being; sense of individuality
रूप -	rūpa-	nature; form, appearance of
अनुगमात्	anugamāt	[*through*] accompaniment (of);
अनु - anu-: following, after, behind + √गम् gam: to go		[*because*] accompanied by the form of; [*due to*] connection
सम्प्रज्ञातः	samprajñātaḥ	lower samādhi; cognitive samādhi;
सम् - sam-: together with, completely, perfectly +		samādhi of wisdom;
प्र - pra-: in front, forth + √ज्ञा jñā: to know		meditation w/limited external awareness

ARYA

I.17 Saṃprajñāta samādhi (meditation that still has residue of limited external awareness) (occurs) through the accompaniment of gross objective thought, feeling of (mystic) ecstasy and an experience of "I am"-ness (progressively in these four stages).

BAILEY

I.17 The consciousness of an object is attained by concentration upon its fourfold nature:
the form, through examination;
the quality (or guna), through discriminative participation;
the purpose, through inspiration (or bliss); and the soul, through identification.

DVIVEDI

I.17 Consciousness is that which is attended by argumentation, deliberation, joy, and the sense of being.

FEUERSTEIN

I.17 [The enstasy arising out of the state of restriction] is cognitive [i.e. object-oriented] by being connected with [the forms of] cogitation, reflection, joy or I-am-ness.

HOUSTON

I.17 (*Nirodha*, the process of ending *vṛtti* is) *samprajñāta*- cognitive, when connecting with forms which are sense-perceived or subtle, having a feeling of bliss or the (individual) sense of "I am".

JNANESHVARA

I.17 The deep absorption of attention on an object is of four kinds, 1) gross (vitarka), 2) subtle (vichara), 3) bliss accompanied (ananda), and 4) with I-ness (asmita), and is called samprajnata samadhi.

PRABHAVANANDA

I.17 Concentration upon a single object may reach four stages: examination, discrimination, joyful peace and simple awareness of individuality.

PUROHIT

I.17 Sampradnyāta Samādhi is that condition of conscious illumination, where mind is mixed up with consciousness of sentiment (sawitarka) or consciousness of discrimination (sawichāra) or consciousness of joy (sānanda) or consciousness of personality (sāsmita).

SATCHIDANANDA

I.17 Samprajnata samadhi (distinguished contemplation) is accompanied by reasoning, reflecting, rejoicing and pure I-am-ness.

SHEARER

I.17 The settled mind is known as *samādhi*. In *samprajnāta samādhi*, the settled state is accompanied by mental activity: first on the gross level, then on the subtle level, then a feeling of bliss and finally the sense of pure "I-am-ness."

TAIMNI

I.17 Saṃprajñāta Samādhi is that which is accompanied by reasoning, reflection, bliss and sense of pure being.

VIVEKANANDA

I.17 The samādhi endowed with right knowledge is that which is attended by reasoning, discrimination, bliss, unqualified egoism.

I.18

विरामप्रत्ययाभ्यासपूर्वः संस्कारशेषोऽन्यः ॥ १८ ॥

virāma-pratyayābhyāsa-pūrvaḥ saṃskāra-śeṣo'nyaḥ

विराम -	virāma-	complete cessation
वि - vi-: intensity + √रम् ram: to stop		
प्रत्यय -	pratyaya-	content of mind-field;
प्रति - prati-: towards, in direction of + √इ i: to go		presented-idea; cognition principle; cognition; causal/awareness principle; *immediate arising thought directed to an object–Houston*
अभ्यास -	abhyāsa-	(persistent) personal
*अभि - abhi-: to, towards, into + √आस् ās: to apply oneself **OR** to sit*		application/practice
पूर्वः	pūrvaḥ	preceded by; conditioned by; having as a precondition or prerequisite
संस्कारशेषः	saṃskāraśeṣaḥ	
संस्कार	saṃskāra-	habitual wave in citta;
सम् - sam-: together with, completely, perfectly + √कृ kṛ: to do		conditioned mental response from habit and memory impression/imprint in the subtle domain (karmāśaya); subliminal activator
शेषः	śeṣaḥ	residue
अन्यः	anyaḥ	the other (asamprajñāta samādhi)

(saṃskāra / śeṣaḥ together: leaving saṃskāra as residue)

ARYA

I.18 (Resulting from) the practice of the cessation awareness, which is its prerequisite, the other (samādhi, i.e. asaṃprajñāta) (is reached) leaving only its impressions.

BAILEY

I.18 A further stage of samadhi is achieved when, through one-pointed thought, the outer activity is quieted. In this stage, the citta is responsive only to subjective impressions.

DVIVEDI

I.18 The other is that which consists only of *Samskāras*, being brought on by the practice of the cause of complete suspension.

FEUERSTEIN

I.18 The other [type of enstacy] has a residuum of subliminal-activators; [it follows] the former [cognitive enstacy] upon the practice of the presented-idea of cessation.

HOUSTON

I.18 The other (*nirodha*), preceded by the practice (*abhyāsa*) of the *pratyayas*-immediate arising thought of *virāma*-cessation, has a residuum of *sanskāra*-subliminal activators.

JNANESHVARA

I.18 The other kind of samadhi is asamprajnata samadhi, and has no object in which attention is absorbed, wherein only latent impressions remain; attainment of this state is preceded by the constant practice of allowing all of the gross and subtle fluctuations of mind to recede back into the field from which they arose.

PRABHAVANANDA

I.18 The other kind of concentration is that in which the consciousness contains no object—only subconscious impressions, which are like burnt seeds. It is attained by constantly checking the thought-waves through the practice of non-attachment.

PUROHIT

I.18 Asampradnyāta Samādhi is that unmixed condition of conscious illumination, where by constant renunciation of all knowledge, mind retains past impressions only.

SATCHIDANANDA

I.18 By the firmly convinced practice of the complete cessation of the mental modifications, the impressions only remain.
This is the other samadhi [asamprajnata or non-distinguished].

SHEARER

I.18 After the repeated experience of the settling and ceasing of mental activity comes another *samādhi*. In this, only the latent impressions of past experience remain.

TAIMNI

I.18 The remnant impression left in the mind on the dropping of the *Pratyaya* after previous practice is the other (i.e. *Asaṃprajñāta Samādhi*).

VIVEKANANDA

I.18 There is another samādhi, which is attained by the constant practice of the cessation of all mental activity, and in which the chitta retains only the unmanifested impressions.

I.19

भवप्रत्ययो विदेहप्रकृतिलयानाम् ॥ १९ ॥

bhava-pratyayo videha-prakṛti-layānām

भवप्रत्ययः	bhavapratyayaḥ		
भव -	bhava-	becoming	
√भु *bhū: to be*			
प्रत्ययः	pratyayaḥ	content of mind-field;	at (re)birth
प्रति - *prati-: towards, in direction of* +		presented-idea;	(the samādhi)
√इ *i: to go*		cognition principle;	of causal
		cognition; causal/ awareness principle;	cognition of being
		immediate arising thought directed to an object–Houston	

विदेह -	videha-	(of) videha: bodiless yogis who died
वि - *vi-: apart, reverse to* +		after achieving ecstatic samādhi
√दिह् *dih: to cover, smear* + देह *deha: body*		(sa-vitarka samādhi)

प्रकृतिलयानाम्	prakṛtilayānām		
प्रकृति -	prakṛti-	unmanifest, unevolved	*[possessed of]*
प्र - *pra-: before, in front* +		primordial matter with	those who
√कृ *kṛ: to make*		the three guṇas in a	have merged/
		state of equilibrium	been absorbed
		prior to universal	(the awareness)
		manifestation	into prakṛti:
लयानाम्	layānām	absorbed; dissolved;	undifferentiated nature
√ली *lī: to clasp/be absorbed*		merged	

ARYA

I.19 The Samādhi naturally experienced at re-birth comes to the *videha* (yogis who die after perfecting the *ānandānugata*, the ecstatic meditation) and to the *prakṛti-laya* (yogis who have accomplished the *asmitānugata*, the meditation accompanied by "I-am-ness") having dissolved the awareness of Matter but without the final self-realisation.

BAILEY

I.19 The samadhi just described passes not beyond the bound of the phenomenal world; it passes not beyond the Gods, and those concerned with the concrete world.

DVIVEDI

I.19 Of those who are *Videha* and *Prakritilaya* the concrete universe is the cause.

FEUERSTEIN

I.19 [The enstacy of those who have] merged with the world-ground [and those who are] bodiless [is due to the persistence of] the presented-idea of becoming.

HOUSTON

I.19 In the case of those who are out of body, or absorbed in *prakṛti*-unmanifest primary matter, it (the other *nirodha* is preceded by) the *pratyaya*-immediate rising thought (directed towards) becoming.

JNANESHVARA

I.19 Some who have attained higher levels (videhas) or know unmanifest nature (prakritilayas), are drawn into birth in this world by their remaining latent impressions of ignorance, and more naturally come to these states of samadhi.

PRABHAVANANDA

I.19 When such concentration is not accompanied by non-attachment, and ignorance therefore retains, the aspirant will reach the state of the discarnate gods or become merged with the forces of Nature.

PUROHIT

I.19 They who have lost attachment to body or who have merged in nature, attain this condition when they are born again.

SATCHIDANANDA

I.19 Those who merely leave their physical bodies and attain the state of celestial deities, or those who get merged in Nature, have rebirth.

SHEARER

I.19 This is the nature of existence for beings without gross physical bodies and for those who are absorbed in the womb of all life waiting rebirth.

TAIMNI

I.19 Of those who are *Videhas* and *Prakṛtilayas* birth is the cause.

VIVEKANANDA

I.19 [This samādhi, when not followed by extreme non-attachment] becomes the cause of the remanifestation of the gods and of those who become merged in nature.

I.20

श्रद्धावीर्यस्मृतिसमाधिप्रज्ञापूर्वक इतरेषाम् ॥ २० ॥

śraddhā-vīrya-smṛti-samādhi-prajñā-pūrvaka itareṣām

श्रद्धा -	śraddhā-	faith
√श्रत् śrat: to assure + √धा dhā: to put		
वीर्य -	vīrya-	strength; power; vigor;
√वीर् vīr: to be powerful		indomitable energy
स्मृति -	smṛti-	memory; remembrance;
√स्मृ smṛ: to recall/remember		also: mindfulness; intentness, awareness or presence of mind; contemplation, meditation; *awakening of ekāgratā—Arya*
समाधि -	samādhi-	meditation; contemplation;
सम् - sam-: together with, completely, perfectly + आ - ā-: near to, all around + √धा dhā: to put		meta-cognitive absorption with various stages
प्रज्ञा -	prajñā-	wisdom; transcendent insight;
प्र - pra-: before, in front + √ज्ञा jñā: to know		consciousness (higher state of); awakening of wisdom (samprajñāta samādhi); supra-cognition; primary insight
पूर्वकः	pūrvakaḥ	preceded by; conditioned by; having them as a precondition or prerequisite
इतरेषाम्	itareṣām:	others'; of others

ARYA

I.20 The samādhi of others (in whose case it does not come right from birth requires effort, in other words, it is) preceded by (the practice and application of) faith, strength, memory (of practices and purifications undertaken in previous lives), (undertaking the practice of) meditation, and development of) wisdom.

BAILEY

I.20 Other yogins achieve samadhi and arrive at a discrimination of pure Spirit through belief, followed by energy, memory, meditation and right perception.

DVIVEDI

I.20 In others (it) is preceded by faith, energy, memory, and discrimination.

FEUERSTEIN

I.20 [The enstacy] of others [i.e. *yogins* whose path is described in I.18] is preceded by faith, energy, mindfulness, enstacy and supra-cognition.

HOUSTON

I.20 In the case of others, it (the other *nirodha*), is preceded by faith, energy, memory (*akliṣṭa*-unobstructed), *samādh*-cognitive absorption and *prajñā*-primary insight.

JNANESHVARA

I.20 Others follow a five-fold systematic path of 1) faithful certainty in the path, 2) directing energy towards the practices, 3) repeated memory of the path and the process of stilling the mind, 4) training in deep concentration, and 5) the pursuit of real knowledge, by which the higher samadhi (asamprajnata samadhi) is attained.

PRABHAVANANDA

I.20 The concentration of the true spiritual aspirant is attained through faith, energy, recollectedness, absorption and illumination.

PUROHIT

I.20 But others have to attain it through faith, effort, recollection, concentration, discrimination.

SATCHIDANANDA

I.20 To the others, this Asamprajnata samadhi could come through faith, strength, memory, contemplation or by discernment.

SHEARER

I.20 For others, this *samādhi* is preceded by trust, perseverance, recollection, tranquillity and wisdom.

TAIMNI

I.20 (In the case) of others (*Upāya-Pratyaya Yogis*) it is preceded by faith, energy, memory and high intelligence necessary for *Samādhi*.

VIVEKANANDA

I.20 By others [this samādhi) is attained through faith, energy, memory, concentration and discrimination of the real [from the unreal].

I.21

तीव्रसंवेगानामासन्नः ॥ २१ ॥

tīvra-saṃvegānām āsannaḥ

तीव्र - tīvra- acute; intense; fast; speedy; keen; extreme or extremely; strong; unlimited

संवेगानाम् saṃvegānām [*of those with/possessing*] intensity: speed; velocity; force; momentum; vehemence; intent

सम्- sam-: greatly, fully, completely, perfectly +

√विज् vij: to be agitated

आसन्नः āsannaḥ near; very close; impending; imminent; near at hand

आ - ā-: near to; from all sides, all around +

√सद् sad: to sit; to apply oneself

ARYA

I.21 In the case of those whose (spiritual) force is intense, the samādhi is very near.

BAILEY

I.21 The attainment of this state (spiritual consciousness) is rapid for those whose will is intensely alive.

DVIVEDI

I.21 (It is) nearest to those whose feeling is most ardent.

FEUERSTEIN

I.21 [This supreme enstacy] is near to [him who is] extremely vehement [in his practice of Yoga].

HOUSTON

I.21 In the case of those whose frequency is intense, it (the other *nirodha*) is near.

JNANESHVARA

I.21 Those who pursue their practices with intensity of feeling, vigor, and firm conviction achieve concentration and the fruits thereof more quickly, compared to those of medium or lesser intensity.

PRABHAVANANDA

I.21 Success in yoga comes quickly to those who are intensely energetic.

PUROHIT

I.21 Success is immediate where effort is intense.

SATCHIDANANDA

I.21 To the keen and intent practitioner this [Samadhi] comes very quickly.

SHEARER

I.21 It is near for those who ardently desire it.

TAIMNI

I.21 It (*Samādhi*) is nearest to those whose desire (for *Samādhi*) is intensely strong.

VIVEKANANDA

I.21 Success is speedy for the extremely emergetic.

I.22

मृदुमध्याधिमात्रत्वात्ततोऽपि विशेषः ॥ २२ ॥

mṛdu-madhyādhimātratvāt tato 'pi viśeṣaḥ

मृदु √मृद् *mṛd: to crush*	mṛdu-	mild; slow; modest	[*due to/because*] (there exists) (distinction in) intensity
मध्य -	madhya-	moderate; medium	
अधिमात्रत्वात् *अधि - adhi-: over, above +* √*मात्र mātra: measure*	adhimātratvāt	intense; extreme; powerful	

ततः	tataḥ	from that; hence	further
अपि	api	even, also	

विशेषः *वि - vi-: apart, separate from + √शिष् śiṣ: to remain*	viśeṣaḥ	distinction; difference; gradation

ARYA

I.22 There is further distinction, there being slow, middle and extreme (rates of growth).

BAILEY

I.22 Those who employ the will likewise differ, for its use may be intense, moderate or gentle. In respect to the attainment of true spiritual consciousness, there is yet another way.

DVIVEDI

I.22 A further distinction arises on account of mild, moderate, and excessive.

FEUERSTEIN

I.22 Because [this vehemence can be] modest, medium or excessive, [there is] hence also a difference [in the proximity of the *yogins* to the superior enstacy].

HOUSTON

I.22 Because of degree of mild, moderate, or extreme (frequency), thence there is also a difference (in nearness).

JNANESHVARA

I.22 Because the methods may be applied in slow, medium, or speedy ways, even among those who have such commitment and conviction, there are differences in the rate of progress, resulting in nine grades of practice.

PRABHAVANANDA

I.22 Success varies according to the means adopted to obtain it—mild, medium or intense.

PUROHIT

I.22 Success varies according to whether the effort is mild, moderate or intense.

SATCHIDANANDA

I.22 The time necessary for success further depends on whether the practice is mild, medium or intense.

SHEARER

I.22 Yet even among them there are degrees—mild, moderate, and intense.

TAIMNI

I.22 A further differentiation (arises) by reason of the mild, medium and intense (nature of means employed).

VIVEKANANDA

I.22 The success of yogis differs according as the means they adopt are mild, medium or intense.

I.23

ईश्वरप्रणिधानाद्वा ॥ २३ ॥

īśvara-praṇidhānād vā

ईश्वरप्रणिधानात	Īśvarapraṇidhānāt		
ईश्वर -	Īśvara-	God; Lord; Knower;	[*due to*] (placing oneself in) in the Lord; *perfect alignment of attention and intention with the Divine — Houston*
√ईष् *īs: to own, be master of +*		Seer; Teacher; Ultimate;	
वर *vara (√वृ vṛ: to choose): the best, choicest*		Divine Presence	
प्रणिधानात्	praṇidhānāt	[*due to*] devotion;	
प्र - *pra-: forward, in front, onward +*		[*by*] practicing	
-नि - *-ni-: into; intensity +*		the Presence (of)	
√धा *dhā: to put*			

वा	vā	or

ARYA

I.23 Or, the samādhi may be attained very quickly through surrender to God.

BAILEY

I.23 By intense devotion to Ishvara, knowledge of Ishvara is gained.

DVIVEDI

I.23 Or by devotion to *Īśvara*.

FEUERSTEIN

I.23 Or [enstacy is gained] through devotion to the Lord.

HOUSTON

I.23 Or, because of *īśvara-praṇidhāna*-the perfect aligning of attention in *īśvara*-the ultimate seer (there is a difference in nearness of the other *nirodha*).

JNANESHVARA

I.23 From a special process of devotion and letting go into the creative source from which we emerged (ishvara pranidhana), the coming of samadhi is imminent.

PRABHAVANANDA

I.23 Concentration may also be attained through devotion to Ishwara.

PUROHIT

I.23 Illumination is also attained by devotion to God.

SATCHIDANANDA

I.23 Or [Samadhi is attained] by devotion with dedication to God [Isvara].

SHEARER

I.23 It can also come from complete surrender to the almighty Lord.

TAIMNI

I.23 Or by self-surrender to God.

VIVEKANANDA

I.23 Or [this samādhi is attained] by devotion to Iśvara.

I.24

क्लेशकर्मविपाकाशयैरपरामृष्टः पुरुषविशेष ईश्वरः ॥ २४ ॥

kleśa-karma-vipākāśayair a-parā-mṛṣṭaḥ puruṣa-viśeṣa īśvaraḥ

क्लेश –	kleśa-	core/root/primary obstructions;
√क्लिश् kliś: to trouble, to be troubled		causes-of-afflictions or misery; impurity: afflictions; misery
कर्म –	karma-	actions and reactions
√कृ kṛ: to do		
विपाक –	vipāka-	results; maturing; ripening;
वि – vi-: intensity + √पच् pac: to cook, to roast		fruition of actions
आशयैः	āśayaiḥ	[*with*] propensities/accumulations/
आ – ā-: near to, from all sides, all around + √शी śī: to lie down/recline/rest		domains; seed impressions of latent desires
अपरामृष्टः	a-parā-mṛṣṭaḥ	unsmeared/unaffected/
अ – a-: un-/non-/not/without + परा parā: opposed to, back + √मृश् mṛś: to touch		untouched (by)
पुरुषविशेषः	puruṣa-viśeṣaḥ	a special or unique puruṣa
पुरुष puruṣa: the Eternal Witness + -वि – -vi-: apart, separate from + √शिष् śiṣ: to remain		
ईश्वरः	Īśvaraḥ	God; Lord; Knower; Seer;
√ईष् īs: to own, be master of + वर vara: the best, choicest (√वृ vṛ: to choose)		Teacher; Ultimate Divine Presence

ARYA

I.24 A special Conscious Being unsmeared by painful defilements, actions (their) fruitions and accumulated propensities is God.

BAILEY

I.24 This Ishvara is the soul, untouched by limitation, free from karma, and desire.

DVIVEDI

I.24 *Iśvara* is a particular soul untouched by affliction, works, fruition, and impressions.

FEUERSTEIN

I.24 The Lord is a special Self [because he is] untouched by the causes-of-affliction, action [and its] fruition [and by] the deposit [in the depth-memory].

HOUSTON

I.24 *Īśvara* is distinction of *Puruṣa*-self, untouched by accumulations of the fruitions of *karma*-action (arising) from *kleśa*-root obstructions(causes of pain).

JNANESHVARA

I.24 That creative source (ishvara) is a particular consciousness (purusha) that is unaffected by colorings (kleshas), actions (karmas), or results of those actions that happen when latent impressions stir and cause those actions.

PRABHAVANANDA

I.24 Ishwara is a special kind of being, untouched by ignorance and the products of ignorance, not subject to karmas or samskaras or the results of action.

PUROHIT

I.24 God is the One unique Personality, untouched by desire, affliction, action or its result.

SATCHIDANANDA

I.24 Isvara is the supreme Purusha, unaffected by any afflictions, actions, fruits of actions or by any inner impressions of desires.

SHEARER

I.24 The Lord is a unique being who exists beyond all suffering. Unblemished by action, He is free of both its cause and effects.

TAIMNI

I.24 *Iśvara* is a particular *Puruṣa* who is untouched by the afflictions of life, actions and the results and impressions produced by these actions.

VIVEKANANDA

I.24 Iśvara (the Supreme Ruler) is a special Purusha, untouched by misery, actions, their results and desires.

I.25

तत्र निरतिशयं सर्वज्ञत्वबीजम् ॥ २५ ॥

tatra nir-atiśayaṃ sarvajñatva-bījam

तत्र	tatra	there; in that (God); in (Him)	
निरतिशयं	nir-atiśayaṃ	ultimate; not exceeded (by any other);	
निर - nir-: without, free from +		unexcelled; complete manifestation;	
-अति - -ati-: beyond, over +		unsurpassed; Absolute Supremacy;	
√शी śī: to lie down/recline/rest		beyond the highest	
सर्वज्ञत्वबीजम्	sarvajñatvabījam		
सर्वज्ञत्व -	sarvajñatva-	(of) omniscient;	seed of
सर्व - sarva: all + √ज्ञा jñā: to know		all-knowing	omniscience
बीजम्	bījam	seed; core principle	

ARYA

I.25 In that God is the seed of omniscience unexceeded (by any other).

BAILEY

I.25 In Ishvara, the Gurudeva, the germ of all knowledge expands into infinity.

DVIVEDI

I.25 In him is the highest limit of the seed of omniscience.

FEUERSTEIN

I.25 In Him the seed of omniscience is unsurpassed.

HOUSTON

I.25 There (in *īśvara*), the seed of omniscience is unsurpassed.

JNANESHVARA

I.25 In that pure consciousness (ishvara) the seed of omniscience has reached its highest development and cannot be exceeded.

PRABHAVANANDA

I.25 In Him, knowledge is infinite; in others it is only a germ.

PUROHIT

I.25 In Him lies the seed of omniscience.

SATCHIDANANDA

I.25 In Him is the complete manifestation of the seed of omniscience.

SHEARER

I.25 In Him lies the finest seed of all knowledge.

TAIMNI

I.25 In Him is the highest limit of Omniscience.

VIVEKANANDA

I.25 In Him becomes infinite that all-knowingness which in others is [only] a germ.

I.26

स पूर्वेषामपि गुरुः कालेनानवच्छेदात् ॥ २६ ॥

sa pūrveṣām api guruḥ kālenānavacchedāt

सः	saḥ	that; this
पूर्वेषाम्	pūrveṣām	ancients' (teachers); [*of*] the ancient/ previous/first (gurus/teachers);
अपि	api	even; also
गुरुः √गुर् *gur: to call upon*	guruḥ	guru; mentor; teacher
वालेन √कल् *kal: to count, impel/urge*	kālena	[*by/with*] time; temporal consideration
अनवच्छेदात् *अन्* - *an-: not, non-* + - *अव* - *-ava-: away, off, down* + √छिद् *chid: to cut/separate*	an-avacchedāt:	[*due to/because of*] (being) boundless/unlimited/without limit/break/division; unconditioned continuity

ARYA

I.26 Because he is not delimited in (divided by) time, he is the guru of even the ancient teachers.

BAILEY

I.26 Ishvara the Gurudeva, being unlimited by time conditions, is the teacher of the primeval Lords.

DVIVEDI

I.26 Being unconditioned by time he is the greatest of the great.

FEUERSTEIN

I.26 [The Lord] was also the mentor of the earlier [*yogins*] by virtue of [His] temporal continuity.

HOUSTON

I.26 That (*īśvara*), being unlimited by time, is also the teacher of the ancients.

JNANESHVARA

I.26 From that consciousness (ishvara) the ancient-most teachers were taught, since it is not limited by the constraint of time.

PRABHAVANANDA

I.26 He was the teacher of even the earliest teachers, since He is not limited by time.

PUROHIT

I.26 He is master of even the ancient masters, being beyond the limits of time.

SATCHIDANANDA

I.26 Unconditioned by time, He is the teacher of even the most ancient teachers.

SHEARER

I.26 Being beyond time, He is the Teacher of even the ancient tradition of teachers.

TAIMNI

I.26 Being unconditioned by time He is Teacher even of the Ancients.

VIVEKANANDA

I.26 He is the Teacher of even the ancient teachers, being not limited by time.

I.27

तस्य वाचकः प्रणवः ॥ २७ ॥

tasya vācakaḥ praṇavaḥ

तस्य	tasya	His; Īśvara's; [*of*] Īśvara/ belonging to Īśvara
वाचकः √वच् *vac: to speak*	vācakaḥ	signifier; symbol; signifying syllable; word or name (is); word expressive (of)
प्रणवः प्र- *pra-: forward, in front, onward* + √नु *nu: to shout/exult*	praṇavaḥ	His Word His Pronouncement His Syllable His Mantra inner sound current } *AUM* or *OM*

ARYA

I.27 The word *Om* is His signaficator (name).

BAILEY

I.27 The Word of Ishvara is AUM (or OM). This is the Pranava.

DVIVEDI

I.27 His indicator is the "word of glory".

FEUERSTEIN

I.27 His symbol is the *praṇava* [i.e. the syllable *oṃ*].

HOUSTON

I.27 The expression of that (*īśvara*) is OM (*praṇava*- primary sound frequency of creation heard as an inner ringing sound current).

JNANESHVARA

I.27 The sacred word designating this creative source is the sound OM, called pranava.

PRABHAVANANDA

I.27 The word which expresses Him is Om.

PUROHIT

I.27 His name is Ōm.

SATCHIDANANDA

I.27 The word expressive of Isvara is the mystic sound OM. [Note: OM is God's name as well as form.]

SHEARER

I.27 He is expressed through the sacred syllable *OM*.

TAIMNI

I.27 His designator is "Om."

VIVEKANANDA

I.27 The word that manifests Him is Om.

I.28

तज्जपस्तदर्थभावनम् ॥ २८ ॥

taj-japas tad-artha-bhāvanam

तज्जपः	taj-japaḥ	repetition/recitation of that (and)	
तद् tad-: that + √जप् jap: to repeat			
तदर्थभावनम्	tadarthabhāvanam		
तद् -	tad-	of that/ its	cultivating, absorbing
अर्थ -	artha-	meaning	(in meditation)
√अर्थ् arth: to intend			the meaning of
भावनम्	bhāvanam	absorbing;	that (praṇava)
√भू bhū: to become		cultivating	(is Īśvara praṇidhāna)

ARYA

I.28 Ishvara praṇidhāna (in Sūtra I.23, is to be defined as) the recitation of that name and (mentally) absorbing its meaning.

BAILEY

I.28 Through the sounding of the Word and through reflection upon its meaning, the Way is found.

DVIVEDI

I.28 Its constant repetition, and intent meditation on its meaning (should be practiced).

FEUERSTEIN

I.28 The recitation of that [syllable] [leads to] the contemplation of its meaning.

HOUSTON

I.28 The repetition of that (*om-praṇava*) (leads to) the realization of its meaning.

JNANESHVARA

I.28 This sound is remembered with deep feeling for the meaning of what it represents.

PRABHAVANANDA

I.28 This word must be repeated with meditation upon its meaning.

PUROHIT

I.28 Repeat it constantly; meditate on its meaning.

SATCHIDANANDA

I.28 To repeat it with reflection upon its meaning is an aid.

SHEARER

I.28 It should be repeated and its essence realized.

TAIMNI

I.28 Its constant repetition and meditation on its meaning.

VIVEKANANDA

I.28 The repetition of this [Om] and meditating on its meaning [is the way].

I.29

ततः प्रत्यक्चेतनाधिगमोऽप्यन्तरायाभावश्च ॥ २९ ॥

tataḥ pratyak-cetanādhigamo'pyantarāyabāvaś ca

ततः	tataḥ	then, from this; through that practice: (practice of Īśvarapraṇidhānād – the presence of God)

प्रत्यक्चेतनाधिगमाः	pratyakcetanādhigamaḥ		*attainment of inward consciousness or realization of the inwardly conscious [self]* – *Arya*
प्रत्यक् -	pratyak-	inward, inner;	
प्रति - prati-: toward, in direction of + √अच् ac: to bend		in-turned	
चेतना -	cetanā-	consciousness;	
√चित् cit: to be conscious		mindedness; self	
अधिगमः	adhigamaḥ	attainment;	
अधि - dhi-: over, above + √गम् gam: to go		realization	

अपि -	api-	too; also
अन्तराय -	antarāya-	(going between) obstacles;
अन्तर् - antar-: between; internal inward, within, + √इ i: to go		impediments; obstructions; hindrances; blockages
अभाव	abhāva	absence; negation;
अ - a-: un-/non-/not/without + √भू bhū: to be/become		nothingness; non-occurrence; absence; removal; disappearance
च	ca	also; and

ARYA

I.29 Then (to the yogi occurs the) attainment of inward consciousness (or) realisation of the inwardly conscious (self), and absence of obstructions (on this path).

BAILEY

I.29 From this comes the realisation of the Self (the soul) and the removal of obstacles.

DVIVEDI

I.29 Thence arises cognition of the subjective, and absence of obstacles.

FEUERSTEIN

I.29 Thence [follows] the attainment of [habitual] inward-mindedness and also the disappearance of the obstacles [mentioned below].

HOUSTON

I.29 From that (comes) the attainment of inward directed consciousness, and also the disappearance of the blocks.

JNANESHVARA

I.29 From that remembering comes the realization of the individual Self and the removal of obstacles.

PRABHAVANANDA

I.29 Hence comes knowledge of the *Atman* and destruction of the obstacles to that knowledge.

PUROHIT

I.29 Devotion to God enlightens the soul, removes every obstacle.

SATCHIDANANDA

I.29 From this practice all the obstacles disappear and simultaneously dawns knowledge of the inner Self.

SHEARER

I.29 Then the mind will turn inward and the obstacles which stand in the way of progress will disappear.

TAIMNI

I.29 From it (result) the disappearance of obstacles and turning inward of consciousness.

VIVEKANANDA

I.29 From that is gained introspection, and the destruction of obstacles.

I.30

व्याधिस्त्यानसंशयप्रमादालस्याविरतिभ्रान्तिदर्शनालब्धभूमिकत्वानवस्थितत्वानि चित्तविक्षेपास्तेऽन्तरायाः ॥ ३० ॥

vyādhi-styāna-saṃśaya-pramādālasyāvirati-bhrānti-darśanālabdha-bhūmikatvānavasthitatvāni citta-vikṣepās te'ntarāyāḥ

व्याधि - vyādhi- — illness; disease; sickness

वि - vi-: apart, separate from + आ - ā-: near to, from all sides + √धा dhā: to put

स्त्यान - styāna- — mental laziness; procrastination; mind's idleness; dullness; inertia

√स्त्या styā: to grow dense

संशय - saṃśaya- — doubt; wrong questioning

सम् - sam-: fully, completely + √शी śī: to lie, rest

प्रमाद् - pramāda- — negligence; carelessness

प्र - pra-: forward, away + √मद् mad: to be intoxicated

आलस्य - ālasya- — laziness; languor; sloth; lethargy

आ - ā-: reverse of action + √लस् las: to shine

अविरति - a-virati- — failing to turn away from the world and the senses; sensuality; non-abstention; dissipation; sexual preoccupation

अ - a-: un-/non-/not/without +
वि - vi-: apart, separate from, reverse to +
√रम् ram: to be excited, to take pleasure

भ्रान्तिदर्शन - bhrānti-darśana- — wrong views; false perception; confusion of philosophies; delusion

भ्रान्ति bhrānti- wrong, false, erroneous:
√भ्रम् bhram: to wander about + दर्शन darśana: viewpoint, perception, philosophy: √दृश् dṛś: to see

अलब्धभूमिकत्व - a-labdha-bhūmikatva- — failing to gain a (higher) ground (and)

अ - a-: un-/non-/not/without + लब्ध् labdh: to obtain + √भू bhū: to become

अनवस्थितत्वानि an-avasthitatvāni — instability; inability to maintain the ground or level when attained

अन - an-: without + √स्था sthā: to stand

चित्तविक्षेपाः citta-vikṣepāḥ — (are) distractions/disruptions (of the) mind-field

√चित् cit: to be conscious +
वि - vi-: apart, separate from + √क्षिप् kṣip: to throw/cast

ते - te- — these

अन्तरायाः antarāyāḥ — obstacles; impediments; obstructions; hindrances; blockages

अन्तर् - antar: inner, other, between + √इ i: to go

ARYA

I.30 Sickness, mental laziness, doubt, negligence, (physical and mental) heaviness, not turning away from sense desires, wrong views, not gaining a (higher) ground (in meditation), and not remaining (at that ground for long) are the disturbances of the mind (and) are the obstacles.

BAILEY

I.30 The obstacles to soul cognition are: bodily disability, mental inertia, wrong questioning, carelessness, laziness, lack of dispassion, erroneous perception, inability to achieve concentration, failure to hold the meditative attitude when achieved.

DVIVEDI

I.30 Disease, Dullness, Doubt, Carelessness, Sloth, Worldly-mindedness, False notion, Missing the point and Instability are the causes of distracting the mind, and they are the obstacles.

FEUERSTEIN

I.30 Sickness, languor, doubt, heedlessness, sloth, dissipation, false vision, non-attaining of the stages [of Yoga] and instability [in these stages] are the distractions of consciousness; these are the obstacles.

HOUSTON

I.30 Sickness, density, doubt, carelessness, lethargy, sexual preoccupation, erroneous perception, failure to obtain grounding (in abhyāsa-yoga practice), and instability are disruptions in *citta*-the field. These are the blocks.

JNANESHVARA

I.30 Nine kinds of distractions come that are obstacles naturally encountered on the path, and are physical illness, tendency of the mind to not work efficiently, doubt or indecision, lack of attention to pursuing the means of samadhi, laziness in mind and body, failure to regulate the desire for worldly objects, incorrect assumptions or thinking, failing to attain stages of the practice, and instability in maintaining a level of practice once attained.

PRABHAVANANDA

I.30 Sickness, mental laziness, doubt, lack of enthusiasm, sloth, craving for sense-pleasure, false perception, despair caused by failure to concentrate and unsteadiness in concentration: these distractions are the obstacles to knowledge.

PUROHIT

I.30 Disease, lack of enthusiasm, doubt, irregularity, lethargy, yearning for sensual pleasure, hallucination, failure to attain a step, failure to maintain that step, are obstacles that distract the mind.

SATCHIDANANDA

I.30 Disease, dullness, doubt, carelessness, laziness, sensuality, false perception, failure to reach firm ground and slipping from the ground gained—these distractions of the mind stuff are the obstacles.

SHEARER

I.30 These obstacles are: illness, fatigue, doubt, carelessness, laziness, attachment delusion, the failure to achieve samādhi and the failure to maintain samādhi.
They are the distractions from the path of yoga.

TAIMNI

I.30 Disease, languor, doubt, carelessness, laziness, worldly-mindedness, delusion, non-achievement of a stage, instability; these (nine) cause the distraction of the mind and they are the obstacles.

VIVEKANANDA

I.30 Disease, mental laziness, doubt, lack of enthusiasm, lethargy, clinging to sense-enjoyments, false perception, non-attaining concentration, and falling away from concentration when obtained—these are the obstructing distractions.

I.31

दुःखदौर्मनस्याङ्गमेजयत्वश्वासप्रश्वासा विक्षेपसहभुवः ॥ ३१ ॥

duḥkha-daurmanasyāṅgam-ejayatva-śvāsa-praśvāsā vikṣepa-saha-bhuvaḥ

दुःख -	duḥkha-	pain; sorrow, suffering; distress; those suffering	
दुस् dus: bad + ख kha: space, e.g. axle-hole			
दौर्मनस्य -	daur-manasya-	frustration; anguish; despair; depression	
दुस् dus: bad + √मन् man: to think + √अस् as: to be + -य ya: one who goes/moves			
अङ्गमेजयत्व -	aṅgamejayatva-		
अङ्गम् -	aṅgam-	(of) limbs	uncontrolled movement of body or limbs
अङ्ग aṅga: parts			
एजयत्व -	ejayatva-	trembling; unsteadiness	
√एज् ej: to tremble			
श्वासप्रश्वासा	śvāsapraśvāsā		
श्वास -	śvāsa-	inhalation (and)	breathing (when disturbed or uncontrolled)
√श्वस् śvas: to pant			
प्रश्वासाः	pra-śvāsāḥ	exhalation	
प्र - vi away + √श्वस् śvas: to breathe			
विक्षेप -	vikṣepa-	(of) distractions; disruptions; agitations	
वि - vi-: apart, separate from + √क्षिप् kṣip: to throw/cast			
सहभुवः	saha-bhuvaḥ	natural accompaniments; correlates	
सह saha: jointly + √भु bhu: to become			

ARYA

I.31 Pain, frustration (or anguish), unsteadiness of limbs (during meditation), uncontrolled exhalation and inhalation: these are the correlates of the obstructions.

BAILEY

I.31 Pain, despair, misplaced bodily activity and wrong direction (or control) of life currents are the results of the obstacles in the lower psychic nature.

DVIVEDI

I.31 Pain, Despair, Nervousness, Inspiration, Expiration are the accompaniments of the causes of distraction.

FEUERSTEIN

I.31 Pain, depression, tremor of the limbs, [wrong] inhalation and exhalation are the accompanying [symptoms] of the distractions.

HOUSTON

I.31 They (the blocks) have the accompanying disruptions of pain, depression, restlessness of the body, inhalation and exhalation.

JNANESHVARA

I.31 From these obstacles, there are four other consequences that also arise, and these are:
1) mental or physical pain,
2) sadness or dejection,
3) restlessness, shakiness, or anxiety, and 4) irregularities in the exhalation and inhalation of breath.

PRABHAVANANDA

I.31 These distractions are accompanied by grief, despondency, troubling of the body, and irregular breathing.

PUROHIT

I.31 Pain, nervousness, sulkiness, irregular breathing, follow.

SATCHIDANANDA

I.31 Accompaniments to the mental distractions include distress, despair, troubling of the body and disturbed breathing.

SHEARER

I.31 Such distractions make the body restless, the breathing coarse and the mind agitated. They result in suffering.

TAIMNI

I.31 (Mental) pain, despair, nervousness and hard breathing are the symptoms of a distracted condition of mind.

VIVEKANANDA

I.31 Grief, mental distress, tremor of the body, irregular breathing accompany non-retention of concentration.

I.32

तत्प्रतिषेधार्थमेकतत्त्वाभ्यासः ॥ ३२ ॥

tat-pratiṣedhārtam eka-tattvābhyāsaḥ

तद् -	tad-	that; these
प्रतिषेध -	pratiṣedha-	preventing; counteracting;
प्रति - prati-: counter + √सिध् sidh: to be accomplished		opposing; negating; voiding; prohibiting; nullifying; removing
अर्थम्	artham	(having as its) purpose;
√अर्थ artha: to intend		for the purpose of; in order to
एक -	eka-	one; single
तत्त्व -	tattva-	lit.: that-ness: here: true or real state; essence; reality; principle; factor
अभ्यासः	abhyāsaḥ	(persistent) personal practice/
अभि - abhi-: to, towards, into +		application
*√आस् - ās: to apply oneself **OR** to sit*		

ARYA

I.32 For the prevention of these (one should observe the) practice of (one-pointed concentration on) one essence, (or some one object of concentration).

BAILEY

I.32 To overcome the obstacles and their accompaniments, the intense application of the will to some one truth (or principle) is required.

DVIVEDI

I.32 To prevent these (there should be) intense application to any one thing.

FEUERSTEIN

I.32 In order to counteract these [distractions] [the *yogin* should resort to] the practice [of concentration] on a single principle.

HOUSTON

I.32 In order to prevent those blocks, the *abhyāsa*-practice of a single truth.

JNANESHVARA

I.32 To prevent or deal with these nine obstacles and their four consequences, the recommendation is to make the mind one-pointed, training it how to focus on a single principle or object.

PRABHAVANANDA

I.32 They can be removed by the practice of concentration upon a single truth.

PUROHIT

I.32 To destroy these, meditate on one object.

SATCHIDANANDA

I.32 The practice of concentration on a single subject [or the use of one technique] is the best way to prevent the obstacles and their accompaniments.

SHEARER

I.32 But they can be eliminated if the mind is brought to a single focus.

TAIMNI

I.32 For removing these obstacles there (should be) constant practice of one truth or principle.

VIVEKANANDA

I.32 To remedy this [one should] practice on one object.

I.33

मैत्रीकरुणामुदितोपेक्षाणां सुखदुःखपुन्यापुन्यविषयाणां भावनातश्चित्तप्रसादनम् ॥ ३३ ॥

maitrī-karuṇā-muditopekṣāṇāṃ sukha-duḥkha-puṇyāpuṇya-
viṣayānāṃ bhāvanātaś citta-prasādanam

मैत्री -	maitrī-	[*possessing*] friendships; amity; loves
√*मिद् mid: to adhere*		
करुणा -	karunā-	[*possessing*] compassion
√*कृ kṛ: to do*		
मुदित -	mudita-	[*experiencing*] delight; joy; gladness
√*मुद् mud: to rejoice*		
उपेक्षाणां	upekṣāṇāṃ	[*holding*] equanimity; indifference;
उप - upa-: towards + √ईक्ष īkṣ: to see		dispassion; disregard
सुख -	sukha-	[*of*] pleasure/comfort;
सु su: well + ख kha: axle-hole		those comfortable, joyful, happy
दुःख -	duḥka-	pain; sorrow; suffering; distress;
दुस् dus: bad + ख kha: space, e.g. axle-hole		those suffering
पुण्य -	puṇya-	with virtue/virtuousness; goodness;
√*पुण् puṇ: to do good*		merit/meritoriousness
अपुण्य -	a-puṇya-	without virtue or merit: vice; wickedness
अ - a-: un-/non-/not/without + √पुण् puṇ: to do good		
विषयाणां	viṣayāṇāṃ	[*possessing*] [*having in relation with/*
√*विष् viṣ: to be active + अय - aya-: going*		*in regard to/in the case of*] objects (of experience) subject-matter
भावनातः	bhāvanātaḥ	(through) cultivating; projection
√*भू bhu: to become*		by impressing into/upon oneself
चित्त -	citta-	(of) energy field called mind
√*चित् cit: to perceive; to be bright*		in all aspects
प्रसादनम्	pra-sādanam	purifying; rendering clear; making
प्र - pra-: towards, into + √सद् sad: to sit; to apply oneself		happy, serene, pleasing, pleasant; undisturbed calm; pacification; clarification

ARYA

I.33 The purification (clarity, or joyfulness) of the mind (is gained) by cultivating love, compassion, joy and equanimity, respectively, in relation to (those who are happy, good and evil).

BAILEY

I.33 The peace of the citta (or mind stuff) can be brought about through the practice of sympathy, tenderness, steadiness of purpose, and dispassion in regard to pleasure or pain, or towards all forms of good or evil.

DVIVEDI

I.33 The mind (becomes) cheerful by the practice of sympathy, compassion, complacency and indifference, respectively, towards happiness, misery, vice, and virtue.

FEUERSTEIN

I.33 The projection of friendliness, compassion, gladness and equanimity towards objects—[be they] joyful, sorrowful, meritorious or demeritorious—[bring about] the pacification of consciousness.

HOUSTON

I.33 The clarification of *citta*-the field comes about due to the realization of friendship with regard to the experiences (*viṣaya*-objects) of happiness, compassion with pain, elation with virtue, and neutrality with non-virtue (negativity).

JNANESHVARA

I.33 In relationships, the mind becomes purified by cultivating feelings of friendliness towards those who are happy, compassion for those who are suffering, goodwill towards those who are virtuous, and indifference or neutrality towards those we perceive as wicked or evil.

PRABHAVANANDA

I.33 Undisturbed calmness of mind is attained by cultivating friendliness toward the happy, compassion for the unhappy, delight in the virtuous and indifference toward the wicked.

PUROHIT

I.33 Mind attains peace by associating with the happy, pitying the miserable, appreciating the virtuous, and avoiding the vicious.

SATCHIDANANDA

I.33 By cultivating attitudes of friendliness toward the happy, compassion for the unhappy, delight in the virtuous and disregard for the wicked, the mind-stuff retains its undisturbed calmness.

SHEARER

I.33 The mind becomes clear and serene when the qualities of the heart are cultivated: friendliness towards the joyful, compassion towards the suffering, happiness towards the pure and impartiality towards the impure.

TAIMNI

I.33 The mind becomes clarified by cultivating attitudes of friendliness, compassion, gladness and indifference respectively towards happiness, misery, virtue and vice.

VIVEKANANDA

I.33 The feelings of friendship, mercy, gladness and indifference, in regard to objects, happy, unhappy, good, and evil, respectively, pacify the chitta.

I.34

प्रच्छर्दनविधारणाभ्यां वा प्राणस्य ॥ ३४ ॥

pracchardana-vidhāraṇābhyāṃ vā prāṇasya

प्रच्छर्दन – *प्र – pra-: towards, into + √छृद् chṛd: to vomit*	pracchardana-	expulsion (here: exhalation)
विधारणाभ्यां *वि – vi-: apart, separate + √धृ dhṛ: to hold/carry/bear*	vidhāraṇābhyāṃ	[*by means of*] control; disciplined restraint
वा	vā	or
प्राणस्य *प्र – pra-: forward, in front + √अन् an: to breathe*	prāṇasya	[*of*] prāṇa/prāṇa's (subtle life-force counterpart of the external breath)

ARYA

I.34 Or by controlled exhalation and retention of breath (the mind is purified).

BAILEY

I.34 The peace of the citta is also brought about by regulation of the prana or life breath.

DVIVEDI

I.34 Or by the expiration and retention of the breath.

FEUERSTEIN

I.34 Or [restriction is achieved] by [the controlled] expulsion and retention of the breath.

HOUSTON

I.34 (*Citta*-the field is clarified) also by the holding in or out of breath.

JNANESHVARA

I.34 The mind is also calmed by regulating the breath, particularly attending to exhalation and the natural stilling of breath that comes from such practice.

PRABHAVANANDA

I.34 The mind may also be calmed by expulsion and retention of the breath.

PUROHIT

I.34 Also by expulsion and retention of breath.

SATCHIDANANDA

I.34 Or that calm is retained by the controlled exhalation or retention of the breath.

SHEARER

I.34 Or through the practice of various breathing exercises.

TAIMNI

I.34 Or by the expiration and retention of breath.

VIVEKANANDA

I.34 By expelling and restraining the breath [the chitta is pacified].

I.35

विषयवती वा प्रवृत्तिरुत्पन्ना मनसः स्थितिनिबन्धनी ॥ ३५ ॥

viṣayavatī vā pravṛttir utpannā manasaḥ sthiti-nibandhanī

विषयवती	viṣayavatī		
विषय - *√विष् viṣ: to be active +* *अय - aya-: going*	viṣaya-	objects (of experience); subject-matter	having sense objects/experiences/ perceptions; object centered
वती	vatī	having	
वा	vā	also, or	
प्रवृत्तिः *प्र - pra-: forward + √वृत् vṛt: to turn*	pravṛttiḥ	inclination; manifestation; direct perception; apprehension; activity; experienced by the senses	
उत्पन्ना मनसः	utpannā manasaḥ		
उत्पन्ना *उद् - ud-: up + √पद् pad: to fall*	utpannā	born; appeared; occurred; become manifest; arising; born of	born of mind
मनसः *√मन् man: to think*	manasaḥ	[*of*] mind; mind's	
स्थिति - *√स्था sthā: to stand*	sthiti-	stability; steadiness	
निबन्धनी *नि - ni-: into + √बन्ध् bandh: to bind*	ni-bandhanī	that which binds/holds/seals/ firmly establishes	

ARYA

I.35 The natural mental tendency of concentrating (even) on an object of senses, when developed, stills and purifies the mind.

BAILEY

I.35 The mind can be trained to steadiness through those forms of concentration which have relation to the sense perceptions.

DVIVEDI

I.35 Or engrossing cognition of any sensuous enjoyment, brought about, is the cause of steadying the mind.

FEUERSTEIN

I.35 Or [restriction comes about when] an object-centred activity has arisen which holds the mind in steadiness.

HOUSTON

I.35 Also, a *pravṛtti*-cognition which has arisen, related to a sensory object, holding the steadiness of the mind, (clarifies *citta*).

JNANESHVARA

I.35 The inner concentration on the process of sensory experiencing, done in a way that leads towards higher, subtle sense perception; this also leads to stability and tranquility of the mind.

PRABHAVANANDA

I.35 Those forms of concentration which result in extra-ordinary perceptions encourage perseverance of the mind.

PUROHIT

I.35 Mind attains peace, when meditation produces extra-ordinary sense-perceptions.

SATCHIDANANDA

I.35 Or the concentration on subtle sense perception can cause steadiness of mind.

SHEARER

I.35 Experience of the finer levels of the senses establishes the settled mind.

TAIMNI

I.35 Coming into activity of (higher) senses also becomes helpful in establishing steadiness of the mind.

VIVEKANANDA

I.35 Those forms of concentration which bring extraordinary sense perceptions cause perseverance of the mind.

I.36

विशोका वा ज्योतिष्मती ॥ ३६ ॥

viśhokā vā jyotiṣmatī

विशोका	viśokā	blissful; serene;
वि - vi-: apart, separate + √शुच् śuc: to burn		free of grief, suffering or sorrow
वा	vā	or
ज्योतिष्मती	jyotiṣmatī	luminous; full of light (sattva)
ज्योतिष् jyotiṣ: light/√ज्युत् jyut: to shine +		supreme light; illumination
- मन्त् mant: having, consisting of		

ARYA

I.36 Or, the (natural mental state: pravṛttiḥ) which is full of (sāttvic) light and (therefore) free of grief (and exhilaration) (stills and purifies the mind).

BAILEY

I.36 By meditation upon Light and upon Radiance, knowledge of the Spirit can be reached and thus peace can be achieved.

DVIVEDI

I.36 Or that sorrowless condition of the mind, full of light (would conduce to *Samādhi*).

FEUERSTEIN

I.36 Or [restriction is achieved by mental activities which are] sorrowless and illuminating.

HOUSTON

I.36 Also, (a *pravṛtti*-cognition) which is sorrowless and luminous (clarifies *citta*).

JNANESHVARA

I.36 Or concentration on a painless inner state of lucidness and luminosity also brings stability and tranquility.

PRABHAVANANDA

I.36 Concentration may also be attained by fixing the mind upon the Inner Light, which is beyond sorrow.

PUROHIT

I.36 Or by meditation on the inner light that leads beyond sorrow.

SATCHIDANANDA

I.36 Or by concentrating on the supreme, everblissful Light within.

SHEARER

I.36 So does experience of the inner radiance which is free from sorrow.

TAIMNI

I.36 Also (through) serene or luminous (states experienced within).

VIVEKANANDA

I.36 Or [the chitta is pacified by meditation on] the Effulgent Light, which is beyond all sorrow.

I.37

वीतरागविषयं वा चित्तम् ॥ ३७ ॥

vīta-rāga-viṣayaṃ vā cittam

वीतरागविषयं	vīta-rāga-viṣayaṃ		
वीत -	vīta-	devoid of; free from; transcended; conquered	*…those from whose mind the attraction toward sense objects is gone – Arya*
Past Participle			
राग -	rāga-	desire; attraction; attachment	
√रज् *raj: to be excited*			
विषयं	viṣayaṃ	sense objects	

वा	vā	or; also
चित्तम्	cittam	(of) energy field called mind in all aspects; mind-field; field of consciousness; consciousness; mind-stuff
√चित् *cit: to perceive; to be bright*		

ARYA

I.37 Or, the mind-stuff from which (all) attraction toward sense-objects is gone (stills and purifies the active–manas–mind).

BAILEY

I.37 The citta is stabilised and rendered free from illusion as the lower nature is purified and no longer indulged.

DVIVEDI

I.37 Or the mind intent upon those free from attachment, etc., (will lead to the end).

FEUERSTEIN

I.37 Or [restriction is achieved when] consciousness is directed to [those beings who] have conquered attachment.

HOUSTON

I.37 Also, *citta* (whose) *Viṣaya*-object is that which transcends attachment (is clarified).

JNANESHVARA

I.37 Or contemplating on having a mind that is free from desires, the mind gets stabilized and tranquil.

PRABHAVANANDA

I.37 Or by meditating on the heart of an illumined soul, that is free from passion.

PUROHIT

I.37 Or by meditation on saints who have attained desirelessness.

SATCHIDANANDA

I.37 Or by concentrating on a great soul's mind which is totally freed from attachment to sense objects.

SHEARER

I.37 So does being attuned to another mind which is itself unperturbed by desire.

TAIMNI

I.37 Also the mind fixed on those who are free from attachment (acquires steadiness).

VIVEKANANDA

I.37 Or (by meditation on) the heart that has given up all attachment to sense-objects.

I.38

स्वप्ननिद्राज्ञानालम्बनं वा ॥ ३८ ॥

svapna-nidrā-jñānālambanaṃ vā

स्वप्न -	svapna-	dream-state
√स्वप् *svap: to sleep*		
निद्रा -	nidrā-	sleep; deep or dreamless sleep
नि - *ni-: in, into, downward motion, great +*		
√द्रा *drai: to sleep*		
ज्ञान -	jñāna-	knowledge; concept; idea;
√ज्ञा *jñā to know*		insight; awareness; observation;
		ordinary knowledge based on sense perception and reasoning
आलम्बनं	ālambanaṃ	supportive device; object or factor;
आ - *ā-: near to, all around +*		object of meditation
√लम्ब् *lamb: to rest on, to hang*		
वा	vā	and; or; also

ARYA

I.38 Or, resorting to the knowledge of dream and sleep (states) (stills the mind).

BAILEY

I.38 Peace (steadiness of the chitta) can be reached through meditation on the knowledge which dreams give.

DVIVEDI

I.38 Or depending on the experience of dream and sleep (will lead to the result).

FEUERSTEIN

I.38 Or [restriction is achieved when consciousness] is resting on the insight [arising from] dreams and sleep.

HOUSTON

I.38 Also (*citta* is clarified) having as its supporting object the knowledge of dreams or sleep.

JNANESHVARA

I.38 Or by focusing on the nature of the stream in the dream state or the nature of the state of dreamless sleep, the mind becomes stabilized and tranquil.

PRABHAVANANDA

I.38 Or by fixing the mind upon a dream experience, or the experience of deep sleep.

PUROHIT

I.38 Or by meditation on the knowledge gained through dream or sleep.

SATCHIDANANDA

I.38 Or by concentrating on an experience had during dream or deep sleep.

SHEARER

I.38 So does witnessing the processing of dreaming or dreamless sleep.

TAIMNI

I.38 Also (the mind) depending upon the knowledge derived from dreams or dreamless sleep (will acquire steadiness).

VIVEKANANDA

I.38 Or [by meditation on] the knowledge that comes in in dreams or the happiness experienced in deep sleep.

I.39

यथाभिमतध्यानाद्वा ॥ ३९ ॥

yathābhimata-dhyānād vā

यथा -	yathā-	as; whichever way
अभिमत -	abhimata-	desired; favorite; attractive;
अभि - abhi-: to, toward, into + √मन् man: to think		agreeable; appealing; object of choice
ध्यानात्	dhyānāt	[*by/from/because of*] meditation;
√ध्यै dhyai: meditate		[*by/from/because of*] meditative absorption
वा	vā	or; also

ARYA

I.39 Or, by meditating upon an object of one's choice, (the mind is stilled and purified).

BAILEY

I.39 Peace can also be reached through concentration upon that which is dearest to the heart.

DVIVEDI

I.39 Or by meditating according to one's predilection.

FEUERSTEIN

I.39 Or [restriction is achieved] through meditative-absorption as desired.

HOUSTON

I.39 Also, by *dhyāna*-meditation as desired (*citta* is clarified).

JNANESHVARA

I.39 Or by contemplating or concentrating on whatever object or principle one may like, or towards which one has a predisposition, the mind becomes stable and tranquil.

PRABHAVANANDA

I.39 Or by fixing the mind upon any divine form or symbol that appeals to one as good.

PUROHIT

I.39 Or by meditation on anything you will.

SATCHIDANANDA

I.39 Or by meditating on anything one chooses that is elevating.

SHEARER

I.39 So does any meditation that is held in high esteem.

TAIMNI

I.39 Or by meditation as desired.

VIVEKANANDA

I.39 Or by the meditation on anything that appeals to one as good.

I.40

परमाणुपरममहत्त्वान्तोऽस्य वशीकारः ॥ ४० ॥

paramāṇu-parama-mahattvānto'sya vaśīkāraḥ

परमाणु	paramāṇu		
परम -	parama-	ultimate; infinite	(from)
√पॄ *pṛ: to surpass*			infinitely minute;
अणु -	aṇu-	smallness; minutest	subatomic field
परममहत्त्व	paramamahattva		
परम -	parama-	ultimate; infinite	(up to)
√पॄ *pṛ: to surpass*			infinite
महत्त्व -	mahattva-	greatness; magnitude	magnitude;
√मह् *mah: to magnify*			cosmic field
अन्तः	antaḥ	ending in; extending up to	
अस्य	asya	His; of this one; this one's	
वशीकारः -	vaśīkāraḥ	mastery; power;	
वश् *vaś: to will* + √कृ *kṛ: to make*		bringing under complete control	

ARYA

I.40 This (stilled and purified mind's) control (is established and covers everything from the) minutest atom to the first field of cosmic material energy.

BAILEY

I.40 Thus, his realisation extends from the infinitely small to the infinitely great, and from the annu (the atom or speck) to atma (or spirit) his knowledge is perfected.

DVIVEDI

I.40 His mastery extends from the finest atom to Infinity.

FEUERSTEIN

I.40 His mastery [extends] from the most minute to the greatest magnitude.

HOUSTON

I.40 The mastery of this (*dhyāna*-meditation and hence desirelessness for its objects) extends from the greatest magnitude to the greatest minuteness.

JNANESHVARA

I.40 When, through such practices (as previously described in I.33-I.39), the mind develops the power of becoming stable on the smallest size object as well as on the largest, then the mind truly comes under control.

PRABHAVANANDA

I.40 The mind of a yogi can concentrate upon any object of any size, from the atomic to the infinitely great.

PUROHIT

I.40 Thus mind masters everything from the smallest to the greatest.

SATCHIDANANDA

I.40 Gradually, one's mastery in concentration extends from the primal atom to the greatest magnitude.

SHEARER

I.40 The sovereignty of the mind that is settled, extends from the smallest of the small to the greatest of the great.

TAIMNI

I.40 His mastery extends from the finest atom to the greatest infinity.

VIVEKANANDA

I.40 The yogi's mind thus meditating, becomes unobstructed from the atomic to the infinite.

I.41

क्षीणवृत्तेरभिजातस्येव मणेर्ग्रहीतृग्रहणग्राह्येषु
तत्स्थतदञ्जनता समापत्तिः ॥ ४१ ॥

kṣīṇa-vṛtter abhijātasyeva maṇer grahītṛ-grahaṇa-grāhyeṣu
tat-stha-tad-añjanatā samāpattiḥ

क्षीणवृत्ते	kṣīṇa-vṛtteḥ	lit.: vṛtti's disappearance:
क्षीण -	kṣīṇa- weakening to disappearance	of one whose vṛttis have:
√क्षि *kṣi: decrease*		subsided/waned/totally weakened/
वृत्तेः	vṛtteḥ vṛtti's	dwindled/diminished/are vanishing/
√वृत् *vṛt: whirl*		almost annihilated
अभिजातस्य -	abhijātasya-	[*of*] pure-born; naturally pure;
अभि - abhi-: to, toward, into + √*जन् jan: to beget*		transparent; beautiful/perfect
इव	iva	like; as though; as it were
मणेः	maṇeḥ	[*due to/because of*] jewel, crystal, gem
ग्राहीतृ -	grahītṛ-	the knower; apprehender;
√*ग्रह् grah: to seize*		experiencer
ग्रहण -	grahaṇa-	[*in, towards*] knowable; cognition
√*ग्रह् grah: to seize*		process of apprehension; instrument of apprehension
ग्राह्येषु	grāhyeṣu	[*in, towards*] the known; the experienced;
√*ग्रह् grah: to seize*		apprehended objects
तत्स्थ -	tat-stha-	becoming stable/focused on that;
तद् tad-: that + √*स्था sthā : to stand*		on that which it rests/abides
तदञ्जनता	tad-añjanatā	coalescence/taking the color of/
तद् tad-: that + √*अञ्ज् añj: to anoint*		saturation/ anointed with that
समापत्तिः	samāpattiḥ	samādhi; encounter; transmutation;
सम् - sam-: together with +		attainment of a state of consciousness;
आ - ā-: towards, near to + √*पत् pat: to fall*		coalescence; proficiency; balanced state; consummation; fusion; simultaneous occurrence; cognitive blending

ARYA

I.41 When a mind's vṛttis have subsided, it attains the state of consciousness in which there is assimilation and coalescence of the subject apprehending, the process or instrument of apprehension and the object apprehended, like pure crystal (which takes on the reflection and color of the objects in its proximity).

BAILEY

I.41 To him whose vrittis (modifications of the substance of the mind) are entirely controlled, there eventuates a state of identity with, and similarity to, that which is realized.
The knower, knowledge and the field of knowledge become one, just as the crystal takes to itself the colors of that which is reflected in it.

DVIVEDI

I.41 In the case of one the transformations of whose mind have been annihilated, there is entire identity with, and complete absorption in, the cogniser, the cognition and the cognised, like a transparent jewel.

FEUERSTEIN

I.41 [In the case of consciousness whose] fluctuations have dwindled [and which has become] like a transparent jewel, [there results]—[with reference to] the 'grasper', 'grasping' and the 'grasped'—[a state of] coincidence with that on which [consciousness] abides and by which [consciousness] is "anointed."

HOUSTON

I.41 In the case (of a *citta*) whose *vṛtti*-definitions have diminished, which is like a perfect gemstone, *samāpatti*-cognitive blending is the focusing on that (object) and the saturation by that in reference to the experiencer, the experience, and what is experienced.

JNANESHVARA

I.41 When the modifications of mind have become weakened, the mind becomes like a transparent crystal, and thus can easily take on the qualities of whatever object observed, whether that object be the observer, the means of observing, or an object observed, in a process of engrossment called samapattih.

PRABHAVANANDA

I.41 Just as the pure crystal takes colors from the object which is nearest to it, so the mind, when it is cleared of thought-waves, achieves sameness or identity with the object of its concen- tration. This may be either a gross object, or the organ of perception, or the sense of ego. This achievement of sameness or identity with the object of concentration is known as samādhi.

PUROHIT

I.41 When mind's activity is controlled, illumination results; mind the nature of either the seer, the seen, or the seeing, as pure crystal reflects the color of whatever is placed on it.

SATCHIDANANDA

I.41 Just as the naturally pure crystal assumes shapes and colors of objects placed near it, so the Yogi's mind, with its totally weakened unifications, becomes clear and balanced and attains the state devoid of differentiation between knower, knowable, and knowledge. This culmination of meditation is Samadhi.

SHEARER

I.41 As a flawless crystal absorbs what is placed before it, so the settled mind is transparent to whatever it meets—the seer, the process of seeing or the object seen. This is *samāpatti*—the state of mental absorption.

TAIMNI

I.41 In the case of one whose Citta-Vṛttis have been almost annihilated, fusion or entire absorption in one or another of the cogizer, cognition and cognized is brought about as in the case of a transparent jewel (resting on a colored surface).

VIVEKANANDA

I.41 The yogi whose vrittis have thus become powerless [controlled] obtains in the receiver, [the instrument of] receiving, and the received [the soul, the mind and external objects], concentratedness and sameness, like the crystal [before different colored objects].

I.42

तत्र शब्दार्थज्ञानविकल्पैः सङ्कीर्णा सवितर्का समापत्तिः ॥ ४२ ॥

tatra śabdārtha-jñāna-vikalpaiḥ saṅkīrṇā sa-vitarkā samāpattiḥ

तत्र	tatra	there; in that; among them
शब्द -	śabda-	[*with/by means of*] word/sound/name
शब्द् śabd: sound		
अर्थ -	artha-	[*with/by/due to*] purpose; intent;
√अर्थ् arth: to intend		object denoted or signified; form; (real meaning through true knowledge —meditation)
ज्ञान -	jñāna-	[*with/by/due to*] knowledge; concept;
√ज्ञा jñā: to know		idea, etc.; ordinary knowledge based on sense perception and reasoning
विकल्पैः	vi-kalpaiḥ	here: [*with/by/due to*] abstraction/
वि - vi-: apart, separate from, reverse to +		imaginary cognition/conceptualization;
√क्लृप् kḷp: be fit/serve		*alteration of occurences between two or more factors—Arya*
सङ्कीर्णा	saṅkīrṇā	mixed; mingled; commingled;
सम् - sam-: together with + √कॄ kṝ: to scatter		alloyed; interspersed

सवितर्का समापत्तिः sa-vitarkā samāpattiḥ

सवितर्का	sa-vitarkā	(samādhi with) vitarkā;	
स - sa-: with, accompanied +		samādhi accompanied with gross thought,	
वि - vi-: difference, division +		reasoning, deliberation;	
√तर्क् tark: to reflect		cogitation w/sense perception	savitarkā
समापत्तिः	samāpattiḥ	samādhi; encounter; transmutation;	
सम् - sam-: together with +		attainment of a state of consciousness;	samādhi
आ - ā-: towards, near to +		coalescence; proficiency; balanced state;	
√पत् pat: to fall		consummation; fusion; simultaneous occurence; cognitive blending	

ARYA

I.42 At that stage, the meditative state of consciousness is accompanied with the thought of gross objects, mixed with concepts of the (signified) word, objects (signified) and the process of signification (i.e. knowledge).

BAILEY

I.42 When the perceiver blends the word, the idea (or meaning) and the object, this is called the mental condition of judicial reasoning.

DVIVEDI

I.42 The argumentative condition (of the concentrated mind) is that which is mixed with thoughts of word, meaning and understanding.

FEUERSTEIN

I.42 [So long as there is] conceptual knowledge [based on] the intent of words in this [enstasy], [then this state is called] coincidence interspersed with cogitation.

HOUSTON

I.42 There (in such a case), *samāpatti*-cognitive blending which is *savitarkā*-with thought, is mixed with words, meaning, knowledge and conceptualization.

JNANESHVARA

I.42 One type of such an engrossment (samapattih) is one in which there is a mixture of three things, a word or name going with the object, the meaning or identity of that object, and the knowledge associated with that object; this engrossment is known as savitarka samapattih (associated with gross objects).

PRABHAVANANDA

I.42 When the mind achieves identity with a gross object of concentration, mixed with awareness of name, quality and knowledge, this is called savitarka samadhi.

PUROHIT

I.42 It is Sawitarka Samādhi, illumination with sentiment, when mind is still muddled with doubt as to word and its meaning.

SATCHIDANANDA

I.42 The samadhi in which name, form and knowledge of them is mixed is called savitarka samadhi, or samadhi with deliberation.

SHEARER

I.42 The first stage of absorption is when the object of attention is gross and its name and other thoughts are mingled together in the mind.

TAIMNI

I.42 Savitarka Samādhi is that in which knowledge based only on words, real knowledge and ordinary knowledge-based sense perception or reasoning are present in a mixed state and the mind alternates between them.

VIVEKANANDA

I.42 [The samādhi in which] sound, meaning and resulting knowledge, being mixed up, is [called] "samādhi with question."

I.43

स्मृतिपरिशुद्धौ स्वरूपशून्येवार्थमात्रनिर्भासा निर्वितर्का ॥ ४३ ॥

smṛti-pariśuddhau svarūpa-śūnyevārtha-mātra-nirbhāsā nir-vitarkā

स्मृति -	smṛti-	memory		
√स्मृ smṛ: to remember				
परिशुद्धौ	pari-śuddhau	[*upon*] complete purification; clarification (of memory)		
परि - pari-: all around + √शुध् śudh: to purify				
स्वरूपशून्या	svarūpaśūnyā			
स्वरूप -	svarūpa-	own form or essential nature		empty/devoid of its own form or essential nature
शून्या	śūnyā	empty/devoid		
√श्वि śvi: to swell				
इव	iva	as it were; as though		
अर्थमात्र -	artha-mātra-			
अर्थ -	artha-	object/purpose		(of) only object or purpose meant
√अर्थ् arth: to intend				
मात्र -	mātra-	alone; solely; only		
निर्भासा	nir-bhāsā	illuminative; shining; shining forth		
निर् - nir-: without, unaccompanied + √भास् bhās: to be bright				
निर्वितर्का	nir-vitarkā	(samādhi) without gross thought; (samādhi) with subtle thought; ultra-cognitive; meta-cognitive; trans-cognitive		
निर् - nir-: without, unaccompanied + वि - vi-: difference, division + √तर्क् tark: to reflect				

ARYA

I.43 When the memory (also) is purified, (that is, the knowledge of words has subsided), (the meditative state of consciousness is) without the awareness of form (object of apprehension and) there is only the flash of a meaning; (such state is called) devoid of gross thought (nir-vitarkā).

BAILEY

I.43 Perception without judicial reasoning is arrived at when the memory no longer holds control, the word and the object are transcended and only the idea is present.

DVIVEDI

I.43 Non-argumentative is that in which the meaning alone is present, as if quite unlike itself, on memory being dissolved.

FEUERSTEIN

I.43 On the purification of the depth-memory [which has become], as it were, empty of its essence, [and when] the object alone is shining forth-[then this state is called] ultra-cognitive [coincidence].

HOUSTON

I.43 Upon the purification of memory, *samāpatti*-cognitive blending is *nirvitarkā*-beyond thought when, as if of its (*citta*'s) own form, it shines forth as the object alone.

JNANESHVARA

I.43 When the memory or storehouse of modifications of mind is purified, then the mind appears to be devoid of its own nature and only the object on which it is contemplating appears to shine forward; this type of engrossment is known as nirvitarka samapattih.

PRABHAVANANDA

I.43 When the mind achieves identity with a gross object of concentration, unmixed with awareness of name, quality, and knowledge, so that the object alone remains, this is called nirvitarka samadhi.

PUROHIT

I.43 It is Nirwitarka Samādhi, illumination above sentiment, when doubt disappears, mind forgets itself, only meaning remains.

SATCHIDANANDA

I.43 When the memory is well purified, the knowledge of the object in concentration shines alone, devoid of the distinction of name and quality. This is nirvitarka samadhi, or samadhi without deliberation.

SHEARER

I.43 The second stage is when the memory is purified and the mind is quiet enough to be absorbed in the object of attention.

TAIMNI

I.43 On the clarification of memory, when the mind loses its essential nature (subjectivity), as it were, and the real knowledge of the object alone shines (through the mind) *Nirvitarka Samādhi* is attained.

VIVEKANANDA

I.43 The samādhi called "without question" [is attained] when the memory is purified, or devoid of qualities, expressing only the meaning [of the object meditated on].

I.44

एतयैव सविचारा निर्विचारा च सूक्ष्मविषया व्याख्याता ॥ ४४ ॥

etayaiva savicārā nirvicārā ca sūkṣma-viṣayā vyākhātā

एतया	etayā	by this; due to; in the same way
एव	eva	thus, only; just; alone; very one; specifically
सविचारा	sa-vicārā	(samādhi) with vicārā; vicārā accompanied; accompanied by subtle thought, with reflection
स - *sa-: with, accompanied* +		
वि - *vi-: difference, division* +		
√चर् *car: to move*		
निर्विचारा	nir-vicārā	(samādhi) without/devoid of vicārā (subtle thought); samādhi beyond or without reflection
निर् - *nir-: without, unaccompanied* +		
वि - *vi-: difference, division* +		
√चर् *car: to move*		
च	ca	also
सूक्ष्मविषया	sūkṣma-viṣayā	having more subtle objects as domain
सूक्ष्म -	sūkṣma-	subtle
√सिव् *siv: to sew*		
विषया	viṣayā	objects (of experience); subject-matter
√विष् *viṣ: to be active* +		
अय - *aya-: going*		
व्याख्याता	vyākhyātā	defined; explained; described

वि - *vi-: difference, division* + आ - *ā-: towards, near to* + √ख्या *khyā: to be mentioned*

ARYA

I.44 In the same way, the definition of (the meditative states) whose objects are subtler, accompanied by or devoid of, subtle thought, are implied.

BAILEY

I.44 The same two processes of concentration, with and without judicial action of the mind, can be applied also to things subtle.

DVIVEDI

I.44 By these, the deliberative having reference to the subtle elements are also explained.

FEUERSTEIN

I.44 Thus by this [above-mentioned form of coincidence] [the other two types of enstacy]—[viz.] the reflexive and the ultra-reflexive are explained; [these have] subtle objects [as props for concentration].

HOUSTON

I.44 Specifically, by this (the previous 2 sutras), *savicārā* (with reflection), and *nirvicārā* (beyond reflection), *samāpatti*-cognitive blending is explained with regard to subtle *viṣaya*-objects.

JNANESHVARA

I.44 In the same way that these engrossments operate with gross objects in savitarka samapattih, the engrossment with subtle objects also operates, and is known as savichara and nirvichara samapattih.

PRABHAVANANDA

I.44 When the object of concentration is a subtle object, two kinds of samadhi, called savichara and nirvichara, may be distinguished in the same manner.

PUROHIT

I.44 In the same way, illumination with discrimination, illumination in regard to each of the finer objects can all be defined and described.

SATCHIDANANDA

I.44 In the same way, savichara (reflective) and nirvichara (super or non-reflective) samadhis, which are practiced on subtle objects are explained.

SHEARER

I.44 In the same way the third and fourth stages of absorption are explained: these occur when the object of attention is subtle.

TAIMNI

I.44 By this (what has been said in the two previous *Sūtras*) *Samādhis* of *Savicāra*, *Nirvicāra* and subtler stages (I.17) have also been explained.

VIVEKANANDA

I.44 By this process [thesamādhis] "with discrimination" and "without discrimination", whose objects are finer, are [also] explained.

I.45

सूक्ष्मविषयत्वं चालिङ्गपर्यवसानम् ॥ ४५ ॥

sūkṣma-viṣayatvaṃ cāliṅga-paryavasānam

सूक्ष्मविषयत्वं	sūkshmaviṣayatvaṃ		
सूक्ष्म -	sūkshma-	subtle	the state of having subtle objects
सिव् siv: to sew			
विषयत्वं	viṣayatvaṃ	the state of having objects; "objectness"; objects of experience	
√विष् viṣ: to be active +			
अय - aya-: going			
च	ca	and	
अलिङ्ग -	a-liṅga-	unmodified/ undifferentiate/ unmanifest prakṛti (primary matter); indefinable	
अ - a-: un-/non-/not/without +			
√लिङ्ग् liṅg: to be attached to			
पर्यवसानम्	pary-avasānam	extending up to; ending at; termination	
परि - pari-: all around, about +			
- अव - -ava-: to lead, to bring to +			
√सै sai: to loosen, deliver, finish			

ARYA

I.45 And "having subtle objects" extends up to unmodified Matter.

BAILEY

I.45 The gross leads into the subtle and the subtle leads in progressive stages to that state of pure spiritual being called Pradhana.

DVIVEDI

I.45 The province of the subtle ends with the indissoluble.

FEUERSTEIN

I.45 And the subtle objects terminate in the Undifferentiate.

HOUSTON

I.45 And the subtlety of objects extends to *alinga*-the unmanifest state of primary matter.

JNANESHVARA

I.45 Having such subtle objects extends all the way up to unmanifest prakriti.

PRABHAVANANDA

I.45 Behind all subtle objects is Prakriti, the primal cause.

PUROHIT

I.45 The finer objects end with the unmanifested seed.

SATCHIDANANDA

I.45 The subtlety of possible objects of concentration ends only at the undefinable.

SHEARER

I.45 The range of subtle objects includes all levels of creation, extending the limits of the *gunas*.

TAIMNI

I.45 The province of *Samādhi* concerned with subtle objects extends up to the *Alinga* stages of the *Guṇas*.

VIVEKANANDA

I.45 The finer objects end with the pradhāna.

I.46

ता एव सबीजः समाधिः ॥ ४६ ॥

tā eva sa-bījaḥ samādhiḥ

ताः	tāḥ	those, these
एव	eva	specifically; only; very ones
सबीजः *स - sa-: with + बीज bīja: seed*	sa-bījaḥ	with seed > having an object (gross or subtle) (as in meditation)
समाधिः *सम् - sam-: together with, completely, perfectly +* *आ - ā-: near to, all around + √धा dhā: to put*	samādhiḥ	meditation; contemplation; meta-cognitive absorption with various stages

ARYA

I.46 Those very four states (come under the category of) samādhi with seed.

BAILEY

I.46 All this constitutes meditation with seed.

DVIVEDI

I.46 These constitute seeded-meditation.

FEUERSTEIN

I.46 These [kinds of coincidence] verily [belong to the class of] enstacy with seed.

HOUSTON

I.46 These particular (*samāpatti*-cognitive blendings) constitute *sabīja samādhi*-cognitive absorption with seed.

JNANESHVARA

I.46 These four varieties of engrossment are the only kinds of concentrations (samadhi) which are objective, and have a seed of an object.

PRABHAVANANDA

I.46 These kinds of samadhi are said to be "with seed."

PUROHIT

I.46 These are all types of illumination.

SATCHIDANANDA

I.46 All these samadhis are sabija (with seed), which could bring one back into bondage or mental disturbance.

SHEARER

I.46 These levels of *samādhi* are concerned only with external objects.

TAIMNI

I.46 They (stages corresponding to subtle objects) constitute only *Samādhi* with 'seed'.

VIVEKANANDA

I.46 These samādhis are "with seed".

I.47

निर्विचारवैशारद्येऽध्यात्मप्रसादः ॥ ४७ ॥

nirvicāra-vaiśāradye' dhyātma-prasādaḥ

निर्विचारवैशारद्य	nirvicāra-vaiśāradye		
		[*upon*]	
निर्विचारा -	nir-vicārā-	(samādhi) devoid of vicara	[*upon*]
निर् - nir-: without, unaccompanied +		(subtle thought);	the
वि - vi-: difference, division +		non-reflective;	purification
√चर् car: to move		beyond/without reflection	and proficiency
वैशारद्ये	vaiśāradye	lucidity	of
वै - vai-: clearly, indeed + शरद् śarad: autumn			nir-vicāra
(lit.: autumnal brightness—Feuerstein)			(samādhi)

अध्यात्म -	adhyātma-	in regard to atman;
अधि - adhi-: over, above + आत्म ātma: self		supreme/higher Self; inner/spiritual being
प्रसादः	prasādaḥ	clarity; lucidity; shining;
प्र - pra-: towards, into + √सद् sad: to sit; to apply oneself		pleasant clearness; pacification

ARYA

I.47 Upon the purification (and mastery) of the nir-vicārā state, spiritual purity is attained.

BAILEY

I.47 When this super-contemplative state is reached; the Yogi acquires pure spiritual realisation through the balanced quiet of the citta (or the mind-stuff).

DVIVEDI

I.47 The purity of the non-deliberative being reached, internal contentment follows.

FEUERSTEIN

I.47 When there is lucidity in the ultra-reflexive [enstacy], [then this is called] the clarity of the inner-being.

HOUSTON

I.47 The clarity of the higher self occurs in the lucidity of the *nirvicāra samāpatti*, (*samāpatti* beyond subtle reflection).

JNANESHVARA

I.47 As one gains proficiency in the undisturbed flow in nirvichara, a purity and luminosity of the inner instrument of mind is developed.

PRABHAVANANDA

I.47 In reaching nirvichara samadhi, the mind becomes pure.

PUROHIT

I.47 Illumination above discrimination, being pure, brings spiritual contentment.

SATCHIDANANDA

I.47 In the purity of nirvichara samadhi, the supreme Self shines.

SHEARER

I.47 But on refinement of the fourth stage of absorption, there is the dawning of the spiritual light of the Self.

TAIMNI

I.47 On attaining the utmost purity of the *Nirvicāra* stage (of *Samādhi*) there is the dawning of the spiritual light.

VIVEKANANDA

I.47 When the yogi becomes established in the samādhi "without discrimination," his chitta becomes firmly fixed.

I.48

ऋतम्भरा तत्र प्रज्ञा ॥ ४८ ॥

ṛtambharā tatra prajñā

ऋतम्भरा	ṛtambharā		
ऋतम् -	ṛtam-	Truth	Truth-bearer/Truth bearing;
भरा	bharā	bearing	bearer of Supreme Truth
√भृ bhṛ: bear			
तत्र	tatra		there
प्रज्ञा	prajñā		wisdom; transcendent insight;
प्र - pra-: before, in front + √ज्ञा jñā: to know			consciousness (higher state of); awakening of wisdom (samprajñāta); supra-cognition; primary insight

ARYA

I.48 At that state (of spiritual development is received) wisdom (which is the) bearer of supreme truth.

BAILEY

I.48 His perception is unfailingly exact (or his mind reveals only the Truth).

DVIVEDI

I.48 The intellect is there truth-bearing.

FEUERSTEIN

I.48 In this [state of utmost lucidity] insight is truth-bearing.

HOUSTON

I.48 There, *prajñā*-insight is truth-bearing.

JNANESHVARA

I.48 The experiential knowledge that is gained in that state is one of essential wisdom and is filled with truth.

PRABHAVANANDA

I.48 In that samadhi, knowledge is said to be "filled with truth."

PUROHIT

I.48 In this condition, the intellect becomes pregnant with truth.

SATCHIDANANDA

I.48 This is ritambhara prajna, or the absolute true consciousness.

SHEARER

I.48 This level is *ritambharā*, where consciousness perceives only the truth.

TAIMNI

I.48 There, the consciousness is Truth-and-Right-bearing.

VIVEKANANDA

I.48 The knowledge through it is called "filled with Truth."

I.49

श्रुतानुमानप्रज्ञाभ्यामन्यविषया विशेषार्थत्वात् ॥ ४९ ॥

śrutānumāna-prajñābhyām anya-viṣayā viśeṣārthatvāt

श्रुत -	śruta-	[*from*] revelation: testimony of sages;
√*श्रु śru: to hear*		[*heard in*] study of the scriptures; [*from*] tradition; learning; hearing
अनुमान -	anumāna-	[*due to/from*] inference and logical
अनु - anu-: following, after, behind + √मा mā: to measure		processes
प्रज्ञाभ्याम्	prajñābhyām	[*due to/from*](two kinds or levels of)
प्र - pra-: forward, in front + √ज्ञा jñā: to know		wisdom; transcendent insight; higher consciousness
अन्यविषया	anya-viṣayā	
अन्य -	anya-	(having) another/different/ distinct } special truth
विषया	viṣayā	objects (of experience);
√विष् viṣ: to be active + -अय - aya-: going		subject-matter; content; realm; scope; field object domain

विशेषार्थत्वात्	viśeṣārthatvāt		
विशेष -	viśeṣa-	distinct; different;	[*because of*] having
वि - vi-: apart, separate from + √शिष् śiṣ: to remain		special; unique; gradation	a special purpose/ aim/significance/
अर्थत्वात् -	arthatvāt	[*because of/due to*]	cognition of
√अर्थ् arth: to intend + -त्व -tva: -ness		nature of	object/purpose

ARYA

I.49 This (higher) wisdom is (completely) different in scope from the knowledge gained from learning and logical processes because its aim is entirely a different one.

BAILEY

I.49 This particular perception is unique and reveals that which the rational mind (using testimony, inference and deduction) cannot reveal.

DVIVEDI

I.49 Its subject is different from that of revelation and inference, for it refers to particulars.

FEUERSTEIN

I.49 The scope [of this gnostic insight] is distinct from the insight [gained from] tradition and inference [owing to its] particular purposiveness.

HOUSTON

I.49 Due to the nature of its purpose being distinction (between *Puruṣa*-self and the *guṇas*-primary forces of creation), that *prajñā*-insight has another *viṣaya*-object than both the insights from tradition and inference.

JNANESHVARA

I.49 That knowledge is different from the knowledge that is commingled with testimony or through inference, because it relates directly to the specifics of the object, rather than to those words or other concepts.

PRABHAVANANDA

I.49 The knowledge which is gained from inference and the study of scriptures is knowledge of one kind. But the knowledge which is gained from samadhi is of a much higher order. It goes beyond inference and scriptures.

PUROHIT

I.49 Instead of knowledge gained through evidence and inference, it brings direct knowledge of objects and their meaning in its entirety.

SATCHIDANANDA

I.49 This special truth is totally different from knowledge gained by hearing, study of scripture or inference.

SHEARER

I.49 The knowledge gained in *ritambharā* is of qualitatively different from that gained in the usual way through testimony and inference. The former means is intuitive and sees things as they are in their totality, whereas the latter means is partial.

TAIMNI

I.49 The knowledge based on inference or testimony is different from direct knowledge obtained in the higher states of consciousness (I.48) because it is confined to a particular object (or aspect).

VIVEKANANDA

I.49 The knowledge that is gained from testimony and inference is about common objects. That from the samādhi just mentioned is of a much higher order, being able to penetrate where inference and testimony cannot go.

तज्जः संस्कारोऽन्यसंस्कारप्रतिबन्धी ॥ ५० ॥

taj-jaḥ saṃskāro 'nya-saṃskāra-pratibandhī

तद् -	tad-	that	arising, born of or produced from that (samādhi)
जः √जन् *jan: to beget*	jaḥ	born; arising	
संस्कारः सम् - *sam-: together with, completely, perfectly +* √कृ *kṛ: to do*	saṃskāraḥ	habitual/standing wave in citta; conditioned mental response from habit and memory; impression/imprint in the subtle domain (karmāśaya); subliminal activator	
अन्य -	anya-	(of) other	
संस्कार -	saṃskāra-	saṃskāra (see above)	
प्रतिबन्धी प्रति - *prati-: in direction of, in opposition to +* √बन्ध् *bandī: to bind*	prati-bandhī	that which impedes/hinders/resists/ opposes/checks/inhibits/blocks/ prevents/annuls/obstructs/ wipes out	

ARYA

I.50 The mental impression created from that prevents all other impressions (from forming).

BAILEY

I.50 It is hostile to, or supersedes all other impressions.

DVIVEDI

I.50 The impression thereof stands in the way of other impressions.

FEUERSTEIN

I.50 The subliminal-activator born from that [gnostic flash] obstructs the other subliminal-activators.

HOUSTON

I.50 The *sanskāra*-subliminal activator, born of that (*prajñā*-insight) checks other *sanskāra*.

JNANESHVARA

I.50 This type of knowledge that is filled with truth creates latent impressions in the mind-field, and those new impressions tend to reduce the formation of other less useful forms of habitual latent impressions.

PRABHAVANANDA

I.50 The impression which is made upon the mind by that samādhi wipes out all other past impressions.

PUROHIT

I.50 The impression remaining after this illumination excludes every other impression.

SATCHIDANANDA

I.50 The impression produced by this samadhi wipes out all other impressions.

SHEARER

I.50 The impression born of *ritambharā* prevents the accumulation of further latent impressions.

TAIMNI

I.50 The impression produced by it (*Sabīja Samādhi*) stands in the way of other impressions.

VIVEKANANDA

I.50 The resulting impression from this samādhi obstructs all other impressions.

I.51

तस्यापि निरोधे सर्वनिरोधान्निर्बीजः समाधिः ॥ ५१ ॥

tasyāpi nirodhe sarva-nirodhān nir-bījaḥ samādhiḥ

तस्य -	tasya-	of that; of this
तद् tad-: that		
अपि	api	even; also
निरोधे	nirodhe	[*upon*] nirodha: cessation/ending/ dissolution/disappearance/ restraint/suppression/control/ restriction/inhibition/annihilation/ process of ending
नि - ni-: under + √रुध् rudh: to restrict or suppress		
सर्व -	sarva-	(of) all
निरोधात्	nirodhāt	[*owing to/due to/because of/ through*] nirodha
√रुध् rudh: to restrict or suppress		
निर्बीजः	nir-bījaḥ	seedless; without seed; having no object
निर् - nir-: without + बीज bīja: seed		
समाधिः	samādhiḥ	samādhi; meditation; contemplation; meta-cognitive absorption with various stages
सम् - sam-: together with, completely, perfectly + आ - ā-: near to, all around + √धा dhā: to put		

ARYA

I.51 Upon the cessation of even that saṃskāra there is cessation of all (else) and thereby seedless samādhi (is attained).

BAILEY

I.51 When this state of perception is itself also restrained (or superseded), then is pure Samadhi achieved.

DVIVEDI

I.51 The prevention of that even, leads to the prevention of all, and thus to meditation without seed.

FEUERSTEIN

I.51 Upon the restriction also of this [regressive subliminal-activator] [there ensues], owing to the restriction of all [contents of consciousness], the enstasy without seed.

HOUSTON

I.51 Upon the *nirodha*-ending of even that (*sanskāra* born of insight), owing to the *nirodha* of all (*sanskāra*), *nirbīja samādhi* (*samādhi* without seed).

JNANESHVARA

I.51 When even these latent impressions from truth-filled knowledge recede along with the other impressions, then there is objectless concentration.

PRABHAVANANDA

I.51 When the impression made by that samādhi is also wiped out, so that there are no more thought-waves at all in the mind, then one enters the samadhi which is called "seedless."

PUROHIT

I.51 When even this has been suppressed, seedless Samādhi is attained.

SATCHIDANANDA

I.51 When even this impression is wiped out, every impression is totally wiped out and there is nirbija [seedless] samadhi.

SHEARER

I.51 And when even the latent impression of *ritambharā* has been brought to a settled state, then all activity ceases and *nirbīja samādhi*—the unbounded consciousness of the Self—alone remains.

TAIMNI

I.51 On suppression of even that owing to suppression of all (modifications of the mind) 'Seedless' *Samādhi* (is attained).

VIVEKANANDA

I.51 By the restraint of even this [impression, which obstructs all other impressions], all being restrained, comes the seedless samādhi.

॥ इति प्रथमः पादः ॥

iti prathamaḥ pādaḥ

इति	iti	thus; herewith [concludes]
प्रथमः	prathamaḥ	first
पादः	pādaḥ	chapter; part

Thus [Concludes] the First Chapter

SĀDHANA PĀDAḤ

Arya	Sādhana-pāda: The Chapter on Means
Bailey	Book II: The Steps to Union
Dvivedi	Section II
Feuerstein	Chapter Two: Sādhana Pāda
Houston	Now, The Chapter on Sādhana
Jnaneshvara	Practice
Prabhavananda	Yoga and Its Practice
Purohit	Practice
Satchidananda	Book II: Sadhana Pada Portion on Practice
Shearer	Treading the Path
Taimni	Sādhana Pāda
Vivekananda	Concentration: Its Practice

Now, The Chapter on Sādhana

॥ अथ साधनपादः ॥

atha sādhanapādaḥ

अथ	atha	Now
साधन -	sādhana-	spiritual practice
पादः	pādaḥ	chapter, part

तपःस्वाध्यायेश्वरप्रणिधानानि क्रियायोगः ॥ १ ॥

tapaḥ-svādhyāyeśvara-praṇidhānāni kriyā-yogaḥ

तपः -	tapaḥ-	ascetic observances; austerity;
√तप् tap: heat, to be hot		intensity in spiritual practice; accepting pain as purification
स्वाध्याय -	svādhyāya-	japa: silent recitation (of mantra);
स्व - sva: own +		Self-study; study of scripture;
-अधि - adhi-: over, above +		learning/application of mantra
-आ - ā-: near to, from all sides, all around +		
√इ i: to go; here: one's going into		
ईश्वर -	Īśvara-	God; Lord; Knower; Seer;
√ईष् īs: to own, be master of +		Teacher; Ultimate Divine Presence
वर vara: the best, choicest (√वृ vṛ: to choose)		
प्रणिधानानि	praṇidhānāni	surrender (to) (Īśvara)
प्र - pra-: forward, in front, before +		dedicated devotion; surrender;
-नि - ni-: intensity + √धा dhā: to put		placing oneself in (God); *perfect alignment of attention and intention with the Divine—Houston*
क्रियायोगः	kriyāyogaḥ	
क्रिया -	kriyā-	practice/action (is called)
√कृ kṛ: to do		
योगः	yogaḥ	yoga; samādhi; union;
√युज् yuj: lit.: to yoke; to unite/dissolve; samādhi		integration; blending (of consciousness)

} yoga of practice/action

ARYA

II.1 Ascetic observances, silent recitation, and surrender to God is called yoga of practice.

BAILEY

II.1 The Yoga of action, leading to union with the soul is fiery aspiration, spiritual reading and devotion to Ishvara.

DVIVEDI

II.1 Preliminary *Yoga* (consists of) mortification, study and resignation to *Iśvara*.

FEUERSTEIN

II.1 Ascesis, self-study and devotion to the Lord [constitute] Kriyā-Yoga.

HOUSTON

II.1 *Tapas*-intensity in spiritual practice, *svādhyāya*-learning and application of personal mantras, and *īśvara-praṇidhāna*—the perfect aligning of attention in the omniscient seer within (*īśvara*) is *Kriyā Yoga*.

JNANESHVARA

II.1 Yoga in the form of action (kriya yoga) has three parts: 1) training and purifying the senses (tapas), 2) self-study in the context of teachings (svadhyaya), and 3) devotion and letting go into the creative source from which we emerged (ishvara pranidhana).

PRABHAVANANDA

II.1 Austerity, study, and the dedication of the fruits of one's work to God: these are the preliminary steps toward yoga.

PUROHIT

II.1 Austerity, study, devotion to God, constitute Practical yoga.

SATCHIDANANDA

II.1 Accepting pain as a help for purification, study of spiritual books, and surrender to the Supreme Being constitute Yoga in practice.

SHEARER

II.1 Purification, refinement, surrender. These are the practical steps on the path of yoga.

TAIMNI

II.1 Austerity, Self-study and resignation to *Īśvara* constitute preliminary *Yoga*.

VIVEKANANDA

II.1 Mortification, study and surrendering fruits of work to God are called kriyā-yoga.

II.2

समाधिभावनार्थः क्लेशतनूकरणार्थश्च ॥ २॥

samādhi-bhāvanārthaḥ kleśa-tanū-karaṇārthaś ca

समाधिभावनार्थः samādhibhāvanārthaḥ

समाधि -	samādhi-	samādhi; meditation;	
सम् - sam-: together with, completely, perfectly +		contemplation;	
आ - ā-: near to, all around + √धा dhā: to put		meta-cognitive absorption with various stages	(for the) purpose (of) cultivating samādhi
भावना -	bhāvanā-	developing; cultivating;	
√भू bhū ; to become		realizing	
अर्थः	arthaḥ	(for the) purpose (of)	
√अर्थ् arth: to intend			

क्लेशतनूकरणार्थः kleśatanūkaraṇārthaḥ

क्लेश -	kleśa-	core/root/primary obstructions;	
√क्लिश् kliś: to trouble, to be troubled		cause of afflictions or misery; impurity: afflictions; misery	(for the)
तनू -	tanū-	diminution; weakening; attenuating; minimizing	purpose (of) diminishing/
करण -	karaṇa-	cause; causing	weakening
√कृ kṛ: to do			kleśa
अर्थः	arthaḥ	purpose	
√अर्थ् arth: to intend			

च	ca	and

ARYA

II.2 (The kriyā yoga is practiced) for the purpose of developing samādhi and to weaken the (strength and remove the presence of) the kleśhas.

BAILEY

II.2 The aim of these three is to bring about soul vision and to eliminate obstructions.

DVIVEDI

II.2 (They are practised) for acquiring habitual *Samādhi* and for attenuating distractions.

FEUERSTEIN

II.2 [This Yoga has] the purpose of cultivating enstacy as also the purpose of attenuating the causes-of-affliction.

HOUSTON

II.2 It has the purpose of realizing *samādhi*-cognitive absorption, and also the purpose of weakening the *kleśas*-root causes of pain.

JNANESHVARA

II.2 That Yoga of action (kriya yoga) is practiced to bring about samadhi and to minimize the colored thought patterns (kleshas).

PRABHAVANANDA

II.2 Thus we may cultivate the power of concentration and remove the obstacles to enlightenment which cause all our sufferings.

PUROHIT

II.2 The aim is to attain Illumination and to destroy afflictions.

SATCHIDANANDA

II.2 They help us minimize obstacles and attain samadhi.

SHEARER

II.2 They nourish the state of *samādhi* and weaken the causes of suffering.

TAIMNI

II.2 (*Kriyā-Yoga*) is practised for attenuating *Kleśas* and bringing about *Samādhi*.

VIVEKANANDA

II.2 [Kriyā-yoga leads to] samādhi and attenuates the pain-bearing obstructions.

II.3

अविद्यास्मितारागद्वेषाभिनिवेशाः क्लेशाः ॥ ३ ॥

avidyāsmitā-rāga-dveṣābhiniveśāḥ kleśāḥ

अविद्या -	avidyā-	lit.: without knowledge/wisdom:
अ - a-: un-/non-/not/without +		absence of self-awareness; ignorance;
√विद् vid: to know		lack of awareness of Reality;
		unawareness (of His [Puruṣa's]) real nature
अस्मिता -	asmitā-	"I-am-ness"; pure ego;
अस्मि asmi-: I am + -ता -tā: -ness		sense of being;
		sense of individuality
राग -	rāga-	desire; attraction; attachment
√रज् raj: to be excited		
द्वेष -	dveṣa-	aversion; dislike; repulsion
√द्विष् dviṣ: to dislike		
अभिनिवेशाः	abhiniveśāḥ	fear of separation from body;
अभि - abhi-: to, toward, into +		will-to-live; drive-to-survive;
-नि - -ni-: downward motion, opposed to, intensity +		clinging to bodily life;
√विश् viś: to dwell		"May I not cease to be"
क्लेश	kleśāḥ	core/root/primary obstructions;
√क्लिश् kliś: to trouble, to be troubled		causes-of-afflictions or misery

ARYA

II.3 Ignorance, "I-am"-ness, attraction, aversion, and fear of death are the kleśhas.

BAILEY

II.3 These are the difficulty producing hindrances: avidya (ignorance), the sense of personality, desire, hate and the sense of attachment.

DVIVEDI

II.3 The distractions are five, *viz.*, Ignorance, the Sense of being, Desire, Aversion and Attachment.

FEUERSTEIN

II.3 Nescience, I-am-ness, attachment, aversion and the will-to-live are the five causes-of-affliction.

HOUSTON

II.3 *Avidyā*-
absence of self-awareness,
asmitā-sense of "I-am",
raga-attachment,
dveṣa-dislike,
and *abhiniveśa*- the will to live,
are the *kleśa*-root causes of pain.

JNANESHVARA

II.3 There are five kinds of coloring (kleshas): 1) forgetting, or ignorance about the true nature of things (avidya), 2) I-ness, individuality, or egoism (asmita), 3) attachment or addiction to mental impressions or objects (raga), 4) aversion to thought patterns or objects (dvesha), and 5) love of these as being life itself, as well as fear of their loss as being death.

PRABHAVANANDA

II.3 These obstacles—the causes of man's sufferings—are ignorance, egoism, attachment, aversion, and the desire to cling to life.

PUROHIT

II.3 Ignorance, egoism, desire, aversion, fear are afflictions.

SATCHIDANANDA

II.3 Ignorance, egoism, attachment, hatred, and clinging to life are the five obstacles.

SHEARER

II.3 The causes of suffering are five: ignorance of our real nature, egoism, attachment, aversion, and the fear of death, which makes us cling to life.

TAIMNI

II.3 The lack of awareness of Reality, the sense of egoism or "I-am-ness," attractions and repulsions towards objects and the strong desire for life are the great afflictions or causes of all miseries in life.

VIVEKANANDA

II.3 The pain-bearing obstructions are ignorance, egoity, attachment, aversion, and clinging to life.

II.4

अविद्या क्षेत्रमुत्तरेषां प्रसुप्ततनुविच्छिन्नोदाराणाम् ॥ ४ ॥

avidyā-kṣetram uttareṣāṃ prasupta-tanu-vicchinnodārāṇām

अविद्या -	avidyā-	possessed of:
अ - a-: un-/non-/not/without +		lit.: without knowing/knowledge:
√विद् vid: to know		here: without wisdom – true ignorance;
		lack of awareness of Reality, which is, unawareness of (His [Puruṣa's]) true nature
क्षेत्रम्	kṣetram	field
√क्षि kṣi: to dwell		
उत्तरेषां	uttareṣāṃ	other; of the others;
		for the others (that follow); of the following ones (divided into various stages of their growth)
प्रसुप्त -	prasupta-	dormant
प्र - pra-: forward, onward + √स्वप् svap: to sleep		
तनु -	tanu-	weak; feeble
√तन् tan: to stretch out		
विच्छिन्न -	vicchinna-	contrasted; intercepted;
वि - vi-: apart, separate from, reverse to +		interrupted; scattered
√छिद् chid: to cut		
उदाराणाम्	udārāṇām	strongly active; sustained;
उद् - ud-: go up + √ऋ mṛ: to go/move/rise		aroused

ARYA

II.4 Ignorance is the field of the (other) following ones (in which they grow in these stages: they are) dormant, weak, contrasted and strongly active.

BAILEY

II.4 Avidya (ignorance) is the cause of all other obstructions whether they be latent, in process of elimination, overcome, or in full operation.

DVIVEDI

II.4 Ignorance is the source of those that follow, whether they be in the dormant, attenuated, overpowered or expanded condition.

FEUERSTEIN

II.4 Nescience is the field of the other [causes-of-affliction]; [they can be] dormant, attenuated, intercepted or aroused.

HOUSTON

II.4 *Avidyā*-absence of self-awareness is the field for the others. They can be *prasupta*-dormant, *tanu*-weakened, *vichinna*-interrupted, or *udāra*-aroused.

JNANESHVARA

II.4 The root forgetting or ignorance of the nature of things (avidya) is the breeding ground for the other of the five colorings (kleshas), and each of these is in one of four states: 1) dormant or inactive, 2) attenuated or weakened, 3) interrupted or separated from temporarily, or 4) active and producing thoughts or actions to varying degrees.

PRABHAVANANDA

II.4 Ignorance creates all the other obstacles. They may exist either in a potential or a vestigial form, or they may have been temporarily overcome or fully developed.

PUROHIT

II.4 Ignorance is the cause, the others are the effects, whether they are dormant, weak, suppressed or aggravated.

SATCHIDANANDA

II.4 Ignorance is the field for the others mentioned after it, whether they be dormant, feeble, intercepted, or sustained.

SHEARER

II.4 Ignorance of our real nature is the source of the other four, whether they be dormant, weak, suspended or fully active.

TAIMNI

II.4 *Avidyā* is the source of those that are mentioned after it, whether they be in the dormant, attenuated, alternating or expanded condition.

VIVEKANANDA

II.4 Ignorance is the productive field of all those that follow, whether they are dormant, attenuated, overpowered, or expanded.

अनित्याशुचिदुःखानात्मसु नित्यशुचिसुखात्मख्यातिरविद्या ॥ ५ ॥

anityāśuci-duḥkhānātmasu nitya-śuci-sukhātma-khyātir avidyā

अनित्य -	anitya-	[*in*/*upon*] (the) non-eternal/ephemeral/
अ - a-: un-/non-/not/without +		impermanent
नित्य nitya: (नि - ni-: intensity + -त्य -tya: being there = everlasting, eternal)		
अशुचि -	aśuci-	impure
अ - a-: un-/non-/not/without + √शुच् śuc: to glow		
दुःख -	duḥkha-	pain; sorrow, suffering; distress;
दुस् dus: bad + ख kha: space, e.g. axle-hole		misery; those suffering
अनात्मसु	anātmasu	[*in*/*upon*] (the) non-self (respectively)
अन - an-: not, non-, absence + आत्मन् ātman: Eternal Self		
नित्य -	nitya-	permanent; eternal
शुचि -	śuci-	pure
√शुच् śuc: to glow		
सुख -	sukha-	pleasure/comfort;
सु - su: well, good + ख kha: space, e.g. axle-hole		those comfortable, joyful, happy
आत्म -	ātma-	Self
ख्यातिः	khyātiḥ	here: false or mistaken cognition appearing as:
√ख्या khyā: to be known		(through discernment) (of Puruśa); (through vision) (of Puruśa); (due to identity) (with Puruśa); (due to realization) (of Puruśa);
अविद्या	avidyā	ignorance; absence of self-awareness;
अ - a-: un-/non-/not/without +		lack of awareness of Reality
√विद् vid: to know		

ARYA

II.5 (False) cognition of permanent, pure, pleasant and self in (what is) impermanent, impure, painful and non-self (is called) ignorance.

BAILEY

II.5 Avidya is the condition of confusing the permanent, pure, blissful and the Self with that which is impermanent, impure, painful and the not-self.

DVIVEDI

II.5 Ignorance is taking the non-eternal, impure, evil and non-*ātmā* to be eternal, pure, good and *ātmā*.

FEUERSTEIN

II.5 Nescience is the seeing of [that which is] eternal, pure, joyful and the Self in [that which is] ephemeral, impure, sorrowful and the non-self.

HOUSTON

II.5 *Avidya*-absence of self-awareness, is an identification of permanance in the impermanant, purity in impurity, happiness in pain, and self in non-self.

JNANESHVARA

II.5 Ignorance (avidya) is of four types: 1) regarding that which is transient as eternal, 2) mistaking the impure for pure, 3) thinking that which brings misery to bring happiness, and 4) taking that which is not-self to be self.

PRABHAVANANDA

II.5 To regard the noneternal as eternal, the impure as pure, the painful as pleasant and the non-Atman as the Atman—this is ignorance.

PUROHIT

II.5 Ignorance thinks of the perishable as inperishable, of the pure as impure, of the painful as pleasurable, of the non-Self as Self.

SATCHIDANANDA

II.5 Ignorance is regarding the impermanent as permanent, the impure as pure, the painful as pleasant, and the non-Self as the Self.

SHEARER

II.5 Ignorance is the failure to discriminate between the permanent and the impermanent, the pure and the impure, bliss and suffering,
the Self and the non-Self.

TAIMNI

II.5 *Avidyā* is taking the non-eternal, impure, evil and non-*Ātman* to be eternal, pure, good and *Ātman* respectively.

VIVEKANANDA

II.5 Ignorance is to take the non-eternal, the impure, the painful, and the non-Self for what is eternal, the pure, the happy and the Atman or Self (respectively).

II.6

दृग्दर्शनशक्त्योरेकात्मतेवास्मिता ॥ ६ ॥

drg-darśana-śaktyor ekātmatevāsmitā

दृक् -	dṛk-	the consciousness force (of Puruṣa);	
√दृश् *dṛś: to see*		power of consciousness	
दर्शनशक्त्यो	darśanaśaktyoḥ		
दर्शन -	darśana-	seeing	possessing
√दृश् *dṛś: to see*			the capacity of buddhi
शक्त्योः	śaktyoḥ	[*two*]	as an instrument;
√शक् *śak: to be able*		powers	[*two*] powers of consciousness;
			power of seeing
एकात्मता -	ekātmatā-		
एक -	eka	one	self-sameness;
आत्मता	ātmatā	identity;	self identity
		self-ness	
इव -	iva-	as it were; as if; seemingly	
अस्मिता	asmitā	"I-am-ness"; pure ego;	
अस्मि *asmi: I am* + - ता *tā: -ness*		sense of being;	
		sense of individuality	

ARYA

II.6 When there appears, as it were, identity of the consciousness-force and (what is essentially the buddhi's) instrumentality of consciousness, it is called "I-am"-ness.

BAILEY

II.6 The sense of personality is due to the identification of the knower with the instruments of knowledge.

DVIVEDI

II.6 The Sense of being is the blending together of the power that knows with the instruments thereof.

FEUERSTEIN

II.6 I-am-ness is the identification as it were of the powers of vision and 'visioner' [i.e. the Self].

HOUSTON

II.6 The sense of "I am" is the seeming identity single identity of the two (distinct) powers of the seer and the act of seeing (something).

JNANESHVARA

II.6 The coloring (klesha) of I-ness or egoism (asmita), which arises from the ignorance, occurs due to the mistake of taking the intellect (buddhi, which knows, decides, judges, and discriminates) to itself be pure consciousness (purusha).

PRABHAVANANDA

II.6 To identify consciousness with that which merely reflects consciousness—this is egoism.

PUROHIT

II.6 Egoism is the identification of the Seer with the limitations of the eye.

SATCHIDANANDA

II.6 Egoism is the identification, as it were, of the power of the Seer (Purusha) with that of the instrument of seeing [body-mind].

SHEARER

II.6 Egoism, the limiting sense of "I," results from the individual intellect's attributing the power of consciousness to itself.

TAIMNI

II.6 Asmitā is the identity or blending together, as it were, of the power of consciousness (Puruṣa) with the power of cognition (Buddhi).

VIVEKANANDA

II.6 Egoity is the identification of the Seer with the instrument of seeing.

II.7

सुखानुशयी रागः ॥ ७ ॥

sukhānuśayī rāgaḥ

सुख -	sukha-	lit.: good space: pleasant; pleasurable;
सु - *su: well, good* + ख *kha: space, e.g. axle-hole*		joy; happiness; comfort
अनुशयी	anuśayī	what remains (as residue);
अनु - *anu-: following, after, behind* +		following; follows with;
√शी *śī: to rest*		accompanying; having the result
रागः	rāgaḥ	desire; attraction; attachment
√रज् *raj: to be excited*		

ARYA

II.7 What remains (as residue) after pleasure (is) attraction.

BAILEY

II.7 Desire is attachment to objects of pleasure.

DVIVEDI

II.7 That which dwells on pleasure is Desire.

FEUERSTEIN

II.7 Attachment is [that which] rests on the pleasant [experiences].

HOUSTON

II.7 *Rāga*-attachment is holding on to (prior) happiness.

JNANESHVARA

II.7 Attachment (raga) is a separate modification of mind, which follows the rising of the memory of pleasure, where the three modifications of attachment, pleasure, and the memory of the object are then associated with one another.

PRABHAVANANDA

II.7 Attachment is that which dwells upon pleasure.

PUROHIT

II.7 Desire is the longing for pleasure.

SATCHIDANANDA

II.7 Attachment is that which follows identification with pleasurable experiences.

SHEARER

II.7 Attachment is clinging to pleasure.

TAIMNI

II.7 That attraction, which accompanies pleasure, is Rāga.

VIVEKANANDA

II.7 Attachment is that which dwells on pleasure.

II.8

दुःखानुशयी द्वेषः ॥ ८ ॥

duḥkhānuśayī dveṣaḥ

दुःख - *दुस् dus: bad + ख kha: space, e.g. axle-hole*	duḥkha-	lit.: bad space: pain; sorrow, suffering; distress; misery; those suffering
अनुशयी *अनु - anu-: following, after, behind +* *√शी śī: to rest*	anuśayī	what remains (as residue); following; follows with; accompanying; having the result
द्वेषः *√द्विष् dviṣ: to dislike*	dveṣaḥ	aversion; dislike; repulsion

ARYA

II.8 What remains (as residue) after pain (is) aversion.

BAILEY

II.8 Hate is aversion for any object of the senses.

DVIVEDI

II.8 That which dwells on pain is Aversion.

FEUERSTEIN

II.8 Aversion is [that which] rests on sorrowful [experiences].

HOUSTON

II.8 *Dveṣa*-dislike is holding on to (prior) pain.

JNANESHVARA

II.8 Aversion (dvesha) is a modification that results from misery associated with some memory, whereby the three modifications of aversion, pain, and the memory of the object or experience are then associated with one another.

PRABHAVANANDA

II.8 Aversion is that which dwells upon pain.

PUROHIT

II.8 Aversion is recoiling from pain.

SATCHIDANANDA

II.8 Aversion is that which follows identification with painful experiences.

SHEARER

II.8 Aversion is clinging to pain.

TAIMNI

II.8 That repulsion which accompanies pain is Dveṣa.

VIVEKANANDA

II.8 Aversion is that which dwells on pain.

II.9

स्वरसवाही विदुषोऽपि तथारूढोऽभिनिवेशः ॥ ९॥

sva-rasa-vāhī viduṣo'pi tathārūḍho 'bhiniveśaḥ

स्वरस -	sva-rasa-		
स्व -	sva-	own	by its own potency; flowing on automatically,
रस -	rasa-	lit.: juice:	by its own momentum;
√रस् *ras: to taste*		inclination	sustained by its own forces; automatically; of its own accord

वाही √वह् *vah: to flow*	vāhī	flowing
विदुषः - √विद् *vid: to know*	viduṣaḥ-	[*of*] a learned or wise man; sage's
अपि	api	even; also
तथा -	tathā-	the same way; thus
रूढः √रुह् *ruh: to grow (here: out of samādhi)*	rūḍhaḥ	grown strong; dominating; rooted; grounded; established
अभिनिवेशाः *अभि - abhi-: to, toward, into +* *-नि - -ni-: downward motion, opposed to, intensity +* *√विश् viś: to dwell*	abhiniveśāḥ	fear of separation from body; will-to-live; drive-to-survive; clinging to bodily life; "May I not cease to be"

ARYA

II.9 The fear of death (that "may I not cease to be") is strong even in a learned man that same way (as it is in an ordinary person), flowing of its own accord (for no apparent cause).

BAILEY

II.9 Intense desire for sentient existence is attachment. This is inherent in every form, is self-perpetuating, and known even to the very wise.

DVIVEDI

II.9 The strong desire for life, seen even in the learned, and ever sustained by its own force, is Attachment.

FEUERSTEIN

II.9 The will-to-live, flowing along [by its] own momentum, is rooted thus even in the sages.

HOUSTON

II.9 *Abhiniveśa*-the will to live, is carried on by its own inclination, rooted in that way even in the wise.

JNANESHVARA

II.9 Even for those people who are learned, there is an ever-flowing, firmly established love for continuation and a fear of cessation, or death, of these various colored modifications (kleshas).

PRABHAVANANDA

II.9 The desire to cling to life is inherent both in the ignorant and in the learned. This is because the mind retains impressions of the death experience from many previous incarnations.

PUROHIT

II.9 Fear is that constant natural terror of death, that is rooted even in the minds of the learned.

SATCHIDANANDA

II.9 Clinging to life, flowing by its own potency [due to past experience], exists even in the wise.

SHEARER

II.9 And the fear of death is a spontaneous feeling, deeply rooted in us all, no matter how learned we may be.

TAIMNI

II.9 Abhiniveśa is the strong desire for life which dominates even the learned (or the wise).

VIVEKANANDA

II.9 Abiding in its own nature [due to past experience of death], and established even in the learned, is the clinging to life.

II.10

ते प्रतिप्रसवहेयाः सूक्ष्माः ॥ १० ॥

te prati-prasava-heyāḥ sūkṣmāḥ

ते	te	those; these (here: kleśāḥ)
प्रतिप्रसव - *प्रति - prati-: towards, back, in opposition to +* *प्र - pra-: forth, onward +* *√सू sū: to set in motion*	prati-pravasa-	(through) counter-production, gradual reabsorption into primal origins/sources/causes
हेयाः *√हा hā: to leave/abandon*	heyāḥ	should be dissolved/destroyed/ ended/overcome/abolished
सूक्ष्म *√सिव् siv: to sew*	sūkṣma	subtle; fine; refined; attenuated

ARYA

II.10 Those kleśhas (being made gradually) subtle should be destroyed through (the process) counter (to their) production, (that is) through gradual dissolution into their own causes.

BAILEY

II.10 These five hindrances, when subtly known, can be overcome by an opposing mental attitude.

DVIVEDI

II.10 These, the subtle ones, must be suppressed by a contrary course.

FEUERSTEIN

II.10 These [causes-of-affliction], [in their] subtle [form], are to be overcome by the process-of-involution.

HOUSTON

II.10 Those (*kleśa*-root cause of pain), (in their) subtle (form), are to be ended (*heya*) by *pratiprasava*-inverse propagation (non-activation).

JNANESHVARA

II.10 When the five types of colorings (kleshas) are in their subtle, merely potential form, they are then destroyed by their disappearance or cessation into and of the field of mind itself.

PRABHAVANANDA

II.10 When these obstacles have been reduced to a vestigial form, they can be destroyed by resolving the mind back into its primal cause.

PUROHIT

II.10 The finer afflictions disappear as mind disappears in illumination.

SATCHIDANANDA

II.10 In subtle form, these obstacles can be destroyed by resolving then back into their primal cause [the ego].

SHEARER

II.10 The subtle causes of suffering are destroyed when the mind merges back into the unmanifest.

TAIMNI

II.10 These, the subtle ones, can be reduced by resolving them backward into their origin.

VIVEKANANDA

II.10 The fine samskāras are to be conquered by resolving them into their causal state.

II.11

ध्यानहेयास्तद्वृत्तयः ॥ ११ ॥

dhyāna-heyās tad-vṛttayaḥ

ध्यान - *√ध्यै dhyai: to meditate*	dhyāna-	(by) meditation/ meditative-absorption
हेयाः *√हा hā: to leave/abandon*	heyāḥ	(to be) dissolved/destroyed/ ended/overcome/abolished (through)
तद्वृत्तयः *तद् tad: that, this + √वृत् vṛt: to whirl*	tad-vṛttayaḥ	these vṛttis

ARYA

II.11 Their vṛttis are to be dissolved through meditation.

BAILEY

II.11 Their activities are to be done away with, through the meditation process.

DVIVEDI

II.11 Their transformations are to be suppressed by meditation.

FEUERSTEIN

II.11 The fluctuation of these [causes-of-affliction] are to be overcome by meditative-absorption.

HOUSTON

II.11 *Vṛtti*-definitions (of *citta*-the field arising from) those (*kleśa*) are to be ended (*heya*) by *dhyāna*-meditation.

JNANESHVARA

II.11 When the modifications still have some potency of coloring (klishta), they are brought to the state of mere potential by meditation (dhyana).

PRABHAVANANDA

II.11 In their fully developed form, they can be overcome through meditation.

PUROHIT

II.11 The grosser afflictions disappear through meditation.

SATCHIDANANDA

II.11 In the active state, they can be destroyed by meditation.

SHEARER

II.11 The gross effects of suffering are discarded through meditation.

TAIMNI

II.11 Their active modifications are to be suppressed by meditation.

VIVEKANANDA

II.11 By meditation their [gross] modifications are to be rejected.

II.12

क्लेशमूलः कर्माशयो दृष्टादृष्टजन्मवेदनीयः ॥ १२ ॥

kleśa-mūlaḥ karmāśyo dṛṣṭādṛṣṭa-janma-vedanīyaḥ

क्लेश -	kleśa-	affliction,	the root cause
√क्लिश् *kliś: to trouble, to be troubled*		obstruction, etc.	of obstruction/
मूलः	mūlaḥ	root; origin;	affliction (is)
√मूर् *mūr: to become rigid*		source; cause	
कर्म -	karma-	action; deed;	the propensity
√कृ *kṛ: to do*		work; performance	of accumulated
आशयाः	āśayaḥ	reservoir; accumulation	karmas (residue
आ - *ā-: near to, from all sides, all around* +			of actions);
√शी *śī: to lie down/recline/rest*			reservoir or womb of
			residual karmas
दृष्ट -	dṛṣṭa-	seen (in the present)	
√दृश् *dṛś: to see*			(is to be)
अदृष्ट -	adṛṣṭa-	unseen; future	experienced
अ - *a-: connoting absence* + √दृश् *dṛś: to see*		(past, future, pralaya)	in seen
जन्म -	janma-	births; lives; incarnation	and unseen
√जन् *jan: to beget*			lives
वेदनीयः	vedanīyaḥ	(to be) experienced;	
√विद् *vid: to know, be conscious of*		is to be experienced in	
		(past, future)	

ARYA

II.12 The karmāśhaya is the root of kleśhas (and) comes to experience in the current life (or has in the past, or may come) in the future lives.

BAILEY

II.12 Karma itself has its root in these five hindrances and must come to fruition in this life or in some later life.

DVIVEDI

II.12 The impressions of works have their root in distractions, and are experienced in the seen or the unseen.

FEUERSTEIN

II.12 The causes-of-affliction are the the root of the action-deposit, and [this] may be experienced in the seen [i.e. the present] birth or in an unseen [i.e. future] [birth].

HOUSTON

II.12 Having its root in the *kleśa*-root causes of pain, the accumulation of *karma*-actions can be experienced in births, seen and unseen.

JNANESHVARA

II.12 Latent impressions that are colored (karmashaya) result from other actions (karmas) that were brought about by colorings (kleshas), and become active and experienced in a current life or a future life.

PRABHAVANANDA

II.12 A man's latent tendencies have been created by his past thoughts and actions. These tendencies will bear fruits, both in this life and in lives to come.

PUROHIT

II.12 Karma, whether fulfilled in present or future life, has its root in affliction.

SATCHIDANANDA

II.12 The womb of karmas (actions and reactions) has its root in these obstacles, and the karmas bring experiences in the seen [present] or in the unseen [future] births.

SHEARER

II.12 The impression of past action, stored deep in the mind, are the seeds of desire. They ripen into action in seen and unseen ways—if not in this life, then in another.

TAIMNI

II.12 The reservoir of Karmas which are rooted in Kleśas brings all kinds of experiences in the present and future lives.

VIVEKANANDA

II.12 The "receptacle of works" has its root in the aforesaid pain-bearing obstructions, and their experience is in this visible (present) life or in the unseen (next) life.

II.13

सति मूले तद्विपाको जात्यायुर्भोगाः ॥ १३ ॥

sati mūle tad-vipāko jātyāyur-bhogāḥ

सति	sati	[*upon*] there being	[*upon*]
√अस् *as: to be*		present; exists;	there being
		with the existence of	the root
मूले	mule	(of the) root, cause/	
√मूर् *mūr: to become rigid*		origin	
तद् -	tad-	there; that	(there occurs)
विपाकः	vipākah	fruition; ripening	its fruition
वि - vi-: intensity + √*पच् pac: to cook, to roast*			in the form of
जाति -	jāti-	species; birth, incarnation class;	
√जन् *jan: to beget*		station of life	
आयुः -	āyuḥ-	life-span; life-time	
आ - ā-: near to, from all sides + √*इ i: to go*			
भोगाः	bhogāḥ	(life) experience; worldly enjoyment	
√भुज् *bhuj: to enjoy*			

ARYA

II.13 When the root (karmāśhaya) is present, there (naturally) occurs its fruition (in the form of) the species (in which one is re-born), lifespan (during that birth and painful or pleasant) experiences (during that lifespan).

BAILEY

II.13 So long as the roots (or samskaras) exist, their fruitition will be birth, life, and experiences resulting in pleasure or pain.

DVIVEDI

II.13 The root being there, their fruition (consists in) class, life and experience.

FEUERSTEIN

II.13 [So long as] the root exists, [there is also] fruition from it: birth, life and enjoyment.

HOUSTON

II.13 As long the root (of *karma*-actions) exists, there is fruition from that-birth, life-time, and life-experience.

JNANESHVARA

II.13 As long as those colorings (kleshas) remain at the root, three consequences are produced: 1) birth, 2) span of life, and 3) experiences in that life.

PRABHAVANANDA

II.13 So long as the cause exists, it will bear fruits—such as rebirth, a long or a short life, and the experiences of pleasure and of pain.

PUROHIT

II.13 So long as the root is present, karma remains, creates re-birth, governs its fulfillment and durations of fulfilment.

SATCHIDANANDA

II.13 With the existence of the root, there will be fruits also: namely, the births of different species of life, their life spans and experiences.

SHEARER

II.13 As long as action leaves its seed in the mind, this seed will grow, generating more births, more lives, more actions.

TAIMNI

II.13 As long as the root is there it must ripen and result it in lives of different class, length and experiences.

VIVEKANANDA

II.13 The root being there, the fruition comes in [the form of] species, longevity, and experience of pleasure and pain.

II.14

ते ह्लादपरितापफलाः पुण्यापुण्यहेतुत्वात् ॥ १४ ॥

te hlāda-paritāpa-phalāḥ puṇyāpuṇya-hetutvāt

ते	te	those; these; here: life/life-span/species/experiences	
ह्लाद -	hlāda-	joyful; delightful;	(accompanied
√ह्लाद् hlād: to rejoice		pleasurable	with) fruit
परिताप -	paritāpa-	suffering; anxious;	(of two kinds):
परि - pari-: all around, in addition to +		sorrow; distress	joyful or anxious,
√तप् tap: to be hot/distressed			gladness or sorrow
फलाः	phalāḥ	fruits; results	
√फल् phal: to ripen, bear fruit			
पुण्य -	puṇya-	virtuous; pure	
√पुण् puṇ: to do good		meritorious	depending on
अपुण्य -	a-puṇya-	unvirtuous; impure;	whether they are
अ - a-: un-/non-/not/without + √पुण् puṇ: to do good		degraded	[*effects of or because of*]
हेतुत्वात्	hetutvāt	[*having*] as cause	merit or vice
√हि hi: to incite			

ARYA

II.14 Those (developments in the form of species, lifespan and experiences) are accompanied with fruits (of two kinds): joyful or anxious, depending on whether they result in meritorious or evil actions.

BAILEY

II.14 These seeds (or samskaras) produce pleasure or pain according as their originating cause was good or evil.

DVIVEDI

II.14 They have pleasure or pain for their fruit according as their cause in virtue or vice.

FEUERSTEIN

II.14 These [three] have delight or distress as results, according to the causes, [which may be] meritorious or demeritorious.

HOUSTON

II.14 These (birth etc.) have delight or distress as results, according to the virtuous or non-virtuous nature of their cause.

JNANESHVARA

II.14 Because of having the nature of merits or demerits (virtue or vice), these three (birth, span of life, and experiences) may be experienced as either pleasure or pain.

PRABHAVANANDA

II.14 Experiences of pleasure and of pain are the fruits of merit and demerit, respectively.

PUROHIT

II.14 It creates pleasure or pain as it springs from virtue or vice.

SATCHIDANANDA

II.14 The karmas bear fruit of pleasure and pain caused by merit and demerit.

SHEARER

II.14 In these too, the fruit of wrong action is sorrow, the fruit of right action is joy.

TAIMNI

II.14 They have joy or sorrow for their fruit according as their cause is virtue or vice.

VIVEKANANDA

II.14 They (i.e actions) bear fruit as pleasure or pain, caused by virtue or vice.

II.15

परिणामतापसंस्कारदुःखैर्गुणवृत्तिविरोधाच्च दुःखमेव सर्वं विवेकिनः ॥ १५ ॥

pariṇāma-tāpa-saṃskāra-duḥkair guṇa-vṛtti-virodhāc ca duḥkham eva sarvaṃ vivekinaḥ

परिणाम -	pariṇāma-	outcomes; effects;	
परि - *pari-: all around, in addition to* +		results; consequences;	
√नम् *nam: to bend*		transformation; change	[*because of*]
ताप -	tāpa-	acute anxiety/anguish/suffering	the (three-
√तप् *tap: to be hot/distressed*			fold) pains
संस्कार -	saṃskāra-	habitual/standing wave in citta;	of effects,
सम् - *sam-: together with, completely, perfectly* +		conditioned mental	anxiety and
√कृ *kṛ: to do*		response from habit	mental
		and memory; impression/imprint in the subtle domain (karmāśaya); subliminal activator	residue (of all actions and involvements)
दुःखैः	duḥkaiḥ	[*because of*] pain; sorrow	
दुस् *dus: bad* + ख *kha: space, e.g. axle-hole*			
गुण -	guṇa-	attributes of Nature; qualities;	[*due to*]
गुण *guṇa: strand*		primary forces of creation	(mutual)
वृत्ति -	vṛtti-	(with) states; operations; activities;	conflicts
√वृत् *vṛt: to whirl*		waves; fluctuations; modifications definitions (of the mind-field)	among the tendencies of
विरोधात्	virodhāt	(mutual) (internal) opposition;	of the
वि - *vi-: apart, reverse to* + √रुध् *rudh: to stop*		[*due to*] opposition/obstruction conflict; contradiction	attributes of prakṛti
च	ca	and	
दुःखम्	duḥkham	painful; sorrowful	
दुस् *dus: bad* + ख *kha: space, e.g. axle-hole*			
एव	eva	only; but; merely	
सर्वं	sarvaṃ	all; everything	
विवेकिनः	vivekinaḥ	[*of*] the/[*to*] the wise man/discerner/	
वि - *vi-: apart from, particular* + √विच् *vic: to examine/discern*		enlightened one; wise man's; discerner's	

ARYA

II.15 To a wise man all (even apparently pleasant things are) painful because (he sees) their painful (nature) in (their) effects, in the anxieties (they produce) and the residue of saṃskāras (which is the cause of kleśhas they leave behind) (as well as he sees) mutual conflict of all vṛttis (activities and involvements arising) from the guṇas.

BAILEY

II.15 To the illuminated man all existence (in the three worlds) is considered pain owing to the activities of the gunas. These activities are threefold, producing consequences, anxieties and subliminal impressions.

DVIVEDI

II.15 To the enlightened *all* is *misery* on account of consequences, anxiety and impressions; as also on account of the opposition of the action of qualities.

FEUERSTEIN

II.15 Because of the sorrow in the [continual] transformation [of the world-ground], [in] the anguish [and in] the subliminal-activators and on account of the conflict between the movements of the primary-constituents—to the discerner all is but sorrow.

HOUSTON

II.15 Because of the pains caused by *sanskara*-subliminal activation of suffering due to change and on account of the obstruction of *vṛtti*-activity due to the *guṇa*-primary forces of nature - to the discerner, all is but pain.

JNANESHVARA

II.15 A wise, discriminating person sees all worldly experiences as painful, because of reasoning that all these experiences lead to more consequences, anxiety, and deep habits (samskaras), as well as acting in opposition to the natural qualities.

PRABHAVANANDA

II.15 But the man of spiritual discrimination regards all these experiences as painful. For even the enjoyment of present pleasure is painful, since we already fear its loss. Past pleasure is painful because renewed cravings arise from the impressions it has left upon the mind. And how can any happiness be lasting if it depends only upon our moods? For these moods are constantly changing, as one or another of the ever-warring gunas seizes control of the mind.

PUROHIT

II.15 To the discriminating mind, all karma is painful, for pain follows them all in the end; they cause irritation, leave impressions behind, create the conflict between the three Qualities.

SATCHIDANANDA

II.15 To one of discrimination, everything is painful indeed, due to its consequences: the anxiety and fear over losing what is gained; the resulting impressions left in the mind to create renewed cravings; and the constant conflict among the three gunas which control the mind.

SHEARER

II.15 Life is uncertain, change causes fear, and latent impressions bring pain—all is indeed suffering to one who has developed discrimination.

TAIMNI

II.15 To the people who have developed discrimination all is misery on account of the pains resulting from change, anxiety and tendencies, as also on account of the conflicts between the functioning of the Guṇas and the Vṛttis (of the mind).

VIVEKANANDA

II.15 To the discriminating, all is, as it were, painful because everything brings pain, either as consequence or as anticipation of loss of happiness or as fresh craving arising from impressions of happiness, and also because the gunas counteract one another.

II.16

हेयं दुःखमनागतम् ॥ १६ ॥

heyaṃ duḥkham anāgatam

हेयं *√हा hā: to leave/abandon*	heyaṃ	(to be) dissolved/overcome/ avoided/ended
दुःखम् *दुस् dus: bad + ख kha: space, e.g. axle-hole*	duḥkham	lit.: bad space: pain; sorrow; misery
अनागतम् *अन्- an-: non-, not, absence +* *आ- ā-: near to +* *√गम् gam: to go*	anāgatam	(that) has not (yet) occurred; (is) yet to come (in the future)

ARYA

II.16 The pain that has not as yet occurred (is what) should be prevented.

BAILEY

II.16 Pain which is yet to come may be warded off.

DVIVEDI

II.16 The misery which is not yet come is to be warded off.

FEUERSTEIN

II.16 [That which is] to be overcome is sorrow yet-to-come.

HOUSTON

II.16 Pain, not yet come, is to be ended (*heya*).

JNANESHVARA

II.16 Because the worldly experiences are seen as painful, it is the pain, which is yet to come, that is to be avoided and discarded.

PRABHAVANANDA

II.16 The pain which is yet to come may be avoided.

PUROHIT

II.16 Future misery is to be avoided.

SATCHIDANANDA

II.16 Pain that is not yet come is avoidable.

SHEARER

II.16 But the suffering yet to come should be averted.

TAIMNI

II.16 The misery which is not yet come can and is to be avoided.

VIVEKANANDA

II.16 The misery which is not yet come is to be avoided.

II.17

द्रष्टृदृश्ययोः संयोगो हेयहेतुः ॥ १७ ॥

draṣṭṛ-dṛśyayoḥ saṃyogo heya-hetuḥ

द्रष्टृ -	draṣṭṛ-	Puruṣas' > Witness'; Seers'; Indwellers'
√दृश् *dṛś: to see*		
दृश्ययोः	dṛśyayoḥ	[*of*] the [*two*] perceptible objects seen;
√दृश् *dṛś: to see*		the [*dual*] seen/seeable
संयोगः	saṃyogaḥ	yoga/union (is)

सम्- sam-: together with, fully, completely + √युज् yuj: lit.: to yoke; to unite/dissolve; samādhi

हेय -	heya-	what should be avoided;
√हा *hā: to leave/abandon*		to be overcome; to be ended; that which is to be avoided
हेतुः	hetuḥ	cause
√हि *hi: to incite*		

ARYA

II.17 The cause of the (pain to) be avoided is the union of the seer and the objects of (his) seeing.

BAILEY

II.17 The illusion that the Perceiver and that which is perceived are one and the same is the cause (of the pain producing effects) which must be warded off.

DVIVEDI

II.17 The cause of that which is to be warded off is the junction of the seer and the sight.

FEUERSTEIN

II.17 The correlation between the seer [i.e. the Self] and the seen [i.e. Nature] is the cause [of that which is] to be overcome.

HOUSTON

II.17 The cause of *heya*-what is to be ended, is the *sanyoga*-correlation between the *draṣṭṛ*-seer and the *dṛśya*-the seeable.

JNANESHVARA

II.17 The uniting of the seer (the subject, or experiencer) with the seen (the object, or that which is experienced) is the cause or connection to be avoided.

PRABHAVANANDA

II.17 This pain is caused by false identification of the experiencer with the object of experience. It may be avoided.

PUROHIT

II.17 The link between the Seer and the seen, creates misery, is to be broken.

SATCHIDANANDA

II.17 The cause of that avoidable pain is the union of the Seer (Purusha) and the seen (Prakriti, or Nature).

SHEARER

II.17 The cause of this suffering is that the unbounded Self is overshadowed by the world.

TAIMNI

II.17 The cause of that which is to be avoided is the union of the Seer and the Seen.

VIVEKANANDA

II.17 The cause of that [misery] which is to be avoided is the junction of the Seer and the seen.

II.18

प्रकाशक्रियास्थितिशीलं भूतेन्द्रियात्मकं भोगापवर्गार्थं दृश्यम् ॥ १८ ॥

prakāśa-kriyā-sthiti-śīlaṃ bhūtendriyātmakaṃ bhogāpavargārthaṃ dṛśyam

प्रकाश -	prakāśa-	illumination; light;
प्र - pra-: forward, onward, away +		luminosity; brightness;
√प्रकाश् prakāś: to be visible		manifestation: as of sattva
क्रिया -	kriyā-	activity: as of rajas
√कृ kṛ: to do		
स्थिति -	sthiti-	inertia: as of tamas
√स्था sthā: to stand		
शीलं	śīlaṃ	(having as) nature; character;
		properties; qualities
भूत -	bhūta-	elements
√भू bhū: to become		
इन्द्रिय -	indriya-	senses; sense organs
इन्द्रि indri: senses + -य -ya: non-between-ness		
आत्मकं	ātmakaṃ	consisting of; embodied in;
आत्मन् ātman: spiritual self + क ka: body		being of nature; having the nature of
भोग -	bhoga-	(life) experience; worldly enjoyment
√भुज् bhuj: to enjoy		
अपवर्ग -	apavarga-	lit.: to turn away: liberation; emancipation
अप - apa-: away from + √वृज् vṛj: to bend, to turn		
अर्थं	artham	(having as its) purpose; (for the sake of;
√अर्थ् arth: to intend		in order to) (regarding) purpose
दृश्यम्	dṛśyam	perceivable; object seen; the seen/the seeable
√दृश् dṛś: to see		

ARYA

II.18 (The world) seen has three natures, light, activity and stability; it consists of elements and senses and exists for the purpose of the seer's worldly enjoyment or liberation.

BAILEY

II.18 That which is perceived has three qualities, sattva, rajas and tanas (rhythm, mobility and inertia); it consists of the elements and the sense organs. The use of these produces experience and eventual liberation.

DVIVEDI

II.18 The sight consists of the elements and the organs, is of the nature of illumination, action and position and is of use so far as experience and absolution are concerned.

FEUERSTEIN

II.18 The seen [i.e. Nature] has the character of brightness, activity and inertia; it is embodied in elements and sense-organs [and it serves] the [dual] purpose of enjoyment and emancipation.

HOUSTON

II.18 *Dṛśya*-the seeable, has the characteristics of brightness (*sattva-guṇa*) activity (*rajas-guṇa*) and inertia (*tamas-guṇa*). It is embodied in the *bhūta*-elements and *indriya*-sense- organs and exists for the (dual) purpose of experience and emancipation.

JNANESHVARA

II.18 The objects (or knowables) are by their nature of:
1) illumination or sentience,
2) activity or mutability, or
3) inertia or stasis; they consist of the elements and the powers of the senses, and exist for the purpose of experiencing the world and for liberation or enlightenment.

PRABHAVANANDA

II.18 The object of experience is conposed of the three gunas—the principles of illumination (sattwa), activity (rajas) and inertia (tamas). From these, the whole universe has evolved, together with the instruments of knowledge—such as the mind, senses, etc.—and the objects perceived—such as the physical elements. The universe exists in order that the experiencer may experience it, and thus become liberated.

PUROHIT

II.18 Purity, passion, ignorance constitute the seen; element and sense its modifications, enjoyment and liberation its aim.

SATCHIDANANDA

II.18 The seen is of the nature of the gunas: illumination, activity and inertia; and consists of the elements and sense organs, whose purpose is to provide both experiences and liberation to the Purusha.

SHEARER

II.18 The world is the play of the *gunas*—the universal energies of light, motion and mass. They take form as the elements and the senses. The purpose of the world is to provide us with experience and thus lead us to liberation.

TAIMNI

II.18 The Seen (objective side of manifestation) consists of the elements and sense-organs, is of the nature of cognition, activity and stability (Sattva, Rajas and Tamas) and has for its purpose (providing the Puruṣa with) experience and liberation.

VIVEKANANDA

II.18 The seen which is composed of elements and organs, and characterized by illumination, action, and inertia, is for the purpose of experience and release (of the Seer).

विशेषाविशेषलिङ्गमात्रालिङ्गानि गुणपर्वाणि ॥ १९ ॥

viśeṣāviśeṣa-liṅga-mātrāliṅgāni guṇa-parvāṇi

विशेष –	viśeṣa-	distinction; difference;
वि – vi-: apart, separate from + √*शिष्* śiṣ: to remain		gradation; specific; particular; particularized evolutes (gross elements and senses)

अविशेष –	a-viśeṣa-	non-specific; general evolutes
अ – a-: without + √*विशेष* viśeṣa (see above)		(subtle elements; mental sense; antahkarana); universal; archetypal

लिङ्ग –	liṅga-	mark; characteristic; definition	merely named; only indicated
√*लिङ्* liṅg: to attach oneself			
मात्र –	mātra-	only; mere	(primary manifestations)

अलिङ्गानि	a-liṅgāni	states: undefined; undefinable;
अ – a-: without + √*लिङ्* liṅg: to attach oneself		unmanifest; unmodified; undifferentiated; unindicated

गुणपर्वाणि   guṇaparvāṇi

गुण –	guṇa-	(for) the attributes of matter (prakṛti): sattva, rajas, tamas; primary-constituents of Nature	stages/phases of unfoldment of the evolutes of the guṇas
गुण guṇa: strand			
पर्वाणि	parvāṇi	level/stage/phase	
√*पृ* pṛ: to fill			

ARYA

II.19 Particularised evolutes, general evolutes, assignation-measure and unassigned Matter: these are evolutes of guṇas.

BAILEY

II.19 The divisions of the gunas (or qualities of matter) are fourfold; the specific, the non-specific, the indicated and the untouchable.

DVIVEDI

II.19 The stages of the *Guṇas* are the defined, the undefined, the dissoluble and the indissoluble.

FEUERSTEIN

II.19 The levels of the primary-constituents are
the particularised,
the unparticularised,
the differentiate and
the undifferentiate.

HOUSTON

II.19 The phases of the *guṇa*-primary forces of creation, are the particularized (visible), the unparticularized (atomic), the *linga*-only-indicated (primary manifestation and *alinga*-the unmanifest (*prakṛti*-primary matter).

JNANESHVARA

II.19 There are four states of the elements (gunas), and these are: 1) diversified, specialized, or particularized (vishesha), 2) undiversified, unspecialized, or unparticularized (avishesha), 3) indicator-only, undifferentiated phenomenal, or marked only (linga-matra), and 4) without indicator, noumenal, or without mark (alingani).

PRABHAVANANDA

II.19 The gunas pass through four states—gross, subtle, primal and unevolved.

PUROHIT

II.19 Gross, fine, manifest, unmanifest, are the four conditions of the three qualities.

SATCHIDANANDA

II.19 The stages of the gunas are specific, non-specific, defined and undefinable.

SHEARER

II.19 The *gunas* operate on various levels: gross, subtle, causal and unmanifest.

TAIMNI

II.19 The stages of the *Guṇas* are the particular, the universal, the differentiated and the undifferentiated.

VIVEKANANDA

II.19 The states of the gunas are the defined (the gross elements), the undefined (the subtle elements), the indicated only, and the signless (prakriti).

II.20

द्रष्टा दृशिमात्रः शुद्धोऽपि प्रत्ययानुपश्यः ॥ २० ॥

draṣṭā dṛśi-mātraḥ śuddo 'pi pratyayānupaśyaḥ

द्रष्टा	draṣṭā	Puruṣa: the Witness—Seer—Knower	
√ दृश् *dṛś: to see*		Imperishable Indweller	
दृशिमात्रः	dṛśimātraḥ		
दृशि -	dṛśi-	seeing	consciousness alone;
√दृश् *dṛś: to see*			seeing alone;
मात्रः	mātraḥ	only; alone	only seeing;
			pure consciousness force; power of seeing
शुद्धः	śuddhaḥ	pure	
अपि	api	although; even	
प्रत्यय -	pratyaya-	content of mind-field;	
प्रति - *prati-: towards, in direction of* + √इ *i : to go*		presented-idea;	
		cognition principle; cognition; causal/awareness principle; awareness perceiving (through the mind); buddhi; discriminatory intelligence; *immediate arising thought directed to an object—Houston*	
अनुपश्यः	anupaśyaḥ	appears as if seeing;	
		appears to see along with; witnessing	

ARYA

II.20 The seer is the consciousness-force only; though pure, (he) perceives in accordance with the awareness of *buddhi* faculty.

BAILEY

II.20 The seer is pure knowledge (gnosis). Though pure, he looks upon the presented idea through the medium of the mind.

DVIVEDI

II.20 The seer is pure gnosis, and though pure, (appears to) see through intellect.

FEUERSTEIN

II.20 The seer [which is] the sheer [power of] seeing, although pure, apperceives the presented-idea.

HOUSTON

II.20 The *draṣṭṛ*-seer is *dṛśi-mātra*-seeing alone. It is pure, even (when) witnessing *pratyayas*-thoughts directed toward an object.

JNANESHVARA

II.20 The Seer is but the force of seeing itself, appearing to see or experience that which is presented as a cognitive principle.

PRABHAVANANDA

II.20 The Atman—the experiencer—is pure consciousness. It appears to take on the changing colors of the mind. In reality, it is unchangeable.

PUROHIT

II.20 The Seer is sight itself, but though untainted, appears as if tainted through the vagaries of the intellect.

SATCHIDANANDA

II.20 The Seer is nothing but the power of seeing which, although pure, appears to see through the mind.

SHEARER

II.20 But the Self is boundless. It is the pure consciousness that illumines the contents of the mind.

TAIMNI

II.20 The Seer is pure consciousness but though pure, appears to see through the mind.

VIVEKANANDA

II.20 The Seer is intelligence only, and though pure, sees through the colouring of the intellect.

II.21

तदर्थ एव दृश्यस्यात्मा ॥ २१ ॥

tad-artha eva dṛśyasyātmā

तद् -	tad-	(of) That	(for the) purpose/ sake of That (Puruṣa)
अर्थः √अर्थ् *arth: to intend*	arthaḥ	(for the) purpose/ sake	
एव	eva	only; alone	
दृश्यस्य - √दृश् *dṛś: to see*	dṛśyasya-	[*of*] the perceived; the seen; the seeable; the perceiveable's	
आत्मा	ātmā	form; nature; being; essence; existence	

ARYA

II.21 The essence of the objects of perception (exists) only for the purpose of that (seer).

BAILEY

II.21 All that is exists for the sake of the soul.

DVIVEDI

II.21 The being of the sight is for him.

FEUERSTEIN

II.21 The essence of the seen is only for the sake of this [seer].

HOUSTON

II.21 The existence of *dṛśya*-the seeable, is solely for the purpose of that (*draṣṭṛ*-seer).

JNANESHVARA

II.21 The essence or nature of the knowable objects exists only to serve as the objective field for pure consciousness.

PRABHAVANANDA

II.21 The object of experience exists only to serve the purpose of the Atman.

PUROHIT

II.21 The seen exists for the Seer alone.

SATCHIDANANDA

II.21 The seen exists only for the sake of the Seer.

SHEARER

II.21 It is only for the sake of the Self that the world exists.

TAIMNI

II.21 The very being of the Seen is for his sake (i.e. Prakṛti exists only for his sake).

VIVEKANANDA

II.21 The [transformation that takes place in the] nature of the seen (i.e. the prakriti) is for Him (i.e. the Purusha).

II.22

कृतार्थं प्रति नष्टमप्यनष्टं तदन्यसाधारणत्वात् ॥ २२ ॥

kṛtārthaṃ prati naṣṭam apy a-naṣṭaṃ tad-anya-sādhāraṇatvāt

कृतार्थं	kṛtāthaṃ		
कृत - √कृ *kṛ: to do*	kṛta-	accomplished	one who has accomplished his purpose: attained liberation, entered enlightenment
अर्थं	arthaṃ	purpose	
प्रति	prati	towards; to; for; with regard to	
नष्टम् √नश् *naś: to perish*	naṣṭaṃ	ceased; lost; destroyed; made to disappear	
अपि	api	although; even; nevertheless	
अनष्टं अ - *a-: un-/non-/not/without* + √नश् *naś: to perish*	a-naṣṭaṃ	not destroyed; not-ceased; existent	
तत् -	tat-	that	
अन्य -	anya-	here: (for) others	
साधारणत्वात् स - *sa-: with* + आ - *ā-: (indicates intensification)* + √धृ *dhṛ: to hold/carry/bear* + - त्व *-tva: -ness*	sādhāraṇatvāt	[*because of*] being common; [*due to*] commonality	

ARYA

II.22 Even when the objects of perceptions have disappeared so far as the (individual) who has fulfilled his purpose is concerned, they are not destroyed because they are still common in other (people's perceptions).

BAILEY

II.22 In the case of the man who has achieved yoga (or union) the objective universe has ceased to be. Yet it existeth still for those who are not yet free.

DVIVEDI

II.22 It, though destroyed in the case of him whose purpose has been fulfilled, is yet not destroyed for it is common to others besides him.

FEUERSTEIN

II.22 Although [the seen] has ceased [to exist] for [the yogin whose] purpose has been accomplished, it has nevertheless not ceased (to exist altogether], since it is common-experience [with respect to all] other [beings].

HOUSTON

II.22 With regard to that (*draṣṭṛ*-seer) whose purpose is accomplished, (*dṛśya*-the seeable) has ceased - although (at the same time) it has not ceased since it is common (to others).

JNANESHVARA

II.22 Although knowable objects cease to exist in relation to one who has experienced their fundamental, formless true nature, the appearance of the knowable objects is not destroyed, for their existence continues to be shared by others who are still observing them in their grosser forms.

PRABHAVANANDA

II.22 Though the object of experience becomes unreal to him who has reached the state of liberation, it remains real all to other beings.

PUROHIT

II.22 The seen is dead to him who has attained liberation, but is alive to others, being common to all.

SATCHIDANANDA

II.22 Although destroyed for him who has attained liberation, it [the seen] still exists for others, being common to them.

SHEARER

II.22 Although the limitations of the world disappear for one who knows the Self, they are not destroyed, because they continue to exist for others.

TAIMNI

II.22 Although it becomes non-existent for him whose purpose has been fulfilled it continues to exist for others on account of being common to others (besides him).

VIVEKANANDA

II.22 Though destroyed for him whose goal has been gained, yet prakriti is not destroyed for others, being common to them.

II.23

स्वस्वामिशक्त्योः स्वरूपोपलब्धिहेतुः संयोगः ॥ २३ ॥

sva-svāmi-śaktyoḥ svarūpopalabdhi-hetuḥ saṃyogaḥ

स्व -	sva-	own; object of possession; something owned
स्वामि - *स्व - sva-: own*	svāmi-	Master/Owner/Possessor of Oneself
शक्त्योः *√शक् śak: to be able*	śaktyoḥ	[*of*] the (as in possession) [*two*] forces/powers; the two powers'

स्वरूप - svarūpa-

स्व -	sva-	own	(in) (His) own essential or fundamental nature or form
रूप -	rūpa-	nature; essence; form; essential or fundamental nature or form	

उपलब्धि - *उप - upa-: towards, near to + √लब्ध् labdh: to obtain*	upalabdhi-	finding; realization; apprehension; recognition
हेतुः *√हि hi: to incite*	hetuḥ	cause; reason; purpose; precedent
संयोगः *सम् - sam-: together with, fully, completely + √युज् yuj: lit.: to yoke; to unite/dissolve; samādhi*	saṃyogaḥ	yoga/union; correlation (is)

ARYA

II.23 The union of the forces of the objects of ownership (buddhi and the objects reflecting in it) and the (force of) ownership (itself) power of puruṣa has only one end: the realisation of the true nature (and at that the union ceases).

BAILEY

II.23 The association of the soul with the mind and thus with that which the mind perceives, produces an understanding of the nature of that which is perceived and likewise of the Perceiver.

DVIVEDI

II.23 Junction is the cause of the self-recognition of its, as well as its lord's, power.

FEUERSTEIN

II.23 The correlation [between the seer and the seen] is the reason for the apprehension of the own-form of the power of the owner and that of the owned [i.e. Nature].

HOUSTON

II.23 The *sanyoga*-correlation (between *draṣṭṛ*-seer and *dṛśya*-seeable) is the cause of the apprehension of the *svarūpa*-distinct essences of the powers (*śakti*) of the master (I, *svāmin-draṣṭṛ*), and what is mine (my domain-*dṛśya*).

JNANESHVARA

II.23 Having an alliance, or relationship between objects and the Self is the necessary means by which there can subsequently be realization of the true nature of those objects by that very Self.

PRABHAVANANDA

II.23 The Atman—the experiencer—is identified with Prakriti— the object of experience—in order that the true nature of both Prakriti and Atman may be known.

PUROHIT

II.23 The Seer and the seen are linked together that the real nature of each may be known.

SATCHIDANANDA

II.23 The union of Owner (Purusha) and owned (Prakriti) causes the recognition of the nature and powers of them both.

SHEARER

II.23 The Self is obscured by the world in order that the reality of both may be discovered.

TAIMNI

II.23 The purpose of the coming together of the Puruṣa and Prakṛti is gaining by the Puruṣa of the awareness of his true nature and the unfoldment of powers inherent in him and Prakṛti.

VIVEKANANDA

II.23 Junction [of prakriti and Purusha] is the cause of the realisation of the nature of the powers of both the seen and its Lord.

II.24

तस्य हेतुरविद्या ॥ २४ ॥

tasya hetur avidyā

तस्य	tasya	of that; its (possessive)
हेतुः *√हि hi: to incite*	hetuḥ	cause; reason; purpose (is)
अविद्या - *अ - a-: un-/non-/not/without, lacking +* *√विद् vid: to know*	avidyā-	lit.: without knowledge: true ignorance = absence of self-awareness; lack of awareness of Reality; unawareness of (His [Puruṣa's]) real nature

ARYA

II.24 The cause of that (union) is ignorance.

BAILEY

II.24 The cause of this association is ignorance or avidya.
This has to be overcome.

DVIVEDI

II.24 Its cause is ignorance.

FEUERSTEIN

II.24 The cause of this [correlation] is nescience.

HOUSTON

II.24 The cause of that (*sanyoga*-correlation) is *avidyā*- absence of self-awareness.

JNANESHVARA

II.24 Avidya or ignorance (II.3-II.5), the condition of ignoring, is the underlying cause that allows this alliance to appear to exist.

PRABHAVANANDA

II.24 This identification is caused by ignorance.

PUROHIT

II.24 The cause of this link is ignorance.

SATCHIDANANDA

II.24 The cause of this union is ignorance.

SHEARER

II.24 It is ignorance of our real nature that Causes the Self to be obscured.

TAIMNI

II.24 Its cause is the lack of awareness of his Real nature.

VIVEKANANDA

II.24 Ignorance is its cause.

II.25

तदभावात् संयोगाभावो हानं तद्दृशेः कैवल्यम् ॥ २५ ॥

tad-abhāvāt saṃyogābhāvo hānaṃ tad dṛśeḥ kaivalyam

तद् -	tad-	that; here: ignorance
अभावात् *अ - a-: un-/non-/not/without + √भू bhū: to be*	abhāvāt	[*through/owing/due to*] absence/ disappearance/elimination (of that [ignorance])
संयोग - *सम् - sam-: together with, fully, completely + √युज् yuj: lit.: to yoke; to unite/dissolve; samādhi*	saṃyoga-	(of) yoga/union
अभावः *अ - a-: un-/non-/not/without + √भू bhū: to be*	abhāvaḥ	absence; dissolution; disappearance (of that union [occurs])
हानं *√हा hā: to leave/abandon*	hānaṃ	final avoidance; cessation; removal; end
तत्	tat	that (is)
दृशेः *√दृश् dṛś: to see*	dṛśeḥ	[*of*] the Consciousness Principle; Consciousness Principle's; [*of*] Seeing
कैवल्यम् *केवल kevala: alone*	kaivalyam	Isolated Unity; Final Liberation; Cosmic Freedom; Independence; *Freedom—Houston*

ARYA

II.25 When ignorance disappears the union (of the two forces) is dissolved (and that is) the consciousness-principle's (realisation, attainment of) the absolute state.

BAILEY

II.25 When ignorance is brought to an end through non-association with the things perceived, this is the great liberation.

DVIVEDI

II.25 The break of the junction, through the dispersion of ignorance, is the (thing) to be warded off; it is the *Kaivalya* of the Seer.

FEUERSTEIN

II.25 With the disappearance of this [nescience] the correlation [also] disappears; this is [total] cessation, the aloneness of the [sheer power] of seeing.

HOUSTON

II.25 Owing to the disappearance of that (*avidyā*-absence of self-awareness), there is the disappearance of the *sanyoga*-correlation, the *hāna*-end (of what is to be ended-*heya*).
That is *Kaivalya*-the aloneness of seeing.

JNANESHVARA

II.25 By causing a lack of avidya, or ignorance there is then an absence of the alliance, and this leads to a freedom known as a state of liberation or enlightenment for the Seer.

PRABHAVANANDA

II.25 When ignorance has been destroyed, this identification ceases. Then bondage is at an end and the experiencer is independent and free.

PUROHIT

II.25 No ignorance, no link. The breaking of the link reveals the independence of the Seer.

SATCHIDANANDA

II.25 Without this ignorance, no such union occurs. This is the independence of the Seer.

SHEARER

II.25 When ignorance is destroyed, the Self is liberated from its identification with the world. This liberation is Enlightenment.

TAIMNI

II.25 The dissociation of *Puruṣa* and *Prakṛti* brought about by the dispersion of *Avidyā* is the real remedy and that is the Liberation of the Seer.

VIVEKANANDA

II.25 There being absence of that (i.e. ignorance), there is absence of junction. This is the destruction of ignorance, and this is the independence of the Seer.

II.26

विवेकख्यातिरविप्लवा हानोपायः ॥ २६ ॥

viveka-khyātir a-viplavā hānopāyaḥ

विवेक -	viveka-	here: distinction (between Seer and seeable);
वि - vi-: apart from, particular + √विच् vic: to examine/discern		discriminatory cognition between Self and not-Self; discrimination; discernment
ख्यातिः	khyātiḥ	discernment (of Puruṣa);
√ख्या khyā: to be known		knowledge; wisdom; intuitive unfoldment; illumination; vision
अविप्लवा	a-viplavā	unagitated; unaffected;
अ - a-: un-/non-/not/without +		uninterrupted; permanent;
वि - vi-: to and fro, different directions, etc. +		unceasing; unbroken; flowing;
√प्लु plu: to swim		incessant
हान -	hāna-	dissolution; cessation;
√हा hā: to leave/abandon		prevention; removal; end
उपायः	upāyaḥ	means; method; way
उप - upa-: towards, near to + √इ i: to go		

ARYA

II.26 The illumination of discriminatory wisdom, not affected (or agitated by anything) is the means of prevention (of sorrow).

BAILEY

II.26 The state of bondage is overcome through perfectly maintained discrimination.

DVIVEDI

II.26 The means of dissolving is continuous discrimination.

FEUERSTEIN

II.26 The means of [attaining] cessation is the unceasing vision of discernment.

HOUSTON

II.26 The unceasing *viveka-khyāti*-identification of *viveka*, is the way to the *hāna*-end.

JNANESHVARA

II.26 Clear, distinct, unimpaired discriminative knowledge is the means of liberation from this alliance.

PRABHAVANANDA

II.26 Ignorance is destroyed by awakening to knowledge of the Atman, until no trace of illusion remains.

PUROHIT

II.26 Unwavering discrimination between Self and non-Self, destroys ignorance.

SATCHIDANANDA

II.26 Uninterrupted discriminative discernment is the method for its removal.

SHEARER

II.26 Ignorance is destroyed by the undisturbed discrimination between the Self and the world.

TAIMNI

II.26 The uninterrupted practice of the awareness of the Real is the means of dispersion (of *Avidyā*).

VIVEKANANDA

II.26 The means of destruction of ignorance is unbroken practice of discrimination.

II.27

तस्य सप्तधा प्रान्तभूमिः प्रज्ञा ॥ २७ ॥

tasya saptadhā prānta-bhūmiḥ prajñā

तस्य	tasya	of that/it	
तद् tad-: that/it			
सप्तधा	saptadhā	sevenfold	
सप्त sapta: seven + √धा dhā: to place/hold			
प्रान्तभूमिः	prāntabhūmiḥ		
प्रान्त -	prānta-	ultimate/final	final/
प्र - pra-: forth, onward + अन्त anta: end			last stage
भूमिः	bhūmiḥ	ground; level; stage	(in yoga)
√भू bhū: to become			
प्रज्ञा	prajñā	wisdom; transcendent insight;	
प्र - pra-: before, in front + √ज्ञा jñā: to know		consciousness (higher state of); awakening of wisdom (samprajñāta); supra-cognition; primary insight	

ARYA

II.27 The wisdom of such a (realized one) is of ultimate level, sevenfold.

BAILEY

II.27 The knowledge (or illumination) achieved is sevenfold and is attained progressively.

DVIVEDI

II.27 The enlightenment which is the last stage, is seven fold in his case.

FEUERSTEIN

II.27 For him [who possesses this unceasing vision of discernment] there arises, in the last stage, transcendental-insight [which is] sevenfold.

HOUSTON

II.27 Of that (*hāna-upāya*-way to the end), there is seven-fold *prajñā*-insight, as the final stage.

JNANESHVARA

II.27 Seven kinds of ultimate insight come to one who has attained this degree of discrimination.

PRABHAVANANDA

II.27 The experiencer gains this knowledge in seven stages, advancing toward the highest.

PUROHIT

II.27 The enlightenment that comes to a yogi at the last step is sevenfold.

SATCHIDANANDA

II.27 One's wisdom in the final stage is seven-fold.
[One experiences the end of
1) desire to know anything more;
2) desire to stay away from anything;
3) desire to gain anything new;
4) desire to do anything;
5) sorrow;
6) fear;
7) delusion.]

SHEARER

II.27 There are seven stages in the growth of this wisdom.

TAIMNI

II.27 In his case the highest stage of Enlightenment is reached by seven stages.

VIVEKANANDA

II.27 His knowledge is attained in seven supreme steps.

II.28

योगाङ्गानुष्ठानादशुद्धिक्षये ज्ञानदीप्तिराविवेकख्यातेः ॥ २८ ॥

yogāṅgānuṣṭhānād aśuddhi-kṣaye jñāna-dīptir āviveka-khyāteḥ

योगाङ्गानुष्ठानात्	yogāṅgānuṣṭhānāt		
योग -	yoga-	(of) yoga	[*through*] the practice of the limbs/steps of yoga
√युज् *yuj: lit.: to yoke; to unite/dissolve; samādhi*			
अङ्ग -	aṅga-	(of) the steps/limbs	
अङ्ग *aṅga: parts*			
अनुष्ठानात्	anuṣṭhānāt	[*because of/through/from*] observance; practice; performance	
अनु - *anu-: following, after, behind +*			
√स्था *sthā: to stand*			

अशुद्धि -	aśuddhi-	(of) impurities
अ - *a-: un-/non-/not/without* + √शुध् *śudh: to purify*		
क्षये	kṣaye	[*upon*] elimination: dwindling; gradual diminishing; destruction
√क्षि *kṣi: to destroy*		
ज्ञान -	jñāna-	knowledge; concept; idea
√ज्ञा *jñā: to know*		
दीप्तिः	dīptiḥ -	kindling; gradual shining force; light; brilliance
√दीप् *dīp: to blaze*		

आविवेकख्यातेः	āvivekakhyāteḥ		
आ -	ā-	leads to; up to; until; as far as	leads to the illumination of discriminatory wisdom
विवेक -	viveka-	discrimination; discernment; discriminatory cognition between Self and not-Self	
वि - *vi-: apart from, particular +*			
√विच् *vic: to examine/discern*			
ख्यातेः	khyāteḥ	faculty of discriminating objects by appropriate designation	
√ख्या *khyā: to be known*			

ARYA

II.28 As the impurities are eliminated through the practice of yoga a (gradual) awakening of knowledge takes place until the (full) illumination of discriminatory wisdom (occurs).

BAILEY

II.28 When the means to yoga have been steadily practised, and when impurity has been overcome, enlightenment takes place, leading up to full illumination.

DVIVEDI

II.28 From the practice of the accessories of *Yoga* (arises) enlightenment, by the destruction of impurity leading to discrimination.

FEUERSTEIN

II.28 Through the performance of the members of Yoga, and with the dwindling of impurity, [there comes about] the radiance of gnosis [which develops] up to the vision of discernment.

HOUSTON

II.28 By practicing the (eight) limbs of yoga - upon diminishing of impurities, there is a light of knowing, up to (leading to) *viveka-khyati*-the identification of *viveka*.

JNANESHVARA

II.28 Through the practice of the different limbs, or steps to Yoga, whereby impurities are eliminated, there arises an illumination that culminates in discriminative wisdom, or enlightenment.

PRABHAVANANDA

II.28 As soon as all impurities have been removed by the practice of spiritual disciplines—the "limbs" of yoga—a man's spiritual vision opens to the light-giving knowledge of the Atman.

PUROHIT

II.28 Impurities having been washed away by the practice of meditation, the light of knowledge shines till discrimination is complete.

SATCHIDANANDA

II.28 By the practice of the limbs of Yoga, the impurities dwindle away and there dawns the light of wisdom, leading to discriminative discernment.

SHEARER

II.28 The distinction between pure consciousness and the world is revealed by the light of knowledge, when the nervous system has been purified by the practice of yoga.

TAIMNI

II.28 From the practice of the component exercises of Yoga, on the destruction of impurity, arises spiritual illumination which develops into awareness of Reality.

VIVEKANANDA

II.28 Through the practice of the different parts of yoga the impurities are destroyed and knowledge is kindled. leading up to discrimination.

II.29

यमनियमासनप्राणायामप्रत्याहारधारणाध्यानसमाधयोऽष्टावङ्गानि ॥ २९ ॥

yama-niyamāsana-prāṇāyāma-pratyāhāra-dhāraṇā-dhyāna-samādhayo-'ṣṭav aṅgāni

यम -	yama-	(the five) commands/
√*यम्* *yam: to expand/restrain*		injunctions of self-restraints; universal disciplines
नियम -	niyama-	(the five) injunctions/rules/
नि - *ni-: in, into* + √*यम्* *yam: to expand/restrain*		fixed observances
आसन -	āsana-	posture
√*आस्* *ās: to sit; to be present*		
प्राणायाम -	prāṇāyāma-	command of prāṇa; expansion of prāṇa
प्राण *prāṇa: vital force* + *आ -* *ā-: from all sides, all around* + √*यम्* *yam: to restrain* ***OR*** *प्राण* *prāṇa: vital force* + *अयम्* *ayam: to expand*		(life-force [breath]) (see sūtra II.49)
प्रत्याहार -	pratyāhāra-	withdrawal of the senses; abstraction
प्रति - *prati-: toward* + *आ -* *ā-: from all sides, all around* + √*हृ* *hṛ: to hold*		
धारणा -	dhāraṇā-	holding a focus; concentration
√*धृ* *dhṛ: to hold*		
ध्यान -	dhyāna-	meditation; meditative process/absorption
√*ध्यै* *dhyai: to meditate*		
समाधयः	samādhayaḥ	samādhi, meta-cognitive absorption with various stages
सम् - *sam-: together with, completely, perfectly* + *आ -* *ā-: near to, all around* + √*धा* *dhā: to put*		
अष्टौ	aṣṭau	eight
अङ्गानि	aṅgāni	limbs/steps/parts (of yoga)
अङ्ग *aṅga: parts*		

ARYA

II.29 Yamas, niyamas, posture, control of prāṇa (and breath), withdrawal of senses, holding a focus, meditative process, (and) highest meditation, (these are) eight limbs, steps (of yoga).

BAILEY

II.29 The eight means of yoga are, the Commandments or Yama, the Rules or Nijama, posture or Asana, right control of life force or Pranayama, abstraction or Pratyahara, attention or Dharana, Meditation or Dhyana, Contemplation or Samadhi.

DVIVEDI

II.29 Forbearance, observance, posture, regulation of breath, abstraction, contemplation, absorption, trance, are the eight accessories of *yoga*.

FEUERSTEIN

II.29 Restraint,
observance,
posture,
breath-control,
sense-withdrawal,
concentration,
meditative absorption
and enstacy are the
eight members
[of Yoga].

HOUSTON

II.29 *Yama, niyama, āsana, prāṇāyāma, pratyāhāra, dhāraṇā, dhyāna, and samādhi* are the eight limbs.

JNANESHVARA

II.29 The eight rungs, limbs, or steps of Yoga are the codes of self-regulation or restraint (yamas), observances or practices of self-training (niyamas), postures (asana), expansion of breath and prana (pranayama), withdrawal of the senses (pratyahara), concentration (dharana), meditation (dhyana), and perfected concentration (samadhi).

PRABHAVANANDA

II.29 The eight limbs of yoga are; the various forms of abstention from evil-doing (yama), the various observances (niyamas), posture (asana), control of the prana (pranayama), withdrawal of the mind from sense objects (pratyahara), concentration (dharana), meditation (dhyana) and absorption in the Atman (samadhi).

PUROHIT

II.29 Yama, Niyama, Āsana, Prānāyāma, Pratyāhāra, Dhāranā, Dhyāna, Samādhi, are the eight steps of Yôga.

SATCHIDANANDA

II.29 The eight limbs of Yoga are:
1) yama (abstinence)
2) niyama (observance)
3) asana (posture)
4) pranayama (breath control)
5) pratyahara (sense withdrawal)
6) dharana (concentration)
7) dhyana (meditation)
8) samadhi (contemplation, absorption or superconscious state)

SHEARER

II.29 There are eight limbs of yoga: *yama*—the laws of life, *niyama*—the rules for living, *asana*—the physical postures, *prāṇāyāma*—the breathing exercises, *pratyāhāra*—the retirement of the senses, *dhāraṇā*—steadiness of mind, *dhyāna*—meditation, *samādhi*—the settled mind.

TAIMNI

II.29 Self-restraints, fixed observances, posture, regulation of breath, abstraction, concentration, contemplation, trance are the eight parts (of the self discipline of *Yoga*).

VIVEKANANDA

II.29 Yama, niyama, āsana, prāṇāyāma, pratyāhāra, dhāraṇā, dhyāna and samādhi, are the eight limbs of yoga.

II.30

अहिंसासत्यास्तेयब्रह्मचर्यापरिग्रहा यमाः ॥ ३० ॥

ahiṃsā-satyāsteya-brahmacaryāparigrahā yamāḥ

अहिंसा -	ahiṃsā-	harmlessness; non-violence
अ - a-: without + √हन् han: to hurt		
सत्य -	satya-	truthfulness; honesty
√अस् as: to be		
अस्तेय -	a-steya-	non-theft; appropriate acquistion
अ - a-: without + √स्ता stā: to steal		
ब्रह्मचर्य -	brahma-carya-	control of sexual passions;
ब्रह्म brahma + √चर् car: to move		continence; chastity;
(lit.: walking/moving in Brahma)		*spiritual resolution of desires —Houston*
अपरिग्रहाः	a-parigrahāḥ	non-possessiveness; greedless
अ - a-: without + परि - pari-: all around, about + √ग्रह् grah: to grasp		non-indulgence of senses
यमाः	yamāḥ	(constitutes) (the five) commands/
√यम् yam: to restrain		injunctions of self-restraints; universal disciplines

ARYA

II.30 (These are five) yamas:
non-violence, truth, non-theft,
walking in brahman,
control over sexual passion,
avoidance of pleasures,
not indulging the senses.

BAILEY

II.30 Harmlessness,
truth to all beings,
abstention from theft,
from incontinence and
from avarice, constitute yama
or the five commandments.

DVIVEDI

II.30 Forbearance consists in
abstaining from killing, falsehood,
theft, incontinence, and greediness.

FEUERSTEIN

II.30 Non-harming,
truthfulness,
non-stealing,
chastity and
greedlessness are
the restraints.

HOUSTON

II.30 *Ahinsā*-
non-hurtfulness,
satya-truth,
asteya-non-stealing,
brahmacarya-spiritual resolution
of desires, and
aparigraha-
non-possessiveness
are the *yama*-universal disciplines.

JNANESHVARA

II.30 Non-injury or non-harming
(ahimsa), truthfulness (satya),
abstention from stealing (asteya),
walking in awareness of the
highest reality (brahmacharya),
and non-possessiveness or non-
grasping with the senses
(aparigraha) are the five yamas, or
codes of self-regulation or
restraint, and are the first of the
eight steps
of Yoga.

PRABHAVANANDA

II.30 Yama is abstention from
harming others, from falsehood,
from theft, from incontinence, and
from greed.

PUROHIT

II.30 Refusal of violence,
refusal of stealing, refusal of
covetousness, with telling truth,
and continence constitute the
Rules (yamas).

SATCHIDANANDA

II.30 Yama consists of
non-violence,
truthfulness,
non-stealing,
continence and
non-greed.

SHEARER

II.30 The laws of life are five:
non-violence,
truthfulness,
integrity,
chastity,
nonattachment.

TAIMNI

II.30 Vows of self-restraint
comprise abstention from
violence, falsehood,
theft, incontinence and
acquisitiveness.

VIVEKANANDA

II.30 Non-killing,
truthfulness,
non-stealing,
continence and
non-receiving [of gifts],
are called yama.

II.31

एते जातिदेशकालसमयानवच्छिन्नाः सार्वभौमा महाव्रतम् ॥ ३१ ॥

ete jāti-deśa-kāla-samayānavacchinnāḥ sārva-bhaumā mahāvratam

एते	ete	these
जाति - √जन् *jan: to beget*	jāti-	(by) birth; species; incarnation; class; station of life
देश - √दिश् *diś: to point out*	deśa-	(by) locus; place
काल - √कल् *kal: to impel*	kāla-	(by) time period/epoch/era
समय - सम् - *sam-: together with, completely, perfectly* + √इ *i: to go*	samaya-	(by) condition; situation; circumstance; occasion
अनवच्छिन्नाः अन् - *an-: not, absent* + - अव - *-ava-: away, off* + √छिद् *chid: to cut*	an-avacchinnāh	not limited; unconditioned; unconditional; irrespective no conditions pertaining
सार्वभौमा	sārvabhaumā	
सार्व -	sārva-	all } universal; applicable to all levels/spheres
भौमाः	bhaumāḥ	level; spheres; ground
महाव्रतम्	mahāvratam	
महा -	mahā-	great } Great Vow or Observance; great/universal vow/observance
व्रतम्	vratam	vow

ARYA

II.31 (These *yamas*) are the universal great vow, (unconditionally applicable to and) not delimited by (any consideration) as to species, locus, time or situation.

BAILEY

II.31 Yama (or the five commandments) constitutes the universal duty and is irrespective of race, place, time or emergency.

DVIVEDI

II.31 These, not qualified by class, place, time, or utility, are called great vows, being universal.

FEUERSTEIN

II.31 [These are valid] in all spheres, irrespective of birth, place, time and circumstance [and constitute] the great vow.

HOUSTON

II.31 Irrespective of life state, place, time, and circumstance, these (*yama*) are universal - the great vow.

JNANESHVARA

II.31 These codes of self-regulation or restraint become a great vow when they become universal and are not restricted by any consideration of the nature of the kind of living being to whom one is related, nor in any place, time or situation.

PRABHAVANANDA

II.31 These forms of abstention are basic rules of conduct. They must be practiced without any reservations as to time, place, purpose, or caste rules.

PUROHIT

II.31 These are the sacred vows, to be observed, independent of time, place, class or occasion.

SATCHIDANANDA

II.31 These Great Vows are universal, not limited by class, place, time or circumstance.

SHEARER

II.31 These laws are universal. Unaffected by time, place, birth or circumstance, together they constitute the "Great Law of Life."

TAIMNI

II.31 These (the five vows), not conditioned by class, place, time or occasion and extending to all stages constitute the Great Vow.

VIVEKANANDA

II.31 These, unbroken by time, place, purpose and caste-rules are universal great vows.

II.32

शौचसन्तोषतपःस्वाध्यायेश्वरप्रणिधानानि नियमाः ॥ ३२ ॥

śauca-santoṣa-tapaḥ-svādhyāyeśvara-praṇidhānāni niyamāḥ

शौच -	śauca-	purity
√शुच् śuc: to be radiant		
सन्तोष -	santoṣa-	contentment
सम्- sam-: together with, completely, perfectly + √तुष् tuṣ: to be satisfied		
तपः -	tapaḥ-	ascetic practices; austerity;
√तप् tap: heat, to be hot, to make hot		intensity in spiritual practice; accepting discomfort/even pain for spiritual unfoldment/purification
स्वाध्याय -	svādhyāya-	study of scripture and
स्व- sva-: own + आधि ā-dhī-: to meditate on +		inspiring text;
यायति yāyati-: to study, recite, read to +		japa (repetition of mantra);
√इ i: to go, (here: one's going into)		learning and practice of personal mantra; self-observation/study; witnessing

ईश्वरप्रणिधानानि	īśvarapraṇidhānāni		
ईश्वर -	īśvara-	God; the Lord:	surrender/devotion to/
ईश् īś: to own, be master of +		immanent or	worship of God;
वर vara: the best, choicest (√वृ vṛ: to choose)		transcendent	alignment/focus of
प्रणिधानानि	praṇidhānāni	surrenders; devotions	attention in God
प्र- pra-: forward, in front, before + -नि- -ni-: intensity + √धा dhā: to put			

नियमाः	niyamāḥ	(the five) rules; injunctions;
नि- ni-: in, into + √यम् yam: to restrain		spiritual observances; fixed observances; internal disciplines

ARYA

II.32 (These) (are five) niyamas; (mental) purity, (physical) cleanliness, contentment, ascetic practice, study of inspiring texts, silent repetition of mantras such as *Om*, (and) surrender to God.

BAILEY

II.32 Internal and external purification, contentment, fiery aspiration, spiritual reading and devotion to Ishvara constitutes nijama (or the five rules).

DVIVEDI

II.32 Observances consist in purity, contentment, mortification, study and resignation to *Iśvara*.

FEUERSTEIN

II.32 Purity, contentment, austerity, self-study and devotion to the Lord are the observances.

HOUSTON

II.32 *Śauca*-purity, *santoṣa*-contentment, *tapas*-intensity in spiritual practice, *svādhyāya*-learning and practice of personal mantra, and *īśvara-praṇidhāna*-perfect aligning of attention in the omniscient seer within (*īśvara*) are the *niyama*-internal disciplines.

JNANESHVARA

II.32 Cleanliness and purity of body and mind (shaucha), an attitude of contentment (santosha), ascesis or training of the senses (tapas), self-study and reflection on sacred words (svadhyaya), and an attitude of letting go into one's source (ishvarapranidhana) are the observances or practices of self-training (niyamas), and are the second rung on the ladder of Yoga.

PRABHAVANANDA

II.32 The niyamas (observances) are purity, contentment, mortification, study and devotion to God.

PUROHIT

II.32 Purity, austerity, contentment, repetition of sacred words, devotion to God, constitute the Regulations (niyama).

SATCHIDANANDA

II.32 Niyama consists of purity, contentment, accepting but not causing pain, study of spiritual books and worship of God [self-surrender].

SHEARER

II.32 The rules of living are five: simplicity, contentment, purification, refinement, surrender to the Lord.

TAIMNI

II.32 Purity, contentment, austerity, self-study and self-surrender constitute observances.

VIVEKANANDA

II.32 Internal and external purification, contentment, mortification, study, and worship of God, are the niyamas.

II.33

वितर्कबाधने प्रतिपक्षभावनम् ॥ ३३ ॥

vitarka-bādhane pratipakṣa-bhāvanam

वितर्क -	vitarka-	negative, even evil,
वि - vi-: particular, distinct, intensity + √तर्क् tark: to reflect		troubling thoughts (as of violence)
बाधने	bādhane	in disturbance/in repelling
प्रतिपक्ष -	pratipakṣa-	opposite thought/principle
भावनम्	bhāvanam	cultivate; realize; ponder

ARYA

II.33 In case of disturbance (arising through) troublesome thoughts (such as of violence) one should become intent on (their respective) opposites (e.g., love opposed to violence).

BAILEY

II.33 When thoughts which are contrary to yoga are present there should be the cultivation of their opposite.

DVIVEDI

II.33 The constant pondering upon the opposites (is necessary) when (these) are obstructed by inadequate thoughts.

FEUERSTEIN

II.33 For the repelling of unwholesome deliberation [the *yogin* should pursue] the cultivation of the opposite.

HOUSTON

II.33 Upon the suspending of *vitarka*-opposing beliefs -there is the realizing of (their) opposites.

JNANESHVARA

II.33 When these codes of self-regulation or restraint (yamas) and observances or practices of self-training (niyamas) are inhibited from being practiced due to perverse, unwholesome, troublesome, or deviant thoughts, principles in the opposite direction, or contrary thought should be cultivated.

PRABHAVANANDA

II.33 To be free from thoughts that distract one from yoga, thoughts of an opposite kind must be cultivated.

PUROHIT

II.33 If wrong sentiments disturb, cultivate right thoughts.

SATCHIDANANDA

II.33 When disturbed by negative thoughts, opposite [positive] ones should be thought of. This is pratipaksha bhavana.

SHEARER

II.33 When negative feelings constrict us, the opposite should be cultivated.

TAIMNI

II.33 When the mind is disturbed by improper thoughts, constant pondering over the opposites (is the remedy).

VIVEKANANDA

II.33 When thoughts obstructive to Yoga arise, contrary thoughts should be employed.

II.34

वितर्का हिंसादयः कृतकारितानुमोदिता लोभक्रोधमोहपूर्वका मृदुमध्याधिमात्रा दुःखाज्ञानानन्तफला इति प्रतिपक्षभावनम् ॥ ३४ ॥

vitarkā hiṃsādayaḥ kṛta-kāritānumoditā lobha-krodha-moha-pūrvakā
mṛdu-madhyādhimātrā duḥkhājñānānanta-phalā iti pratipakṣa-bhāvanam

वितर्काः	vitarkāḥ	negative thoughts (are)
वि - vi-: particular, distinct, intensity + √तर्क् tark: to reflect		
हिंसा -	hiṃsā-	violence; intent to harm; hurtfulness
√हन् han: to hurt		
आदयः	ādayaḥ	beginning with; etc.
कृत -	kṛta-	committed (by oneself)
√कृ kṛ: to do		
कारित -	kārita-	caused to be done through others (or)
√कृ kṛ: to do		
अनुमोदिताः	anu-moditāḥ	consented to; approved; abetted
अनु - anu-: following, after, behind + √मुद् mud: to rejoice		
लोभ -	lobha-	greed; avarice
√लुभ् lubh: to desire		
क्रोध -	krodha-	anger
√क्रुध् krudh: to be angry		
मोह -	moha-	delusion; infatuation; confusion
√मुह् muh: to be deluded		
पूर्वकाः	pūrvakāḥ	preceded by; arising from; conditioned by
मृदु -	mṛdu-	mild
मध्य -	madhya-	middling; medium; moderate
अधिमात्राः	adhimātrāḥ	intense
दुःख -	duḥkha-	suffering; sorrow; pain
अज्ञान -	ajñāna-	ignorance
अनन्त -	ananta-	unending; infinite
फलाः	phalāḥ	(having as) fruit; results
इति	iti	thus
प्रतिपक्ष -	pratipakṣa-	opposite principle/thoughts
भावनम्	bhāvanam	cultivating; realizing; dwelling in mind

ARYA

II.34 The troubling thoughts such as of violence (whether) conmitted (by oneself), caused to be done (through others) or (just) consented to, whether preceded by (or motivated through) greed, anger or delusion, (whether) mild, medium or intense, (they all) result in unending sorrow and ignorance—thus (should one) cultivate the (thoughts of principles) opposite (to violence, etc.).

BAILEY

II.34 Thoughts contrary to yoga are harmfulness, falsehood, theft, incontinence, and avarice, whether comitted personally, caused to be committed or approved of, whether arising from avarice, anger or delusion (ignorance); whether slight in the doing, middling or great. These result always in excessive pain and ignorance. For this reason, the contrary thoughts must be cultivated.

DVIVEDI

II.34 Inadequate thoughts are killing, etc.; whether done, caused to be done, or approved of; whether arising from covetousness, anger or delusion; whether slight middling or great;—(always) resulting in endless and innumerable misery and ignorance. Hence the (necessity of) pondering upon the opposites.

FEUERSTEIN

II.34 The unwholesome deliberations, [such as] harming *et cetera*, [whether] done, caused to done or approved, [whether] rising from greed, anger or infatuation, [whether] modest, medium or excessive—[these find their] unending fruition in nescience and sorrow; thus [the *yogin* should devote himself to] the cultivation of [their] opposites.

HOUSTON

II.34 *Vitarka*-opposing beliefs, such as *hinsā*-hurtfulness etc. whether done, caused to be done, or approved of, are conditioned upon greed, anger, and confusion, are mild, moderate or excessive, and have their unending results in pain and ignorance. Thus the realizing of their opposites.

JNANESHVARA

II.34 Actions arising out of such negative thoughts are performed directly by oneself, caused to be done through others, or approved of when done by others. All of these may be preceded by, or performed through anger, greed or delusion, and can be mild, moderate or intense in nature. To remind oneself that these negative thoughts and actions are the causes of unending misery and ignorance is the contrary thought, or principle in the opposite direction that was recommended in the previous sutra.

PRABHAVANANDA

II.34 The obstacles to yoga—such as acts of violence and untruth—may be directly created or indirectly caused or approved, they may be motivated by greed, anger or self-interest, they may be small or moderate or great, but they never cease to result in pain and ignorance. One should over-come distracting thoughts by remembering this.

PUROHIT

II.34 Think that wrong actions, violence and the like, whether committed, caused or abetted, whether provoked by anger, avarice or infatuation, whether they seem important or unimportant, bring endless ignorance and misery.

SATCHIDANANDA

II.34 When negative thoughts or acts such as violence, etc. are caused to be done or even approved of, whether incited by greed, anger or infatuation, whether indulged in with mild, medium or extreme intensity, they are based on ignorance and bring certain pain. Reflecting thus is also pratipaksha bhavanam.

SHEARER

II.34 Negative feelings, such as violence, are damaging to life, whether we act upon them our-selves, or cause or condone them in others. They are born of greed, anger or delusion, and may be slight, moderate or intense. Their fruit is endless ignorance and suffering. To remember this is to cultivate the opposite.

TAIMNI

II.34 As improper thoughts, emotions (and actions) such as those of violence, etc. whether they are done (indulged in), caused to be done or abetted, whether caused by greed, anger or delusion, whether present in mild, medium or intense degree, result in endless pain and ignorance; so there is the necessity of pondering over the opposites.

VIVEKANANDA

II.34 The obstructions to Yoga are killing, falsehood, and so forth—whether committed, caused, or approved—either through avarice, or anger, or ignorance—whether slight, middling, or great; they result in infinite ignorance and misery. This is [the method of] thinking the contrary.

II.35

अहिंसाप्रतिष्ठायां तत्सन्निधौ वैरत्यागः ॥ ३५॥

ahiṃsā-pratiṣṭhāyāṃ tat-sannidhau vaira-tyāgaḥ

अहिंसा -	ahiṃsā-	[*upon*] harmlessness; non-violence

अ - a-: without + √हन् han: to hurt

प्रतिष्ठायां	pratiṣṭhāyāṃ	[*upon*] firm establishment; being grounded

प्र - pra-: forward, onward + √स्था sthā: to stand

तद् -	tad-	(of) that
सन्निधौ	sannidhau	here: [*in*] (the yogi's) presence

सम् - sam-: together with, completely + -नि - -ni-: into + √धा dhā: to put

वैर -	vaira-	enmity; hostility

वीर् vīr: to be powerful + √ईर् īr : to move = to split/divide, to break into pieces

त्यागः	tyāgaḥ	ceases/disappears

√त्यज् tyaj: to abandon

ARYA

II.35 When (the yogi has) firmly established (in himself the principle of) non-violence; in his presence (there accrues a natural) loss of enmity (from the minds of others).

BAILEY

II.35 In the presence of him who has perfected harmlessness, all enmity disappears.

DVIVEDI

II.35 Abstinence from killing being confirmed, there is suspension of antipathy in the presence of him (who has acquired the virtue).

FEUERSTEIN

II.35 When [the *yogin*] is grounded in [the virtue of] non-harming, [all] enmity is abandoned in his presence.

HOUSTON

II.35 Upon being established in *ahinsā*-
non-hurtfulness-
there is a relinquishing of hostility in the presence of that (*ahinsā*).

JNANESHVARA

II.35 As a Yogi becomes firmly grounded in non-injury (ahimsa), other people who come near will naturally lose any feelings of hostility.

PRABHAVANANDA

II.35 When a man becomes steadfast in his abstention from harming others, then all living creatures will cease to feel enmity in his presence.

PUROHIT

II.35 When non-violence is firmly rooted, enmity ceases in the yogi's presence.

SATCHIDANANDA

II.35 In the presence of one firmly established in non-violence, all hostilities cease.

SHEARER

II.35 When we are firmly established in nonviolence, all beings around us cease to feel hostility.

TAIMNI

II.35 On being firmly established in non-violence there is abandonment of hostility in (his) presence.

VIVEKANANDA

II.35 When the yogi is established in non-killing, in all enmities [in others] cease his presence.

II.36

सत्यप्रतिष्ठायां क्रियाफलाश्रयत्वम् ॥ ३६ ॥

satya-pratiṣṭhāyāṃ kriyā-phalāśrayatvam

सत्य -	satya-	Truth; truthfulness
√अस् *as: to be* + -य- *-ya-: -ness*		
प्रतिष्ठायां	pratiṣṭhāyāṃ	[*upon*] firm establishment;
प्र- *pra-: forward, onward* + √स्था *sthā: to stand*		being grounded
क्रिया -	kriyā-	action/practice
√कृ *kṛ: to do*		
फल -	phala-	fruit; fruition; results
√फल् *phal: to ripen, bear fruit*		
आश्रयत्वम्	āśrayatvam	being the resort of;
आ- *ā-: from all sides, around* + √श्रि *śri: to rest on*		become subservient to; dependent on

ARYA

II.36 When (the yogi has) firmly established (in himself the principle of truth) (his) actions (such as speech) become the resort of (unfailing) fruition (i.e., his words always come true).

BAILEY

II.36 When truth to all beings is perfected, the effectiveness of his words and acts is immediately to be seen.

DVIVEDI

II.36 Veracity being confirmed, there is the result of the fruits of acts (in him who has acquired the virtue).

FEUERSTEIN

II.36 When grounded in truthfulness, action [and its] fruition depend [on him].

HOUSTON

II.36 Upon being established in *satya*–truth – there is surety in the result of actions/practice.

JNANESHVARA

II.36 As truthfulness (satya) is achieved, the fruits of actions naturally result according to the will of the Yogi.

PRABHAVANANDA

II.36 When a man becomes steadfast in his abstention from falsehood he gets the power of obtaining for himself and others the fruits of good deeds, without having to perform the deeds themselves.

PUROHIT

II.36 When truth is firmly rooted, the yogi attains the result of action without acting.

SATCHIDANANDA

II.36 To one established in truthfulness, actions and their results become subservient.

SHEARER

II.36 When we are finally established in truthfulness, action accomplishes its desired end.

TAIMNI

II.36 On being firmly established in truthfulness, fruit (of action) rests on action (of the *Yogi*) only.

VIVEKANANDA

II.36 By being established in truthfulness, the yogi gets the power of attaining for himself and others the fruits of work without the work.

II.37

अस्तेयप्रतिष्ठायां सर्वरत्नोपस्थानम् ॥ ३७ ॥

asteya-pratiṣṭhāyāṃ sarva-ratnopasthānam

अस्तेय -	asteya-	lit.: without theft
अ - a-: without + √स्ता stā: to steal		
प्रतिष्ठायां	pratiṣṭhāyāṃ	[*upon*] firm establishment;
प्र - pra-: forward, onward + √स्था sthā: to stand		being grounded
सर्व -	sarva-	all
रत्न -	ratna-	jewels; gems; wealth
√रा rā: to bestow		
उपस्थानम्	upasthānam	approach; come; present;
उप - upa-: towards, near to + √स्था sthā: to stand		appear; attain; attend; avail themselves

ARYA

II.37 Upon mastering (the principle of) non-theft all jewels attend upon him (i.e., become available to) him.

BAILEY

II.37 When abstention from theft is perfected the yogi can have whatever he desires.

DVIVEDI

II.37 Abstinence from theft being confirmed, all jewels approach (him who has acquired the virtue).

FEUERSTEIN

II.37 When grounded in non-stealing, all [kinds of] jewels appear [for him].

HOUSTON

II.37 Upon being established in *asteya*– non-stealing –
the attainment of all prosperity.

JNANESHVARA

II.37 When non-stealing (asteya) is established, all jewels, or treasures present themselves, or are available to the Yogi.

PRABHAVANANDA

II.37 When a man becomes steadfast in his abstention from theft, all wealth comes to him.

PUROHIT

II.37 When non-stealing is firmly rooted, riches are attained.

SATCHIDANANDA

II.37 To one established in non-stealing, all wealth comes.

SHEARER

II.37 When we are firmly established in integrity, all riches present themselves freely.

TAIMNI

II.37 On being firmly established in honesty all kinds of gems present themselves (before the Yogi).

VIVEKANANDA

II.37 By being established of non-stealing, the yogi obtains all wealth.

II.38

ब्रह्मचर्यप्रतिष्ठायां वीर्यलाभः ॥ ३८ ॥

brahmacarya-pratiṣṭhāyāṃ vīrya-lābhaḥ

ब्रह्मचर्य -	brahma-carya-	control of sexual passions;
ब्रह्म brahma + √चर् car: to move		continence; chastity;
(lit.: walking/moving in Brahma)		*course of action/desires leading to Brahma—Houston*
प्रतिष्ठायां	pratiṣṭhāyāṃ	[*upon*] firm establishment;
प्र - pra-: forward, onward + √स्था sthā: to stand		being grounded
वीर्य -	vīrya-	vigor; vitality; virility;
√वीर् vīr-: to be powerful + -य- -ya-: -ness		energy; strength; capacity
लाभः	lābhaḥ	attained; gained; acquired
√लभ् labh: to obtain		

ARYA

II.38 When the (practice) (of) control over sexual passion is mastered, growth of virility (accrues).

BAILEY

II.38 By abstention from incontinence, energy is acquired.

DVIVEDI

II.38 Vigour is obtained on the confirmation of continence.

FEUERSTEIN

II.38 When grounded in chastity, [great] vitality is acquired.

HOUSTON

II.38 Upon being established in *brahmacarya*-the obtainment of vital energy.

JNANESHVARA

II.38 When walking in the awareness of the highest reality (brahmacharya) is firmly established, then a great strength, capacity, or vitality (virya) is acquired.

PRABHAVANANDA

II.38 When a man becomes steadfast in his abstention from incontinence, he acquires spiritual energy.

PUROHIT

II.38 When continence is firmly rooted, the yogi becomes potent.

SATCHIDANANDA

II.38 By one established in continence, vigor is gained.

SHEARER

II.38 When we are firmly established in chastity, subtle potency is generated.

TAIMNI

II.38 On being firmly established in sexual continence, vigour (is) gained.

VIVEKANANDA

II.38 By being established in continence, the yogi gains energy.

II.39

अपरिग्रहस्थैर्ये जन्मकथंतासम्बोधः ॥ ३९ ॥

aparigraha-sthairye janma-kathaṃtā-sambodhaḥ

अपरिग्रह -	aparigraha-	non-possessiveness; greedlessness;
अ - a-: without + - परि - pari-: all around, about +		non-indulgence of the senses;
√ग्रह् grah: to grasp		avoidance of pleasures
स्थैर्ये	sthairye	[*upon*] stability;
√स्था sthā: to stand		[*upon*] the foundation being confirmed, settled
जन्म -	janma-	births; incarnations } "how and why" of incarnation
√जन् jan: to beget		
कथंता -	kathaṃtā-	wherewithal } "how and why" of incarnation
कथ katha: why (nature of), wherefore		
सम्बोधः	sambodhaḥ	(through) awareness/illumination;
सम् - sam-: fully, completely, perfectly + √बुध् budh: to know		knowledge; understanding

ARYA

II.39 Upon (attaining the) stability of the practice of not indulging the senses, (one gains the) knowledge of "how and why" of incarnations.

BAILEY

II.39 When abstention from avarice is perfected, there comes an understanding of the law of rebirth.

DVIVEDI

II.39 Abstinence from greediness being confirmed there arises knowledge of the how and wherefore of existence.

FEUERSTEIN

II.39 When steadied in greedlessness [he secures] knowledge of the wherefore of [his] birth(s).

HOUSTON

II.39 Upon a foundation in *aparigraha*-
non-possessiveness -
the understanding of the wherefore of birth.

JNANESHVARA

II.39 When one is steadfast in non-possessiveness or non-grasping with the senses (aparigraha), there arises knowledge of the why and wherefore of past and future incarnations.

PRABHAVANANDA

II.39 When a man becomes steadfast in his abstention from greed, he gains knowledge of his past, present and future existences.

PUROHIT

II.39 When non-covetousness is firmly rooted the yogi knows his past, present, future.

SATCHIDANANDA

II.39 When non-greed is confirmed, a thorough illumination of the how and why of one's birth comes.

SHEARER

II.39 When we are established in non-attachment, the nature and purpose of existence is understood.

TAIMNI

II.39 Non-possessiveness being confirmed, there arises knowledge of the 'how' and 'wherefore' of existence.

VIVEKANANDA

II.39 When the yogi is established in non-receiving he gets the memory of past life.

II.40

शौचात्स्वाङ्गजुगुप्सा परैरसंसर्गः ॥ ४० ॥

śaucāt svāṅga-jugupsā parair a-saṃsargaḥ

शौचात्	śaucāt	[*through/owing to*] purity
√शुच् śuc: to be radiant		
स्वाङ्ग -	svāṅga-	
स्व -	sva-	own
अङ्ग -	aṅga-	limbs; body
अङ्ग aṅga: parts		
जुगुप्सा	jugupsā	aversion (towards);
√गुप् gup: to protect		distancing; disgust; desire to protect
परैः -	paraiḥ	[*with/by means of*] others
असंसर्गः	a-saṃsargaḥ	non-contact/contamination

अ - a-: un-/non-/not/without + -सम् - -sam-: fully, completely, perfectly + √सृग् sṛg: to emit

ARYA

II.40 Through the practice of purity and cleanliness (one develops) aversion towards (his/her) own limbs and (an inclination) not (to have) contact (with others' bodies).

BAILEY

II.40 Internal and external purification produces aversion for form, both one's own and all forms.

DVIVEDI

II.40 From purity (arises) disgust for one's own body, and non-intercourse with others.

FEUERSTEIN

II.40 Through purity [he gains] distance toward his own limbs [and also] [the desire for] non-contamination by others.

HOUSTON

II.40 Owing to *śauca*-purity, there is a desire to protect one's own body, being the non-contact with whatever is adverse (to that).

JNANESHVARA

II.40 Through cleanliness and purity of body and mind (shaucha), one develops an attitude of distancing, or disinterest towards one's own body, and becomes disinclined towards contacting the bodies of others.

PRABHAVANANDA

II.40 As a result of purity there arises indifference toward the body and disgust for physical intercourse with others.

PUROHIT

II.40 When purity is attained, the yogi shrinks from his body, avoids the touch of others.

SATCHIDANANDA

II.40 By purification arises disgust for ones own body and for contact with other bodies.

SHEARER

II.40 Simplicity destroys identification with the body and brings freedom from contact with other bodies.

TAIMNI

II.40 From physical purity (arises) disgust for one's own body and disinclination to come in physical contact with others.

VIVEKANANDA

II.40 When he is established in internal and external cleanliness, there arises in him disgust for one's own body and desire for non-intercourse with others.

II.41 सत्त्वशुद्धिसौमनस्यैकाग्र्येन्द्रियजयात्मदर्शनयोग्यत्वानि च ॥ ४१ ॥

sattva-śuddhi-saumanasyaikāgryendriya-jayātma-darśana-yogyatvāni ca

सत्त्वशुद्धि -	sattvaśuddhi-		
सत्त्व -	sattva-	luminosity; brightness;	(upon)
√अस् *as: to be*		mental personality	purification
शुद्धि -	śuddhi-	(upon) purity; clarification	of sattva
√शुध् *śudh: to purify*			
सौमनस्य -	saumanasya-	happiness and clarity of mind;	
सु- *su: good* + √मन् *man: to think* / मनस् *manas: mind* + √अस् *as: to be* + -य- *-ya-: -ness*		cheerfulness; gladness; inspiration	
एकाग्र्य -	ekāgrya-		
एक -	eka-	one	intentness;
अग्र्य -	agrya-	pointed(ness)	ability to
अग्र *agra: point* + -य- *-ya-: -ness*			focus/concentrate
इन्द्रियजय -	indriyajaya-		
इन्द्रिय -	indriya-	senses; sense organs	
इन्द्र *indra: senses* + -य- *-ya-: -ness*			mastery of
जय -	jaya-	mastery; conquest (of)	senses
√जि *ji: to win*			
अत्मदर्शन	ātmadarśana		
आत्म -	ātma-	Self; inner-Self	Realization
दर्शन -	darśana-	view; vision;	of
√दृश् *dṛś: to see*		seeing; realization	Self
योग्यत्वानि	yogyatvāni	becoming worthy of; fitness for;	
√युज् *yuj: lit.: to yoke; to dissolve/unite; samādhi;*		capacity/capability for; readiness	
योग्य *yogya: fit (for)* + -त्व *-tva: -ness*			
च	ca	and	

ARYA

II.41 And (through the practice of purity and cleanliness), upon the purification of mental personality (there accrue) happiness and clarity of mind, ability to concentrate, conquest over senses and (finally) readiness (or worthiness) to realise the self.

BAILEY

II.41 Through purification comes also a quiet spirit, concentration, conquest of the organs, and ability to see the Self.

DVIVEDI

II.41 Moreover, (there arise) clear passivity, pleasantness of mind, fixity of attention, subjugation of the senses and fitness for communion with soul.

FEUERSTEIN

II.41 [Furthermore:] purity of *sattva*, gladness, one-pointedness, mastery of the sense-organs and the capability for self-vision [are achieved].

HOUSTON

II.41 And (due to *śauca*-purity), there is the force of clarity of *sattva* (the primary force of brightness/ intelligence), inspiration, one-pointedness, mastery of the sense organs, and readiness for the seeing of the self.

JNANESHVARA

II.41 Also through cleanliness and purity of body and mind (shaucha) comes a purification of the subtle mental essence (sattva), a pleasantness, goodness and gladness of feeling, a one-pointedness with intentness, the conquest or mastery over the senses, and a fitness, qualification, or capability for self-realization.

PRABHAVANANDA

II.41 Moreover, one achieves purification of the heart, cheerfulness of mind, the power of concentration, control of the passions and fitness for vision of the Atman.

PUROHIT

II.41 He attains as well clarification of intellect, cheerfulness of mind, subjugation of sense, power of concentration, that fit him for Self-experience.

SATCHIDANANDA

II.41 Moreover, one gains purity of sattva, cheerfulness of mind, one-pointedness, mastery over the senses, and fitness for Self-realization.

SHEARER

II.41 Purity of mind, cheerfulness, mastery of the senses, one-pointedness, and fitness for Self-realization follow.

TAIMNI

II.41 From mental purity (arises) purity of *Sattva*, cheerful-mindedness, one-pointedness, control of the senses and fitness for the vision of the Self.

VIVEKANANDA

II.41 There also arise purification of the sattva, cheerfulness of the mind, concentration, conquest of the organs, and fitness for the realisation of the Self.

II.42

सन्तोषादनुत्तमः सुखलाभः ॥ ४२ ॥

santoṣād an-uttamaḥ sukha-lābhaḥ

सन्तोषात्	santoṣāt	[*through*] contentment
सम्- sam-: together with, completely, perfectly + √तुष् tuṣ: to be satisfied		
अनुत्तमः	an-uttamaḥ	supreme; unexcelled;
अन्- an-: not, absent, differing +		ultimate; highest;
-उद्- -ud-: up, onwards: implying superiority + -तम -tama: -est		unsurpassed; incomparable
सुख -	sukha-	pleasure; joy; mental comfort;
सु- su: well, good + ख kha: space, e.g. axle-hole		happiness
लभः	labhaḥ	attainment; achievement; gain
√लभ् labh: to obtain		

ARYA

II.42 Through contentment (one) gains unexcelled mental comfort.

BAILEY

II.42 As a result of contentment, bliss is achieved.

DVIVEDI

II.42 Superlative happiness (arises) from contentment.

FEUERSTEIN

II.42 Through contentment unexcelled joy is gained.

HOUSTON

II.42 Owing to *santoṣa*-contentment, there is an unexcelled attainment of happiness.

JNANESHVARA

II.42 From an attitude of contentment (santosha), unexcelled happiness, mental comfort, joy, and satisfaction is obtained.

PRABHAVANANDA

II.42 As the result of contentment, one gains supreme happiness.

PUROHIT

II.42 Contentment brings supreme happiness.

SATCHIDANANDA

II.42 By contentment, supreme joy is gained.

SHEARER

II.42 From contentment, unsurpassed happiness is gained.

TAIMNI

II.42 Superlative happiness from contentment.

VIVEKANANDA

II.42 From contentment comes superlative happiness.

II.43

कायेन्द्रियसिद्धिरशुद्धिक्षयात् तपसः ॥ ४३ ॥

kāyendriya siddhir aśuddhi-kṣayāt tapasaḥ

काय -	kāya-	body
इन्द्रिय -	indriya-	senses; sense-organs
इन्द्र indra: senses + -य ya: -ness		
सिद्धिः	siddhiḥ	esoteric powers/accomplishments/
√सिध् sidh: to succeed		attainments/achievements/ perfections; mastery
अशुद्धि -	aśuddhi-	impurities
अ- a-: without + √शुध् śudh: to purify		
क्षयात्	kṣayāt	[*due to*/*because of*/*as result of*]
√क्षि kṣi: to destroy		elimination; dwindling
तपसः	tapasaḥ	[*from*] ascetic practice/austerities/
√तप् tap: heat, to be hot		fiery aspiration; [*due to*] intensity of spiritual practice

ARYA

II.43 From ascetic practice, through gradual) elimination of impurities (there occurs) the mastery over body and (its) senses.

BAILEY

II.43 Through fiery aspiration and through the removal of all impurity, comes the perfecting of the bodily powers and of the senses.

DVIVEDI

II.43 (There arise) from mortification, after the destruction of impurities, occult powers in the body and the senses.

FEUERSTEIN

II.43 Through austerity, on account of the dwindling of impurity, perfection of the body and the sense organs [is attained].

HOUSTON

II.43 The perfection of the body and sense organs is due to *tapas*-intensity in spiritual practice, being the elimination of impurities.

JNANESHVARA

II.43 Through ascesis or training of the senses (tapas), there comes a destruction of mental impurities, and an ensuing mastery or perfection over the body and the mental organs of senses and actions (indriyas).

PRABHAVANANDA

II.43 As the result of mortification, impurities are removed. Then special powers come to the body and the sense-organs.

PUROHIT

II.43 Austerity destroys impurity, awakens physical and mental powers.

SATCHIDANANDA

II.43 By austerity, impurities of body and senses are destroyed and occult powers gained.

SHEARER

II.43 By purification, the body and the senses are perfected.

TAIMNI

II.43 Perfection of the sense-organs and the body after destruction of impurity by austerities.

VIVEKANANDA

II.43 The mortification of the organs and the body, through the destruction of their impurities, brings powers to them.

II.44

स्वाध्यायादिष्टदेवतासम्प्रयोगः ॥ ४४ ॥

svādhyāyād iṣṭa-devatā-samprayogaḥ

स्वाध्यायात्	svādhyāyāt	[*through/from/because of*] sacred study and japa; mantra recitation (silent and aloud); integration and application of mantra; study of scripture; self-observation/self-study
स्व - sva: own +		
अधि - adhi-: over, above +		
आ - ā-: near to, from all sides, all around +		
√इ i: to go; (here: one's going into)		
इष्ट -	iṣṭa-	beloved; worshipped; desired; chosen; favorite
√इष् iṣ: to desire		
देवता -	devatā-	deity
√दिव् div: to shine		
सम्प्रयोगः	samprayogaḥ	(comes) union/concert; communion (with)
सम् - sam-: fully, completely, perfectly +		
प्र - pra-: forward, onward + √युज् yuj: lit.: to yoke; to unite/dissolve; samādhi		

ARYA

II.44 Through sacred study and silent recitation (of appropriate mantra) one attains concert with (his) chosen deity.

BAILEY

II.44 Spiritual reading results in a contact with the soul (or divine One).

DVIVEDI

II.44 By study (is produced) communion with the desired deity.

FEUERSTEIN

II.44 Through self-study [the yogin establishes] contact with the chosen diety.

HOUSTON

II.44 Owing to *svādyaya-* learning and application of personal mantras, there is union with (one's) beloved deity (source of inspiration).

JNANESHVARA

II.44 From self-study and reflection on sacred words (svadhyaya), one attains contact, communion, or concert with that underlying natural reality or force.

PRABHAVANANDA

II.44 As the result of study, one obtains the vision of that aspect of God which one has chosen to worship.

PUROHIT

II.44 Repetition of sacred words brings you in direct contact with the God you worship.

SATCHIDANANDA

II.44 By study of spiritual books comes communion with one's chosen diety.

SHEARER

II.44 Refinement brings communion with the desired celestial being.

TAIMNI

II.44 By (or from) self-study, union with the desired deity.

VIVEKANANDA

II.44 By the repetition of the mantra comes the realisation of the Chosen Deity.

II.45

समाधिसिद्धिरीश्वरप्रणिधानात् ॥ ४५ ॥

samādhi-siddhir īśvara-praṇidhānāt

समाधि - samādhi- — samādhi; meditation; contemplation; meta-cognitive absorption with various stages

सम् - sam-: together with, completely, perfectly +
आ - ā-: near to, all around + √धा dhā: to put

सिद्धिः siddhiḥ — esoteric powers/accomplishments/attainments/achievements/perfections; mastery

√सिध् sidh: to succeed

ईश्वरप्रणिधानात् Īśvarapraṇidhānāt — [*due to/because of*] surrender/devotion to/worship of God; alignment/focus of attention in God

ईश्वर - īśvara- — God; the Lord: immanent or transcendent

√ईष् īs: to own, be master of +
वर vara: the best, choicest (√वृ vṛ: to choose)

प्रणिधानात् praṇidhānāt — surrender; devotion

प्र - pra-: onward, forward + -णि - ṇi-: downward motion +
√धा dhā: to put

ARYA

II.45 Through surrender to God achievement of highest meditation takes place.

BAILEY

II.45 Through devotion to Ishvara the goal of meditation (or samadhi) is reached.

DVIVEDI

II.45 From resignation to *Iśvara* (follows) the accomplishment of *Samādhi*.

FEUERSTEIN

II.45 Through devotion to the Lord [comes about] the attainment of enstasy.

HOUSTON

II.45 The perfection of *samādhi*-cognitive absorption is due to *īśvara-praṇidhāna*-perfect aligning of attention with the omniscient seer within (*īśvara*).

JNANESHVARA

II.45 From an attitude of letting go into one's source (ishvarapranidhana), the state of perfected concentration (samadhi) is attained.

PRABHAVANANDA

II.45 As the result of devotion to God, one achieves samadhi.

PUROHIT

II.45 Illumination is attained by devotion to God.

SATCHIDANANDA

II.45 By total surrender to God, samadhi is attained.

SHEARER

II.45 From surrender to the Lord, the state of *samādhi* is perfected.

TAIMNI

II.45 Accomplishment of *Samādhi* from resignation to God.

VIVEKANANDA

II.45 Through the sacrificing of all to Iśvara comes samādhi.

II.46

स्थिरसुखमासनम् ॥ ४६ ॥

sthira-sukham āsanam

स्थिर -	sthira-	steady; stable

√स्था sthā: to stand

सुखम्	sukham	comfortable; easy

सु - su: well, good + ख kha: space, e.g. axle-hole

आसनम्	āsanam	posture

√आस् ās: to sit; to be present

ARYA

II.46 A posture (should be) steady and comfortable.

BAILEY

II.46 The posture assumed must be steady and easy.

DVIVEDI

II.46 Posture is that which is steady and easy.

FEUERSTEIN

II.46 The posture [should be] steady and comfortable.

HOUSTON

II.46 *Āsana*-posture is that which is stable and comfortable.

JNANESHVARA

II.46 The posture (asana) for Yoga meditation should be steady, stable, and motionless, as well as comfortable, and this is the third of the eight rungs of Yoga.

PRABHAVANANDA

II.46 Posture (asana) is to be seated in a position which is firm but relaxed.

PUROHIT

II.46 Āsana (Posture) implies steadiness and comfort.

SATCHIDANANDA

II.46 Asana is a steady, comfortable posture.

SHEARER

II.46 The physical postures should be steady and comfortable.

TAIMNI

II.46 Posture (should be) steady and comfortable.

VIVEKANANDA

II.46 Posture is that which is firm and pleasant.

II.47

प्रयत्नशैथिल्यानन्तसमापत्तिभ्याम् ॥ ४७ ॥

prayatna-śaithilyānanta-samāpattibhyām

प्रयत्न -	prayatna-	[*through/by/due to*] effort
प्र - *pra-: forward, onward, in front* + √यत् *yat: to endeavor*		
शैथिल्य -	śaithilya-	relaxation; release; let-go
शिथिल *śithila: loose*		
अनन्त -	ananta-	boundless; eternal; infinite; the unending
समापत्तिभ्याम्	samāpattibhyām	[*by/from/due to*] samādhi: state of consciousness; attainment of a state of consciousness by meditation; focus for meditation; coalescence; proficiency; balanced state; consummation; fusion; simultaneous occurence; cognitive blending
सम् - *sam-: together with* + -आ - *-ā-: towards, near to* + √पत् *pat: to fall*		

ARYA

II.47 (The posture is perfected, made steady and comfortable) through relaxing (not forcing) the effort and by fixing the consciousness on the infinite.

BAILEY

II.47 Steadiness and ease of posture is to be achieved through persistent slight effort and through the concentration of the mind upon the infinite.

DVIVEDI

II.47 By mild effort and meditation on the endless.

FEUERSTEIN

II.47 [It is accompanied] by the relaxation of tension and the coinciding with the infinite [consciousness-space].

HOUSTON

II.47 *Āsana*-posture (becomes stable and comfortable) owing to the relaxation of effort and *samāpatti*-cognitive blending with the infinite.

JNANESHVARA

II.47 The means of perfecting the posture is that of relaxing or loosening of effort, and allowing attention to merge with endlessness, or the infinite.

PRABHAVANANDA

II.47 Posture becomes firm and relaxed through control of the natural tendencies of the body and through meditation on the Infinite.

PUROHIT

II.47 It requires relaxation and meditation on the Immovable.

SATCHIDANANDA

II.47 By lessening the natural tendency for restlessness and by meditating on the infinite, posture is mastered.

SHEARER

II.47 They are mastered when all effort is relaxed and the mind is absorbed in the Infinite.

TAIMNI

II.47 By relaxation of effort and meditation on the 'Endless' (posture is mastered).

VIVEKANANDA

II.47 Through the lessening of the natural tendency [for activity, caused by identification with the body,] and through meditation on the Infinite, [posture becomes firm and pleasant].

II.48

ततो द्वन्द्वानभिघातः ॥ ४८ ॥

tato dvandvānabhighātaḥ

ततः	tataḥ	then; thence; thereafter
द्वन्द्व -	dvandva-	(by) dichotomies; dualities;
द्व dva: two, both + द्व dva: two, both		pairs of opposites
अनभिघातः	an-abhighātaḥ	undisturbed; unassailed;
अन् - an-: not, non-, differing +		unhurt; unafflicted;
-अभि - -abhi-: over, above, in addition + √हन् han: to strike		free from suffering

ARYA

II.48 Then one no (longer) suffers from pairs of opposites (such as heat and cold).

BAILEY

II.48 When this is attained, the pairs of opposites no longer limit.

DVIVEDI

II.48 Then no assaults from the pairs of opposites.

FEUERSTEIN

II.48 Thence [results] unassailability by the pairs-of-opposites.

HOUSTON

II.48 From that (*āsana*), non-affliction from the pairs of opposites (pleasure and pain, etc.)

JNANESHVARA

II.48 From the attainment of that perfected posture, there arises an unassailable, unimpeded freedom from suffering due to the pairs of opposites (such as heat and cold, good and bad, or pain and pleasure).

PRABHAVANANDA

II.48 Thereafter, one is no longer troubled by the dualities of sense-experience.

PUROHIT

II.48 Then opposing sensations cease to torment.

SATCHIDANANDA

II.48 Thereafter, one is not disturbed by the dualities.

SHEARER

II.48 Then we are no longer upset by the play of opposites.

TAIMNI

II.48 From that, no assaults from the pairs of opposites.

VIVEKANANDA

II.48 Posture being conquered, the dualities do not obstruct.

II.49

तस्मिन् सति श्वासप्रश्वासयोर्गतिविच्छेदः प्राणयामः ॥ ४९ ॥

tasmin sati śvāsa-praśvāsayor gati-vicchedaḥ prāṇāyāmaḥ

तस्मिन्	tasmin	upon this/that
सति	sati	being; having been (accomplished);
√*अस् as: to be*		there being (present); being (achieved); existing (as) (achievement)
श्वास -	śvāsa-	(of) inhalation (and)
√*श्वस् śvas: to breathe*		
प्रश्वासयोः	praśvāsayoḥ	(of) exhalation (that)
प्र - pra-: forward, onward, in front + √श्वस् śvas: to breathe		
गति -	gati-	flow; force; movement; motion
√*गम् gam: to go*		
विच्छेदः	vicchedaḥ	regulation/control/braking/
वि - vi-: apart, separate from, reverse to +		restraining/suspension
√*छिद् chid: to cut*		
प्राणायामः	prāṇāyāmaḥ	

प्राण	prāṇā	prāṇa	expansion
प्राण prāṇa: vital force			of prāṇa
आयामः	āyāmaḥ	command	(through)
आ - ā-: from all sides, all around + √यम् yam: to restrain			breath control
OR/AND			
आयम् āyam: to expand	āyāmaḥ	expansion	

ARYA

II.49 When that (posture) has been accomplished, then braking the force of inhalation and exhalation is called prāṇāyama.

BAILEY

II.49 When right posture (asana) has been attained there follows right control of prana and proper inspiration and expiration of the breath.

DVIVEDI

II.49 This being (accomplished), *prāṇāyāma* (follows)—the cutting off of the course of inspiration and expiration (of the breath).

FEUERSTEIN

II.49 When this is [achieved], breath-control [which is] the cutting-off of the flow of inhalation and exhalation [should be practiced].

HOUSTON

II.49 That (*āsana*-posture) being achieved, *prāṇāyāma*-breath regulation is interruption of the (normal) motion of inhalation and exhalation.

JNANESHVARA

II.49 Once that perfected posture has been achieved, the slowing or braking of the force behind, and of unregulated movement of inhalation and exhalation is called breath control and expansion of prana (pranayama), which leads to the absence of the awareness of both, and is the fourth of the eight rungs.

PRABHAVANANDA

II.49 After mastering posture, one must practice control of the prana (pranayama) by stopping the motions of inhalation and exhalation.

PUROHIT

II.49 The next step is Prānāyāma (Control of Breath), the cessation of exhalation and inhalation.

SATCHIDANANDA

II.49 That [firm posture] being acquired, the movements of inhalation and exhalation should be controlled.
This is pranayama.

SHEARER

II.49 Next come the breathing exercises which suspend the flow of breath and increase the life energy.

TAIMNI

II.49 This having been (accomplished) Prāṇāyāma which is cessation of inspiration and expiration (follows).

VIVEKANANDA

II.49 Control of the motion of the exhalation and the inhalation follows after this.

II.50

बाह्याभ्यन्तरस्तम्भवृत्तिर्देशकालसङ्ख्याभिः परिदृष्टो दीर्घसूक्ष्मः ॥ ५० ॥

bāhyābhyantara-stambha-vṛttir deśa-kāla-saṅkhyābhiḥ paridṛṣṭo dīrgha-sūkṣmaḥ

बाह्य -	bāhya-	external; outward
बहिस् bahis: outer, outside		
अभ्यन्तर -	abhyantara-	internal; inward
√अभि - abhi-: to, towards, into + अन्तर antara: inner		
स्तम्भ -	stambha-	suspended; retention;
√स्तम्भ् stambh: to stop		stationary; fixed
वृत्तिः	vṛttiḥ	mind-field operations/states/activities/
√वृत् vṛt: to whirl		fluctuations
देश -	deśa-	[*by*] place/locus/point (of focus)
√दिश् diś: to point out		
काल -	kāla-	[*by*] time
√कल् kal: to impel		
सङ्ख्याभिः	saṅkhyābhiḥ	[*by*] numbers
सम् - sam-: fully, completely, perfectly + √ख्या khyā: to be mentioned		
परिदृष्टः	paridṛṣṭaḥ	(breath pattern) regulated; measured;
परि - pari-: all around + √दृश् dṛś: to see		observed/viewed with intent to regulate
दीर्घ -	dīrgha-	(they are) long; prolonged; protracted
सूक्ष्मः	sūkṣmaḥ	(they are) fine; subtle; attenuated
√सिव् siv: to sew		

ARYA

II.50 That prāṇāyama (has) (three) ways: outward flow, inward flow, and (the way of) retention. Observed by place (spot concentration in the body), (length of) time, number of times, (the breath) should be (made) long and fine.

BAILEY

II.50 Right control of prana (or the life currents) is external, internal or motionless; it is subject to place, time and number and is also protracted or brief.

DVIVEDI

II.50 (It is) external, internal or steady; regulated by place, time and number; and is long or short.

FEUERSTEIN

II.50 [Breath-control is] external, internal and fixed in its movement, [and it is] regulated by place, time and number; [it can be] protracted or contracted.

HOUSTON

II.50 (Prāṇāyāma has) external, internal or suspended modifications, (which become) long and subtle, when observed by means of location (of the breath's motion in the body), time (length of inhalation, exhalation and interveningspaces), and number.

JNANESHVARA

II.50 That pranayama has three aspects of external or outward flow (exhalation), internal or inward flow (inhalation), and the third, which is the absence of both during the transition between them, and is known as fixedness, retention, or suspension. These are regulated by place, time, and number, with breath becoming slow and subtle.

PRABHAVANANDA

II.50 The breath may be stopped externally, or internally, or checked in mid-motion, and regulated according to place, time and a fixed number of moments, so that the stoppage is either protracted or brief.

PUROHIT

II.50 Exhalation, inhalation, cessation of breath, may be short or long, according to length, duration and number of breaths.

SATCHIDANANDA

II.50 The modifications of the life-breath are either external, internal or stationary. They are to be regulated by space, time and number and are either long or short.

SHEARER

II.50 The life energy is increased by regulation of the out-breath, or the in-breath, or the breath in mid-flow. Depending upon the volume, and the length and frequency of holding, the breathing becomes slow and refined.

TAIMNI

II.50 (It is in) external, internal or suppressed modification; is regulated by place, time and number, (and becomes progressively) prolonged and subtle.

VIVEKANANDA

II.50 Its modifications are threefold, namely, external, internal, and motionless; they are regulated by place, time, and number; and further, they are either long or short.

II.51

बाह्याभ्यन्तरविषयाक्षेपी चतुर्थः ॥ ५१ ॥

bāhyābhyantara viṣayākṣepī caturthaḥ

बाह्य -	bāhya-	(on) outward, external
बहिस् *bahis: outer, outside*		
अभ्यन्तर	abhyantara	inward, internal (as in movement)
अभि - *abhi-: to, towards, into* + *अन्तर* *antara: inner*		
विषय -	viṣaya-	objects (of experience); areas; range;
√विष् *viṣ: to be active* + *-य* *-ya:-ness*		field object domain; sphere; subject/subject-matter; content; object of sensory experience; realm; scope; matters of enjoyment or experience
आक्षेपी	ākṣepī	transcending; going beyond;
आ - *ā-: from all sides* + *√क्षिप्* *kṣip: to cast*		(gradually) moving in
चतुर्थः	caturthaḥ	(is the) fourth
चतुर् *catur: four*		

ARYA

II.51 The fourth (prāṇāyām is that in which the prāṇa) gradually moving with outward (concentrations such as on the nostrils) or inward (concentrations such as on the heart center) (then ceases to move and becomes centered).

BAILEY

II.51 There is a fourth stage which transcends those dealing with the internal and external phases.

DVIVEDI

II.51 The fourth is that which has reference to the internal and external subject.

FEUERSTEIN

II.51 [The movement of breath] transcending the external and internal sphere is the 'fourth'.

HOUSTON

II.51 The fourth (modification) transcends the reference to external and internal.

JNANESHVARA

II.51 The fourth pranayama is that continuous prana which surpasses, is beyond, or behind those others that operate in the exterior and interior realms or fields.

PRABHAVANANDA

II.51 The fourth kind of pranayama is the stoppage of the breath which is caused by concentration upon external or internal objects.

PUROHIT

II.51 A fourth method of breathing is that which is determined by a uniform external or internal measure.

SATCHIDANANDA

II.51 There is a fourth kind of pranayama that occurs during concentration on an internal or external object.

SHEARER

II.51 The fourth kind of *prānāyāma* takes us beyond the domain of inner and outer.

TAIMNI

II.51 That *Prāṇāyāma* which goes beyond the sphere of internal and external is the fourth (variety).

VIVEKANANDA

II.51 The fourth is the restraining of the prāna by directing it either to external or internal objects.

II.52

ततः क्षीयते प्रकाशावरणम् ॥ ५२ ॥

tataḥ kṣīyate prakāśāvaraṇam

ततः	tataḥ	then; thence; thereafter (as a result)
क्षीयते *√क्षि kṣi: to decrease*	kṣīyate	diminishes, then vanishes; disappears; dissolves; disperses
प्रकाश - *प्र - pra-: forward, onward + √काश् kāś: to shine*	prakāśa-	light
आवरणम् *आ - ā-: near to, from all sides + √वृ vṛ: to cover*	āvaraṇam	veil/covering (over)

ARYA

II.52 Then (gradually) vanishes the veil (that is covering) the light.

BAILEY

II.52 Through this, that which obscures the light is gradually removed.

DVIVEDI

II.52 Thence is destroyed the covering of light.

FEUERSTEIN

II.52 Thence the covering of the [inner] light disappears.

HOUSTON

II.52 Due to that, the covering of light is dispersed.

JNANESHVARA

II.52 Through that pranayama the veil of karmasheya (II.12) that covers the inner illumination or light is thinned, diminishes and vanishes.

PRABHAVANANDA

II.52 As the result of this, the covering of the Inner Light is removed.

PUROHIT

II.52 Then the cloud that obscures the light, melts away.

SATCHIDANANDA

II.52 As its result, the veil over the inner Light is destroyed.

SHEARER

II.52 Then the light of the intellect is unveiled.

TAIMNI

II.52 From that is dissolved the covering of light.

VIVEKANANDA

II.52 By that the covering of the light of the citta is attenuated.

II.53

धारणासु च योग्यता मनसः ॥ ५३ ॥

dhāranāsu ca yogyatā manasaḥ

धारणासु √धृ *dhṛ: to hold*	dhāraṇāsu	[*upon/in the matter of/with regard to*] holding a focus re: dhāraṇā/concentration
च	ca	and
योग्यता	yogyatā	[*possessed of*] capability/readiness/fitness/ability
मनसः √मन् *man: to think*	manasaḥ	mind's; [*of*] the minds;

ARYA

II.53 Then also develops mind's fitness as regards holding a focus (through the practice of prāṇāyāma).

BAILEY

II.53 And the mind is prepared for concentrated meditation.

DVIVEDI

II.53 The mind becomes fit for absorption.

FEUERSTEIN

II.53 And [the *yogin* gains] the fitness of the mind for concentration.

HOUSTON

II.53 And readiness of the mind for *dhāranā*-focusings.

JNANESHVARA

II.53 Through these practices and processes of pranayama, which is the fourth of the eight steps, the mind acquires or develops the fitness, qualification, or capability for true concentration (dharana), which is itself the sixth of the steps.

PRABHAVANANDA

II.53 The mind gains the power of concentration (dharana).

PUROHIT

II.53 And mind becomes fit for attention.

SATCHIDANANDA

II.53 And the mind becomes fit for concentration.

SHEARER

II.53 And the mind becomes fit for steadiness.

TAIMNI

II.53 And the fitness of the mind for concentration.

VIVEKANANDA

II.53 The mind becomes fit for dhāranā.

II.54

स्वविषयासम्प्रयोगे चित्तस्य स्वरूपानुकार इवेन्द्रियाणां प्रत्याहारः ॥ ५४ ॥

sva-viṣayāsamprayoge cittasya svarūpānukāra ivendriyāṇāṃ pratyāhāraḥ

स्व - sva- own

विषय - viṣaya- (with) objects (of sensory experience); areas; range; field object domain; sphere; subject/subject-matter; content; object of sensory experience; realm; scope; matters of enjoyment or experience

√विष् viṣ: to be active + -य -ya:-ness

असम्प्रयोगे a-samprayoge [*upon*] non-communication; non-intercourse; withdrawal; disuniting; disconnecting

अ - a-: un-/non-/not + सम् - sam-: fully, completely, perfectly + प्र - pra-: forward, onward + √युग् yuj: lit.: to yoke; to unite; samādhi

चित्तस्य cittasya [*of*] the mind's field; mind-field's; all aspects [*possessed by*] energy field called mind

√चित् cit: perceive; be bright

स्वरूप - svarūpa- own form; essential nature

अनुकारः anukāraḥ following; imitating

अनु - anu-: following, after, behind + √कृ kṛ: to do

इव - iva- as it were; as if

इन्द्रयाणां indriyāṇāṃ [*of*] senses; sense's

इन्द्र indra: senses + -य -ya: -ness

प्रत्याहारः pratyāhāraḥ (is called) withdrawal of the senses; abstraction

प्रति - prati-: toward + आ - ā-: from all sides, all around + √हृ hṛ: to hold

ARYA

II.54 When the senses (are made to) cease intercourse with their objects (and thereby) become, as it were, assimilated with the nature of the mind-pool, (that is called) pratyāhāra, withdrawal of the senses.

BAILEY

II.54 Abstraction (or Pratyahara) is the subjugation of the senses by the thinking principle and their withdrawal from that which has hitherto been their object.

DVIVEDI

II.54 Abstraction is, as it were, the imitating by the senses, the thinking principle, by withdrawing themselves from their objects.

FEUERSTEIN

II.54 Sense-withdrawal is the imitation as it were of the own-form of consciousness [on the part] of the sense-organs by disuniting [themselves] from their objects.

HOUSTON

II.54 *Pratyāhāra*-sense withdrawal is as if imitating *citta*'s *svarūpa*-essential nature (*sattva-guṇa*-brightness, clarity) on the part of the senses, in disconnecting with their sensory objects.

JNANESHVARA

II.54 When the mental organs of senses and actions (indriyas) cease to be engaged with the corresponding objects in their mental realm, and assimilate or turn back into the mind-field from which they arose, this is called pratyahara, and is the fifth step.

PRABHAVANANDA

II.54 When the mind is withdrawn from sense-objects, the sense-organs also withdraw themselves from their respective objects and thus are said to imitate the mind. This is known as pratyahara.

PUROHIT

II.54 Pratyāhāra is the restoration of sense to the original purity of mind, by renouncing its objects.

SATCHIDANANDA

II.54 When the senses withdraw themselves from the objects and imitate, as it were, the nature of the mind-stuff, this is pratyahara.

SHEARER

II.54 The senses retire from their objects by following the natural inward movement of the mind.

TAIMNI

II.54 Pratyāhāra or abstraction is, as it were, the imitation by the senses of the mind by withdrawing themselves from their objects.

VIVEKANANDA

II.54 Pratyāhāra, or the drawing in of the organs, is effected by their giving up their own objects and taking, as it were, the form of the mind-stuff.

II.55

तत: परमा वश्यतेन्द्रियाणाम् ॥ ५५ ॥

tataḥ paramā vaśyatendriyāṇām

ततः	tataḥ	then; thereby; thence
परमा	paramā	final/supreme/highest perfection
वश्यता *√वश् vaś: to will + -त -tā: -ness*	vaśyatā	to be mastered/controlled; brought to obedience
इन्द्रियाणाम् *इन्द्रि indri: senses + -य -ya: -ness*	indriyāṇām	[*of*] the senses/sense-organs; senses'

ARYA

II.55 Through that (pratyāhāra), final control over the senses (is established).

BAILEY

II.55 As a result of these means there follows the complete subjugation of the sense organs.

DVIVEDI

II.55 Then follows the greatest mastery over the senses.

FEUERSTEIN

II.55 Thence [results] the supreme obedience of the sense-organs.

HOUSTON

II.55 From that, the perfect mastery of the senses.

JNANESHVARA

II.55 Through that turning inward of the organs of senses and actions (indriyas) also comes a supreme ability, controllability, or mastery over those senses inclining to go outward towards their objects.

PRABHAVANANDA

II.55 Thence arises complete mastery over the senses.

PUROHIT

II.55 Then follows the complete subjugation of sense.

SATCHIDANANDA

II.55 Then follows supreme mastery over the senses.

SHEARER

II.55 From this comes supreme mastery of the senses.

TAIMNI

II.55 Then follows the greatest mastery over the senses.

VIVEKANANDA

II.55 Thence arises supreme control of the organs.

॥ इति द्वितीयः पादः ॥

iti dvitīyaḥ pādaḥ

इति	iti	thus; herewith [concludes]
द्वितीयः	dvitīyaḥ	second
पादः	pādaḥ	chapter, part

Thus [Concludes] the Second Chapter

VIBHŪTI PĀDAḤ

Arya	Vibhuti-pāda: The Chapter on Attainments
Bailey	Book III: Union Achieved and its Result
Dvivedi	Section III
Feuerstein	Chapter Three: Vibhūti Pāda
Houston	Now, The Chapter on Powers
Jnaneshvara	Progressing
Prabhavananda	Powers
Purohit	Powers
Satchidananda	Book III: Vibhuti Pada Portion on Accomplishments
Shearer	Expansion
Taimni	Vibhūti Pāda
Vivekananda	Powers

Now, The Chapter on Powers

॥ अथ विभूतिपादः ॥

atha vibhūti-pādaḥ

अथ	atha	Now
विभूति -	vibhūti-	powers
पादः	pādaḥ	chapter, part

III.1

देशबन्धश्चित्तस्य धारणा ॥ १ ॥

deśa-bandhaś cittasya dhāraṇā

देश - √दिश् *diś: to point out*	deśa-	point; locus; place; bodily spot	focusing on one spot
बन्धः √बन्ध् *bandh: to bind*	bandhaḥ	binding; fixing; confining; concentrating on	
चित्तस्य √चित् *cit: perceive; be bright*	cittasya	[*of*] the mind's field; mind-field's; all aspects [*possessed by*] energy field called mind	
धारणा √धृ *dhṛ: to hold*	dhāraṇā	holding a focus; concentration	

ARYA

III.1 Fixing the mind at a locus is called holding a focus.

BAILEY

III.1 Concentration is fixing the citta (mind stuff) upon a particular object.
This is dharana.

DVIVEDI

III.1 Contemplation is fixing the mind on something.

FEUERSTEIN

III.1 Concentration is the binding of consciousness to a [single] spot.

HOUSTON

III.1 *Dhāraṇā*-focusing is fixation of *citta*- (the energy of) the field of consciousness within a focal point.

JNANESHVARA

III.1 Concentration (dharana) is the process of holding or fixing the attention of mind onto one object or place, and is the sixth of the eight rungs.

PRABHAVANANDA

III.1 Concentration (dharana) is holding the mind within a center of spiritual consciousness in the body, or fixing it on some divine form, either within the body or outside it.

PUROHIT

III.1 Attention fixed upon an object is Dhāranā.

SATCHIDANANDA

III.1 Dharana is binding of the mind to one place, object or idea.

SHEARER

III.1 When the attention is held focused on an object, this is known as *dhāranā*.

TAIMNI

III.1 Concentration is the confining of the mind within a limited mental area (object of concentration).

VIVEKANANDA

III.1 Dhāranā is holding the mind on to some particular object.

III.2

तत्र प्रत्ययैकतानता ध्यानम् ॥ २ ॥

tatra pratyayaika-tānatā dhyānam

तत्र	tatra	here; there; therein; (with regard to) that
प्रत्यय - प्रति - *prati-: towards, in direction of* + √इ *i: to go*	pratyaya-	content of mind-field; presented-idea; cognition principle; cognition; causal/awareness principle; awareness perceiving (through the mind); buddhi; discriminatory intelligence; *immediate arising thought directed to an object—Houston*
एक -	eka-	single
तानता √तन् *tan: to stretch*	tānatā	continuous (flow); stream; continuity; directionality
ध्यानम् √ध्यै *dhyai: to meditate*	dhyānam	meditation; meditational process; meditational absorption

ARYA

III.2 In that (concentration or its locus) single (unbroken) continuous (flow) (is called) meditational process (dhyāna).

BAILEY

III.2 Sustained concentration (dharana) is meditation (dhyana).

DVIVEDI

III.2 The unity of the mind with it is absorption.

FEUERSTEIN

III.2 The one-directionality of the presented-ideas with regard to that [object of concentration] is meditative-absorption.

HOUSTON

III.2 The single directionality of a *pratyaya* there (to the chosen focal point) is *Dhyāna*-meditation.

JNANESHVARA

III.2 The repeated continuation, or uninterrupted stream of that one point of focus is called absorption in meditation (dhyana), and is the seventh of the eight steps.

PRABHAVANANDA

III.2 Meditation (dhyana) is an unbroken flow of thought toward the object of concentration.

PUROHIT

III.2 Union of mind and object is Dhyāna.

SATCHIDANANDA

III.2 Dhyana is the continuous flow of cognition toward that object.

SHEARER

III.2 When awareness flows evenly towards the point of attention, this is known as *dhyāna*.

TAIMNI

III.2 Uninterrupted flow (of the mind) towards the object (chosen for meditation) is contemplation.

VIVEKANANDA

III.2 An unbroken flow of knowledge about that object is dhyāna.

III.3

तदेवार्थमात्रनिर्भासं स्वरूपशून्यमिव समाधिः ॥ ३ ॥

tad evārtha-mātra-nirbhāsaṃ svarūpa-śūnyam iva samādhiḥ

तत्	tat	that (meditation)	
एव	eva	definitely; verily; specifically	
अर्थमात्र -	arthamātra-		
अर्थ - √अर्थ् *arth: to intend*	artha-	object; purpose	(having) the object/purpose alone
मात्र -	mātra-	only; alone	
निर्भासं निर् - *nir-: without, unaccompanied* + √भास् *bhās: to be bright*	nirbhāsaṃ	(as) apparent; shining forth; reflecting	
स्वरूप -	svarūpa-	of its own/true form/essence/ essential nature	
शून्यम् √श्वि *śvi: to swell*	śūnyam	void; emptiness	
इव	iva	as it were; as if	
समाधिः सम् - *sam-: together with, completely, perfectly* + आ *ā-: near to, all around* + √धा *dhā: to put*	samādhiḥ	samādhi	

ARYA

III.3 That (dhyāna), too, when only the object of signification (remains) apparent (in the mind and it is) devoid of (its) own form is tensed samādhi.

BAILEY

III.3 When the citta becomes absorbed in that which is the reality (or idea embodied in the form), and is unaware of separateness or the personal self, this is contemplation or samadhi.

DVIVEDI

III.3 The same, when conscious only of the object, as if unconscious of itself, is trance.

FEUERSTEIN

III.3 [That consciousness], [when] shining forth as the object only as if empty of [its] essence, is enstacy.

HOUSTON

III.3 That (*citta*) specifically, reflecting as the object alone, as if empty of its own form, is *samādhi*-cognitive absorption.

JNANESHVARA

III.3 When only the essence of that object, place, or point shines forth in the mind, as if devoid even of its own form, that state of deep absorption is called deep concentration or samadhi, which is the eighth rung.

PRABHAVANANDA

III.3 When, in meditation, the true nature of the object shines forth, not distorted by the mind of the perceiver, that is absorption (samadhi).

PUROHIT

III.3 Samādhi is that condition of illumination where union disappears, only the meaning of the object on which the attention is fixed being present.

SATCHIDANANDA

III.3 Samadhi is the same meditation when there is the shining of the object alone, as if devoid of form.

SHEARER

III.3 And when that same awareness, its essential nature shining forth in purity, is as if unbounded, this is known as *samādhi*.

TAIMNI

III.3 The same (contemplation) when there is consciousness only of the object of meditation and not of itself (the mind) is *Samādhi*.

VIVEKANANDA

III.3 When that (i.e. dhyāna) gives up all forms and reveals only the meaning, it is samādhi.

III.4

त्रयमेकत्र संयमः ॥ ४ ॥

trayam ekatra saṃyamaḥ

त्रयम् त्रि *tri: three*	trayam	the triad; the three (taken together)
एकत्र एक *eka: one*	ekatra	together as one (is called); upon one object; synthesized; jointly; in one place
संयमः सम्- *sam-: together with, completely, perfectly* + √यम् *yam: to restrain*	saṃyamaḥ	three-fold focus/synthesis: simultaneous dhārana, dhyāna, samādhi; *perfect regulation of citta—Houston*

ARYA

III.4 When the triad (of holding a focus, meditational process and final meditation) is (focussed) together in one object, it is called saṃyama.

BAILEY

III.4 When concentration, meditation and contemplation form one sequential act, then sanyama is achieved.

DVIVEDI

III.4 The three together constitute *Samyama*.

FEUERSTEIN

III.4 The three [practiced] together [on the same object] are constraint.

HOUSTON

III.4 The group of three (*dhāraṇā*, *dhyāna*, and *samādhi*, practiced) together as one, is *sanyama*-the perfect regulation of *citta*.

JNANESHVARA

III.4 The three processes of dharana, dhyana, and samadhi, when taken together on the same object, place or point is called samyama.

PRABHAVANANDA

III.4 When these three—concentration, meditation and absorption—are brought to bear upon one subject, they are called samyama.

PUROHIT

III.4 The three together (attention, union, illumination) form (Samyama) Concentration.

SATCHIDANANDA

III.4 The practice of these three [dharana, dhyana and samadhi] upon one object is called samyama.

SHEARER

III.4 *Dhāranā*, *dhyāna* and *samādhi* practiced together are known as *sanyama*.

TAIMNI

III.4 The three taken together constitute *Saṃyama*.

VIVEKANANDA

III.4 [These] three [when practised] in regard to one object is samyama.

III.5

तज्जयात् प्रज्ञालोकः ॥ ५ ॥

taj-jayāt prajñālokaḥ

तज्जयात्	tajjayāt		
तद् -	tad-	that; this, it	[*through*] this mastery
जयात् √जि *ji: to win*	jayāt	[*through*] mastery; conquest	
प्रज्ञा - *प्र - pra-: before, in front + √ज्ञा jñā: to know*	prajñā-	(of) wisdom; transcendent insight	
आलोकः *आ - ā-: near to, from all sides + √लोक् lok: to perceive*	ālokaḥ	radiance/brilliance (shines forth); flashing forth	

ARYA

III.5 Through the mastery of that (saṃyama) the brilliance of wisdom (shines forth).

BAILEY

III.5 As a result of sanyama comes the shining forth of the light.

DVIVEDI

III.5 By mastering it (results) lucidity of the intellect.

FEUERSTEIN

III.5 Through mastery of that [practice of] [constraint] [there ensues] the flashing-forth of transcendental-insight.

HOUSTON

III.5 Owing to the success of that (*sanyama*), the brilliance of *prajñā*-insight.

JNANESHVARA

III.5 Through the mastery of that three-part process of samyama, the light of knowledge, transcendental insight, or higher consciousness (prajna) dawns, illumines, flashes, or is visible.

PRABHAVANANDA

III.5 Through mastery of samyama comes the light of knowledge.

PUROHIT

III.5 Successful concentration is direct knowledge.

SATCHIDANANDA

III.5 By the mastery of samyama comes the light of knowledge.

SHEARER

III.5 When *sanyama* is mastered, the light of supreme knowledge dawns.

TAIMNI

III.5 By mastering it (*Saṃyama*) the light of the higher consciousness.

VIVEKANANDA

III.5 Through the attainment of that (i.e samyama) comes light of knowledge.

III.6

तस्य भूमिषु विनियोगः ॥ ६ ॥

tasya bhūmiṣu viniyogaḥ

तस्य	tasya	of this/that; that's; its; here: saṃyama
भूमिषु √भू *bhū: to become*	bhūmiṣu	[*into*] the levels gradually, by stages (of citta-manas/mind-field and dhāraṇā/concentration)
विनियोगः	viniyogaḥ	practice; application; progression

वि- *vi-: particular, distinct, intense* + -नि- *ni-: into, great, intensity* +

√युज् *yuj: lit.: to yoke; to unite/dissolve; samādhi*

ARYA

III.6 That saṃyama (should be) applied to (the various) levels (of mind and concentration).

BAILEY

III.6 This illumination is gradual; it is developed stage by stage.

DVIVEDI

III.6 It is used by stages.

FEUERSTEIN

III.6 Its progression is gradual.

HOUSTON

III.6 Its (*sanyama*'s) application is in stages.

JNANESHVARA

III.6 That three-part process of samyama is gradually applied to the finer planes, states, or stages of practice.

PRABHAVANANDA

III.6 It must be applied stage by stage.

PUROHIT

III.6 Concentration is necessary to mount the various steps.

SATCHIDANANDA

III.6 Its practice is to be accomplished in stages.

SHEARER

III.6 But, *sanyama* has its application at every stage of the development of this knowledge.

TAIMNI

III.6 Its (of *Saṃyama*) use by stages.

VIVEKANANDA

III.6 That (i.e. samyama) should be practiced in stages.

III.7

त्रयमन्तरङ्गं पूर्वेभ्यः ॥ ७ ॥

trayam-antar-aṅgaṃ pūrvebhyaḥ

त्रयम् -	trayam	(this) triad; the three (taken together)	
त्रि tri: three			
अन्तरङ्गं	antaraṅgaṃ		
अनतर् -	antar-	inner; inward	inner /internalized
अङ्गं	aṅgaṃ	step; limb; member	step
अङ्ग aṅga: parts			
पूर्वेभ्यः	pūrvebhyaḥ	[*due to/because of/from the*] previous (ones [here: limbs]) or (distinct from) the previous (five aṅga: steps, limbs)	

ARYA

III.7 This triad is more internal than the five (steps that) precede it.

BAILEY

III.7 These last three means of yoga have a more intimate subjective effect than the previous means.

DVIVEDI

III.7 The three are more intimate than the others.

FEUERSTEIN

III.7 [In relation to] the previous [five techniques of Yoga] the three [components of constraint] are inner members.

HOUSTON

III.7 The group of three (*dhāraṇā*, *dhyāna*, and *samādhi*) is the inner limb(s) distinct from the previous (five limbs of yoga).

JNANESHVARA

III.7 These three practices of concentration (dharana), meditation (dhyana), and samadhi are more intimate or internal than the previous five practices.

PRABHAVANANDA

III.7 These three are more direct aids to experience than the five limbs previously described.

PUROHIT

III.7 Attention, union, illumination, are more internal than the preceding five steps. (II.29)

SATCHIDANANDA

III.7 These three [dharana, dhyana and samadhi] are more internal than the preceding five limbs.

SHEARER

III.7 It is the heart of yoga, more intimate than the preceding limits.

TAIMNI

III.7 The three are internal in relation to the preceding ones.

VIVEKANANDA

III.7 These three disciplines are more internal than those that precede.

III.8

तदपि बहिरङ्गं निर्बीजस्य ॥ ८ ॥

tad api bahir-aṅgaṃ nirbījasya

तत्	tat	that	
अपि	api	too; also	
बहिरङ्गं	bahiraṅgaṃ		
बहिर् -	bahir-	external	external
अङ्गं	aṅgaṃ	step; limb; member	step
अङ्ग *aṅga: parts*			
निर्बीजस्य	nir-bījasya	*[of]* the seedless/seedless's; here: samādhi	
निर् - *nir-: without* + बीज *bīja: seed*			

ARYA

III.8 This (triad) too is external (as compared with the) seedless (samādhi).

BAILEY

III.8 Even these three, however, are external to the true seedless meditation (or samadhi) which is not based on an object. It is free from the effects of the discriminative nature of the citta (or mind stuff).

DVIVEDI

III.8 Even it is foreign to the unconscious.

FEUERSTEIN

III.8 Yet they are outer members [in relation to] the seedless [enstacy].

HOUSTON

III.8 That (inner limb) however is an external limb of *nirbija*-the seedless (*samādhi*-cognitive absorption).

JNANESHVARA

III.8 However, these three practices are external, and not intimate compared to nirbija samadhi, which is samadhi that has no object, nor even a seed object on which there is concentration.

PRABHAVANANDA

III.8 But even these are not direct aids to the seedless samadhi.

PUROHIT

III.8 But they are external, compared with seedless Samādhi.

SATCHIDANANDA

III.8 Even these are external to the seedless samadhi.

SHEARER

III.8 Yet even *sanyama* is outside that pure unboundedness.

TAIMNI

III.8 Even that (*Sabīja Samādhi*) is external to the Seedless (*Nirbīja Samādhi*).

VIVEKANANDA

III.8 But even they (i.e. dhāranā, dhyāna, and samādhi) are external to the seedless [samadhi].

III.9 व्युत्थाननिरोधसंस्कारयोरभिभवप्रादुर्भावौ
निरोधक्षणचित्तान्वयो निरोधपरिणामः ॥ ९॥

vyutthāna-nirodha-saṃskārayor abhibhava-prādur-bhāvau
nirodha-kṣana-cittānvayoh nirodha-pariṇāmaḥ

व्युत्थान -	vyutthāna-	emergence; externalization;
वि - vi-: apart, separate from + -उद् - -ud-: up, upwards + √स्था sthā: to stand		outgoing; rising; waking state
निरोधः	nirodhaḥ	(vṛtti) cessation/dissolution/
नि - ni-: under + √रुध् rudh: to restrict or suppress		disappearance/restraint/ suppression/control/ restriction/inhibition/annihilation/ process of ending
संस्कारयोः	saṃskārayoḥ	saṃskāras'; impressions';
सम् - sam-: together with, completely, perfectly + √कृ kṛ: to do		[*possessed of*] propensities of the mental residue of impressions; subliminal activators
अभिभव -	abhibhava-	subduing; subjugating; submergence;
अभि - abhi-: to, towards, into + √भू bhū: to become		disappearing; moving into latency
प्रादुर्भावौ	prādurbhāvau	appear; manifest; emerge;
प्र - pra-: onward, away + दुर् dur: door + √भू bhū: to become		become apparent; rise
निरोध -	nirodha-	cessation, etc.
नि - ni-: under + √रुध् rudh: to restrict or suppress		
क्षण -	kṣaṇa-	moment
√क्षण् kṣan: to break		
चित्त -	citta-	mind-field
√चित् cit: to perceive/be bright		
अन्वयः	anvayaḥ	accompaniment; association;
अनु - anu-: following, after, behind + √इ i: to go		conjunction; connection; permeation
निरोध -	nirodha-	cessation, etc.
नि - ni-: under + √रुध् rudh: to restrict or suppress		
परिणामः	pariṇāmaḥ	transformation; alteration; resulting;
परि - pari-: all around, in addition to + √नम् nam: to bend		modifying; altering

ARYA

III.9 The subduing of the propensities of vyutthāna (lower consciousness) and rise of the propensity of cessations, this association of the mind with the moment of cessation is called nirodha-pariṇāma (the mind's alteration to a state of the cessation of vṛttis).

BAILEY

III.9 The sequence of mental states is as follows; the mind reacts to that which is seen; then follows the moment of mind control. Then ensues a moment wherein the citta (mind stuff) responds to both these factors. Finally these pass away, and the perceiving consciousness has full sway.

DVIVEDI

III.9 Intercepted transformation is the transformation of the mind into the moment of interception: the impression of distraction and interception going out and rising up respectively.

FEUERSTEIN

III.9 [When there is] subjugation of the subliminal-activators of emergence and the manifestation of the subliminal-activators of restriction— [this is] the restriction transformation which is connected with consciousness [in its] moment of restriction.

HOUSTON

III.9 The submergence of the *sanskāra*-sublimal activator of externalization and the emergence of the *sanskāra* of nirodha-the act of ending (*citta-vṛtti*) is the *nirodha-pariṇāma* (*nirodha*-transformation) which is connected to *citta*-the energy field of consciousness at the moment of *nirodha*.

JNANESHVARA

III.9 That high level of mastery called nirodhah-parinamah occurs in the moment of transition when there is a convergence of the rising tendency of deep impressions, the subsiding tendency, and the attention of the mind field itself.

PRABHAVANANDA

III.9 When the vision of the lower samadhi is suppressed by an act of conscious control, so that there are no longer any thoughts or visions in the mind, that is the achievement of control of the thought-waves of the mind.

PUROHIT

III.9 At every moment distractions and impressions of distractions lessen, control and impressions of control increase, until mind clings to the condition of control.

SATCHIDANANDA

III.9 The impressions which normally arise are made to disappear by the appearance of suppressive efforts, which in turn create new mental modifications. The moment of conjunction of mind and new modifications is nirodha parinama.

SHEARER

III.9 *Nirodha pariṇāma*, the transformation of the bounded state, occurs when the attention moves from the rise and fall of the mind's impressions to the silence which pervades when its activity is settled.

TAIMNI

III.9 Nirodha Pariṇama is that transformation of the mind in which it becomes progressively permeated by that condition of Nirodha which intervenes momentarily between an impression which is disappear- ing and the impression which is taking its place.

VIVEKANANDA

III.9 By the suppression of the disturbing impressions of the mind, and by the rise of impressions of control, the mind which persists in that moment of control is said to attain the controlling modifications.

III.10

तस्य प्रशान्तवाहिता संस्कारात् ॥ १० ॥

tasya praśānta-vāhitā saṃskārāt

तस्य	tasya	of this/that; that's; its (mind at that stage—nirodha-pariṇāma)
प्रशान्त - *प्र - pra-: forward, onward + √शम् śam: to be calm*	praśānta-	lit.: breathe forth: calm; steady; tranquil; peaceful; undisturbed
वाहिता *√वह् va: to bear along*	vāhitā	flowing-ness
संस्कारात् *सम् - sam-: together with, completely, perfectly + √कृ kṛ: to do*	saṃskārāt	[*because of/through*] the force of saṃskāra: habitual wave in citta/ conditioned mental response from habit and memory

ARYA

III.10 The mind at that stage flows calm through the force of that cessation-propensity.

BAILEY

III.10 Through the cultivation of this habit of mind there will eventuate a steadiness of spiritual perception.

DVIVEDI

III.10 Its flow becomes steady by impressions.

FEUERSTEIN

III.10 The calm flow of this [consciousness][is effected] thru subliminal-activators.

HOUSTON

III.10 The calm flow of that (*nirodha-pariṇāma*-transformation) occurs due to the *sanskāra*-subliminal activator (of *nirodha*).

JNANESHVARA

III.10 The steady flow of this state (nirodhah-parinamah) continues by the creation of deep impressions (samskaras) from doing the practice.

PRABHAVANANDA

III.10 When this suppression of thought-waves becomes continuous, the mind's flow is calm.

PUROHIT

III.10 When impressions of control prevail, mind flows peacefully.

SATCHIDANANDA

III.10 The flow of nirodha parinama becomes steady through habit.

SHEARER

III.10 This silence flows evenly into the mind, because it becomes a latent impression itself.

TAIMNI

III.10 Its flow becomes tranquil by repeated impression.

VIVEKANANDA

III.10 Its flow becomes steady by habit.

III.11

सर्वार्थतैकाग्रतयोः क्षयोदयौ चित्तस्य समाधिपरिणामः ॥ ११ ॥

sarvārthataikāgratayoḥ kṣayodayau cittasya samādhi-pariṇāmaḥ

सर्वार्थता -	sarvārthatā		
सर्व -	sarva-	all; everything	all-pointedness;
अर्थता -	arthatā-	purpose/object-ness	scattered habit
√अर्थ् arth: to intend			

एकाग्रतयोः	ekāgratayoḥ		
एक -	eka-	one	one-pointed; focused;
अग्रतयो	agratayoḥ	pointed	ability to focus/concentrate; intent state

क्षया -	kṣaya-	subsiding; declining; dwindling; disappearing
√क्षि kṣi: to destroy		
उदयौ	udayau	rising; appearing (is called)
उद् - ud-: up, upwards, over above + √इ i: to go		
चित्तस्य	cittasya	[*of*] the mind's field; mind-field's; all aspects [*possessed by*] energy field called mind
√चित् cit: perceive; be bright		

समाधिपरिणामः	samādhipariṇāmaḥ		
समाधि -	samādhi-	samādhi	transformation to samādhi
सम् - sam-: together with, completely, perfectly + आ - ā-: near to, all around + √धा dhā: to put			
परिणामः	pariṇāmaḥ	transformation alteration	
परि - pari-: all around, in addition to + √नम् nam: to bend			

ARYA

III.11 When the mind's scattered habit subsides and the intent state is on the rise, that is then called the mind's turning to samādhi!

BAILEY

III.11 The establishing of this habit, and the restraining of the mind from its thought-form-making tendency, results eventually in the constant power to contemplate.

DVIVEDI

III.11 Trance-transformation is the setting and rising of distractions and concentration respectively.

FEUERSTEIN

III.11 The dwindling of all-objectness and the upriding of one-pointed-ness is the enstacy transformation of consciousness.

HOUSTON

III.11 The disappearance of *sarvārthatā*-all objectness and arising of *ekāgratā*-one-pointedness is *samādhi-pariṇāma* (*samādhi*-transformation) of *citta*-the energy field of consciousness.

JNANESHVARA

III.11 The mastery called samadhi-parinamah is the transition whereby the tendency to all-pointedness subsides, while the tendency to one-pointedness arises.

PRABHAVANANDA

III.11 When all mental distractions disappear and the mind becomes one-pointed, it enters the state called samadhi.

PUROHIT

III.11 When mind rejects all objects but one, illumination results.

SATCHIDANANDA

III.11 When there is a decline in distractedness and appearance of one-pointedness, then comes samadhi parinamah (development in samadhi).

SHEARER

III.11 *Samādhi parināma*, the transformation of the settled state, is the alternation between the mind's being one-pointed and its being unbounded.

TAIMNI

III.11 *Samādhi* transformation is the (gradual) settling of the distractions and simultaneous rising of one-pointedness.

VIVEKANANDA

III.11 Taking in all sorts of objects and concentrating upon one object are two modifications of the mind. When the first of these is suppressed and the other manifested, the citta acquires the modification called samādhi.

III.12 ततः पुनः शान्तोदितौ तुल्यप्रत्ययौ चित्तस्यैकाग्रतापरिणामः ॥ १२ ॥

tataḥ punaḥ śāntoditau tulya-pratyayau cittasyaikāgratā-pariṇāmaḥ

ततः — tataḥ — then

पुनः — punaḥ — again

शान्त - — śānta- — made tranquil/calm/quiet/subsided/quiescent
√शम् śam: to be calm

उदितौ — uditau — risen
उद् - ud-: up, upwards, over above + √इ i: to go

तुल्य - — tulya- — same; similar; equal
√तुल् tul: to compare with

प्रत्ययौ — pratyayau — content of mind-field; presented-idea; cognition principle; cognition; causal/awareness principle; awareness perceiving (through the mind); buddhi; discriminatory intelligence; *immediate arising thought directed to an object—Houston*
प्रति - prati-: towards, in direction of + √इ i: to go

चित्तस्य — cittasya — [*of*] mind-field; mind-field's (see sūtra II.54)
√चित् cit: to perceive/be bright

एकाग्रतापरिणामः — ekāgratāpariṇāmaḥ — transformation to single-pointedness

- एकाग्रता - — ekāgratā- — one/single point
  एक eka: one + अग्र agra: foremost point, top + ता - tā: -ness
- परिणामः — pariṇāmaḥ — transformation; alteration
  परि - pari-: all around, in addition to + √नम् nam: to bend

ARYA

III.12 Then, again when both the subsiding and (immediately) arising states are equally of the same (samādhi) awareness, (it is termed) the mind's alteration to intentness (one-pointedness).

BAILEY

III.12 When mind control and the controlling factor are equally balanced, then comes the condition of one-ointedness.

DVIVEDI

III.12 Then again the repressed and the revived are equally (present in) consciousness: this is that condition of the mind which is transformation into unity.

FEUERSTEIN

III.12 Then again, when the quiescent and the uprisen ideas are similar, [this is] the one-pointed transformation of consciousness.

HOUSTON

III.12 Then again when the *śānta*-quieted and the *udita*-arisen are the same *pratyaya*, there is *ekāgrata-pariṇām*-one-pointedness transformation of *citta*-the field.

JNANESHVARA

III.12 The mastery called ekagrata-parinamah is the transition whereby the same one-pointedness arises and subsides sequentially.

PRABHAVANANDA

III.12 The mind becomes one-pointed when similar thought-waves arise in succession without any gaps between them.

PUROHIT

III.12 It is the result of concentration that mind's attitude towards the object of concentration remains the same, today as yesterday.

SATCHIDANANDA

III.12 Then again, when the subsiding past and rising present images are identical, there is ekagrata parinama (one-pointedness).

SHEARER

III.12 And from this comes *ekāgratā samādhi*, the transformation of one-pointedness, the state in which activity and silence are equally balanced in the mind.

TAIMNI

III.12 Then, again, the condition of the mind in which the 'object' (in the mind) which subsides is always exactly similar to the 'object' which rises (in the next moment) is called *Ekāgratā Pariṇāma*.

VIVEKANANDA

III.12 The modification called one-pointedness of the chitta is acquired when the impression that which is past and that which is present are similar.

III.13

एतेन भूतेन्द्रियेषु धर्मलक्षणावस्थापरिणामा व्याख्याताः ॥ १३ ॥

etena bhūtendriyeṣu dharma-lakṣaṇāvastha-pariṇāmā vyākhyātāḥ

एतेन	etena	by this
एतद् etad-: this		
भूत -	bhūta-	(subtle and gross) elements
√भू bhū: to become		
इन्द्रियेषु	indriyeṣu	[*upon/into*] senses/sense-organs; senses'
इन्द्र indra: senses + -य -ya: fit for		
धर्म -	dharma-	(of) natures; attributes;
√धृ dhṛ: to hold		essential/visible characteristics; properties; forms
लक्षण -	lakṣaṇa-	(of) time/time-factor/
√लक्ष् lakṣ: to observe		time-variation characteristic
अवस्था -	avasthā-	condition; state
अव - ava-: away, off + √स्था sthā: to stand		
परिणामाः	pariṇāmāḥ	transformations; alterations;
परि - pari-: all around, in addition to + √नम् nam: to bend		changes
व्याख्याताः	vyākhyātāḥ	have been described, explained
वि - vi-: difference, division + आ - ā-: towards, near to + √ख्या khyā: to be mentioned		(by implication)

ARYA

III.13 (In explaining the alterations of the mind) are also implied the alterations of its attributes, times (awareness of changes from past to present to future) and (transitions from conditions to) conditions with reference to (mind's relationships with gross and subtle) elements and the senses.

BAILEY

III.13 Through this process the aspects of every object are known, their characteristics (or form), their symbolic nature, and their specific use in time-conditions (stage of development) are known and realised.

DVIVEDI

III.13 By this the three: property-, character-, and condition-transformations are explained.

FEUERSTEIN

III.13 By this are also explained the transformations of form, time-variation and condition [with regard to] the elements [and] sense-organs.

HOUSTON

III.13 By this are explained the *pariṇāma*-transformations of *dharma*-characteristic form, *lakṣana*-potential change and *avasthā*-condition in regard to the *bhūta*-elements and *indriya*-sense organs.

JNANESHVARA

III.13 These three transition processes also explain the three transformations of form, time, and characteristics, and how these relate to the material elements and senses.

PRABHAVANANDA

III.13 In this state, it passes beyond the three kinds of changes which take place in subtle or gross matter, and in the organs: change of form, change of time and change of condition.

PUROHIT

III.13 In the same way, the three-fold modifications of element and sense into form, age, and condition can be explained.

SATCHIDANANDA

III.13 By this [what has been said in the preceding three Sutras], the transformations of the visible characteristics, time factors and conditions of elements and senses are also described.

SHEARER

III.13 These are the transformations of the mind. The transformations that operate in matter—transformations of quality, form, and state—are similarly explained.

TAIMNI

III.13 By this (by what has been said in the last four Sūtras) the property, character and condition-transformations in the elements and the sense-organs are also explained.

VIVEKANANDA

III.13 In this way (i.e by the three modifications mentioned above) is explained the threefold transformation as to form, time and state, in time or gross matter, and in the organs.

III.14

शान्तोदिताव्यपदेश्यधर्मानुपाती धर्मी ॥ १४ ॥

śāntoditāvyapadeśya-dharmānupātī dharmī

शान्त -	śānta-	made tranquil/quiet/subsided
√शम् śam: to be calm		
उदित -	udita-	risen; manifest; present; active
उद् - ud-: up, upwards, over above + √इ i: to go		
अव्यपदेश्य -	a-vyapadeśya-	unmanifest; dormant; future;
अ - a-: without + वि - vi-: apart, separate from +		indeterminate; latent;
अप - apa-: away from + √दिश् diś: to point out		those/that cannot be pointed to
धर्म -	dharma-	attributes; forms; characteristic form;
√धृ dhṛ: to hold		nature; properties; qualifications
अनुपाती	anupātī	following; conforming; correlated
अनु - anu-: following, after, behind + √पत् pat: to fall		
धर्मी	dharmī	essential characteristic; form bearer;
√धृ dhṛ: to hold		possessor of attributes

ARYA

III.14 A dharmī (possessor of attributes, qualified) is that which maintains the (same) qualification (or attribute, throughout the past, present or future, that is, whether that attribute has some of its aspect) subsided, (some) on the rise (at present, and some lying dormant) to become apparent (in the future).

BAILEY

III.14 The characteristics of every object are acquired, manifesting or latent.

DVIVEDI

III.14 The substratum is that which correlated to properties, tranquil, active or indescribable.

FEUERSTEIN

III.14 The form-bearer [i.e. the substance] is [that which] conforms to the quiescent, uprisen or indeterminable form.

HOUSTON

III.14 The form substratum (*dharmī*) conforms to the characteristic form, which may be quieted, arisen, and indistinguishable (past, present, future).

JNANESHVARA

III.14 There is an unmanifest, indescribable substratum or existence that is common or contained within all of the other forms or qualities.

PRABHAVANANDA

III.14 A compound object has attributes and is subject to change, either past, present or yet to be manifested.

PUROHIT

III.14 Substance is that which is uniform in the past, present and future.

SATCHIDANANDA

III.14 It is the substratum (Prakriti) that by nature goes through latent, uprising and unmanifested phases.

SHEARER

III.14 Each object carries its past, present and future qualities within it.

TAIMNI

III.14 The substratum is that in which the properties—latent, active or unmanifest—inhere.

VIVEKANANDA

III.14 That which is acted upon by transformations, either past, present or yet to be manifested, is the substance qualified.

III.15

क्रमान्यत्वं परिणामान्यत्वे हेतुः ॥ १५ ॥

kramānyatvaṃ pariṇāmānyatve hetuḥ

क्रम - √क्रम् *kram: to step/stride*	krama-	(of) sequence; succession; sequential progression
अन्यत्वं √अन्य *anya: other+* - त्व *-tva: -ness*	anyatvaṃ	lit.: other-ness: difference/differentiation
परिणाम - परि - *pari-: all around, in addition to* + √नम् *nam: to bend*	pariṇāma-	transformation; shift in stage of evolution
अन्यत्वे अन्य *anya: other*	anyatve	[*upon*] difference/differentiation (is the)
हेतुः √हि *hi: to incite*	hetuḥ	cause

ARYA

III.15 Difference of sequence (in step by step alterations) is the cause of (there being) difference in end product.

BAILEY

III.15 The stage of development is responsible for the various modifications of the versatile psychic nature and of the thinking principle.

DVIVEDI

III.15 The cause in the mutability of forms is the change of order.

FEUERSTEIN

III.15 The differentiation in the sequence is the reason for the differentiation in the transformations.

HOUSTON

III.15 The separateness of the *krama*-sequential progression (of each *citta*-field) is the reason for the separateness of *pariṇāma*-transformations.

JNANESHVARA

III.15 Change in the sequence of the characteristics is the cause for the different appearances of results, consequences, or effects.

PRABHAVANANDA

III.15 The succession of these changes is the cause of manifold evolution.

PUROHIT

III.15 Different modifications of substance are due to different orders of sequence.

SATCHIDANANDA

III.15 The succession of these different phases is the cause of the differences in stages of evolution.

SHEARER

III.15 The diversity of matter is caused by the laws of nature which conduct evolution.

TAIMNI

III.15 The cause of the difference in transformation is the difference in the underlying process.

VIVEKANANDA

III.15 The succession of changes is the cause of manifold evolution.

III.16

परिणामत्रयसंयमादतीतानागतज्ञानम् ॥ १६ ॥

pariṇāma-traya-saṃyamād atītānāgata-jñānam

परिणाम -	pariṇāma-	transformation; alteration;
परि - pari-: all around, in addition to + √नम् nam: to bend		stages of evolution
त्रय -	traya-	threefold
त्रिय tri: three		
संयमात्	saṃyamāt	[*due to*/*through*] three-fold
सम् - sam-: together with, completely, perfectly +		focus/synthesis: simultaneous dhāranā,
√यम् yam: to restrain		dhyāna, samādhi;
		perfect regulation of citta—Houston
अतीत -	atīta-	(of) past (and)
अति - atī-: over, beyond + √इ i: to go		
अनागत -	anāgata-	lit.: not come (as yet): future
अन् - an-: not, non- absent + आ - ā-: (here: indicates a reversal of direction) + √गम् gam: to go = to come		
ज्ञानम्	jñānam	knowledge; concept; idea;
√ज्ञा jñā: to know		insight; awareness; observation; ordinary knowledge based on sense perception and reasoning

ARYA

III.16 Through concentration on the (above) three types of alteration, the knowledge of past and present (accrues to a yogi).

BAILEY

III.16 Through concentrated meditation upon the triple nature of every form, comes the revelation of that which has been and that which will be.

DVIVEDI

III.16 The knowledge of past and future, by *Samyama* on the three transformations.

FEUERSTEIN

III.16 Through constraint on the three [forms of] transformation [comes about] knowledge of the past and the future.

HOUSTON

III.16 Due to *sanyama* (perfect regulation of *citta* by *dhāraṇa*, *dhyāna*, *samādhi*), on the three transformations (*dharma*-characteristic, *lakṣaṇa*-potential change, *avastā*-condition) there arises knowledge of the past and future.

JNANESHVARA

III.16 By samyama on the three-fold changes in form, time, and characteristics, there comes knowledge of the past and future.

PRABHAVANANDA

III.16 By making samyama on the three kinds of changes, one obtains knowledge of the past and the future.

PUROHIT

III.16 Concentrate on the above three-fold modifications; know past and future.

SATCHIDANANDA

III.16 By practicing samyama on the three stages of evolution comes knowledge of past and future.

SHEARER

III.16 *Sanyama* on the three transformations brings knowledge of the past and future.

TAIMNI

III.16 By performing *Saṃyama* on the three kinds of transformations (*Nirodha*, *Samādhi* and *Ekāgratā*) knowledge of the past and future.

VIVEKANANDA

III.16 Through the practice of samyama on the three sorts of changes comes the knowledge of past and future.

III.17 शब्दार्थप्रत्ययानामितरेतराध्यासात् सङ्करस्तत्प्रविभागसंयमात् सर्वभूतरुतज्ञानम् ॥ १७ ॥

śabdārtha-pratyayānām-itaretarādhyāsāt saṇkarastat-pravibhāga-saṃyamāt sarva-bhūta-ruta-jñānam

शब्द् -	śabda-	words
अर्थ -	artha-	meanings'; purposes'; objects'
√अर्थ् *arth: to intend*		
प्रत्ययानाम् -	pratyayānām-	significators'; contents of mind-field;
प्रति - *prati-: towards, in direction of* + √इ *i: to go*		cognitions'; perceivings' (through the mind); buddhis'; discriminatory intelligences'
इतरेतर -	itaretara-	on each other; mutual; among themselves
अध्यासात्	adhyāsāt	[*because of*] superimposition (there arises)
आधि - *adhi-: over, above* + √अस् *as: to be or to cast/throw*		
सङ्करः	saṅkaraḥ	confusion; mix-up
सम्कृ *samkṛ:* सम् *sam-: very, fully, greatly* + √कृ *kṛ: to do = to mix/confuse; to pour/scatter*		
तत्प्रविभाग -	tat-pravibhāga-	(on) the distinctions, divisions;
प्र - *pra-: forward, onward* + वि - *vi-: apart, separate from* + √भज् *bhaj: to divide*		differentiation (of that)
संयमात्	saṃyamāt	[*due to/because of*] three-fold
सम् - *sam-: together with, completely, perfectly* + √यम् *yam: to restrain*		focus/synthesis: simultaneous dhāraṇā, dhyāna, samādhi; *perfect regulation of citta—Houston*
सर्व -	sarva-	(of) all
भूत -	bhūta-	being; beings; elements
√भू *bhū: to become*		
रुत -	ruta-	sounds (and their meanings)
√रु *ru: to roar*		
ज्ञानम्	jñānam	knowledge; concept; idea;
√ज्ञा *jñā: to know*		ordinary knowledge based on sense perception and reasoning

ARYA

III.17 Because of mutual superimposition of words, meanings and signification (there arises) confusion (and mix-up of these). Through the concentration on on their separation (the yogi gains) the knowledge (of the meaning of) the sounds of all beings.

BAILEY

III.17 The Sound (or word), that which it denotes (the object) and the embodied spiritual essence (or idea) are usually confused in the mind of the perceiver. By concentrated meditation on these three aspects comes an (intuitive) comprehension of the sound uttered by all forms of life.

DVIVEDI

III.17 The word, its sense, and knowledge are confused with one another on account of their being mutually mistaken for one another; hence by *Samyama* on the proper province of each, (arises) the comprehension of (the meaning of) sounds uttered by any being.

FEUERSTEIN

III.17 [There is a natural] confusion of presented ideas, object and word [on account of an erroneous] superimposition on one another. Through constraint upon the distinction of these [confused elements] knowledge of the sound of all beings [is acquired].

HOUSTON

III.17 The confusion of words, meanings, and *pratyaya* is due to the super-imposition of one upon the other. By *sanyama* (perfect regulation of the *citta*) on the inherent distinctness of these, there arises knowledge of the sound of all beings.

JNANESHVARA

III.17 The name associated with an object, the object itself implied by that name, and the conceptual existence of the object, all three usually interpenetrate or commingle with one another. By samyama on the distinction between these three, the meaning of the sounds made by all beings becomes available.

PRABHAVANANDA

III.17 By taking samyama on the sound of a word, one's perception of its meaning,
and one's reaction to it—
three things which are ordinarily confused—
one obtains understanding of all sounds uttered by living beings.

PUROHIT

III.17 Concentrate separately on the word, the meaning and the object, which are mixed up in the common usage; understand the speech of every creature.

SATCHIDANANDA

III.17 A word, its meaning and the idea behind it are normally confused because of superimposition upon one another. By samyama on the word [or sound] produced by any being, knowledge of its meaning is obtained.

SHEARER

III.17 Perception of an object is usually confused, because its name, its form, and an idea about it are all superimposed upon each other. By doingsanyama on the distinction between these three, we can understand the sound of all living beings.

TAIMNI

III.17 The sound, the meaning (behind it) and the idea (which is present in the mind at the time) are present together in a confused state. By performing Saṃyama (on the sound) they are resolved and there arises comprehension of the meaning of sounds uttered by any living being.

VIVEKANANDA

III.17 Through samyama on word, meaning, and knowledge, which are ordinarily confused, comes the knowledge of all animal sounds.

III.18

संस्कारसाक्षात्करणात् पूर्वजातिज्ञानम् ॥ १८ ॥

saṃskāra-sākṣāt-karaṇāt pūrva-jāti-jñānam

संस्कार -	saṃskāra-	habitual wave in citta;
सम् - *sam-: together with, completely, perfectly* +		conditioned mental response from habit
√*कृ* *kṛ: to do*		and memory;
		(of) the residue of impressions impression/imprint in the subtle domain (karmaṣaya); subliminal activator

साक्षात्करणात्	sākṣātkaraṇāt		
साक्षात् -	sākṣāt-	direct	[*due to*] realization; [*due to*] bringing to the fore;
करणात्	karaṇāt	[*due to*]	[*due to*] bringing to awareness;
√*कृ* *kṛ: to do*		perception	[*due to*] direct perception/ observation

पूर्व -	pūrva-	(of) previous/earlier
जाति -	jāti-	incarnations; births
√*जन्* *jan: to beget*		
ज्ञानम्	jñānam	knowledge, etc.
√*ज्ञा* *jñā: to know*		

ARYA

III.18 By bringing the previous saṃskāras to (his) awareness (the yogi gains) the knowledge of (his) previous incarnations.

BAILEY

III.18 Knowledge of previous incarnations becomes available when the power to see thought-images is acquired.

DVIVEDI

III.18 By mental presentation of the impressions, a knowledge of former class.

FEUERSTEIN

III.18 Through direct-perception of subliminal-activators [the *yogin* gains] knowledge of [his] previous birth(s).

HOUSTON

III.18 By direct perception of *sanskāra*-subliminal activators, knowledge of previous births.

JNANESHVARA

III.18 Through the direct perception of the latent impressions (samskaras) comes the knowledge of previous incarnations.

PRABHAVANANDA

III.18 By making samyama on previous thought-waves, one obtains knowledge of one's past lives.

PUROHIT

III.18 Concentrate on the impressions of the past; know past lives.

SATCHIDANANDA

III.18 By direct perception, through samyama, of one's mental impressions, knowledge of past births is obtained.

SHEARER

III.18 From the direct experience of latent impressions comes knowledge of previous births.

TAIMNI

III.18 By direct perceptions of the impressions a knowledge of the previous birth.

VIVEKANANDA

III.18 Through the perceiving of the impressions [comes] the knowledge of past life.

III.19

प्रत्ययस्य परचित्तज्ञानम् ॥ १९ ॥

pratyayasya para-citta-jñānam

प्रत्ययस्य	pratyayasya	mind-field's content/presented-idea;
प्रति - prati-: towards, in direction of + √इ i: to go		[*of*] cognition principle/cognition/ causal/awareness principle; awareness perceiving (through the mind); buddhi; discriminatory intelligence; *immediate arising thought directed to an object—Houston*
पर -	para-	other; another's
चित्त -	citta-	(of) energy field called mind
√चित् cit: to perceive; to be bright		in all aspects; mind-field; field of consciousness; consciousness; mind-stuff
ज्ञानम्	jñānam	knowledge (of)
√ज्ञा jñā: to know		

ARYA

III.19 By concentration on (some external sign of whatever may be transpiring in) (another's) mind (the yogi gains) the knowledge of another's mind.

BAILEY

III.19 Through concentrated meditation, the thought images in the minds of other people become apparent.

DVIVEDI

III.19 With reference to a sign, the knowledge of the mind of others.

FEUERSTEIN

III.19 [Through direct-perception] of [another's] presented-idea, knowledge of another's consciousness [is obtained].

HOUSTON

III.19 (By direct perception) of a *pratyaya* -knowledge of the *citta* of another.

JNANESHVARA

III.19 By samyama on the notions or presented ideas comes knowledge of another's mind.

PRABHAVANANDA

III.19 By making samyama on the distinguishing marks of another man's body, one obtains knowledge of the nature of his mind.

PUROHIT

III.19 Concentrate on another's mind; know that mind.

SATCHIDANANDA

III.19 By samyama on the distinguishing signs of others' bodies, knowledge of their mental images is obtained.

SHEARER

III.19 And from the direct experience of its state, we can know the quality of another mind.

TAIMNI

III.19 (By direct perception through *Saṃyama*) of the image occupying the mind, knowledge of the mind of others.

VIVEKANANDA

III.19 Through the practice of samyama on the signs in another's body, knowledge of his mind comes.

III.20

न च तत् सालम्बनं तस्याविषयीभूतत्वात् ॥ २० ॥

na ca tat sālambanaṃ tasyāviṣayī-bhūtatvāt

न च	na ca	not however
तत्	tat	that; here: knowledge
सालम्बनं	sālambanaṃ	[*with/having*] support/supporting object/
स - *sa-: with* + *आ -* *ā-: near to, from all sides* +		foundation; [*having*] a base
√लम्ब् *lamb: to rest on*		
तस्य -	tasya-	[*possessing*] of that
अविषयीभूतत्वात्	aviṣayībhūtatvāt	

अविषयी -	a-viṣayī-	lit.: without action:	[*because of*]
अ - *a-: without* + *√विष्* *viṣ: to be active*		which has no object	not being the object
भूतत्वात्	bhūtatvāt	[*due to*] nature of being	(of saṃyama)
√भू *bhū: to become*			

ARYA

III.20 That knowledge of (another's mind as in Sutra 19) does not include the subject of (that mind's) current cogitation but only the totality of that mind) because that was not the object of (this particular type of) concentration.

BAILEY

III.20 As, however, the object of those thoughts is not apparent to the perceiver, he sees only the thought and not the object. His meditation excludes the tangible.

DVIVEDI

III.20 But not with its occupant, for that is not the subject.

FEUERSTEIN

III.20 But [this knowledge] does not [have as its object] that [presented-idea] together with the [respective] support [i.e. object], because of its being absent from [the other's consciousness].

HOUSTON

III.20 And it is not that (*citta*) together with its supporting object, due to its (the *citta*'s) nature of being that which has no object.

JNANESHVARA

III.20 But the underlying support of that knowledge (of the other person's mind, in III.19) remains unperceived or out of reach.

PRABHAVANANDA

III.20 But not of its contents, because that is not the object of the samyama.

PUROHIT

III.20 You cannot know its contents unless you concentrate on those contents.

SATCHIDANANDA

III.20 But this does not include the support in the person's mind [such as the motive behind the thought, etc.] as that is not the object of the samyama.

SHEARER

III.20 We know the quality, but not the content of the mind, because that is not within the sphere of this *sanyama*.

TAIMNI

III.20 But not also of other mental factors which support the mental image, for that is not the object of (*Saṃyama*).

VIVEKANANDA

III.20 But not its contents, that not being the object of the samyama.

III.21

कायरूपसंयमात् तद्ग्राह्यशक्तिस्तम्भे चक्षुःप्रकाशासम्प्रयोगेऽन्तर्धानम् ॥ २१ ॥

kāya-rūpa-saṃyamāt tad-grāhya-śakti-stambhe cakṣuḥ-prakāśāsamprayoge 'ntardhānam

काय -	kāya-	(on or of) body's	[*through*] concentration on body's form
रूप -	rūpa-	form	
संयमात्	saṃyamāt	[*through*] three-fold focus	

सम् - sam-: together with, completely, perfectly + √यम् yam: to restrain

तद् -	tad-	by that	[*upon*] arresting the power of its visibility/ apprehensibility
ग्राह्य -	grāhya-	visible; perceivable	
√ग्रह् grah: to seize		apprehensible; graspable	
शक्ति -	śakti-	power; capacity; ability	
√सक् śak: to be able			
स्तम्भे	stambhe	[*upon*] arresting/ suspension	
√स्तम्भ् stambh: to stop			

चक्षुः -	cakṣuḥ-	(of) eye

√चक्ष् cakṣ: to appear

प्रकाश -	prakāśa-	light

प्र - pra-: forward, onward, away + √काश् kāś: to be visible

असम्प्रयोगे	a-samprayoge	[*upon*] absence of contact; disconnection

अ - a-: non-, without + सम् - sam-: together with, fully, completely

प्र - pra-: forward, onward + √युज् yuj: lit.: to yoke; to dissolve/unite; samādhi

अन्तर्धानम्	antar-dhānam	lit.: put or place within: disappearance; vanish; invisible

अन्तर् - antar-: inner, within + √धा dhā: to put

ARYA

III.21 Through concentration on the body's form when (the yogi) brings to arrest the power of (the body's) being an object of apprehension, there is then (stoppage of) contact with the light in others' eyes, so (the yogi) accomplishes (the power of) becoming invisible.

BAILEY

III.21 By concentrated meditation upon the distinction between form and body, those properties of the body which make it visible to the human eye are negated (or withdrawn) and the yogi can render himself invisible.

DVIVEDI

III.21 By *Samyama* on the form of the body, the power of comprehension being suspended, and the connection between light and the eye being severed, there follows disappearance of the body.

FEUERSTEIN

III.21 Through constraint on the form of the body, upon suspension of the capacity to be perceived, [that is to say] upon the disruption of the light [travelling from that body] to the eye, [there follows] invisibility.

HOUSTON

III.21 By *sanyama* on the form of the body, while suspending its ability to be seen, that is the disconnecting of light to the eye - there arises invisibility (placement within).

JNANESHVARA

III.21 When samyama is done on the form of one's own physical body, the illumination or visual characteristic of the body is suspended, and is thus invisible to other people.

PRABHAVANANDA

III.21 If one makes samyama on the form of one's body, obstructing its perceptibility and separating its power of manifestation from the eyes of the beholder, then one's body becomes invisible.

PUROHIT

III.21 Concentrate on the form of your body, suspend the power of another to see it; and as the light of his eye cannot reach you, become invisible.

SATCHIDANANDA

III.21 By samyama on the form of one's body, [and by] checking the power of perception by intercepting light from the eyes of the observer, the body becomes invisible.

SHEARER

III.21 *Sanyama* on the form of the body makes it imperceptible, by breaking the contact between the eye of the observer and the light reflected by the body. From this *sanyama*, invisibility comes.

TAIMNI

III.21 By performing Saṃyama on Rūpa (one of the five Tanmātras), on suspension of the receptive power, the contact between the eye (of the observer) and light (from the body) is broken and the body becomes invisible.

VIVEKANANDA

III.21 Through the practice of samyama on the form of the body, the power of perceiving forms being obstructed and the power of manifestation in the eye being separated [from the form], the yogi's body becomes unseen.

III.22

एतेन शब्दाद्यन्तर्धानमुक्तम् ॥ २२ ॥

etena śabdādy-antardhānam uktam

एतेन	etena	[*by*] this (here: manner);
एतद् *etad-: this*		[*by*] the same way
शब्द -	śabda-	(of) words; sounds
शब्द् *śabd: sound*		
आदि -	ādi-	and so forth
अन्तर्धानम्	antardhānam	disappearance
अन्तर् - *antar-: inner, within* + √धा *dhā: to put*		
उक्तम्	uktam	is explained/described
√उभ *ukta: to speak*		

[Author's Note: Not all authorities include this sūtra.
From this point, sūtra numbering will vary between translators. S.Z.]

ARYA

III.22 By this (very principle) the disappearance of sounds, etc., is also explained.

BAILEY

III. ---

DVIVEDI

III. ---

FEUERSTEIN

III.22 ---

HOUSTON

III. ---

JNANESHVARA

III.22 In the same way as described in relation to sight (III.21), one is able to suspend the ability of the body to be heard, touched, tasted, or smelled.

PRABHAVANANDA

III.22 Thus, also, its sounds cease to be heard.

PUROHIT

III.22 ---

SATCHIDANANDA

III.22 In the same way, the disappearance of sound [touch, taste, smell, etc.] is explained.

SHEARER

III.22 ---

TAIMNI

III.22 From the above can be understood the disappearance of sound, etc.

VIVEKANANDA

III.22 In this manner the disappearance or concealment of words which are being spoken and such other things, are also explained.

III.23

सोपक्रमं निरुपक्रमं च कर्म तत्संयमादपरान्तज्ञानमरिष्टेभ्यो वा ॥ २३ ॥

sopakramaṃ nirupakramaṃ ca karma tat-saṃyamād aparānta-jñānam ariṣṭebhyo vā

सोपक्रमं — sopakramaṃ — in the process (of fruition); swift result/manifestation/fruition; already in momentum; energetically operative

स - sa-: with + (उप - upa-: towards + √क्रम् kram: to step/stride = √उपक्रम् upakram: to go near)

निरुपक्रमं — nir-upakramaṃ — not yet in momentum; slow result/manifestation/fruition; deferred/dormant progression

निर् - nir-: without + उप - upa-: toward, near to + √क्रम् kram: to step/stride

च — ca — and

कर्म — karma — action; action-fruition; action-reaction response

√कृ kṛ: to do

तत्संयमात् — tatsaṃyamāt — [*by/because of*] three-fold synthetic focus on that

- **तद् -** — tad- — that
- **संयमात्** — saṃyamāt — [*by*] three-fold focus/synthesis: simultaneous dhāranā, dhyāna, samādhi; *perfect regulation of citta—Houston*

  सम् - sam-: completely, perfectly + √यम् yam: to restrain

अपरान्त - — aparānta- — of death (time of)

अ - a-: un-/non-/not + पर - para-: distant, remote + अन्त anta: end

ज्ञानम् — jñānam — knowledge

√ज्ञा jñā: to know

(अपरान्त-ज्ञानम्: knowledge (of time) of death)

अरिष्टेभ्यः — ariṣṭebhyaḥ — [*from/because of/through/on*] omens/portents/signs

अ - a-: un-/non-/not + √ऋष् ṛṣ: to pierce

वा — vā — or

ARYA

III.23 The actions (of the past) (are of two kinds): those which have already started well with their momentum of bringing forth the fruition, and those that have not yet begun to do so. By concentrating on these (two kinds of actions the yogi gains) the knowledge of his death; or (by concentration on) ill omens.

BAILEY

III.22 Karma (or effects) are of two kinds: immediate karma or future karma. By perfectly concentrated meditation on these, the yogi knows the term of his experience in the three worlds. This knowledge comes also from signs.

DVIVEDI

III.22 *Karma* is of two kinds; active and dormant; by *Samyama* on them (results) knowledge of cessation; as also by portents.

FEUERSTEIN

III.22 Karman [is of two kinds]: acute and deferred. Through constraint there on, or from omens, [the yogin acquires] knowledge of death.

HOUSTON

III.22 *Karma* is either *sopakrana*-with the advance of *krama*-sequential progression (fast in fruition) or *nirupakrama*-against the advance of *krama* (slow in fruition). The knowledge of time of death may be known by *sanyama* upon that or by signs.

JNANESHVARA

III.23 Karma is of two kinds, either fast or slow to manifest; by samyama on these karmas comes foreknowledge of the time of death.

PRABHAVANANDA

III.23 By making samyama on two kinds of karma—that which will soon bear fruit and that which will not bear fruit until later—or by recognizing the portents of death, a yogi may know the exact time of his separation from the body.

PUROHIT

III.22 Concentrate on immediate or future karma; know the time and cause of death.

SATCHIDANANDA

III.23 Karmas are of two kinds: quickly manifesting and slowly manifesting.
By samyama on them, or on the portents of death, the knowledge of the time of death is obtained.

SHEARER

III.22 The fruits of an action may return to the doer quickly or slowly. From *sanyama* on the fruit of action comes foreknowledge of the time of death and the understanding of omens.

TAIMNI

III.23 Karma is of two kinds: active and dormant;
by performing Saṃyama on them (is gained) knowledge of the time of death;
also by (performing Saṃyama on) portents.

VIVEKANANDA

III.23 Karma is of two kinds: Some to be fructified soon, and some to be fructified later. By practicing samyama on these, or on the signs called arishta, portents, the yogis know the exact time of separation from their bodies.

III.24

मैत्र्यादिषु बलानि ॥ २४ ॥

maitryādiṣu balāni

मैत्री - *√मिद् mid: to adhere*	maitrī-	[*on*] love; friendship
आदिषु	ādiṣu	and so forth; etcetera; beginning with
बलानि	balāni	powers; strengths

ARYA

III.24 By concentration on (brahma-vihāras) love and so forth (Sutra 1.33) their (respective) powers (accrue).

BAILEY

III.23 Union with others is to be gained through one-pointed meditation upon the three states of feeling—compassion, tenderness and dispassion.

DVIVEDI

III.23 In sympathy, etc., strength.

FEUERSTEIN

III.23 [Through constraint] on friendliness *et cetera*., [he acquires] powers.

HOUSTON

III.23 (By *sanyama*) on friendship, etc. - strengths. (I.33)

JNANESHVARA

III.24 By samyama on friendliness (and the other attitudes of I.33), there comes great strength of that attitude.

PRABHAVANANDA

III.24 By making samyama on friendliness, compassion, etc., one develops the powers of these qualities.

PUROHIT

III.23 Concentrate on friendship, mercy, joy; excel in them.

SATCHIDANANDA

III.24 By samyama on friendliness and other such qualities, the power to transmit them is obtained.

SHEARER

III.23 From *sanyama* on friendliness, compassion and happiness, these qualities blossom.

TAIMNI

III.24 (By performing *Saṃyama*) on friendliness, etc. (comes) strength (of the quality).

VIVEKANANDA

III.24 By practicing samyama on friendship, mercy, etc. (I.33), the Yogi excels in respective qualities.

III.25

बलेषु हस्तिबलादीनि ॥ २५ ॥

baleṣu hasti-balādīni

बलेषु	baleṣu	[*on*] strengths
हस्ति -	hasti-	(of) elephants
हस्त *hasta: hand*		
बल -	bala-	strengths
आदीनि	ādīni	and so forth; et cetera

ARYA

III.25 By concentration on the strengths (of various strong beings) the strengths of elephants and so forth (are gained).

BAILEY

III.24 Meditation, one-pointedly centered upon the power of the elephant, will awaken that force or light.

DVIVEDI

III.24 In strength, that of the elephant, etc.

FEUERSTEIN

III.24 [Through constraint] on powers, [he acquires] powers [comparable to those of] the elephant, etc.

HOUSTON

III.24 On strengths - the strength of an elephant, etc.

JNANESHVARA

III.25 By samyama on the strength of elephants comes a similar strength.

PRABHAVANANDA

III.25 By making samyama on any kind of strength, such as that of the elephant, one obtains that strength.

PUROHIT

III.24 Concentrate on strength like that of the elephant; get that strength.

SATCHIDANANDA

III.25 By samyama on the strength of elephants and other such animals, their strength is obtained.

SHEARER

III.24 From *sanyama* on the strength of an elephant, or other creatures, we gain that strength.

TAIMNI

III.25 (By performing *Saṃyama*) on the strengths (of animals) the strength of an elephant, etc.

VIVEKANANDA

III.25 Through samyama on the strength of the elephant, and other creatures, their respective strength comes to the yogi.

III.26

प्रवृत्त्यालोकन्यासात् सूक्ष्मव्यवहितविप्रकृष्टज्ञानम् ॥ २६ ॥

pravṛtty-āloka-nyāsāt sūkṣma-vyavahita-viprakṛṣṭa-jñānam

प्रवृत्त्यालोकन्यासात् pravṛttyālokanyāsāt

प्रवृत्ति -	pravṛtti-	natural focus	
प्र - pra-: forward + √वृत् vṛt: turn		on sense objects;	
		higher sense activity	[*because of/by*]
आलोक -	āloka-	light, brilliance;	projection to
आ - ā-: near to, from all sides + √लोक् lok: perceive		flashing forth	various objects,
न्यासात्	nyāsāt	[*because of*] projecting/	the light of
नि - ni-: in, into + √आस् ās: sit, be present		directing/focusing; [*by*] placing	pravṛtti

सूक्ष्म - sūkṣma- subtle; fine

√सिव् siv: to sew

व्यवहित - vyavahita- hidden; concealed; obscure

व va: like, as + अ - a-: un-/non-/not + √धा dhā: to put

विप्रकृष्ट - viprakṛṣṭa- distant; remote

वि - vi-: apart, separate from + प्र - pra-: onward, away + √कृष् kṛṣ: to draw

ज्ञानम् jñānam knowledge

√ज्ञा jñā: to know

ARYA

III.26 By projecting (to all things) the light of *pravṛtti* (Sutras 1.35-36) (the yogi gains) the knowledge of (things that are fine) subtle, hidden or distant.

BAILEY

III.25 Perfectly concentrated meditation upon the awakened light will produce the consciousness of that which is subtle, hidden or remote.

DVIVEDI

III.25 The knowledge of the subtle, the obscure, and the remote, by contemplation on the inner light.

FEUERSTEIN

III.25 By focusing the flashing-forth of [those mental] activities [which are sorrowless and illuminating] [on any object] knowledge of the subtle, concealed and distant [aspects of those objects] [is gained].

HOUSTON

III.25 By projecting the brilliancy of the *pravṛtti*-finer activity (of *citta*), knowledge of the subtle, concealed, and distant.

JNANESHVARA

III.26 By directing the flash of inner light of higher sensory activity, knowledge of subtle objects, those hidden from view, and those very distant can be attained.

PRABHAVANANDA

III.26 By making samyama on the Inner Light, one obtains knowledge of what is subtle, hidden, or far distant.

PUROHIT

III.25 Concentrate on the inner Light; know the fine, the obscure, the remote.

SATCHIDANANDA

III.26 By samyama on the Light within, the knowledge of the subtle, hidden and remote is obtained. [Note: subtle as atoms, hidden as treasure, remote as far distant lands.]

SHEARER

III.25 By directing the inner light we can see what is subtle, hidden from view
or far away.

TAIMNI

III.26 Knowledge of the small, the hidden or the distant by directing the light of superphysical faculty.

VIVEKANANDA

III.26 Through samyama on the effulgent light (I.36) comes the knowledge of the fine, the obstructed and the remote.

III.27

भुवनज्ञानं सूर्ये संयमात् ॥ २७ ॥

bhuvana-jñānaṃ sūrye saṃyamāt

भुवन - √भू *bhu: to become*	bhuvana-	(of) worlds; universe; planes of existence
ज्ञानं √ज्ञा *jñā: to know*	jñānaṃ	knowledge
सूर्ये स्वर् *svar: heaven*	sūrye	[*on*] the sun
संयमात् सम् - *sam-: together with, completely, perfectly* + √यम् *yam: restrain*	saṃ-yamāt	[*due to/through*] three-fold focus/synthesis: simultaneous dhāraṇā, dhyāna, samādhi; complete restraint (from distraction) with control

ARYA

III.27 Through concentration on the sun the knowledge of worlds (accrues).

BAILEY

III.26 Through meditation, one-pointedly fixed upon the sun, will come a consciousness (or knowledge) of the seven worlds.

DVIVEDI

III.26 By *Samyama* on the sun, the knowledge of space.

FEUERSTEIN

III.26 Through constraint on the sun [he gains] knowledge of the world.

HOUSTON

III.26 By *sanyama* on the sun - knowledge of the worlds.

JNANESHVARA

III.27 By samyama on the inner sun, knowledge of the many subtle realms can be known.

PRABHAVANANDA

III.27 By making samyama on the sun, one gains knowledge of the cosmic spaces.

PUROHIT

III.26 Concentrate on the Sun; know the world.

SATCHIDANANDA

III.27 By making samyama on the sun, knowledge of the entire solar system is obtained.

SHEARER

III.26 From *sanyama* on the sun comes knowledge of the various realms of the universe.

TAIMNI

III.27 Knowledge of the Solar system by performing *Saṃyama* on the Sun.

VIVEKANANDA

III.27 Through samyama on the sun, (comes) the knowledge of the world.

III.28

चन्द्रे ताराव्यूहज्ञानम् ॥ २८ ॥

candre tārā-vyūha-jñānam

चन्द्रे	candre	[*on*] (the) moon
√चन्द् *cand: to shine*		
तारा -	tārā-	(of the) stars
√तॄ *tṝ: to cross over*		
व्यूह -	vyūha-	order; arrangement;
√व्यूह् *vyūh: to array*		formation; organization
ज्ञानम्	jñānam	knowledge
√ज्ञा *jñā: to know*		

ARYA

III.28 (By concentrating) on the moon the knowledge of the formations of stars is attained.

BAILEY

III.27 A knowledge of all lunar forms arises through one-pointed meditation upon the moon.

DVIVEDI

III.27 In the moon, the knowledge of the starry regions.

FEUERSTEIN

III.27 [Through constraint] on the moon, knowledge of the arrangement of the stars.

HOUSTON

III.27 On the moon - knowledge of the organization of the stars.

JNANESHVARA

III.28 By samyama on the moon, knowledge of the arrangement of the inner stars can be known.

PRABHAVANANDA

III.28 By making samyama on the moon, one gains knowledge of the arrangement of the stars.

PUROHIT

III.27 Concentrate on the Moon; know the planets.

SATCHIDANANDA

III.28 By samyama on the moon comes knowledge of the stars' arrangement.

SHEARER

III.27 From *sanyama* on the moon comes knowledge of the arrangement of the stars.

TAIMNI

III.28 (By performing *Saṃyama*) on the moon, knowledge concerning the arrangement of the stars.

VIVEKANANDA

III.28 On the moon, knowledge of the cluster of stars.

III.29

ध्रुवे तद्गतिज्ञानम् ॥ २९॥

dhruve tad-gati-jñānam

ध्रुवे	dhruve	[*on*] (the) pole star	
√धृ dhṛ: to hold			
तद्गति -	tadgati-		
तद् -	tad-	their	their (stars)
गति -	gati-	movements;	movements
√गम् gam: to go		motion; flow	
ज्ञानम्	jñānam	knowledge	
√ज्ञा jñā: to know			

ARYA

III.29 (By concentrating) on the polar star (one gains) the knowledge of movement of those (stars).

BAILEY

III.28 Concentration upon the Pole Star will give knowledge of the orbits of the planets and the stars.

DVIVEDI

III.28 In the pole-star, knowledge of their motions.

FEUERSTEIN

III.28 [Through constraint] on the pole-star, knowledge of their movement.

HOUSTON

III.28 On the pole star - knowledge of their motion.

JNANESHVARA

III.29 By samyama on the pole-star, knowledge of the movement of those stars can be known.

PRABHAVANANDA

III.29 By making samyama on the polestar, one gains knowledge of the actions of the stars.

PUROHIT

III.28 Concentrate on the pole-star; know the motions of the stars.

SATCHIDANANDA

III.29 By samyama on the pole star, comes the knowledge of the stars' movements.

SHEARER

III.28 From *sanyama* on the pole star, comes knowledge of their motion.

TAIMNI

III.29 (By performing *Saṃyama*) on the pole-star knowledge of their movements.

VIVEKANANDA

III.29 On the pole-star, knowledge of the motions of the stars.

III.30

नाभिचक्रे कायव्यूहज्ञानम् ॥ ३० ॥

nābhi-cakre kāya-vyūha-jñānam

नाभिचक्रे	nābhi-cakre	[*upon*] (the) navel center/cakra/plexus
नाभ् nābh: aperture + √चर् car: to move		
काय -	kāya-	(of) body; anatomy
व्यूह -	vyūha-	organization; function; formation; order; arrangement
√व्यूह् vyūh: to array		
ज्ञानम्	jñānam	knowledge
√ज्ञा jñā: to know		

ARYA

III.30 (By concentrating) on the navel center (one gains) the knowledge of anatomy.

BAILEY

III.29 By concentrated attention upon the centre called the solar plexus, comes perfected knowledge as to the condition of the body.

DVIVEDI

III.29 In the navel-circle, the knowledge of the arrangement of the body.

FEUERSTEIN

III.29 [Through constraint] on the 'navel wheel', knowledge of the organisation of the body.

HOUSTON

III.29 On the navel chakra - knowledge of the organization of the body.

JNANESHVARA

III.30 By samyama on the navel center, knowledge of the arrangement of the systems of the body can be known.

PRABHAVANANDA

III.30 By making samyama on the navel, one gains knowledge of the constitution of the body.

PUROHIT

III.29 Concentrate on the navel; know the organism of the body.

SATCHIDANANDA

III.30 By samyama on the navel plexus, knowledge of the body's constitution is obtained.

SHEARER

III.29 *Sanyama* on the navel centre brings knowledge of the bodily system.

TAIMNI

III.30 (By performing *Saṃyama*) on the navel centre, knowledge of the organization of the body.

VIVEKANANDA

III.30 [Through samyama] on the navel circle [comes] knowledge of the constitution of the body.

III.31

कण्ठकूपे क्षुत्पिपासानिवृत्तिः ॥ ३१ ॥

kaṇṭha-kūpe kṣut-pipāsā-nivṛttiḥ

कण्ठकूपे	kaṇṭhakūpe		
कण्ठ -	kaṇṭha-	throat	[*on*] the pit/
कूपे	kūpe	well; pit	well of the throat
क्षुत् -	kṣut-	(of) hunger (and)	

√क्षुध् kṣudh: to be hungry

पिपासा -	pipāsā-	thirst

√पा pā: to drink

निवृत्तिः	nivṛttiḥ	cessation; turning off

नि - ni-: opposed to, downward motion + √वृत् vṛt: to whirl

ARYA

III.31 (By concentrating) in the pit of the throat hunger and thirst are turned off.

BAILEY

III.30 By fixing the attention upon the throat centre, the cessation of hunger and thirst will ensue.

DVIVEDI

III.30 In the pit of the throat, the cessation of hunger and thirst.

FEUERSTEIN

III.30 [Through constraint] on the 'throat well', the cessation of hunger and thirst.

HOUSTON

III.30 On the well of the throat - the ceasing of hunger and thirst.

JNANESHVARA

III.31 By samyama on the pit of the throat, hunger and thirst leave.

PRABHAVANANDA

III.31 By making samyama on the hollow of the throat, one stills hunger and thirst.

PUROHIT

III.30 Concentrate on the hollow of the throat; go beyond hunger and thirst.

SATCHIDANANDA

III.31 By samyama on the pit of the throat, cessation of hunger and thirst is achieved.

SHEARER

III.30 *Sanyama* on the hollow in the throat brings cessation of hunger and thirst.

TAIMNI

III.31 (By performing *Saṃyama*) on the gullet, the cessation of hunger and thirst.

VIVEKANANDA

III.31 On the hollow of the throat, cessation of hunger.

III.32

कूर्मनाड्यां स्थैर्यम् ॥ ३२ ॥

kūrma-nāḍyāṃ sthairyam

कूर्मनाड्यां	kūrmanāḍyāṃ		
कूर्म -	kūrma-	tortoise	[*upon*] (संयमः / saṃ-yamaḥ)
नाड्यां	nāḍyāṃ	[*on*] subtle duct/ channel	[*on*] the kūrma (tortoise) channel: subtle channel (in the chest below the throat pit in the shape of a tortoise)

स्थैर्यम् √स्था *sthā: to stand*	sthairyam	steadiness; motionlessness; immobility

ARYA

III.32 (By concentrating) on the *kūrma* channel, steadiness (is accomplished).

BAILEY

III.31 By fixing the attention upon the tube or nerve below the throat centre, equilibrium is achieved.

DVIVEDI

III.31 In the *Kurma-nādi*, steadiness.

FEUERSTEIN

III.31 [Through constraint] on the 'tortoise duct', steadiness.

HOUSTON

III.31 On the tortoise duct (tortoise), steadiness.

JNANESHVARA

III.32 By samyama on the tortoise channel, below the throat, steadiness is attained.

PRABHAVANANDA

III.32 By making samyama on the tube within the chest, one acquires absolute motionlessness.

PUROHIT

III.31 Concentrate on the nerve called Koorma; attain steadiness.

SATCHIDANANDA

III.32 By samyama on the kurma nadi (a subtle tortoise-shaped tube located below the throat), motionlessness in the meditative posture is achieved.

SHEARER

III.31 *Sanyama* on the *kūrma* nerve brings steadiness.

TAIMNI

III.32 By performing *Saṃyama*) on the *Kūrma*-nāḍ*i*, steadiness.

VIVEKANANDA

III.32 On the nerve called kurma, fixity of the body.

III.33

मूर्धज्योतिषि सिद्धदर्शनम् ॥ ३३ ॥

mūrdha-jyotiṣi siddha-darśanam

मूर्ध -	mūrdha-	(of) (crown of) head
√मूर् *mūr: to become solid*		
ज्योतिषि	jyotiṣi	[*on*] light
√ज्युत् *jyut: to shine*		
सिद्ध -	siddha-	(of) masters; adepts;
√सिध् *sidh: to succeed*		perfected ones
दर्शनम्	darśanam	vision; seeing

दर्शन darśana-: viewpoint, perception, philosophy (from √दृश् dṛś: to see)

ARYA

III.33 (By concentrating) on the light (in the fontanella part) of the head (one has) the vision of siddhas (masters).

BAILEY

III.32 Those who have attained self-mastery can be seen and contacted through focusing the light in the head. This power is developed in one-pointed meditation.

DVIVEDI

III.32 In the light in the head, the sight of the *siddhas*.

FEUERSTEIN

III.32 [Through constraint] on the light in the head, vision of the perfected ones.

HOUSTON

III.32 On the light in the top of the head - vision of the perfected ones.

JNANESHVARA

III.33 By samyama on the coronal light of the head, visions of the siddhas, the masters can come.

PRABHAVANANDA

III.33 By making samyama on the radiance within the back of the head, one becomes able to see the celestial beings.

PUROHIT

III.32 Concentrate on the Light in the head; meet the Masters.

SATCHIDANANDA

III.33 By samyama on the light at the crown of the head (sahasrara chakra), visions of masters and adepts are obtained.

SHEARER

III.32 From *sanyama* on the light in the head, we see the perfected ones.

TAIMNI

III.33 (By performing S*aṃyama* on) the light under the crown of the head, vision of perfected beings.

VIVEKANANDA

III.33 On the light emanating from the top of the head, sight of the siddhas.

III.34

प्रातिभाद्वा सर्वम् ॥ ३४ ॥

prātibhād vā sarvam

प्रातिभात्	prātibhāt	[*because of/due to/from/through*]
प्र - *pra-: forward, in front* + अति - *ati-: towards* + √भा *bhā: to shine*		intuitive flash/flash of illumination/ spontaneous intuitive insight or vision/ spontaneous enlightenment/ supra-sensory perception
वा	vā	or
सर्वम्	sarvam	all/everything; here: knowledge

ARYA

III.34 Or every (power may be gained) through an intuitive flash.

BAILEY

III.33 All things can be known in the vivid light of the intuition.

DVIVEDI

III.33 Or everything from the result of *pratibhā*.

FEUERSTEIN

III.33 Or through a flash-of-illumination [the *yogin* acquires knowledge of] all.

HOUSTON

III.33 From *prātibha*- the flash of illumination, all knowledge.

JNANESHVARA

III.34 Or, through the intuitive light of higher knowledge, anything might become known.

PRABHAVANANDA

III.34 All these powers of knowledge may also come to one whose mind is spontaneously enlightened through purity.

PUROHIT

III.33 Concentrate on intelligence; know everything.

SATCHIDANANDA

III.34 Or, in the knowledge that dawns by spontaneous enlightenment [through a life of purity], all the powers come by themselves.

SHEARER

III.33 By the clarity of intuitive perception everything can be known.

TAIMNI

III.34 (Knowledge of) everything from intuition.

VIVEKANANDA

III.34 Or by the power of pratibhā [comes] all knowledge.

III.35

हृदये चित्तसंवित् ॥ ३५ ॥

hṛdaye citta-saṃvit

हृदये	hṛdaye	[*in*/*on*] the heart
चित्त -	citta-	(of) energy field called mind
√चित् *cit: to perceive; to be bright*		in all aspects; mind-field; field of consciousness; consciousness; mind-stuff
संवित्	saṃvit	understanding; full knowledge
सम् - *sam-: fully, greatly, completely* + √विद् *vid: to know*		and awareness

ARYA

III.35 (By concentrating) in the heart an understanding of the (one's own and of others') minds (is gained).

BAILEY

III.34 Understanding of the mind-consciousness comes from one-pointed meditation upon the heart centre.

DVIVEDI

III.34 In the heart, knowledge of mind.

FEUERSTEIN

III.34 [Through constraint] on the heart [he gains] understanding of [the nature of] consciousness.

HOUSTON

III.34 On the heart - full knowledge of *citta*-the field.

JNANESHVARA

III.35 By practicing samyama on the heart, knowledge of the mind is attained.

PRABHAVANANDA

III.35 By making samyama on the heart, one gains knowledge of the contents of the mind.

PUROHIT

III.34 Concentrate on the heart; know every mind.

SATCHIDANANDA

III.35 By samyama on the heart, the knowledge of the mind-stuff is obtained.

SHEARER

III.34 From *sanyama* on the heart comes awareness of pure mind.

TAIMNI

III.35 (By performing *Saṃyama*) on the heart, awareness of the nature of the mind.

VIVEKANANDA

III.35 [Through samyama] on the heart [comes] knowledge of minds.

III.36 सत्त्वपुरुषयोरत्यन्तासङ्कीर्णयोः प्रत्ययाविशेषो भोगः परार्थात् स्वार्थसंयमात् पुरुषज्ञानम् ॥ ३६ ॥

sattva-puruṣayor atyantāsaṅkīrṇayoḥ pratyayāviśeṣo bhogaḥ
parārthāt svārtha-saṃyamāt puruṣa-jñānam

सत्त्व -	sattva-	(mental personalities') purity; buddhi; intellect; primary guṇa constituent: brightness; clarity	[*of*] non-distinction between mental personality and the
पुरुषयोः	puruṣayoḥ	Consciousness Principles'	Consciousness
अत्यन्त -	atyanta-	totally; absolutely	Principle
असङ्कीर्णयोः	a-saṅkīrṇayoḥ	separate, different; distinct	(which are, in fact)

अ - a-: un-/non-/not/without + सम् - sam-: together with + √कॄ kṝ: to scatter — totally separate

प्रत्यय -	pratyaya-	content of mind-field; presented-idea; cognition principle; cognition; causal/awareness principle; awareness perceiving (through the mind); buddhi; discriminatory intelligence; *immediate arising thought directed to an object—Houston*

प्रति - prati-: towards, in direction of + √इ i: to go

अविशेषः	a-viśeṣaḥ	non-distinction
भोगः	bhogaḥ	(are called) experience
परार्थात्	parārthāt	
पर -	para- another	[*because of*] what is the object of the other; for another's interest;
अर्थात्	arthāt purpose	distinct from the purpose (of another)
स्वार्थ -	svārtha-	what is (the Consciousness Principle's) own awareness/purpose
संयमात्	saṃyamāt	[*due to/through*] three-fold synthetic focus
पुरुष -	puruṣa-	(of) Conscious Principle
ज्ञानम्	jñānam	knowledge

ARYA

III.36 When there is (a conception of) non-distinction between the mental personality and the Conscious Principle, (which are, in fact) totally distinct (and not at all commingling, that is called) experience. Through concentration on what is the object of the other (the mental personality) and, separate from that, what is the awareness of the Conscious Principle itself, there arises the realisation of the Conscious Principle.

BAILEY

III.35 Experience (of the pairs of opposites) comes from the inability of the soul to distinguish between the personal self and the purusa (or spirit). The objective forms exist for the use (and experience) of the spiritual man. By meditation upon this, arises the intuitive perception of the spiritual nature (the purusa).

DVIVEDI

III.35 Experience is the *Indistinctness of the mild* conception of *sattva* and *puruśa* which are absolutely apart; this enjoyment being for another, of *puruśa* arises from *samyama* on himself.

FEUERSTEIN

III.35 Experience is a presented-idea [which is based on] the non-distinction between the absolutely unblended Self and *sattva*. Through constraint on the [Self's] own-purposive [of Nature], knowledge of the Self [is obtained].

HOUSTON

III.35 Experience is a *pratyaya* which does not distinguish *sattva* (*guṇa* of brightness, a primary constituent of matter) and *puruśa*-the self as absolutely unmixed. By *sanyama* on what exists for its own sake (*puruṣa*) distinct from that (*sattva*) which exists for the other -the knowledge of *puruṣa*.

JNANESHVARA

III.36 The having of experiences comes from a presented idea only when there is a commingling of the subtlest aspect of mind (sattva) and pure consciousness (purusha), which are really quite different. Samyama on the pure consciousness, which is distinct from the subtlest aspect of mind, reveals knowledge of that pure consciousness.

PRABHAVANANDA

III.36 The power of enjoyment arises from a failure to discriminate between the Atman and the sattwa guna, which are totally different. The sattwa guna is merely an agent of the Atman, which is independent, existing only for its own sake. By making samyama on the independence of the Atman, one gains knowledge of the Atman.

PUROHIT

III.35 Sensation is the result of the identification of Self and the intellect; they radically differ from each other, the latter serving the cause of the former; concentrate on the real Self; know that Self.

SATCHIDANANDA

III.36 The intellect and the Purusha (or Atman) are are totally different, the intellect existing for the sake of the Purusha, while the Purusha exists for its own sake. Not distinguishing this is the cause of all experiences;
and by samyama on the distinction, knowledge of the Purusha is obtained.

SHEARER

III.35 The Self and the contents of the mind are completely separate. Our usual experience, which is directed to outer fulfilment, fails to distinguish between them. *Sanyama* on inner fulfilment brings knowledge of the Self.

TAIMNI

III.36 Experience is the result of inability to distinguish between the *Puruṣa* and the *Sattva* though they are absolutely distinct. Knowledge of the *Puruṣa* results from *Saṃyama* on the Self-interest (of the *Puruṣa*) apart from another's interest (of *Prakṛti*).

VIVEKANANDA

III.36 Enjoyment comes through the non-discrimination of the Soul and sattva (buddhi) which are totally different. This enjoyment is for the sake of the Soul. There is another state of the sattva, called svārtha (its own pure state). The practice of samyama on this state gives the knowledge of the Purusha.

III.37

ततः प्रातिभश्रावणवेदनादर्शास्वादवार्त्ता जायन्ते ॥ ३७ ॥

tataḥ prātibha-śrāvaṇa-vedanādarśāsvāda-vārttā jāyante

ततः	tataḥ	[*by*] through that; thence
प्रातिभ - *प्र - pra-: forward, in front + अति - ati-: towards + √भा bhā: to shine*	prātibha-	(through) intuitive flashes; flashes of illumination; spontaneous intuitive insights/visions; spontaneous enlightenments; supra-sensory perceptions
श्रावण - *√श्रु śru: to hear*	śrāvaṇa-	auditory: clairaudience
वेदन - *√विद् vid: to know*	vedana-	tactile sensations: supra-tactile
आदर्श - *आ - ā-: from all sides, all around + √दृश् dṛs: to see*	ādarśa-	visual: clairvoyance
आस्वाद - *आ - ā-: from all sides, all around + √स्वाद् svād: to taste*	āsvāda-	flavours: supra-gustatory
वार्त्ताः *√वृत् vṛt: to stir*	vārttāḥ	fragrances: olfactory; supra-olfactory
जायन्ते *√जन् jan: to beget*	jāyante	are born/emerge/develop/arise/ occur

ARYA

III.37 Through that (concentration, Sutra 35) intuitive, auditory, tactile, visual, flavour related and olfactory (powers) develop.

BAILEY

III.36 As the result of this experience and meditation, the higher hearing, touch, sight, taste and smell are developed, producing intuitional knowledge.

DVIVEDI

III.36 Thence is produced intuitional (cognition of) sound, touch, sight, taste and smell.

FEUERSTEIN

III.36 Thence occur flashes-of illumination [in the sensory areas of] hearing, sensing, sight, taste and smell.

HOUSTON

III.36 From that arise *prātibha*- the flash of illumination, suprasensory hearing, feeling, seeing, tasting, smelling and intelligence.

JNANESHVARA

III.37 From the light of the higher knowledge of that pure consciousness or purusha (III.36) arises higher, transcendental, or divine hearing, touch, vision, taste, and smell.

PRABHAVANANDA

III.37 Hence, one gains the knowledge due to spontaneous enlightenment, and obtains supernatural powers of hearing, touch, sight, taste and smell.

PUROHIT

III.36 Then follows enlightenment; the sublimation of the sense of sight, smell, touch, taste, and hearing.

SATCHIDANANDA

III.37 From this knowledge arises superphysical hearing, touching, seeing, tasting and smelling through spontaneous intuition.

SHEARER

III.36 From this are born intuitive clarity and finest finest hearing, finest touch, finest sight, finest taste, and finest smell.

TAIMNI

III.37 Thence are produced intuitional hearing, touch, sight, taste and smell.

VIVEKANANDA

III.37 From that arises the knowledge of [supernatural] hearing, touching, seeing, tasting and smelling which belng to pratibhā.

III.38

ते समाधावुपसर्गा व्युत्थाने सिद्धयः ॥ ३८ ॥

te samādhāv upasargā vyutthāne siddhayaḥ

ते	te	they; here: siddhis
समाधौ *सम्- sam-: together with, completely, perfectly +* *आ- ā-: near to, all around + √धा dhā: to put*	samādhau	[*upon*/*in*] samādhi: meditation; contemplation; meta-cognitive absorption with various stages
उपसर्गाः *उप- upa-: down, under + √सृज् sṛj: to emit*	upasargāḥ	obstacles
व्युत्थाने *वि- vi-: apart, separate from + उद्- ud-: up, upwards +* *√स्था sthā: to stand*	vyutthāne	[*in*] externalized state of lower consciousness; [*in*] worldly pursuit; external emergence; outgoing; rising; waking state
सिद्धयः *√सिध् sidh: to succeed*	siddhayaḥ	esoteric powers/accomplishments/attainments/achievements/perfections; mastery

ARYA

III.38 They are obstacles in (the way of) samādhi, (though) accomplishments in lower consciousness.

BAILEY

III.37 These powers are obstacles to the highest spiritual realisation, but serve as magical powers in the objective worlds.

DVIVEDI

III.37 These are obstacles in the way of *Samādhi*; and are powers in moments of suspension.

FEUERSTEIN

III.37 These are obstacles to enstacy [but] attainments in the waking-state.

HOUSTON

III.37 These *siddhi*-attainments in the externalized state are obstacles in reference to *samādhi*-cognitive absorption (*nirbīja*-seedless).

JNANESHVARA

III.38 These experiences resulting from samyama are obstacles to samadhi, but appear to be attainments or powers to the outgoing or worldly mind.

PRABHAVANANDA

III.38 They are powers in the worldly state, but they are obstacles to samadhi.

PUROHIT

III.37 These powers of knowledge are obstacles to illumination; but illumination apart, they bring success.

SATCHIDANANDA

III.38 These [superphysical senses] are obstacles to [nirbija] samadhi but are siddhis (powers or accomplishments in the worldly pursuits.

SHEARER

III.37 These are subordinate to the state of pure unboundedness, but are the perfections of a mind still operating on the subtle level.

TAIMNI

III.38 They are obstacles in the way of *Samādhi* and powers when the mind is outward-turned.

VIVEKANANDA

III.38 These are obstacles to samadhi; but they are powers in the worldly state.

III.39

बन्धकारणशैथिल्यात् प्रचारसंवेदनाच्च चित्तस्य परशरीरावेशः ॥ ३९॥

bandha-kāraṇa-śaithilyāt pracāra-saṃvedanāc ca cittasya para-śarīrāveśaḥ

बन्ध - *√बन्ध् bandh: to bind*	bandha-	bondage; attachment: binding; fixing; confining; concentrating on
कारण - *√कृ kṛ: to do*	kāraṇa-	cause
शैथिल्यात् *√शिथिल śithila: loose*	śaithilyāt	[*by/due to*] loosening; relaxation; let-go
प्रचार - *प्र - pra-: forward, onward, forth + √चर् car: to move*	pracāra-	circulation; passages; channels; going forth
संवेदनात् *सम् - sam-: fully, completely, perfectly + √विद् vid: to know*	saṃvedanāt	[*through*] awareness; knowledge of; [*due to*] experience
च	ca	and
चित्तस्य *√चित् cit: perceive; be bright*	cittasya	[*of*] the mind's field; mind-field's; all aspects [*possessed by*] energy field called mind
पर -	para-	(into) other/another's
शरीर - *√श्री śrī: to support*	śarīra-	body
आवेशः *आ - ā-: near to, from all sides + √विश् viś: to enter*	āveśaḥ	entry; entrance; possession

ARYA

III.39 By loosening the cause of bondage and learning the (paths of) circulation (of mental energy) (the yogi learns to) enter and take possession of another body.

BAILEY

III.38 By liberation from the causes of bondage through their weakening and by an understanding of the mode of transference (withdrawal or entrance), the mind stuff (or chitta) can enter another body.

DVIVEDI

III.38 The mind enters another body, by relaxation of the cause of bondage and by knowledge of the method of passing.

FEUERSTEIN

III.38 Through the relaxation of the causes of attachment [to one's body] and through the experience of going-forth, consciousness [is capable of] entering another body.

HOUSTON

III.38 By the relaxation of the cause of relationship (to the body), and the experience of going forth, *citta*'s entry into another body.

JNANESHVARA

III.39 By loosening or letting go of the causes of bondage and attachment, and by following the knowledge of how to go forth into the passages of the mind, there comes the ability to enter into another body.

PRABHAVANANDA

III.39 When the bonds of the mind caused by karma have been loosened, the yogi can enter into the body of another by knowledge of the operation of its nerve currents.

PUROHIT

III.38 When the cause of bondage is removed, the yogi can by knowledge of the nervous system, concentrate his mind upon the body of another and enter into it.

SATCHIDANANDA

III.39 By the loosening of the cause [of the bondage of mind to body] and by knowledge of the procedure of the mind-stuff's functioning, entering another's body is accomplished.

SHEARER

III.38 When attachment to the body is loosened and there is perfect knowledge of the movement of the mind, the ability to enter another's body is gained.

TAIMNI

III.39 The mind can enter another's body on relaxation of the cause of bondage and from knowledge of passages.

VIVEKANANDA

III.39 When the cause of bondage has become loosened, the yogi, by his knowledge of its channels of activity of the chitta, enters another's body.

III.40

उदानजयाज्जलपङ्ककण्टकादिष्वसङ्ग उत्क्रान्तिश्च ॥ ४० ॥

udāna-jayāj jala-paṅka-kaṇṭakādiṣvasaṅga utkrāntiś ca

उदान -	udāna-	(of) udāna (up-breath)
उद् - ud-: upward + √अन् an: to breathe		
जयात्	jayāt	[*because of/through*] mastery/conquest
√जि ji: to win		
जल -	jala-	water
पङ्क -	paṅka-	mud; mire; swamp
कण्टक -	kaṇṭaka-	thorns and thorny branches
आदिषु -	ādiṣu-	and so forth; et cetera
असङ्गः	a-saṅgaḥ	unattached; not getting stuck
अ - a-: non-/un-/not + √सञ्ज् sañj: to adhere		
उत्क्रान्तिः	utkrāntiḥ	ascent; rising above; levitation
उद् - ud-: up, upwards + √क्रम् kram: to step		
च	ca	and

ARYA

III.40 By mastering udāna (the prāṇa force dwelling above the throat) one (is not sunk) in waters and mire (and does) not get stuck in thorny bushes and so forth. (If he does sink or gets stuck he has easy egress and masters death so as to) ascend (to higher levels).

BAILEY

III.39 By subjugation of the upward life (the udana) there is liberation from water, the thorny path, and mire, and the power of ascension is gained.

DVIVEDI

III.39 By mastery over *udāna*, ascension and non-contact with water, mud, thorns, etc.

FEUERSTEIN

III.39 Through mastery of the up-breath [the *yogin* gains the power of] non-adhesion to water, mud or thorns and [the power of] rising.

HOUSTON

III.39 Through mastery of *udāna* - non-contact, and rising above with regard to water, mud, thorns, etc.

JNANESHVARA

III.40 By the mastery over udana, the upward flowing prana vayu, there is a cessation of contact with mud, water, thorns, and other such objects, and there ensues the rising or levitation of the body.

PRABHAVANANDA

III.40 By controlling the nerve-currents that govern the lungs and the upper part of the body, the yogi can walk on water and swamps, or on thorns and similar objects, and he can die at will.

PUROHIT

III.39 By concentration on Udāna, living fire, the yogi remains unaffected in water, in swamps, or amid thorns; leaves his body at will.

SATCHIDANANDA

III.40 By mastery over the udana nerve current (the upward vital air), one accomplishes levitation over water, swamps, thorns, etc. and can leave the body at will.

SHEARER

III.39 On the mastery of *udāna*, the life breath which rises through the body, we can direct it upwards and avoid contact with such things as water, mud and thorns.

TAIMNI

III.40 By mastery over *Udāna*, levitation and non-contact with water, mire, thorns, etc.

VIVEKANANDA

III.40 When he has conquered the current called udāna the yogi does not sink in water or in swamps, he can walk on thorns and so forth, and can die at will.

III.41

समानजयाज्ज्वलनम् ॥ ४१ ॥

samāna-jayāj jvalanam

समान -	samāna-	(of) samāna (nerve current);
सम् - *sam-: fully, greatly, completely* + √अन् *an: to breathe*		mid-breath; prana moving up to navel center
जयात्	jayāt	[*through*] mastery
√जि *ji: to win*		
ज्वलनम्	jvalanam	radiance; brilliance; effulgence
√ज्वल् *jval: to blaze*		

ARYA

III.41 By conquest of samāna (prāṇa force dwelling in navel area)(the yogi attains) brilliance.

BAILEY

III.40 Through subjugation of the samana, the spark becomes the flame.

DVIVEDI

III.40 Effulgence by mastery over *Samāna*.

FEUERSTEIN

III.40 Through mastery of the mid-breath [he acquires] effulgence.

HOUSTON

III.40 Through mastery of *samāna* - radiance.

JNANESHVARA

III.41 By mastery over samana, the prana flowing in the navel area, there comes effulgence, radiance, or fire.

PRABHAVANANDA

III.41 By controlling the force which governs the prana, he can surround himself with a blaze of light.

PUROHIT

III.40 By concentrating on the Samāna, living fire, the yogi creates a halo of light about him.

SATCHIDANANDA

III.41 By mastery over the samana nerve current (the equalizing vital air) comes radiance to surround the body.

SHEARER

III.40 On mastery of *samāna*, the life breath which nourishes the body, the body shines with radiant light.

TAIMNI

III.41 By mastery over *Samāna*, blazing of the gastric fire.

VIVEKANANDA

III.41 Through the conquest of the current samāna he is surrounded by a blaze of light.

III.42

श्रोत्राकाशयोः सम्बन्धसंयमाद्दिव्यं श्रोत्रम् ॥ ४२ ॥

śrotrākāśayoḥ sambandha-saṃyamād divyaṃ śrotram

श्रोत्र -	śrotra-	[*in*] ear/[*upon*] hearing
√श्रु śru: to hear		
आकाशयोः	ākāśayoḥ	[*upon*] ether; space (between)
आ - ā-: near to; towards + √काश् kāś: to be visible		
सम्बन्ध -	sambandha-	(on) relationship/interrelationship
सम् - sam-: complete, fully, completely + √बन्ध् bandh: to bind		
संयमात्	saṃyamāt	[*due to/through*] three-fold focus/synthesis: simultaneous dhāranā, dhyāna, samādhi; *perfect regulation of citta—Houston*
सम् - sam-: together with, completely, perfectly + √यम् yam: to restrain		
दिव्यं	divyaṃ	celestial; divine
√दिव् div: to radiate		
श्रोत्रम्	śrotram	ear/hearing
√श्रु śru: to hear		

ARYA

III.42 Through concentration on the relation between ear and space (one gains an) ear (that hears) celestial (sounds).

BAILEY

III.41 By means of one-pointed meditation upon the relationship between the akasha and sound, an organ for spiritual hearing will be developed.

DVIVEDI

III.41 By *Samyama* on the relation between *ākāśa* and the sense of hearing, (arises) supernatural audition.

FEUERSTEIN

III.41 Through constraint on the relation between ear and ether [he acquires] the divine ear.

HOUSTON

III.41 By *sanyama* on the interrelation between hearing and *ākāśa*-space/ether - divine hearing.

JNANESHVARA

III.42 By samyama over the relation between space and the power of hearing, the higher, divine power of hearing comes.

PRABHAVANANDA

III.42 By making samyama on the relation between the ear and the ether, one obtains supernatural powers of hearing.

PUROHIT

III.41 By concentrating on the relation between air and ear, the yogi hears the divine message.

SATCHIDANANDA

III.42 By samyama on the relationship between ear and ether, supernormal hearing becomes possible.

SHEARER

III.41 From *sanyama* on the relationship of hearing and *ākāsha*, celestial hearing is gained.

TAIMNI

III.42 By performing *Saṃyama* on the relation between *Ākāśa* and the ear, superphysical hearing.

VIVEKANANDA

III.42 Through samyama on the relation between the ear and the ākāśa comes divine hearing.

III.43

कायाकाशयोः सम्बन्धसंयमाल्लघुतूलसमापत्तेश्चाकाशगमनम् ॥ ४३ ॥

kāyākāśayoḥ sambandha-saṃyamāl laghu-tūla-samāpatteś cākāśa-gamanam

काय -	kāya-	(of) body (and)
आकाशयोः	ākāśayoḥ	[*on*] ākāśa: space; ether

आ - ā-: near to; towards + √काश् kāś: to be visible

सम्बन्ध -	sambandha-	(on) relationship
संयमात्	saṃyamāt	[*through*] three-fold synthetic focus

सम् - sam-: together with, completely, perfectly + √यम् yam: to restrain

लघु -	laghu-	(of) light
तूल -	tūla-	cotton fiber
समापत्तेः	samāpatteḥ	[*by/from/due to*] attaining the state

सम् - sam-: together with + आ - ā-: towards, near to + √पत् pat: to fall

च -	ca-	and
आकाश -	ākāśa-	[*through*] space; ether; sky
गमनम्	gamanam	traveling; traversing

√गम् gam: to go

ARYA

III.43 By concentration on the relationship of body and space, (consequently) through attaining the state of (becoming like) light cotton (one gains facility to) travel through the sky.

BAILEY

III.42 By one-pointed meditation upon the relationship existing between the body and the akasha, ascension out of matter (the three worlds) and power to travel in space is gained.

DVIVEDI

III.42 By *Samyama* on the relation between the body and *ākāśa*, as also by being identified with light (things like) cotton, (there follows) passage through space.

FEUERSTEIN

III.42 Through constraint on the relation between body and ether and through the coincidence [of consciousness] with light [objects], such as cotton, [he obtains the power of] traversing the ether.

HOUSTON

III.42 By *sanyama* on the relation between the body and *ākāśa*-space/ether, and *samāpatti*-cognitive blending with light objects like cotton - traversing *ākāśa*.

JNANESHVARA

III.43 By Samyama on the relationship between the body and space (akasha) and by concentrating on the lightness of cotton, passage through space can be attained.

PRABHAVANANDA

III.43 By making samyama on the relation between the body and the ether, or by acquiring through meditation the lightness of cotton fiber, the yogi can fly through the air.

PUROHIT

III.42 By concentrating on the relation between air and body, and identifying himself with light things like cotton wool, the yogi moves in the sky.

SATCHIDANANDA

III.43 By samyama on the relationship between the body and ether, lightness of cotton fibre is attained, and thus traveling through the ether becomes possible.

SHEARER

III.42 From *samyama* on the relationship between body and *ākāsha*, together with absorption in the lightness of cotton fibre, we can move through the air at will.

TAIMNI

III.43 By performing *Saṃyama* on the relation between the body and *Ākāśa* and at the same time bringing about coalescence of the mind with light (things like) cotton down, (there comes the power of) passage through space.

VIVEKANANDA

III.43 By practicing samyama on the relation between the ākāśa and the body and regrding himself to be as light as cotton wool and so forth, the Yogi can go through the skies.

III.44

बहिरकल्पिता वृत्तिर्महाविदेहा ततः प्रकाशावरणक्षयः ॥ ४४ ॥

bahir akalpitā vṛttir mahā-videhā tataḥ prakāśāvaraṇa-kṣayaḥ

बहिर् -	bahir-	outside; external
अकल्पिता	a-kalpitā	actual; real;
अ - a-: un-/non-/not/without + √क्लृप् kḷp: to befit		non-imaginary/unimagined; not active; unidentified with
वृत्तिः	vṛtti	mental state (is called)
वृत् vṛt: to whirl		

महाविदेहा	mahāvidehā		
महा -	mahā-	great	great incorporeality; great non-physicality; great bodilessness
विदेहा	videhā	out-of-body state	
वि - vi-: apart, reverse to + √दिह् dih: to cover, smear + देह deha: body			

ततः	tataḥ	thereby; from that; thence
प्रकाश -	prakāśa-	light; illumination
प्र - pra-: forward, onward, away + √काश् kāś: to be visible		
आवरण -	āvaraṇa-	(of) veils/coverings
आ - ā-: near to, from all sides + √वृ vṛ: to cover		
क्षयः	kṣayaḥ	destroyed; dispersed
√क्षि kṣi: to destroy		

ARYA

III.44 The mental state (in which the mind does) not (go) out (of the body) is called mahā-videhā (and) thereby (there occurs) loss of veils on (inner) light.

BAILEY

III.43 When that which veils the light is done away with, then comes the state of being called discarnate (or disembodied), freed from the modification of the thinking principle. This is the state of illumination.

DVIVEDI

III.43 The external, unthought-of, transformation (of the mind) is the great incorporeal; hence the destruction of the covering of illumination.

FEUERSTEIN

III.43 An external, non-imaginary fluctuation [of consciousness] is the 'great incorporeal' from which [comes] the dwindlings of the coverings of the [inner] light.

HOUSTON

III.43 The non-imaginary (actual) external *vṛtti*-activity (defining *citta*) is the great out-of-body state. From that, the dispersing of the covering of light.

JNANESHVARA

III.44 When the formless thought patterns of mind are projected outside of the body, it is called maha-videha, a great disincarnate one. By samyama on that outward projection, the veil over the spiritual light is removed.

PRABHAVANANDA

III.44 By making samyama on the thought-waves of the mind when it is separated from the body—the state known as the Great Disincarnation—all coverings can be removed from the light of knowledge.

PUROHIT

III.43 By concentrating on the involuntary activity of mind, completely unconscious of the body, the veil that obscures light is drawn aside.

SATCHIDANANDA

III.44 By samyama on the thought waves unidentified by and external to the body [maha-videha, or the great bodilessness], the veil over the light of the Self is destroyed.

SHEARER

III.43 The operation of the mind outside the confines of the body is known as *mahāvidehā*—"the great state beyond the body."
This destroys the veil which covers the light of discrimination.

TAIMNI

III.44 The power of contacting the state of consciousness which is outside the intellect and is therefore inconceivable is called *Mahā-videhā*. From it is destroyed the covering of light.

VIVEKANANDA

III.44 Through samyama on the real modifications of the mind, outside the body, called great disembodied-ness, comes disappearance of the covering to light.

III.45

स्थूलस्वरूपसूक्ष्मान्वयार्थवत्त्वसंयमाद् भूतजयः ॥ ४५ ॥

sthūla-svarūpa-sūkṣmānvayārthavattva-saṃyamād bhūta-jayaḥ

स्थूल -	sthūla-	gross/coarse
स्वरूप -	svarūpa-	own/own nature/essential form
सूक्ष्म - √सिव् *siv: to sew*	sūkṣma-	subtle/fine
अन्वय - अनु - *anu-: following, after, behind* + √इ *i: to go*	anvaya-	composition; correlative; connection; interconnection; all-pervading state
अर्थवत्त्व - अर्थ् *arth: to intend* + √वत *vat: to surround or encompass* + -त्व *-tva: -ness*	arthavattva-	being effective to a purpose; serving a purpose; subservience to a purpose; purposeful-ness
संयमात् सम् - *sam-: together with, completely, perfectly* + √यम् *yam: to restrain*	saṃyamāt	[*due to/through*] three-fold focus/synthesis: simultaneous dhāranā, dhyāna, samādhi; *perfect regulation of citta—Houston*
भूत - √भू *bhū: to become*	bhūta-	(of) elements (subtle and gross)
जयः √जि *ji: to win*	jayaḥ	mastery

ARYA

III.45 By concentrating on the gross (form), nature, finer aspect (known as tan-mātrā), composition (as to the content of sattva, rajas and tamas in each) and their effectiveness to the purpose (of puruṣha, the Conscious Principle), one conquers the elements.

BAILEY

III.44 One-pointed meditation upon the five forms which every element takes, produces mastery over every element. These five forms are the gross nature, the elemental form, the quality, the pervasiveness and basic purpose.

DVIVEDI

III.44 Mastery over the elements, by *Samyama* on the gross, the constant, the subtle, the all-pervading and the fruition-bearing (in them).

FEUERSTEIN

III.44 Through constraint on the coarse, the own-form, the subtle, the connectedness and the purposiveness [of objects][the yogin gains] mastery over the elements.

HOUSTON

III.44 By *sanyama* on (their) gross state, *svarūpa*-essential nature, subtle state, interconnectedness and nature of serving a purpose - mastery of the *bhūta*-elements.

JNANESHVARA

III.45 By samyama on the five forms of the elements (bhutas), which are gross form, essence, subtleness, interconnectedness, and its purpose, then mastery over those bhutas is attained.

PRABHAVANANDA

III.45 By making samyama on the gross and subtle forms of the elements, on their essential characteristics and the inherence of the gunas in them, and on the experiences they provide for the individual, one gains mastery of the elements.

PUROHIT

III.44 By concentrating on the grossness, fineness, nature, relation, and purpose of elements, their conquest is attained.

SATCHIDANANDA

III.45 By samyama on the gross and subtle elements and on their essential nature, correlations and purpose, mastery over them is gained.

SHEARER

III.44 Mastery over the elements comes from *sanyama* on their forms—earth, water, fire, air and space; on their characteristics—mass, fluidity, heat, motion and omnipresence; on their essences—odor, flavor, form, texture and sound; on the relationship between forms, characteristics and essences and on evolutionary purpose.

TAIMNI

III.45 Mastery over Pañca-Bhūtas by performing Saṃyama on their gross, constant, subtle, all-pervading and functional states.

VIVEKANANDA

III.45 Through samyama on the gross and fine forms of the elements, their essential traits, the inherence of the gunas in them, and on their contributing to the experience of the Soul, comes mastery of the elements.

III.46

ततोऽणिमादिप्रादुर्भावः कायसम्पत् तद्धर्मानभिघातश्च ॥ ४६ ॥

tato 'ṇimādi-prādur-bhāvaḥ kāya-sampat tad-dharmānabhighātaś ca

ततः	tatah	then; thence
अणिम -	aṇima-	becoming minute; atomization
आदि -	ādi-	and so forth
प्रादुर्भावः प्र - *pra-: onward, away* + दुर् *dur: door* + √भू *bhū: to become*	prādurbhāvaḥ	development; attainment; manifestation; emergence; appearance
काय -	kāya-	physical body
सम्पत् सम् - *sam-: completely, fully, perfectly* + √पद् *pad: to fall*	sampat	excellence; perfection
तद्ः	tad-	its
धर्मा - √धृ *dhṛ: to hold*	dharma-	functions; constituents; attributes; characteristic forms
अनभिघातः अन् - *an-: not, non-, differing* + अभि - *abhi-: over, above, in addition* + √हन् *han: to strike*	an-abhighātaḥ	non-suppression; non-obstruction unafflicted; not being affected unhurt; unafflicted
च	ca	and

ARYA

III.46 Then there takes place the development of (eight siddhis) such as minuteness; excellence of body develops and its functions (are then) not affected (by anything).

BAILEY

III.45 Through this mastery, minuteness and siddhis (powers) are attained, likewise bodily perfection and freedom from all hindrances.

DVIVEDI

III.45 Then the attainment of *aṇimā* and others, as also of perfection of the body and the corresponding non-obstruction of its functions.

FEUERSTEIN

III.45 Thence [results] the manifestation [of the powers], such as atomisation et cetera., perfection of the body and the indestructibility of its constituents.

HOUSTON

III.45 From that, the emergence of such powers as becoming minute, etc., perfection of the body, and non-affliction by its constituents.

JNANESHVARA

III.46 Through that mastery over the elements, comes the abilities of making the body atomically small, perfect, and indestructible in its characteristics or components, as well as bringing other such powers.

PRABHAVANANDA

III.46 Hence one gains the power of becoming as tiny as an aton and all similar powers; also perfection of the body, which is no longer subject to the obstructions of the elements.

PUROHIT

III.45 Then follows the power to take any form, big or small; a sound body which nothing can destroy.

SATCHIDANANDA

III.46 From that comes attainment of anima and other siddhis, bodily perfection and non-obstruction of bodily functions by the influence of the elements. [Note: The eight major siddhis alluded to here are: anima (to become very small; mahima (to become very big); laghima (very light); garima (heavy); prapti (to reach anywhere); prakamya (to achieve all one's desires); isatva (ability to create anything); vasitva (ability to command and control everything)].

SHEARER

III.45 From mastery over the elements come the eight physical perfections: shrinking the body to the size of an atom, becoming very light, becoming very heavy, becoming very large, developing an irresistible will, controlling the elements, materializing objects and causing them to disappear, fulfilling all desires. In addition, the body becomes perfected and cannot be harmed in its own mortality.

TAIMNI

III.46 Thence, the attainment of Aṇimān etc., perfection of the body and the non-obstruction of its functions (of the body) by the powers (of the elements.

VIVEKANANDA

III.46 From that comes minuteness, and the rest of the powers, glorification of the body, and indestructibility of the bodily qualities.

III.47

रूपलावण्यबलवज्रसंहननत्वानि कायसम्पत् ॥ ४७ ॥

rūpa-lāvaṇya-bala-vajra-saṃhananatvāni kāya-sampat

रूप -	rūpa-	form; nature; here, also: handsomeness; beauty
लावण्य -	lāvaṇya-	charm; grace

√लू *lū: to cut*

बल -	bala-	strength
वज्र -	vajra-	diamond-like; adamantine

√वज् *vaj: to be strong*

संहननत्वानि	saṃhananatvāni	build; structure; texture (these are)

सम्- *sam-: fully, completely, perfectly* + √हन् *han: to strike* + -त्व *-tva: -ness*

काय -	kāya-	body
सम्पत्	sampat	excellence; perfection

सम्- *sam-: completely, fully, perfectly* + √पद् *pad: to fall*

ARYA

III.47 Excellence of body (means) handsomeness (of features), charm, strength and a diamond-like texture.

BAILEY

III.46 Symmetry of form, beauty of colour, strength and compactness of the diamond, constitute bodily perfection.

DVIVEDI

III.46 Beauty, gracefulness, strength, adamantine-hardness constitute perfection of the body.

FEUERSTEIN

III.46 Beauty, gracefulness and adamant robustness [constitute] the perfection of the body.

HOUSTON

III.46 Beauty, gracefulness, strength, and adamantine firmness is the perfection of the body.

JNANESHVARA

III.47 This perfection of the body includes beauty, gracefulness, strength, and adamantine hardness in taking the blows that come.

PRABHAVANANDA

III.47 Perfection of the body includes beauty, grace, strength and the hardness of a thunderbolt.

PUROHIT

III.46 Soundness of body means beauty, grace, strength, hardness like adamant.

SATCHIDANANDA

III.47 Beauty, grace, strength and adamantine hardness constitute bodily perfection.

SHEARER

III.46 The attributes of a perfected body are beauty, grace, strength and adamantine hardness.

TAIMNI

III.47 Beauty, fine complexion, strength, adamantine hardness constitute the perfection of the body.

VIVEKANANDA

III.47 "Glorification of the body" means beauty, complexion, strength, admantine hardness.

III.48

ग्रहणस्वरूपास्मितान्वयार्थवत्त्वसंयमादिन्द्रियजयः ॥ ४८ ॥

grahaṇa-svarūpāsmitānvayārtavattva-saṃyamād indriya-jayaḥ

ग्रहण - √ग्रह् *grah: to sieze*	grahaṇa-	[*upon*] apprehension/ cognition; power of cognition/ perception
स्वरूप -	svarūpa-	own/essential form/nature
अस्मिता - *अस्मि asmi: I am* + *ता tā: -ness*	asmitā-	"I-am"-ness
अन्वय - *अनु- anu-: following, after, behind* + √*इ i: to go*	anvaya-	composition; correlative; connection; interconnection; all-pervading state
अर्थवत्त्व - *अर्थ् arth: to intend* + √*वत् vat: to surround or encompass* + -*त्व -tva:-ness*	arthavattva-	being effective to a purpose; serving a purpose; significance; subservience to a purpose; purposefulness
संयमात् *सम्- sam-: together with, completely, perfectly* + √*यम् yam: to restrain*	saṃyamāt	[*due to/through*] three-fold focus/synthesis: simultaneous dhāranā, dhyāna, samādhi; *perfect regulation of citta—Houston*
इन्द्रिय - *इन्द्र indra: senses* + -*य -ya: -ness*	indriya-	senses/sense-organs
जयः √*जि ji: to win*	jayaḥ	(of) conquest; mastery

ARYA

III.48 (One attains the) conquest over senses by concentration on the (process of senses) grasping (their objects), nature, identification with "I am"-ness principle, their composition (as to sattva, rajas and tamas) and their effectiveness with regard to their purpose (to serve the Consciousness Principle by helping him with worldly experience and liberation therefrom).

BAILEY

III.47 Mastery over the senses is brought about through concentrated meditation upon their nature, peculiar attributes, senses, egoism, pervasiveness and useful purpose.

DVIVEDI

III.47 Mastery over the organs of sense by *samyama* on the power of cognition, nature, egoism, all-pervasiveness and fruition-giving capacity (of them).

FEUERSTEIN

III.47 Through constraint on the process-of-perception, the own-form, I-am-ness, connectedness and purposiveness [he gains] mastery over the sense-organs.

HOUSTON

III.47 By *sanyama* on (their) process of perception, *svarūpa*-essential nature, the sense of "I am", (their) interconnectedness and nature of serving a purpose, mastery of the *indriya*-sense organs.

JNANESHVARA

III.48 By samyama on the process of perception and action, essence, I-ness, connectedness, and purposefulness of senses and acts, mastery over those senses and acts (indriyas) is attained.

PRABHAVANANDA

III.48 By making samyama on the transformation that the sense-organs undergo when they contact objects, on the power of illumination of the sense-organs, on the ego-sense, on the gunas which constitute the organs, and on the experiences they provide for the individual, one gains mastery of the organs.

PUROHIT

III.47 By concentrating on the activity, nature, individuality, relation, purpose of every sense, their conquest is attained.

SATCHIDANANDA

III.48 By samyama on the power of perception and on the essential nature, correlation with the ego sense and purpose of the sense organs, mastery over them is gained.

SHEARER

III.47 Mastery over the senses is gained from *sanyama* on their power of perceiving; on the sense organs themselves; on the feeling of "I-ness" which sense perception creates; on the relationship between these aspects of the senses and on their evolutionary purpose.

TAIMNI

III.48 Mastery over the sense-organs by performing Saṃyama on their power of cognition, real nature, egoism, all-pervasiveness and functions.

VIVEKANANDA

III.48 Through samyama on the perception, by the organs, the knowledge that follows, the "I-consciousness" that accompanies this knowledge, the inherence of the gunas in all of these, and their contributing to the experience of the Soul comes the conquest of the organs.

III.49

ततो मनोजवित्वं विकरणभावः प्रधानजयश्च ॥ ४९ ॥

tato mano-javitvam vikaraṇa-bhāvaḥ pradhāna-jayaś ca

ततः	tataḥ	from that; thence	
मनोजवित्वं	manojavitvam		
मनः -	manaḥ-	mind	become swift or fleet like mind
√मन् *man: to think*			
जवित्वं	javitvam	swift; fleet	
जविन् *javin: quick, fleet* + -त्व *-tva: -ness*			
विकरणभावः	vikaraṇabhāvaḥ		clair-sentience: ability to function independent of the sense-organs
विकरण -	vikaraṇa-	beyond sense-organs	
वि - *vi-: apart, separate from* + √कृ *kṛ: to make*			
भावः	bhāvaḥ	state	
√भू *bhū: to become*			
प्रधानजयः	pradhānajayaḥ		
प्रधान -	pradhāna-	prakṛti: primary matter matrix material energy-field	mastery over material energy-field
प्र - *pra-: forth, forward, in front* + √धा *dhā: to put*			
जयः	jayaḥ	mastery; conquest	
च	ca	and	

ARYA

III.49 Then (the yogi attains the power of) being as speedy as mind, clairsentience (i.e., senses experiencing distant objects without the use of physical body) and conquest over the material energy-field.

BAILEY

III.48 As a result of this perfection, there comes rapidity of action like that of mind, perception independent of the organs, and mastery over root substance.

DVIVEDI

III.48 Thence fleetness (as of) mind, the being unobstructed by instruments and complete mastery over the *pradhāna.*

FEUERSTEIN

III.48 Thence [comes about] fleetness [as of the] mind, the state lacking sense-organs and the mastery over the matrix [of Nature].

HOUSTON

III.48 From that, the swiftness of the mind, the state of transcending the sense organs, and mastery over *pradhāna*-the primary matrix of matter (*prakṛti*).

JNANESHVARA

III.49 By that mastery over the senses and acts (indriyas), there comes quickness of mind, perception with the physical instruments of perception, and mastery over the primal cause out of which manifestation arises.

PRABHAVANANDA

III.49 Hence the body gains the power of movement as rapid as that of the mind, the power of using the sense-organs outside the confines of the body, and the mastery of Prakriti.

PUROHIT

III.48 Then the yogi moves with the speed of thought, causes sense to work without body, conquers nature.

SATCHIDANANDA

III.49 From that, the body gains the power to move as fast as the mind, ability to function without the aid of the sense organs and complete mastery over the primary cause (Prakriti).

SHEARER

III.48 As a result of this, the senses can move with the speed of thought and operate independently of the body. This is mastery over Nature.

TAIMNI

III.49 Thence, instantaneous cognition without the use of any vehicle and complete mastery over *Pradhāna.*

VIVEKANANDA

III.49 From that comes to the body the power of rapid movement like that of the mind, power of the organs independently of the body, and conquest of nature.

III.50

सत्त्वपुरुषान्यताख्यातिमात्रस्य सर्वभावाधिष्ठातृत्वं सर्वज्ञातृत्वं च ॥ ५० ॥

sattva-puruṣānyatā-khyāti-mātrasya sarva-bhāvādhiṣṭātṛtvaṃ sarva-jñātṛtvaṃ ca

सत्त्व -	sattva-	essential purity/brightness (in mental personality)	one who cognizes only the separateness of mental personality and the Consciousness Principle
√अस् *as: to be*			
पुरुष -	puruṣa-	Consciousness Principle; Self	
अन्यता -	anyatā-	separateness; distinction	
अन्य *anya: other*			
ख्यातिमात्रस्य	khyātimātrasya		

ख्याति -	khyāti-	vision's; identification's	[*of*] cognition's alone
√ख्या *khyā: to be known*			
मात्रस्य	mātrasya	only; merely	

सर्व -	sarva-	(over) all
भाव -	bhāva-	states of being; aspects (of) existence
√भू *bhū: to become*		
अधिष्ठातृत्वं	adhiṣṭātṛtvaṃ	authority; supremacy

अधि - adhi-: over, above + √स्था sthā: to stand + तृ tṛ: one who + -त्व -tva: -ness

सर्वज्ञातृत्वं — sarvajñātṛtvaṃ

सर्व -	sarva-	all	omniscient
ज्ञातृत्वं	jñātṛtvaṃ	knowing	
√ज्ञा *jñā: to know* + तृ *tṛ: one who* + -त्व *-tva: -ness*			

च	ca	and

ARYA

III.50 One who cognizes only separateness of mental personality and Consciousness Principle (thereby gains) authority over all aspects of existence, as well as omniscience.

BAILEY

III.49 The man who can discriminate between the soul and the spirit achieves supremacy over all conditions and becomes omniscient.

DVIVEDI

III.49 In him who is fixed upon the distinctive relation of *sattva* and *puruśa*, (arises) mastery over all things and the knowledge of all.

FEUERSTEIN

III.49 [The *yogin* who has] merely the vision of the distinction between the Self and the *sattva* [of consciousness] [gains] supremacy over all states [of existence] and omniscience.

HOUSTON

III.49 Of (that *citta*-field), having only the identification of the separateness of *sattva guṇa*, and *puruṣa*-self, there is supremacy over all states, and omniscience.

JNANESHVARA

III.50 To one well established in the knowledge of the distinction between the purest aspect of mind and consciousness itself, there comes supremacy over all forms or states of existence, as well as over all forms of knowing.

PRABHAVANANDA

III.50 By making samyama on the discrimination between the sattwa guna and the Atman, one gains omnipotence and omniscience.

PUROHIT

III.49 Once the yogi is convinced that Self and intellect are two, he masters the qualities, masters their results, knows everything.

SATCHIDANANDA

III.50 By recognition of the distinction between sattva (pure reflective nature) and the Self, supremacy over all states and forms of existence [omnipotence] is gained as is omniscience.

SHEARER

III.49 He who has realized the distinction between the subtlest level of his mind, which is translucent intellect, and the Self, enjoys supremacy over all creation. Nothing remains unknown to him.

TAIMNI

III.50 Only from the awareness of the distinction between *Sattva* and *Puruṣa* arise supremacy over all states and forms of existence (omnipotence) and knowledge of everything (omniscience).

VIVEKANANDA

III.50 Through samyama on the discrimination between the sattva and the Purusha come omnipotence and omniscience.

III.51

तद्वैराग्यादपि दोषबीजक्षये कैवल्यम् ॥ ५१ ॥

tad-vairāgyād api doṣa-bīja-kṣaye kaivalyam

तद् -	tad-	(of) that	[*through*] non-attachment about even that
वैराग्यात्	vairāgyāt	[*through*] dispassion; [*through*] non-attachment	
वै - *vai-: dis-* + रज् *raj: be attracted/excited*			
अपि	api	even	
दोष -	doṣa-	defilements; bondage; defects; impediments; impurities	[*upon*] the disappearance of the seed of impurity or bondage
√दुस् *duṣ: to be impaired*			
बीज -	bīja-	seed	
क्षये	kṣaye	[*upon*] loss; vanishing	
√क्षि *kṣi: to destroy*			
कैवल्यम्	kaivalyam	Transcendent Solitude; Isolated Unity; Liberation; Independence; Freedom; Absoluteness; Aloneness	
केवल *kevala: alone*			

ARYA

III.51 When (the yogi has developed) dispassion even about that (Sutra I.49) (and consequently) the (very) seeds of impurities vanish (the yogi attains final) absoluteness.

BAILEY

III.50 By a passionless attitude towards this attainment and towards all soul-powers, the one who is free from the seeds of bondage, attains the condition of isolated unity.

DVIVEDI

III.50 By non-attachment even thereto, follows *Kaivalya*, the seeds of bondage being destroyed.

FEUERSTEIN

III.50 Through dispassion towards even this [exalted vision], with the dwindling of the seeds of the defects [he achieves] the aloneness [of the power of seeing].

HOUSTON

III.50 Through *vairāgya*-non-attachment even to this (supremacy and omniscience), upon the disappearance of the seeds of the impediments (*kleśa*), there is *Kaivalya*-the aloneness (of the power of seeing-the seer).

JNANESHVARA

III.51 With non-attachment or desirelessness even for that supremacy over forms and states of existence and the omniscience (III.50), the seeds at the root of those bondages are destroyed, and absolute liberation is attained.

PRABHAVANANDA

III.51 By giving up even these powers, the seed of evil is destroyed and liberation follows.

PUROHIT

III.50 Finally, by renouncing even these powers, the seed of bondage being destroyed, the yogi attains liberation.

SATCHIDANANDA

III.51 By non-attachment even to that [all these siddhis], the seed of bondage is destroyed and thus follows Kaivalya (Independence).

SHEARER

III.50 And when he is unattached even to this state, the very seeds of bondage are destroyed, and Enlightenment follows.

TAIMNI

III.51 By non-attachment to even that, on the very seed of bondage being destroyed, follows *Kaivalya*.

VIVEKANANDA

III.51 Through giving up even these powers comes the destruction of the very seed of evil, and this leads to kaivalya.

III.52

स्थान्युपनिमन्त्रणे सङ्गस्मयाकरणं पुनरनिष्टप्रसङ्गात् ॥ ५२ ॥

sthāny-upanimantraṇe saṅga-smayākaraṇaṃ punar aniṣṭa-prasaṅgāt

स्थानि -	sthāni-	(of) high/well-placed
√स्था sthā: to stand		(as of celestial beings)
उपनिमन्त्रणे	upa-nimantraṇe	[*upon*] invitation; admiration
उप - upa-: towards, near to + -नि - -ni-: in, into, intensity + मन्त्रणम् mantraṇam (√मन् man: to think + त्र tra: protector)		
सङ्ग -	saṅga-	pleasure; attraction; attachment
√सञ्ज् sañj: to adhere		
स्मय -	smaya-	amazement; pride;
√स्मि smi: to smile		smile (as with pride) and self-wonder
अकरणं	a-karaṇaṃ	non-acceptance/rejection;
अ - a-: un-/non-/not/without + √कृ kṛ: to do		avoidance; no cause (for response)
पुनर् -	punar-	again; renewal
अनिष्ट -	aniṣṭa-	(of the) undesirable
अन् - an-: non-, absent, differing + √इष् iṣ: to desire		
प्रसङ्गात्	prasaṅgāt	[*because of/due to*] possibility/
प्र - pra-: forth, forward, onward + √सञ्ज् sañj: to adhere		inclination (leading to re-ensnarement/ recurrence/revival)

ARYA

III.52 Upon receiving invitations from celestial beings (that he should join them in enjoying celestial pleasures) (he should) not respond with attraction (to those invitations and pleasures) or self-amazement because (otherwise there is) possible (danger) of (his falling back) again into undesirable (lower attractions).

BAILEY

III.51 There should be entire rejection of all allurements from the forms of being, even celestial, for the recurrence of evil contacts remains possible.

DVIVEDI

III.51 (There should be) entire destruction of pleasure or pride in the invitations by the powers (of various places), for there is a possibility of a repetition of evil.

FEUERSTEIN

III.51 Upon the invitation of high-placed [beings], [he should give himself] no cause for attachment or pride, because of the renewed and undesired inclination [for lower levels of existence].

HOUSTON

III.51 Upon the invitation of the high-placed, (there should be) no cause for contact or pride because of the renewed, undesired inclination.

JNANESHVARA

III.52 When invited by the celestial beings, no cause should be allowed to arise in the mind that would allow either acceptance of the offer, or the smile of pride from receiving the invitation, because to allow such thoughts to arise again might create the possibility of repeating undesirable thoughts and actions.

PRABHAVANANDA

III.52 When tempted by the invisible beings in high places let the yogi feel neither allured nor flattered; for he is in danger of being caught once more by ignorance.

PUROHIT

III.51 The yogi should not be allured or wonderstruck by the courtship of celestial powers, lest he fall into the undesirable world again.

SATCHIDANANDA

III.52 The Yogi should neither accept nor smile with pride at the admiration of even the celestial beings, as there is the possibility of his getting caught again in the undesirable.

SHEARER

III.51 We should not respond with pleasure or pride to the alluring invitations of celestial beings, because this will obstruct progess, and it is always possible to fall.

TAIMNI

III.52 (There should be) avoidance of pleasure or pride on being invited by the super-physical entities in charge of various planes because there is the possibility of the revival of evil.

VIVEKANANDA

III.52 The yogi should not feel allured or flattered by the overtures of celestial beings, for fear of evil again.

III.53

क्षणतत्क्रमयोः संयमाद्विवेकजं ज्ञानम् ॥ ५३ ॥

kṣaṇa-tat-kramayoḥ saṃyamād vivekajaṃ jñānam

क्षण -	kṣaṇa-	[*upon*] moments (of time) (and)
√क्षन् kṣan: to break or √क्षद् kṣad: to divide		
तद् -	tad-	their
क्रमयोः	kramayoḥ	sequence; sequential progression
√क्रम् kram: to step/stride		
संयमात्	saṃyamāt	[*due to/through*] three-fold
सम् - sam-: together with, completely, perfectly +		focus/synthesis: simultaneous dhāranā,
√यम् yam: to restrain		dhyāna, samādhi;
		perfect regulation of citta—Houston

विवेकजं	vivekajaṃ		
विवेक -	viveka-	discernment	born of discriminating wisdom; discernment-born
जं	ja	born	awareness of reality
√जन् jan: to beget			

ज्ञानम्	jñānam	knowledge
√ज्ञा jña: to know		

ARYA

III.53 Through concentration on moments and their sequence (there arises) knowledge that comes from discriminating wisdom.

BAILEY

III.52 Intuitive knowledge is developed through the use of the discriminative faculty when there is one-pointed concentration upon moments and their continuous succession.

DVIVEDI

III.52 Discriminative knowledge from *Samyama* on moments and their order.

FEUERSTEIN

III.52 Through constraint on the moment [of time] and its sequence [he obtains] the gnosis of discernment.

HOUSTON

III.52 By *sanyama* on the *kṣaṇa*-moment and its *karma*-sequential progression - the knowledge born of *viveka*-discernment (between *sattva guṇa* and *Puruṣa*-the self).

JNANESHVARA

III.53 By samyama over the moments and their succession, there comes the higher knowledge that is born from discrimination.

PRABHAVANANDA

III.53 By making samyama on single moments and on their sequence in time, one gains discriminative knowledge.

PUROHIT

III.52 Concentration on the present moment, the moment gone, and the moment to come, brings enlightenment, the result of discrimination.

SATCHIDANANDA

III.53 By samyama on single moments in sequence comes discriminative knowledge.

SHEARER

III.52 From *sanyama* on moments and their succession, the finest discriminative knowledge is born.

TAIMNI

III.53 Knowledge born of awareness of Reality by performing *Saṃyama* on moment and (the process of) its succession.

VIVEKANANDA

III.53 Through samyama on a particle of time and that which preceeds and succeeds it comes discrimination.

III.54

जातिलक्षणदेशैरन्यतानवच्छेदात् तुल्ययोस्ततः प्रतिपत्तिः ॥ ५४ ॥

jāti-lakṣaṇa-deśair anyatānavacchedāt tulyayos tataḥ pratipattiḥ

जाति -	jāti-	[*by*] genus; species; class; category
√जन् *jan: to beget*		
लक्षण -	lakṣaṇa-	peculiarities of; particulars;
√लक्ष् *lakṣ: to observe*		characteristics; appearance; indication of potential
देशैः	deśaiḥ	[*by*] locus; place; position
√दिश् *diś: to point out*		

अन्यतानवच्छेदात् anyatānavacchedāt

अन्यता -	anyatā-	(of) difference; distinction;	indistinguishable
अन्य *anya: other*		other-ness	
अनवच्छेदात्	an-avacchedāt	[*due to*] non-delimitation or	
अन् - *an-: not, non-* +		indistinguishable demarcation;	
- अव - *-ava-: away, off, down* +		absent definition;	
√छिद् *chid: to cut/separate*		indeterminateness	

तुल्ययोः	tulyayoḥ	[*of*] [*two*] (things) equal or similar;
√तुल् *tul: to compare with*		possessing same-ness
ततः	tataḥ	thereby
प्रतिपत्तिः	pratipatti	determination; distinguishable;
प्रति - *prati-: towards, in direction of* + √पत् *pat: to fall*		ascertainment; awareness

ARYA

III.54 When between two similar objects there is no demarcation (to point to their) being different (other) as to their genus, peculiarities or locus, then they are determined only through (viveka) discriminatory wisdom.

BAILEY

III.53 From this intuitive knowledge is born the capacity to distinguish (between all beings) and to cognize their genus, qualities and position in space.

DVIVEDI

III.53 From it, knowledge of similars, there being non-discrimination by class, characteristic, or position.

FEUERSTEIN

III.53 Thence [arises] the awareness of [the difference between] similars which cannot normally be distinguished due to an indeterminateness of the distinctions of category, appearance and position.

HOUSTON

III.53 From that, the ascertainment of the difference between similars (not normally distinguished), due to not being restricted in their separateness by means of category, potential, and position.

JNANESHVARA

III.54 From that discriminative knowledge (III.53) comes awareness of the difference or distinction between two similar objects, which are not normally distinguishable by category, characteristics, or position in space.

PRABHAVANANDA

III.54 Thus one is able to distinguish between two exactly similar objects, which cannot be distinguished by their species, characteristic marks, or positions in space.

PUROHIT

III.53 It also brings knowledge of the difference between two similar objects, when that difference cannot be known by kind, character or locality.

SATCHIDANANDA

III.54 Thus, the indistinguish- able differences between objects that are alike in species, characteristic marks and positions become distinguishable.

SHEARER

III.53 This enables us to distinguish between two objects that are to all appearances identical.

TAIMNI

III.54 From it (Vivekajaṃ-Jñānam), knowledge of distinction between similars which cannot be distinguished by class, characteristic or position.

VIVEKANANDA

III.54 Those things which cannot be differentiated by species, sign and place—even they will be discriminated by the above samyama.

III.55

तारकं सर्वविषयं सर्वथाविषयमक्रमं चेति विवेकजं ज्ञानम् ॥ ५५ ॥

tārakaṃ sarva-viṣayaṃ sarvathā-viṣayam akramaṃ ceti vivekajaṃ jñānam

तारकं — tārakaṃ — transcendent; self-inspired; deliverer; causing to cross beyond
√तॄ tṝ: to traverse

सर्वविषयं — sarvaviṣayaṃ
- **सर्व -** — sarva- — all; everything
- **विषयं** — viṣayaṃ — object; field; conditions
  √विष् viṣ: to be active

having all (evolutes as its field); cognizing all objects

सर्वथा - — sarvathā- — in all ways

विषयम् — viṣayam — (having them as its) field; conditions
√विष् viṣ: to be active

अक्रमं — akramaṃ — simultaneous; non-sequential
अ - a-: without + √क्रम् kram: to step/stride

in all ways at once or simultaneously

च — ca — and

इति — iti — this (is); so; such

विवेकजं — vivekajaṃ
- **विवेक** — viveka- — discernment
  वि - vi-: apart from, particular + √विच् vic: to examine/discern
- **जं** — jaṃ — born
  √जन् jan: to beget

discernment born of discriminatory wisdom; awareness of reality

ज्ञानम् — jñānam — knowledge
√ज्ञा jñā: to know

ARYA

III.55 Self-inspired, having all (evolutes from gross elements to mahat) as its field, having all their ways (or states) as their field, not in a sequence (of logic): such is the knowledge born of discriminatory wisdom.

BAILEY

III.54 This intuitive knowledge, which is the great Deliverer, is omnipresent and omniscient and includes the past, the present and the future in the Eternal Now.

DVIVEDI

III.54 The knowledge born of discrimination is *tāraka*, relating to all objects, in every condition and simultaneous.

FEUERSTEIN

III.54 The gnosis born of discernment is the 'deliverer', and is omni-objective, omni-temporal and non-sequential.

HOUSTON

III.54 (This knowledge born of *viveka* is) *tāraka*-causing to cross beyond (*kleśa/karma* etc.), *sarva-viṣaya*-omni-objective (encompassing all objects of perception), *sarvathā-viṣaya*-omni-temporal (encompassing objects in all conditions), and is *akrana*-non-sequential. Thus concludes the knowledge born of *viveka*-discernment.

JNANESHVARA

III.55 That higher knowledge is intuitive and transcendent, and is born of discrimination; it includes all objects within its field, all conditions related to those objects, and is beyond any succession.

PRABHAVANANDA

III.55 This discriminative knowledge delivers a man from the bondage of ignorance. It comprehends all objects simultaneously, at every moment of their existence and in all their modifications.

PUROHIT

III.54 Such knowledge, the result of discrimination, extended at the same time to all objects, under all conditions, leads to liberation.

SATCHIDANANDA

III.55 The discriminative knowledge that simultaneously comprehends all objects in all conditions is the intuitive knowledge which brings liberation.

SHEARER

III.54 Knowledge born of the finest discrimination takes us to the farthest shore. It is intuitive, omniscient and beyond all divisions of time and space.

TAIMNI

III.55 The highest knowledge born of the awareness of Reality is transcendent, includes the cognition of all objects simultaneously, pertains to all objects and processes whatsoever in the past, present and future and also transcends the World Process.

VIVEKANANDA

III.55 The saving knowledge is that knowledge of discrimin- ation which simultaneously covers all objects in all their variations.

III.56

सत्त्वपुरुषयोः शुद्धिसाम्ये कैवल्यम् ॥ ५६ ॥

sattva-puruṣayoḥ śuddhi-sāmye kaivalyam

सत्त्व -	sattva-	purity; tranquillity
√अस् *as: to be*		(of) mental personality; primary guṇa constituent: brightness; purity; beingness
पुरुषयोः	puruṣayoḥ	Consciousness Principle
शुद्धि -	śuddhi-	[*upon*] purity
√शुध् *śudh: to purify*		
साम्ये	sāmye	equality
सम *sama: same*		
कैवल्यम्	kaivalyam	Transcendent Solitude; Isolated Unity;
केवल *kevala: alone*		Final Liberation; Cosmic Freedom; Independence; Absoluteness

ARYA

III.56 When the mental personality and the Conscious Principle (become) equally pure (that is, the mental personality is as purified as the Conscious Principle itself, that state is called) absoluteness.

BAILEY

III.55 When the objective forms and the soul have reached a condition of equal purity, then is At-one-ment achieved and liberation results.

DVIVEDI

III.55 *Kaivalya* on the equality of purity between *puruśa* and *sattva*.

FEUERSTEIN

III.55 With [the attainment of] equality in purity of the *sattva* and the Self, the aloneness [of the power of seeing is established].

HOUSTON

III.55 Upon the equal purity of *sattva* and *Puruṣa- Kaivalya-* the aloneness (of seeing).

JNANESHVARA

III.56 With the attainment of equality between the purest aspect of sattvic buddhi and the pure consciousness of purusha, there comes absolute liberation, and that is the end.

PRABHAVANANDA

III.56 Perfection is attained when the mind becomes as pure as the Atman itself.

PUROHIT

III.55 When intellect becomes as pure as Self, liberation follows.

SATCHIDANANDA

III.56 When the tranquil mind attains purity equal to that of the Self, there is Absoluteness.

SHEARER

III.55 And when the translucent intellect is as pure as the Self, there isSelf Realization.

TAIMNI

III.56 *Kaivalya* is attained when there is equality of purity between the *Puruṣa* and *Sattva*.

VIVEKANANDA

III.56 By the similarity of purity between the sattva and the Purusha comes kaivalya.

॥ इति तृतीयः पादः ॥

iti tṛīyaḥ pādaḥ

इति	iti	thus; herewith [concludes]
तृतीयः	tṛīyaḥ	third
पादः	pādaḥ	chapter; part

Thus [Concludes] the Third Chapter

KAIVALYA PĀDAḤ

Arya	Kaivalya-pāda: The Chapter on the State of Absoluteness
Bailey	Book IV: Illumination
Dvivedi	Section IV
Feuerstein	Chapter Four: Kaivalya Pāda
Houston	Now, The Chapter on Kaivalya
Jnaneshvara	Liberation
Prabhavananda	Liberation
Purohit	Liberation
Satchidananda	Book IV: Kaivalya Pada Portion on Absoluteness
Shearer	Self Realization
Taimni	Kaivalya Pāda
Vivekananda	Independence

Now, The Chapter on Kaivalya

॥ अथ कैवल्यपादः ॥

atha kaivalya-pādaḥ

अथ	atha	Now
कैवल्य -	kaivalya-	Kaivalya; Transcendent Solitude; Liberation; Independence; Freedom; Absoluteness; Aloneness
पादः	pādaḥ	chapter, part

IV.1

जन्मौषधिमन्त्रतपःसमाधिजाः सिद्धयः ॥ १ ॥

janmauṣadhi-mantra-tapaḥ-samādhijāḥ siddhayaḥ

जन्म -	janma-	(by) birth
√जन् *jan: to beget*		
औषधि -	auṣadhi-	herbs; drugs
मन्त्र -	mantra-	sacred syllables
√मन् *man: to think*		
तपः -	tapaḥ-	ascetic practices; austerity;
√तप् *tap: to be hot; heat*		intensity in spiritual practice; accepting discomfort/pain for spiritual unfoldment
समाधिजाः	samādhijāḥ	
समाधि -	samādhi-	samādhi } samādhi born
सम् - sam-: together with, completely, perfectly +		
आ - ā-: near to, all around + √धा dhā: to put		
जः	jaḥ	born (of)
√जन् *jan: to beget*		
सिद्धयः	siddhayaḥ	accomplishments;
√सिध् *sidh: to succeed*		attainments; powers

ARYA

IV.1 The siddhis are (innate by) birth, (produced through the application of) herbs, mantras, ascetic pursuit and (samādhi) highest meditation.

BAILEY

IV.1 The higher and lower siddhis (or powers) are gained by incarnation, or by drugs, words of power, intense desire or by meditation.

DVIVEDI

IV.1 The *Siddhis* are the result of birth, herbs, incantations, austerities, or *Samādhi.*

FEUERSTEIN

IV.1 The [para-normal] attainments are the result of birth, herbs, *mantra* [-recitation], ascesis or entasy.

HOUSTON

IV.1 *Siddhi*-attainments result from *samādhi*-cognitive absorption (which may arise) from birth, herbs, mantra, and *tapas*-intensity in spiritual practice.

JNANESHVARA

IV.1 The subtler attainments come with birth or are attained through herbs, mantra, austerities or concentration.

PRABHAVANANDA

IV.1 The psychic powers may be obtained either by birth, or by means of drugs, or by the power of words, or by the practice of austerities, or by concentration.

PUROHIT

IV.1 Powers are either revealed at birth, or acquired by medicinal herbs, or by repetition of sacred words, or through austerity, or through illumination.

SATCHIDANANDA

IV.1 Siddhis are born of practices performed in previous births, or by herbs, mantra repetition, asceticism, or by samadhi.

SHEARER

IV.1 The perfections may already be present at birth, or they may be developed by herbs, *mantras*, by purification and by *samādhi.*

TAIMNI

IV.1 The *Siddhis* are the result of birth, drugs, mantras, austerities or *Samādhi.*

VIVEKANANDA

IV.1 The siddhis or powers are attained by birth, chemical means, power of words, mortification or concentration.

IV.2

जात्यन्तरपरिणामः प्रकृत्यापूरात् ॥ २ ॥

jāty-antara-pariṇāmaḥ prakṛtyāpūrāt

जाति -	jāti-	species; birth, incarnation class,
√जन् *jan: to beget*		station of life
अन्तर -	antara-	different; another; inner
परिणामः	pariṇāmaḥ	transformation; change
परि - pari-: all around, in addition to + √नम् *nam: to bend*		outcomes; effects; results; consequences
प्रकृति -	prakṛti-	primary unmanifest, unevolved
प्र - pra-: before, in front + √कृ *kṛ: to make*		world ground; Nature: its tendencies and potentialities; primordial matter with the three guṇas in a state of equilibrium prior to universal manifestation
आपूरात्	āpūrāt	[*due to*/*because of*] overflowing/flooding;
आ - ā-: near to, from all sides, all around + √पृ *pṛ: to fill*		[*through*] filling; [*from*] inflow/ abundance

ARYA

IV.2 (In siddhis) the change of (one condition into the condition of) another kind (occurs) through the flooding from a finer cause (for example, growth in the powers of senses by their being flooded from the source of their power, their finer cause, *asmitā*).

BAILEY

IV.2 The transfer of the consciousness from a lower vehicle into a higher is part of the great creative and evolutionary process.

DVIVEDI

IV. 2 The transformation into another kind (is) by the flow of *Prakriti*.

FEUERSTEIN

IV.2 The transformation into another category-of-existence [is possible] because of the superabundance of the world-ground.

HOUSTON

IV.2 Transformation into another category of existence is because of the overflowing of *prakṛiti*-the primary unmanifest world ground.

JNANESHVARA

IV.2 The transition or transformation into another form or type of birth takes place through the filling in of their innate nature.

PRABHAVANANDA

IV.2 The transformation of one species into another is caused by the inflowing of nature.

PUROHIT

IV.2 The yogi can transform himself into another life, gathering together the elements and character of that life.

SATCHIDANANDA

IV.2 The transformation of one species into another is brought about by the inflow of Nature.

SHEARER

IV.2 Any change into a new state of being is the result of the fullness of nature unfolding inherent potential.

TAIMNI

IV.2 The transformation from one species or kind into another is by the overflow of natural tendencies or potentialities.

VIVEKANANDA

IV.2 The change into another species is effected by the filling in of nature.

IV.3

निमित्तमप्रयोजकं प्रकृतीनां वरणभेदस्तु ततः क्षेत्रिकवत् ॥ ३ ॥

nimittam-aprayojakaṃ prakṛtīnāṃ varaṇa-bhedas tu tataḥ kṣetrikavat

निमित्तम् -	nimittam-	external means; incidental cause
नि - ni-: in, into + √मा mā: to measure		
अप्रयोजकं	a-prayojakaṃ	not the impeller/motivator
अ - a-: un-/non-/not/without + प्र - pra-: forward, in front + √युज् yuj: lit.: to yoke; to unite/dissolve; samādhi		
प्रकृतीनां	prakṛtīnāṃ	primary unmanifest world grounds';
प्र - pra-: before, in front + √कृ kṛ: to make		toward Nature's evolution: its tendencies and potentialities
वरण -	varaṇa-	here: obstructions; impediments
√वृ vṛ: to obstruct, to cover		
भेदः	bhedaḥ	break; remove
√भिद् bhid: to split		
तु	tu	however; but; verily
ततः	tataḥ	with that/thence (external means)
क्षेत्रिकवत्	kṣetrikavat	
क्षेत्रिक -	kṣetrika-	farmer } like a farmer
√क्षि kṣi: to inhabit		
वत्	vat	like; as } like a farmer

ARYA

IV.3 No external means impel the finer causes (to come forth flooding) but through these (means there occurs a) break through the impediments the way a farmer (does not impel a flow but breaks the dyke with a tool).

BAILEY

IV.3 The practices and methods are not the true cause of the transfer of consciousness but they serve to remove obstacles, just as the husbandman prepares his ground for sowing.

DVIVEDI

IV.3 The incidental cause is not the real cause in the action of *Prakriti*; from thence is the removal of obstacles, like a husbandman.

FEUERSTEIN

IV.3 The incidental cause does not initiate the processes-of-evolution, but [merely is responsible for] the singling-out of possibilities—like a farmer [who irrigates a field by selecting appropriate pathways for the water].

HOUSTON

IV.3 The efficient cause (*samādhi*) does not motivate the processes of *prakṛiti*-primary evolution, but is merely the separating away of obstacles, like a farmer (who irrigates a field by removing obstacles to waterways).

JNANESHVARA

IV.3 Incidental causes or actions do not lead to the emergence of attainments or realization, but rather, come by the removal of obstacles, much like the way a farmer removes a barrier (sluice gate), so as to naturally allow the irrigation of his field.

PRABHAVANANDA

IV.3 Good or bad deeds are not the direct causes of the transformation. They only act as breakers of the obstacles to natural evolution; just as the farmer breaks down the obstacles in a water course, so that water flows through by its own nature.

PUROHIT

IV.3 Elements work of their own accord, good and evil do not cause them to work, but act as implements only; water flows downwards naturally when the farmer removes obstacles in the way.

SATCHIDANANDA

IV.3 Incidental events do not directly cause natural evolution; they just remove obstacles as a farmer [removes obstacles in a water course running to his field].

SHEARER

IV.3 But the apparent causes of a change do not in fact bring it about.
They merely remove the obstacles to natural growth, as a farmer clears the ground for his crops.

TAIMNI

IV.3 The incidental cause does not move or stir up the natural tendencies into activity; it merely removes the obstacles, like a farmer (irrigating a field).

VIVEKANANDA

IV.3 Good and bad deeds are not the direct causes in the transformations of nature, but they act as breakers of obstacles to the evolutions—as a farmer breaks the obstacles to the course of water, which then runs down by its own nature.

IV.4

निर्माणचित्तान्यस्मितामात्रात् ॥ ४ ॥

nirmāṇa-cittāny-asmitā-mātrāt

निर्माण -	nirmāṇa-	created; formed;	
निर् nir-: free from, with + √मा mā: to measure		duplicated; brought into existence	
चित्तानि	cittāni	pl.: citta: mind-fields/minds	
√चित् cit: to perceive/be bright			
अस्मितामात्रात्	asmitāmātrāt		
अस्मिता -	asmitā-	"I-am"-ness	[*due to*] "egoism" >
अस्मि asmi: I am + -ता -tā: -ness			separative sense of self;
मात्रात्	mātrāt	[*due to*]	[*from*] "I-am"-ness/solitude;
		only; alone; here: "egoism"	[*because of*] egoism

ARYA

IV.4 (The yogi creates duplicate minds from his own and these) artificially produced minds created from (his own *asmitā*) "I am"-ness alone (move the duplicate bodies he creates for his use).

BAILEY

IV.4 The "I am" consciousness is responsible for the creation of the organs through which the sense of individuality is enjoyed.

DVIVEDI

IV.4 Created minds proceed from the sense of being alone.

FEUERSTEIN

IV.4 The individualised consciousnesses [proceed] from the primary I-am-ness.

HOUSTON

IV.4 Individually created *citta*-fields proceed only from *asmitā*-the sense of "I am."

JNANESHVARA

IV.4 The emergent mind fields spring forth from the individuality of I-ness (asmita).

PRABHAVANANDA

IV.4 The ego-sense alone can create minds.

PUROHIT

IV.4 The yogi provides minds for the bodies he creates through his personality.

SATCHIDANANDA

IV.4 A Yogi's egoity alone is the cause of [other artificially] created minds.

SHEARER

IV.4 All minds are created by Ego—the separative sense of "I."

TAIMNI

IV.4 Artificially created minds (proceed) from 'egoism' alone.

VIVEKANANDA

IV.4 A yogi can create many minds from his egoity.

IV.5

प्रवृत्तिभेदे प्रयोजकं चित्तमेकमनेकेषाम् ॥ ५॥

pravṛtti-bhede prayojakaṃ cittam ekam-anekeṣām

प्रवृत्ति -	pravṛtti-	tendencies; inclinations;
प्र - pra-: forward + √वृत् vṛt: to turn		activities; functions
भेदे	bhede	[*in/upon*] difference/ distinction
भिद् bhid: to split		
प्रयोजकं	prayojakaṃ	impeller; director; controller;
प्र - pra-: forward, in front +		originator; motivator
√युज् yuj: lit.: to yoke; to unite/dissolve; samādhi		
चित्तम्	cittam	energy field called mind
√चित् cit: to perceive; to be bright		in all aspects; mind-field; field of consciousness; consciousness; mind-stuff
एकम् -	ekam-	one
एक eka: one		
अनेकेषाम्	anekeṣām	one (of) many other; other than one
अन् - an-: without + एक eka: one		

ARYA

IV.5 In the case of (a question on possible) difference of inclinations (in various duplicated minds), the one (original) mind is the controller of (other) many (minds).

BAILEY

IV.5 Consciousness is one, yet produces the varied forms of the many.

DVIVEDI

IV.5 One mind is the cause of all the minds in their various activities.

FEUERSTEIN

IV.5 [Although the multiple individualised consciousnesses are engaged] in distinct activities, the 'one consciousness' is the originator of [all] the other [numerous individualised consciousnesses].

HOUSTON

IV.5 Although there is division in *pravṛtti*-activity, one *citta* is the motivator of many (*citta*-fields).

JNANESHVARA

IV.5 While the activities of the emergent mind fields may be diverse, the one mind is the director of the many.

PRABHAVANANDA

IV.5 Though the activities of the different created minds are various, the one original mind controls them all.

PUROHIT

IV.5 Though the activities of such minds vary, the one original mind of the yogi controls then all.

SATCHIDANANDA

IV.5 Although the functions in the many created minds may differ, the original mind-stuff of the Yogi is the director of them all.

SHEARER

IV.5 All these expressions of individuality, however highly developed, are the impulses of the forces of evolution.

TAIMNI

IV.5 The one (natural) mind is the director or mover of the many (artificial) minds in their different activities.

VIVEKANANDA

IV.5 Though the activities of the different created minds are various, the one original mind is the controller of them all.

IV.6

तत्र ध्यानजमनाशयम् ॥ ६ ॥

tatra dhyāna-jam-anāśayam

तत्र	tatra	of these	
ध्यानजम् -	dhyānajam-		
ध्यान	dhyāna-	meditation	born (of) meditation
√ध्यै *dhyai: to meditate*			
जम्	jam-	born (of)	
जन् *jan: to beget*			
अनाशयम्	an-āśayam	without accumulated residue impressions; free from karmic impression; seed impressions of latent desires	

अन् - an-: without +

आशय āśaya: आ - ā-: near to, from all sides, all around +

√शी śī: to lie down/recline/rest = here: repository (of residual impressions) (see karmāśaya - sūtra II.12)

ARYA

IV.6 Of these (minds, the one) produced in meditation (leaves behind) no impressions (as karmic) residue.

BAILEY

IV.6 Among the forms which consciousness assumes, only that which is the result of meditation is free from latent karma.

DVIVEDI

IV.6 That which is born of contemplation is free from impressions.

FEUERSTEIN

IV.6 Of these [individualised consciousnesses] [that consciousness which is] born of meditative-absorption is without [subliminal] deposit.

HOUSTON

IV.6 There is (in the division of activity), non-accumulation (of *karma*) is the result of *dhyāna*-meditation.

JNANESHVARA

IV.6 Of these mind fields, the one that is born from meditation is free from any latent impressions that could produce karma.

PRABHAVANANDA

IV.6 Of the various types of mind, only that which is purified by samadhi is freed from all latent impressions of karma and from all cravings.

PUROHIT

IV.6 The controlling mind, born of illumination, remains unaffected by the contagion of desire.

SATCHIDANANDA

IV.6 Only the minds born of meditation [the artifically created ones] are free from karmic impressions.

SHEARER

IV.6 And, of these, only the mind born of meditation is free from the latent impressions which generate desire.

TAIMNI

IV.6 Of these the mind born of meditation is free from impressions.

VIVEKANANDA

IV.6 Among the various minds, that which is attained by samādhi is desireless.

IV.7

कर्माशुक्लाकृष्णं योगिनस्त्रिविधमितरेषाम् ॥ ७ ॥

karmāśuklākṛṣṇaṃ yoginas tri-vidham-itareṣām

कर्म	karma	action and reaction; cause and effect
कृ kṛ: to do		
अशुक्ल -	a-śukla-	non-white
अ- a-: without + √शुच् śuc: to be bright		
अकृष्णं	a-kṛṣṇaṃ	non-black
अ- a-: without + कृष्ण kṛṣṇa: black		
योगिनः	yoginaḥ	(a) yogi's; [*of*] a yogi
त्रिविधम् -	tri-vidham-	threefold; of three kinds
त्रि tri: three + विधा vidhā: form, division, part, portion		
इतरेषाम्	itareṣām	others'; [*of*] others

ARYA

IV.7 The action of yogis is neither white nor black but (the action) of others is of three kinds.

BAILEY

IV.7 The activities of the liberated soul are free from the pairs of opposites. Those of other people are of three kinds.

DVIVEDI

IV.7 Actions are neither white nor black in the case of *Yogins*; they are three kinds in the case of others.

FEUERSTEIN

IV.7 The *karman* of the *yogin* is neither black nor white: [the *karman*] of others is threefold.

HOUSTON

IV.7 The *karma* of a *yogin* (of whom there is *nirodha* of *citta-vṛtti*) is neither white nor black. Of others it is threefold.

JNANESHVARA

IV.7 The actions of yogis are neither white nor black, while they are threefold for others.

PRABHAVANANDA

IV.7 The karma of the yogi is neither white nor black. The karma of others is of three kinds: white, black or mixed.

PUROHIT

IV.7 The yogi's karma is neither pure nor impure; that of others is pure, impure or mixed.

SATCHIDANANDA

IV.7 The actions of the Yogi are neither white [good] nor black [bad]; but the actions of others are of three kinds: good, bad and mixed.

SHEARER

IV.7 The actions of an enlightened being are neither black nor white, but those of others are threefold.

TAIMNI

IV.7 *Karmas* are neither white nor black (neither good nor bad) in the case of *Yogis*; they are of three kinds in the case of others.

VIVEKANANDA

IV.7 Works are neither black nor white for the yogis; for others they are threefold: black, white and mixed.

IV.8

ततस्तद्विपाकानुगुणानामेवाभिव्यक्तिर्वासनानाम् ॥ ८ ॥

tatas tad-vipākānuguṇānām evābhivyaktir vāsanānām

ततः	tataḥ	from those
तद् -	tad-	their
विपाक -	vipāka-	fruition; ripening; maturity

वि - vi-: intensity + √पच् pac: to cook, to roast

अनुगुणानाम्	anuguṇānām	[*possessed of*] those conforming in qualities; favorable conditions

अनु - anu-: following, after, behind +

गुण guṇa: constituents of prakṛiti—the constituents of primordial Nature

एव	eva	alone; only; specifically
अभिव्यक्तिः	abhi-vyaktiḥ	manifestation

अभि - abhi-: over, above + वि - vi-: apart + √अञ्ज् añj: to abide

वासनानाम्	vāsanānām	vāsanās'; [*of*] vāsanās: subconscious impressions; potential tendencies/desires; subliminal traits

√वस् vas: to abide

ARYA

IV.8 From those (three kinds of actions) the vāsanās manifest themselves that follow in qualities the maturing (fruits) of those (actions).

BAILEY

IV.8 From these three kinds of karma emerge those forms which are necessary for the fruition of effects.

DVIVEDI

IV.8 From thence, there is development of those impressions alone for which the conditions are favorable.

FEUERSTEIN

IV.8 Thence [follows] the manifestation [of those] subliminal-traits only which correspond to the fruition of their [particular *karman*].

HOUSTON

IV.8 From that (threefold *karma*), the manifestation of *vāsana*-subliminal traits, specifically corresponding to their fruition.

JNANESHVARA

IV.8 Those threefold actions result in latent impressions (vasanas) that will later arise to fruition only corresponding to those impressions.

PRABHAVANANDA

IV.8 Of the tendencies produced by these three kinds of karma, only those are manifested for which the conditions are favorable.

PUROHIT

IV.8 From this three-fold karma desires spring up, that are helpful to its fulfilment.

SATCHIDANANDA

IV.8 Of these [actions], only those vasanas (subconscious impressions) for which there are favourable conditions for producing their fruits will manifest in a particular birth.

SHEARER

IV.8 From their actions are sown the seeds of mental tendencies that bear fruit appropriate to their nature.

TAIMNI

IV.8 From these only those tendencies are manifested for which the conditions are favourable.

VIVEKANANDA

IV.8 From these threefold works are manifested in each state only those desires [which are] fitting to that state alone. [The others are held in abeyance for the time being.]

IV.9

जातिदेशकालव्यवहितानामप्यानन्तर्यं स्मृतिसंस्कारयोरेकरूपत्वात् ॥ ९॥

jāti-deśa-kāla-vyavahitānām-apyānantaryaṃ smṛti-saṃskārayor eka-rūpatvāt

जाति -	jāti-	(by) genus; species;
√जन् *jan: to beget*		class; caste;
		category of existence
देश -	deśa-	(by) locus; place; space
√दिश् *diś: to point out*		
काल -	kāla-	(by) time
√कल् *kāl: to impel*		
व्यवहितानाम् -	vyavahitānām-	[*of*] those separated/distant
वि - vi-: apart + -अव - -ava-: down +		(by) (here: jāti-deśa-kāla)
√धा dhā : to put = to place apart		
अपि	api	even; though
आनन्तर्यं	ān-antaryaṃ	uninterrupted/continuous
अन् - an-: non-, not + अन्तर् antar: inner, inward		relationship without
		interval or distance
स्मृति -	smṛti-	memories'; [*of*] memory/depth memory
√स्मृ smṛ: to remember		
संस्कारयोः	saṃskārayoḥ	saṃskāras'; [*of*] saṃskāras
सम् - sam-: together with, completely, perfectly + √कृ kṛ: to do		
एकरूपत्वात्	ekarūpatvāt	
एक -	eka- one	[*because of*] there being uniformity;
रूपत्वात्	rūpatvāt form	[*because of*] being identical

ARYA

IV.9 Because memory and saṃskāras have the same nature, no distance (or interval) of genus, locus or time, (however) distant, (counts).

BAILEY

IV.9 There is identity of relation between memory and the effect-producing cause, even when separated by species, time and place.

DVIVEDI

IV.9 There is the relation of cause and effect even (among them) though separated by class, space, or time, on account of the unity of memory and impressions.

FEUERSTEIN

IV.9 On account of the uniformity between depth-memory and subliminal activators [there is] a causal-relation [between the manifestation of the subliminal-activator and the karman cause], even though [cause and effect] may be separated [in terms of] place, time and category-of-existence.

HOUSTON

IV.9 Even in the case of those (*vāsana*-subliminal traits) separated by birth, place, and time (from their cause in *karma*), there is a causal relation on account of the uniformity of *smṛti*-memory (*smṛti*) and *sanskāra*-subliminal activators.

JNANESHVARA

IV.9 Since memory (smriti) and the deep habit patterns (samskaras) are the same in appearance, there is an unbroken continuity in the playing out of those traits, even though there might be a gap in location, time, or state of life.

PRABHAVANANDA

IV.9 Because of our memory of past tendencies, the chain of cause and effect is not broken by change of species, space or time.

PUROHIT

IV.9 Since recollections and impressions are the same, desires are awakened automatically, though separated by time, incarnation, country.

SATCHIDANANDA

IV.9 Although desires are separated from their fulfil- ments by class, space and time, they have an uninterrupted relationship because the impressions [of desires] and memories of them are identical.

SHEARER

IV.9 Memory and impression have similiar forms. They give birth to our tendencies, which operate continuously to shape our lives, even if their cause is separated from their effect by time, by place, or by lifetimes.

TAIMNI

IV.9 There is the relation of cause and effect even though separated by class, locality and time because memory and impressions are the same in form.

VIVEKANANDA

IV.9 There is consecutiveness in desires, even though separated by species, space and time, there being identification of memory and impressions.

IV.10

तासामनादित्वं चाशिषो नित्यत्वात् ॥ १० ॥

tāsām anāditvaṃ cāśiṣo nityatvāt

तासाम्	tāsām	of those (impressions)
अनादित्वं	an-āditvaṃ	without beginning (therefore eternal)

अन्- an-: without + आदि ādi: beginning, commencement + -त्व -tva: -ness

च -	ca-	and
आशिषः	āśiṣaḥ	[*possessed of*] primordial will; drive-to-survive; will-to-live; desire to live

आ- ā-: near to, toward + √शास् śās: to order

नित्यत्वात्	nityatvāt	[*because of/due to*] being permanent eternal

नित्य nitya: eternal + -त्व -tva: -ness

ARYA

IV.10 Because expectations are permanent (in a being) the vāsanās (have been there) without a beginning (forever).

BAILEY

IV.10 Desire to live being eternal, these mind-created forms are without known beginning.

DVIVEDI

IV.10 Besides they are without beginning, on account of the eternity of desire.

FEUERSTEIN

IV.10 And these [subliminal-activators] are without beginning because of the perpetuity of the primordial-will [inherent in Nature].

HOUSTON

IV.10 And the beginninglessness of these (*vāsanā*-subliminal traits) is because of the eternality of the will-to-live.

JNANESHVARA

IV.10 There is no beginning to the process of these deep habit patterns (samskaras), due to the eternal nature of the will to live.

PRABHAVANANDA

IV.10 Since our desire to exist has always been present, our tendencies cannot have had any beginning.

PUROHIT

IV.10 Desires have no beginning.

SATCHIDANANDA

IV.10 Since the desire to live is eternal, impressions are also beginningless.

SHEARER

IV.10 And tendencies are without beginning, because the desire for fulfilment, which sustains them, is everlasting.

TAIMNI

IV.10 And there is no beginning of them, the desire to live being eternal.

VIVEKANANDA

IV.10 Thirst for happiness being eternal, desires are without beginning.

IV.11

हेतुफलाश्रयालम्बनैः सङ्गृहीतत्वादेषामभावे तदभावः ॥ ११ ॥

hetu-phalāśrayālambanaiḥ saṅgṛhītatvād-eṣām-abhāve tad-abhāvaḥ

हेतु -	hetu-	[*with*] causes; means
√हा *hā: to leave/abandon*		
फल -	phala-	[*with*]fruits; results; effects
√फल् *phal: to ripen, bear fruit*		
आश्रय -	āśraya-	substrata; resorts; basis
आ - *ā-: from all sides, around* + √श्रि *śri: to rest on*		
आलम्बनैः	ālambanaiḥ	[*by/with*] supporting objects;
आ - *ā-: near to, from all sides* + √लम्ब् *lamb: to rest on*		support with props
सङ्गृहीतत्वात् -	saṅgṛhītatvāt-	[*because of*] being gathered/
सम् - *sam-: fully, completely* + √ग्रह् *grah: to grasp*		bound/being held together
एषाम्	eṣām	of these
अभावे	abhāve	[*upon/with*] the disappearance
अ - *a-: un-/non-/not/without* + √भू *bhū: to be*		
तद् -	tad-	of those (here: vāsanā)
अभ	abhāvaḥ	disappearance; removal; negation
अ - *a-: un-/non-/not/without* + √भू *bhū: to be*		

ARYA

IV.11 Because (the vāsanās) are gathered through (various) causes, their results, resorts (where they may find a substratum) and with (various) supports, in the absence of these (factors), the absence of those (vāsanās) (occurs).

BAILEY

IV.11 These forms being created and held together through desire, the basic cause, personality, the effective result, mental vitality or the will to live, and the support of the outward going life or object, when these cease to attract then the forms cease likewise to be.

DVIVEDI

IV.11 Being bound together by cause, effect, substratum, and support, it is destroyed by their destruction.

FEUERSTEIN

IV.11 Because of the connection [of the subliminal-traits] with cause, fruit, substratum and support, [it follows that] with the disappearance of these [factors], the disappearance [also] of those [subliminal-traits] [is brought about].

HOUSTON

IV.11 Owing to the inter-connectedness by means of the cause (*avidyā*-absence of self awareness), the results (of *karma*), and the supporting objects of the substratum (*citta*) - upon the disappear- ance of these (factors) the disappearance of those (*vāsanā*).

JNANESHVARA

IV.11 Since the impressions (IV.10) are held together by cause, motive, substratum, and object, they disappear when those deep impressions disappear.

PRABHAVANANDA

IV.11 Our subconscious tendencies depend upon cause and effect. They have their basis in the mind, and they are stimulated by the sense-objects. If all these are removed, the tendencies are destroyed.

PUROHIT

IV.11 Desires are the aggregate result of ignorance and vanity, mind and the object of its hunt; they are absent when these are absent.

SATCHIDANANDA

IV.11 The impressions being held together by cause, effect, basis and support, they disappear with the disappearance of these four.

SHEARER

IV.11 They are maintained by the mind's bondage to its objects, through the cycle of cause and effect.

TAIMNI

IV.11 Being bound together as cause-effect, substratum-object, they (effects, i.e. Vāsanās) disappear on their (cause, i.e. Avidyā) disappearance.

VIVEKANANDA

IV.11 [Desire] being held together by cause, effect, support, and objects, in the absence of these it is absent.

IV.12

अतीतानागतं स्वरूपतोऽस्त्यध्वभेदाद्धर्माणाम् ॥ १२ ॥

atītānāgataṃ svarūpato-'styadhva-bhedād-dharmāṇām

अतीत -	atīta-	past (and)
अति atī: over, beyond + √इ i: to go		
अनागतं	anāgataṃ	(that) which has not (yet) come; future
अन् - an-: not + आगम् āgam: अ - ā-: here: indicates reversal + √गम् gam: to go = to come		
स्वरूपतः -	svarūpataḥ-	in own form/essential nature;
स्व - sva-: own, essential + रूप rūpa: form, nature		in fact; in reality; as such
अस्ति -	asti-	here: exists
√अस् as: to be		
अध्व -	adhva-	in the path/conditions
धव् dhav: to flow (along)		(past, present, future)
भेदात् -	bhedāt-	[*owing to/because of*] difference
भिद् bhid: to split		
धर्माणाम्	dharmāṇām	[*possessed of*] characteristics; properties;
धृ dhṛ: to hold		characterized forms

ARYA

IV.12 (The vāsanās do not non-exist; their) past and future remains, there being (a natural process) of attributes (of things to pass on) the three (past, present and future) paths (of time).

BAILEY

IV.12 The past and the present exist in reality. The form assumed in the time concept of the present is the result of developed characteristics and holds latent seeds of future quality.

DVIVEDI

IV.12 Past and future exists in real nature, in consequence of the differences in the conditions of the properties.

FEUERSTEIN

IV.12 Past and future as such exist, because of the [visible] difference in the 'paths' of the forms [produced by Nature].

HOUSTON

IV.12 Past and future essentially exist, owing to the difference in the paths (sequential progressions) of *dharma*-of characterized form.

JNANESHVARA

IV.12 Past and future exist in the present reality, appearing to be different because of having different characteristics or forms.

PRABHAVANANDA

IV.12 There is the form and expression which we call "past," and the form and expression we call "future"; both exist within the object, at all times. Form and expression vary according to time—past, present or future.

PUROHIT

IV.12 In reality, past and future exist as much as present; they are not seen because they exist on different planes.

SATCHIDANANDA

IV.12 The past and future exist in the real form of objects which manifest due to differences in the conditions of their characteristics.

SHEARER

IV.12 The past and the future exist within an object, and are due to the difference in the characteristics of that object.

TAIMNI

IV.12 The past and the future exist in their own (real) form. The difference of *Dharmas* or properties is on account of the difference of paths.

VIVEKANANDA

IV.12 The past and future exist in their own nature, their difference being due to the differences in the gunas.

IV.13

ते व्यक्तसूक्ष्मा गुणात्मानः ॥ १३ ॥

te vyakta-sūkṣmā guṇātmānaḥ

ते	te	they/these; here: the characteristics
व्यभ -	vyakta-	manifest

वि - vi-: apart + √अञ्ज् añj: to cause to appear; to make clear

सूक्ष्माः	sūkṣmāḥ	subtle; fine; unmanifest

√सिव् siv: to sew

गुणात्मानः	guṇa-ātmānaḥ		
गुण -	guṇa-	guṇas; primordial elements	(essentially) consist of nature of guṇas
गुण guṇa: strand			
आत्मानः	ātmānaḥ	(of the) nature; consisting	

ARYA

IV.13 Those (processes or attributes of things, divided into the three paths of time, in fact) consist of the guṇas (of prakrti), whether in manifest or finer (unmanifest) (form).

BAILEY

IV.13 The characteristics, whether latent or potent, partake of the nature of the three gunas (qualities of matter).

DVIVEDI

IV.13 They are manifest or subtle being of the nature of the *Guṇas*.

FEUERSTEIN

IV.13 These [forms] are manifest or subtle and composed of the primary-constituents.

HOUSTON

IV.13 These forms (*dharma*) are manifested or subtle, and conposed of the *guṇa*-primary forces.

JNANESHVARA

IV.13 Whether these ever-present characteristics or forms are manifest or subtle, they are composed of the primary elements called the three gunas.

PRABHAVANANDA

IV.13 They are either manifest or subtle, according to the nature of the gunas.

PUROHIT

IV.13 The present is manifest, the past and the future are obscure, but they all live in the Qualities.

SATCHIDANANDA

IV.13 Whether manifested or subtle, these characteristics belong to the nature of the gunas.

SHEARER

IV.13 Manifested characteristics are the present; unmanifested, the past and future.
All are the workings of the *gunas*.

TAIMNI

IV.13 They, whether manifest or unmanifest, are of the nature of *Guṇas*.

VIVEKANANDA

IV.13 They are manifested or fine, the gunas being their inmost nature.

IV.14

परिणामैकत्वाद्वस्तुतत्त्वम् ॥ १४ ॥

pariṇāmaikatvād vastu-tattvam

परिणाम -	pariṇāma-	transformation; change
परि - pari-: all around, in addition to + √नम् nam: to bend		
एकत्वात्	ekatvāt	(due to) being one/unique/
एक eka: one + -त्व -tva: -ness		(due to) uniformity/homogeneity
वस्तु -	vastu-	(of) object
√वस् vas: to remain		
तत्त्वम्	tattvam	being That; reality; essence

ARYA

IV.14 Because (various) products (of the same) guṇas (are each) unique, an object's being that (object is made possible).

BAILEY

IV.14 The manifestation of the objective form is due to the one-pointedness of the effect-producing cause (the unification of the modifications of the citta or mind stuff).

DVIVEDI

IV.14 In consequence of the unity of transformation (results) the one-ness of things.

FEUERSTEIN

IV.14 The 'that-ness' of an object [derives] from the homogeneity in the transformation [of the primary-constituents].

HOUSTON

IV.14 The reality of an object (derives) from the uniqueness of (its) changes.

JNANESHVARA

IV.14 The characteristics of an object appear as a single unit, as they manifested uniformly from the underlying elements.

PRABHAVANANDA

IV.14 Since the gunas work together within every change of form and expression, there is a unity in all things.

PUROHIT

IV.14 Though the Qualities are more than one, their material is one, their result is one, their work is one.

SATCHIDANANDA

IV.14 The reality of things is due to the uniformity of the gunas' transformations.

SHEARER

IV.14 The state of an object at any moment arises from the unique state of the *gunas* then operating.

TAIMNI

IV.14 The essence of the object consists in the uniqueness of transformation (of the *Guṇas*).

VIVEKANANDA

IV.14 The unity in things follows from the unity in changes [of the gunas].

IV.15

वस्तुसाम्ये चित्तभेदात्तयोर्विभक्तः पन्थाः ॥ १५ ॥

vastu-sāmye citta-bhedāt tayor vibhaktaḥ panthāḥ

वस्तु - *√वस् vas: to remain*	vastu-	objects
साम्ये *सम sama: same*	sāmye	[*upon*] sameness; similarity
चित्त - *√चित् cit: to perceive; to be bright*	citta-	energy field called mind in all aspects; mind-field; field of consciousness; consciousness; mind-stuff
भेदात् *√भिद् bhid: to split*	bhedāt	[*owing to/because of*] difference
तयोः	tayoḥ	of both; [*of*] those [*two*]
विभक्तः *वि - vi-: distinct, apart, separate from + √भज् bhaj: to allot*	vibhaktaḥ	distinct; different; separate; divided
पन्थाः *√पथ् path: to bring into*	panthāḥ	path (in time); ways of perception; ways of being; level of understanding and integration

ARYA

IV.15 Even when the same object (is present) there is a difference of minds (concerning it, because of which) those two (the objects and the mind take to) different paths.

BAILEY

IV.15 These two, consciousness and form, are distinct and separate; though forms may be similar, the consciousness may function on differing levels of being.

DVIVEDI

IV.15 Though things are similar, the cause of mind and things is distinct in consequence of the difference of minds.

FEUERSTEIN

IV.15 In view of the multiplicity of consciousness [as opposed] to the singleness of a [perceived] object, both [belong to] separate levels [of existence].

HOUSTON

IV.15 Owing to the difference of *citta*-fields, while (there is) sameness of an object perceived - the separate way (sequential progression) of both (*citta* and *vastu*-object).

JNANESHVARA

IV.15 Although the same objects may be perceived by different minds, they are perceived in different ways, because those minds manifested differently.

PRABHAVANANDA

IV.15 The same object is perceived in different ways by different minds. Therefore the mind must be other than the object.

PUROHIT

IV.15 Though the object is one, different minds see it differently.

SATCHIDANANDA

IV.15 Due to differences in various minds, perception of even the same object may vary.

SHEARER

IV.15 Two similar objects appear different in the minds that perceive them.

TAIMNI

IV.15 The object being the same, the difference in the two (the object and its cognition) are due to their (of the minds') separate path.

VIVEKANANDA

IV.15 Since perception and desire vary with regard to the same object, mind and object are of different nature.

IV.16

न चैकचित्ततन्त्रं वस्तु तदप्रमाणकं तदा किं स्यात् ॥ १६ ॥

na caika-citta-tantraṃ vastu tad-apramāṇakaṃ tadā kiṃ syāt

न	na	nor
च	ca	and
एक -	eka-	one; single
चित्त - *√चित् cit: to perceive; to be bright*	citta-	(of) energy field called mind in all aspects; mind-field; field of consciousness; consciousness; mind-stuff
तन्त्रं *√तन् tan: to extend*	tantraṃ	dependent
वस्तु *√वस् vas: to remain*	vastu	object
तत्	tat	that
अप्रमाणकं *अ - a-: un-/non-/not/without +* *प्र - pra-: forth, onward, in front +* *√मा mā: to measure/mark off + न - na-: no, not, nor*	apramāṇa-akaṃ	not perceived; non-cognized; unwitnessed; unprovable
तदा	tadā	then; besides
किं	kiṃ	what?; which? (This word is bacically equivalent to a question mark.)
स्यात् *√अस् as: to be*	syāt	could/would/should; becomes

ARYA

IV.16 And an object (that is, its existence) does not depend on (only) one mind, for, if it were so, then at a time when it is not being perceived by that mind, what would (the object) be?

BAILEY

IV.16 The many modifications of the one mind produce the diverse forms, which depend for existence upon those many mind impulses.

DVIVEDI

IV.16 Nor are objects the result of a single mind; (for) what should become of them when not cognised by that mind.

FEUERSTEIN

IV.16 And the object is not dependent on a single consciousness; this is unprovable; besides, what could [such an imaginary object possibly] be?

HOUSTON

IV.16 An object is not dependent on one *citta* (*citta*'s perception); that being without *pramāṇa*-a valid means of assessment, in such a case, would be "what"?

JNANESHVARA

IV.16 However, the object itself does not depend on any one mind, for if it did, then what would happen to the object if it were not being experienced by that mind?

PRABHAVANANDA

IV.16 The object cannot be said to be dependent on the perception of a single mind. For, if this were the case, the object could be said to be non-existent when that single mind was not perceiving it.

PUROHIT

IV.16 No object depends on one mind only; otherwise what becomes of it when that mind sees it no longer?

SATCHIDANANDA

IV.16 Nor does an object's existence depend upon a single mind, for if it did, what would become of that object when that mind did not perceive it?

SHEARER

IV.16 An object does not depend on a single mind for its existence, for if it did, what would become of it when not perceived by that mind?

TAIMNI

IV.16 Nor is an object dependent on one mind. What would become of it when not cognized by that mind?

VIVEKANANDA

IV. - - -

IV.17

तदुपरागापेक्षित्वाच्चित्तस्य वस्तु ज्ञाताज्ञातम् ॥ १७ ॥

tad-uparāgāpekṣitvāc cittasya vastu jñātājñātam

तद् -	tad-	(of) that
उपराग -	uparāga-	reflected coloring
उप - upa-: toward, near to + √रज् raj: to excite		
अपेक्षित्वात्	apekṣitvāt	[*because of*] being dependent on; [*due to*] the need/requirement
अप - apa-: away from + √ईक्ष् īkṣ: to look + -त्व -tva: -ness		
चित्तस्य	cittasya	[*of*] the mind's field; mind-field's; all aspects [*possessed by*] energy field called mind
√चित् cit: perceive; be bright		
वस्तु	vastu	object
√वस् vas: to remain		
ज्ञात -	jñāta-	known (or)
√ज्ञा jñā: to know		
अज्ञातम्	ajñātam	unknown
अ - a-: un-/non-/not/without + √ज्ञा jñā: to know		

ARYA

IV.17 Because the mind is dependent upon the reflection (that falls on it from an object) an object becomes either known or unknown to it.

BAILEY

IV.17 These forms are cognized or not, according to the qualities latent in the perceiving consciousness.

DVIVEDI

IV.17 In consequence of the necessity of being tinged by them, things are known or unknown to the mind.

FEUERSTEIN

IV.17 An object is known or not by reason of the required coloration of consciousness by that object.

HOUSTON

IV.17 An object is known or unknown because of the conditionality of the coloring by that (object) of *citta*-the field.

JNANESHVARA

IV.17 Objects are either known or not known according to the way in which the coloring of that object falls on the coloring of the mind observing it.

PRABHAVANANDA

IV.17 An object is known or unknown, depending upon the moods of the mind.

PUROHIT

IV.17 Object becomes known, when it is reflected in the mind; when it is not reflected it remains unknown.

SATCHIDANANDA

IV.17 An object is known or unknown dependent on whether or not the mind gets colored by it.

SHEARER

IV.17 An object is experienced only when it colors the mind.

TAIMNI

IV.17 In consequence of the mind being coloured or not coloured by it, an object is known or unknown.

VIVEKANANDA

IV.16 Things are known or unknown to the mind, being dependent on the colouring which they give to the mind.

IV.18

सदा ज्ञाताश्चित्तवृत्तयस्तत्प्रभोः पुरुषस्यापरिणामित्वात् ॥ १८ ॥

sadā jñātāś citta-vṛttayas tat-prabhoḥ puruṣasyāpariṇāmitvāt

सदा	sadā	always; perpetually		
ज्ञाताः	jñātāḥ	known (plural)		
√ज्ञा jñā: to know				
चित्तवृत्तयः	cittavṛttayaḥ			
चित्त -	citta-	energy field called mind in all aspects; mind-field; field of consciousness; consciousness; mind-stuff	}	the mental states and activities
√चित् cit: to perceive; to be bright				
वृत्तयः	vṛttayaḥ	(of) states; operations; activities; fluctuations; waves; modifications; definitions		
√वृत् vṛt: to whirl				
तत्प्रभोः	tatprabhoḥ			
तद् -	tad-	that; its	}	its master's
प्रभोः	prabhoḥ	owner's; master's		
प्र - pra-: forth, onward, in front + √भू bhū: to become				
पुरुषस्य	puruṣasya	Consciousness Principle's		
अपरिणामित्वात्	a-pariṇāmitvāt	[*because of*] being changeless/ immutable; [*due to*] (His) changelessness		
अ - a-: without + परि - pari-: all around + √नम् nam: to bend				

ARYA

IV.18 The activities of the mind are always known to the (mind's) master, the Conscious Principle, because (though the mental functions undergo oscillations and alterations, the Consciousness Principle is ever) unchanging.

BAILEY

IV.18 The Lord of the mind, the perceiver, is ever aware of the constantly active mind stuff, the effect-producing cause.

DVIVEDI

IV.18 The functions of the mind are always known on account of the constant nature of its lord, the *Puruśa*.

FEUERSTEIN

IV.18 The fluctuations of consciousness are always known by their 'superior', because of the immutability of the Self.

HOUSTON

IV.18 The *vṛtti*-definitions of *citta*-the field are always known, due to the changelessness of *Puruṣa*-the self, who is the master of those (*citta-vṛtti*).

JNANESHVARA

IV.18 The activities of the mind are always known by the pure consciousness, because that pure consciousness is superior to, support of, and master over the mind.

PRABHAVANANDA

IV.18 Because the Atman, the Lord of the mind, is unchangeable, the mind's fluctuations are always known to it.

PUROHIT

IV.18 The activities of mind are known to the Self; for Self is the Lord, who remains unaffected.

SATCHIDANANDA

IV.18 Due to His changelessness, changes in the mind-stuff are always known to the Purusha, who is its Lord.

SHEARER

IV.18 But the mind itself is always experienced because it is witnessed by the unchanging Self.

TAIMNI

IV.18 The modifications of the mind are always known to its lord on account of the changelessness of the *Puruṣa*.

VIVEKANANDA

IV.17 The states of the mind are always known because the Lord of the mind, the Purusha, is unchangeable.

IV.19

न तत् स्वाभासं दृश्यत्वात् ॥ १९ ॥

na tat svābhāsaṃ dṛśyatvāt

न	na	not	
तत्	tat	that; here: mind (is)	
स्वाभासं	svābhāsaṃ		
स्व -	sva-	own	self-luminous
आभासं	ābhāsaṃ	light; luminosity	
आ - ā-: from all sides + to shine			
√भास् bhās: to shine			
दृश्यत्वात्	dṛśya-tvāt	[*because of/due to*] being perceptible	
√दृश् dṛś: to see + -त्व -tva: -ness or –ible or -ility			

ARYA

IV.19 That (mind) is not self-luminous, for it is perceived (by the Consciousness Principle).

BAILEY

IV.19 Because it can be seen or cognised it is apparent that the mind is not the source of illumination.

DVIVEDI

IV.19 Nor it is self-illuminative, for it is a perceptible.

FEUERSTEIN

IV.19 That [consciousness] has no self-luminosity because of [its] object-character.

HOUSTON

IV.19 That (*citta*) is not self-luminous because of its *dṛśya*-seeable nature.

JNANESHVARA

IV.19 That mind is not self-illuminating, as it is the object of knowledge and perception by the pure consciousness.

PRABHAVANANDA

IV.19 The mind is not self-luminous, since it is an object of perception.

PUROHIT

IV.19 The mind does not shine by itself, being an object of perception.

SATCHIDANANDA

IV.19 The mind-stuff is not self-luminous because it is an object of perception by the Purusha.

SHEARER

IV.19 The mind does not shine by its own light. It too is an object, illumined by the Self.

TAIMNI

IV.19 Nor is it self-illuminative, for it is perceptible.

VIVEKANANDA

IV.18 The mind is not self-luminous, being an object.

IV.20

एकसमये चोभयानवधारणम् ॥ २० ॥

eka-samaye cobhayānavadhāraṇam

एकसमये	ekasamaye		
एक -	eka-	one	simultaneous;
समये	samaye	[*at*] time	[*at*] the same time

सम् - sam-: together with, completely + √इ i: to go

च	ca	and
उभय -	ubhaya-	(of) both
अनवधारणम्	an-avadhāraṇam	non-cognizable

अन् - an-: non-, un-, without + -अव - -ava-: away, off + √धृ dhṛ: to hold

ARYA

IV.20 (If it were suggested that mind recognises both the object as well as itself) (it is) not (possible to have) the recognition of both at one time.

BAILEY

IV.20 Neither can it know two objects simultaneously, itself and that which is external to itself.

DVIVEDI

IV.20 Moreover, it is impossible to cognise two things at one and the same time.

FEUERSTEIN

IV.20 And [this implies] the impossibility-of-cognising both [consciousness and object] simultaneously.

HOUSTON

IV.20 And (because of its non-luminous *dṛśya*-seeable nature), the impossibility of cognizing both (*citta*-the field and an object) at the same time.

JNANESHVARA

IV.20 Nor can both the mind and the illuminating process be cognized simultaneously.

PRABHAVANANDA

IV.20 And since it cannot perceive both subject and object simultaneously.

PUROHIT

IV.20 Mind cannot at the same time know itself and any other object.

SATCHIDANANDA

IV.20 The mind-stuff cannot perceive both subject and object simultaneously [which proves it is not self-luminous].

SHEARER

IV.20 Not being self-luminous, the mind cannot be aware of its object and itself at the same time.

TAIMNI

IV.20 Moreover, it is impossible for it to be of both ways (as perceiver and perceived) at the same time.

VIVEKANANDA

IV.19 On account of its being unable to cognize both at the same time, [the mind is not self-luminous].

IV.21

चित्तान्तरदृश्ये बुद्धिबुद्धेरतिप्रसङ्गः स्मृतिसङ्करश्च ॥ २१ ॥

cittāntara-dṛśye buddhi-buddher ati-prasaṅgaḥ smṛti-saṅkaraś ca

चित्त - — citta- — (of) energy field called mind in all aspects; mind-field; field of consciousness; consciousness; mind-stuff

√चित् cit: to perceive; to be bright

अन्तर - — antara- — lit.: inner: another

(चित्तान्तर: here: another mind)

दृश्ये — dṛśye — [*in*/*upon*] being the object of perception; [*in*/*upon*] being seeable/perceivable

√दृश् dṛś: to see

बुद्धिबुद्धेः — buddhibuddheḥ

- **बुद्धि -** — buddhi - — faculty of citta by which an object is reflected: cognition
  √बुध् budh: to be aware
- **बुद्धेः** — buddheḥ — [*from*] *buddhi*
  √बुध् budh: to be aware

(बुद्धिबुद्धेः: [*because of*] another discriminatory instrument; discriminatory instrumentation; [*due to*] buddhi of buddhi)

अतिप्रसङ्गः — ati-prasaṅgaḥ — infinite regression

अति - ati-: beyond, over + प्र - pra-: forward, onward + √सञ्ज् sañj: to adhere

स्मृति - — smṛti- — memory

√स्मृ smṛ: to remember

सङ्करः — saṅkaraḥ — confusion

समकृ samkṛ: सम् - sam-: together + √कृ kṛ: to do = to mix/confuse; to pour/scatter/disperse

च — ca — and

ARYA

IV.21 (If it were suggested) that (the mind) is the object of perception of another mind then (the argument will suffer) a fallacious stretch (ad infinitum) so as (there will have to be) another buddhi for that buddhi (and for that buddhi, another and so on). Also (there will be) confusion of memories (as to which memory is of which buddhi!)

BAILEY

IV.21 If knowledge of the mind (chitta) by a remoter mind is postulated, an infinite number of knowers must be inferred, and the sequence of memory reactions would tend to infinite confusion.

DVIVEDI

IV.21 If cognition by another mind (be postulated) there would be an infinity of cognisers, and confusion of memory also.

FEUERSTEIN

IV.21 If consciousness [were] perceived by another [consciousness], [this would lead to infinite] regress from cognition to cognition and the confusion of memory.

HOUSTON

IV.21 If citta were seeable by other *citta* (there would be) an infinite regression from one *buddhi*-function of cognition to another *buddhi*, and the confusion of memory.

JNANESHVARA

IV.21 If one mind were illumined by another, as its master, then there would be an endless and absurd progression of cognitions, as well as confusion.

PRABHAVANANDA

IV.21 If one postulates a second mind to perceive the first, then one would have to postulate an infinite number of minds; and this would cause confusion of memory.

PUROHIT

IV.21 If we grant a second mind illuminating the first, we grant what is ridiculous; it would confuse memory.

SATCHIDANANDA

IV.21 If the perception of one mind by another mind be postulated, we would have to assume an endless number of them and the result would be confusion of memory.

SHEARER

IV.21 Nor is the mind illumined by another more subtle mind, for that would imply the absurdity of an infinite series of minds, and the resulting confusion of memories.

TAIMNI

IV.21 If cognition of one mind by another (be postulated) we would have to assume cognition of cognitions and confusion of memories also.

VIVEKANANDA

IV.20 Another cognising mind being assumed, there will be no end to such assumptions, and confusion of memory will be the result.

IV.22

चितेरप्रतिसङ्क्रमायास्तदाकारापत्तौ स्वबुद्धिसंवेदनम् ॥ २२ ॥

citer apratisaṅkramāyās tad-ākārā pattau sva-buddhi-saṃvedanam

चितेः	citeḥ	[*of*] Consciousness Principle;
√चित् *cit: to be aware*		[*of*] transcendental awareness
अप्रतिसङ्क्रमायाः	a-pratisaṅkramāyāḥ	[*because of*] that which passes through;
अ - *a-: without* +		[*due to*] no changes/ transitions;
प्रति - *prati-: in direction of, in return* +		unchanging; immutable
सम् - *sam-: together* + क्रम *krama: action* (√कृ *kṛ: to move)*		
तद् -	tad-	(to) that
आकार	ākāra	form; shape
आ - *ā-: with, near to* + √कृ *kṛ: to make*		
आपत्तौ	āpattau	[*upon*] assuming/appearing/occurring
आ *ā-: (indicates intensification or augmentation)* + √पत् *pat: to fall*		
स्वबुद्धि -	sva-buddhi-	own cognition; own buddhi;
स्व - *sva-: own* + √बुध् *buddh: to be aware*		*faculty by which an object is reflected—Houston*
संवेदनम्	saṃvedanam	knowing; experiencing
सम् - *sam-: fully, completely, perfectly* + √विद् *vid: to know*		

ARYA

IV.22 The Consciousness Principle, which in fact does not undergo changes, (reflects in and) assumes (thereby) the forms of its own buddhi (and thus gains) awareness (of what is reflecting in that buddhi from outside).

BAILEY

IV.22 When the spiritual intelligence which stands alone and freed from objects, reflects itself in the mind stuff, then comes awareness of the Self.

DVIVEDI

IV.22 When the never-changing soul takes its form, then arises knowledge of its own cognition.

FEUERSTEIN

IV.22 When the unchanging transcendental-awareness assumes the shape of that [consciousness], experience of one's own cognitions [becomes possible].

HOUSTON

IV.22 The unchanging awareness (of *puruṣa*-the self), has an experience of its *buddhi*-function of cognition, upon the appearance of a form in that (*citta*-field).

JNANESHVARA

IV.22 When the unchanging consciousness appears to take on the shape of that finest aspect of mind-field (IV.18), then the experience of one's own cognition process is possible.

PRABHAVANANDA

IV.22 The pure consciousness of the Atman is unchangeable. As the reflection of its consciousness falls upon the mind, the mind takes the form of the Atman and appears to be conscious.

PUROHIT

IV.22 Though Self does not move, it is reflected in the mind, and when mind takes the form of that reflection, Self becomes conscious of sensation.

SATCHIDANANDA

IV.22 The consciousness of the Purusha is unchangeable; by getting the reflection of it, the mind-stuff becomes conscious of the Self.

SHEARER

IV.22 When the unmoving consciousness of the Self assumes the form of intellect, it becomes conscious mind.

TAIMNI

IV.22 Knowledge of its own nature through self-cognition (is obtained) when consciousness assumes that form in which it does not pass from place to place.

VIVEKANANDA

IV.21 The Essence of Knowledge (the Purusha) is unchangeable; when the mind takes Its form, it becomes conscious.

IV.23

द्रष्टृदृश्योपरक्तं चित्तं सर्वार्थम् ॥ २३ ॥

draṣṭṛ-dṛśyoparaktaṃ cittaṃ sarvārtham

द्रष्टृ - draṣṭṛ- (by) Seer (and)

√दृश् dṛś: to see

दृश्य - dṛśya- that which is to be seen

√दृश् dṛś: to see

उपरक्तं uparaktaṃ coloured through reflection

उप - upa-: toward, near to + √रञ्ज् raj: to excite

चित्तं cittaṃ energy field called mind in all aspects; mind-field; field of consciousness; consciousness; mind-stuff

√चित् cit: to perceive; to be bright

सर्व - sarva- all; everything

अर्थम् artham (is) scattered towards (all) objects and matters

√अर्थ् arth: to intend

ARYA

IV. 23 The mind coloured with the seer and objects of sight is scattered toward all objects (or matters) (and is not intent or one-pointed).

BAILEY

IV.23 Then the mind stuff, reflecting both the knower and the knowable, becomes omniscient.

DVIVEDI

IV.23 The mind tinged by the seer and seen has everything for its subject.

FEUERSTEIN

IV.23 [Provided that] consciousness is colored by the 'seer' and the 'seen', [it can perceive] any object.

HOUSTON

IV.23 *Citta*-the field, colored because of *draṣṭṛ*-the seer and *dṛśya*-the seeable, (encompasses) all objects.

JNANESHVARA

IV.23 Therefore, the mind field, which is colored by both seer and seen, has the potential to perceive any and all objects.

PRABHAVANANDA

IV.23 The mind is able to perceive because it reflects both the Atman and the objects of perception.

PUROHIT

IV.23 The Seer and the seen are both reflected in the mind, hence it takes any conceivable form.

SATCHIDANANDA

IV.23 The mind-stuff, when colored by both Seer and seen, understands everything.

SHEARER

IV.23 The mind which is colored by both its object and the Self is all-embracing.

TAIMNI

IV.23 The mind coloured by the Knower (i.e., the *Puruṣa*) and the Known is all apprehending.

VIVEKANANDA

IV.22 Coloured by the Seer and the seen, the mind is able to understand everything.

IV.24

तदसङ्ख्येयवासनाभिश्चित्रमपि परार्थं संहत्यकारित्वात् ॥ २४ ॥

tad asaṅkhyeya-vāsanābhiś citram-api parārthaṃ saṃhatya-kāritvāt

तद्	tad		that
असङ्ख्येय -	a-saṅkhyeya-		uncountable; countless; innumerable
अ - a-: un-/non-/not/without + सम् - sam-: fully, completely + √ख्या khyā: to be mentioned			
वासनाभिः	vāsanābhiḥ		[*with/due to*] vāsanā: subconscious desires; subliminal traits
√वस् vas: to abide/reside			
चित्रम्	citram		variegated; multicolored
√चित् cit: to be visible			
अपि	api		even; although
परार्थं	pararthaṃ		
पर -	para-	other	(remains) for the (service) purpose or sake of another
अर्थं	arthaṃ	purpose	
√अर्थ् arth: to intend			
संहत्यकारित्वात्	saṃhatyakāritvāt		
संहत्य -	saṃhatya-	collaborate	[*because of*] being an aggregate; [*due to*] activity acting in association (with Puruṣa)
सम् - sam-: fully, completely + √हन् han: to strike			
कारित्वात्	kāritvāt	[*because of*] activity	
√कृ kṛ: to do			

ARYA

IV.24 That mind, even multi-coloured, with uncountable vāsanās (remains to serve) the purpose of another (i.e., puruṣha) because of being an aggregate (as all things, such as a house, that are composite of many, only exist for the service of another).

BAILEY

IV.24 The mind stuff also, reflecting as it does an infinity of mind impressions, becomes the instrument of the Self and acts as a unifying agent.

DVIVEDI

IV.24 Though variegated by innumerable *vāsanās*, it acts for another, for it acts in association.

FEUERSTEIN

IV.24 That [consciousness], though speckled with countless subliminal-traits, is other-purposed due to [its being limited to] collaborate activity.

HOUSTON

IV.24 That (*citta*), although variegated by uncountable *vāsanā*-subliminal traits, exists for the purpose of another (*puruṣa*-the self) due to its activation by collaboration.

JNANESHVARA

IV.24 That mind field, though filled with countless impressions, exists for the benefit of another witnessing consciousness, as the mind field is operating only in combination with those impressions.

PRABHAVANANDA

IV.24 Though the mind has innumerable impressions and desires, it acts only to serve another, the Atman; for, being a compound substance, it cannot act independently, and for its own sake.

PUROHIT

IV.24 The mind is coloured with innumerable desires, and as mind and desires work hand in hand, it follows that mind works to please someone else.

SATCHIDANANDA

IV.24 Though having countless desires, the mind-stuff exists for the sake of another [the Purusha] because it can act only in association with it.

SHEARER

IV.24 And the mind, despite its countless separative tendencies, exists for the sake of the Self, because it is dependent upon it.

TAIMNI

IV.24 Though variegated by innumerable *Vāsanās*, it (the mind) acts for another (*Puruṣa*) for it acts in association.

VIVEKANANDA

IV.23 The mind, though variegated on acount of innumerable desires, acts for another (i.e. the Purusha), because it acts in combination.

IV.25

विशेषदर्शिन आत्मभावभावनाविनिवृत्तिः ॥ २५ ॥

viśeṣa-darśina ātma-bhāva-bhāvanā-vinivṛttiḥ

विशेषदर्शिनः	viśeṣadarśinaḥ		
विशेष -	viśeṣa-	distinction	[*of*] one who (has realized) (and) sees distinction
वि - vi-: apart, separate from + √शिष् śiṣ: to remain			
दर्शिनः	darśinaḥ	[*of*] one who sees	
√दृश् dṛś: to see			
आत्मभाव -	ātmabhāva-		
आत्म -	ātma-	self	self-sense (concerning the) being; aspects of self; mind as self
भाव -	bhāva-	sense	
√भू bhū: to become			
भावना -	bhāvanā-		thought; mental projection; dwelling in or on the mind
√भू bhū: to become			
विनिवृत्तिः	vinivṛttiḥ		complete cessation; discontinuation; turning of
वि - vi-: apart, separate from, reverse to +			
-नि - -ni-: low, downward motion, greatly opposed to +			
√वृत् vṛt: to whirl			

ARYA

IV.25 Of one who has realised the distinction (between mind and Consciousness Principle), (all) inquiry (full of doubts as to "who am I", "what am I", etc.) is (then) turned off (and ends).

BAILEY

IV.25 The state of isolated unity (withdrawn into the true nature of the Self) is the reward of the man who can discriminate between the mind stuff and the Self, or spiritual man.

DVIVEDI

IV.25 The cessation of the desire of knowing the nature of the soul (takes place) in one who has mastered the difference.

FEUERSTEIN

IV.25 For him who sees the distinction [between *sattva* and Self] [there comes about] the discontinuation of the projection of the [false] self-sense.

HOUSTON

IV.25 Of the one who sees the distinction (between *citta/sattva guṇa* and *puruṣa*), there is a discontinuation of perpetuating the sense of self (defined by *vṛtti*).

JNANESHVARA

IV.25 For one who has experienced this distinction between seer and this subtlest mind, the false identities and even the curiosity about the nature of one's own self come to an end.

PRABHAVANANDA

IV.25 The man of discrimination ceases to regard the mind as Atman.

PUROHIT

IV.25 He who sees clearly, refuses to identify mind with Self.

SATCHIDANANDA

IV.25 To one who sees the distinction between the mind and the Atman, thought of mind as the Atman ceases forever.

SHEARER

IV.25 All confusion about the nature of the Self vanishes for one who has seen its glory.

TAIMNI

IV.25 The cessation (of desire) for dwelling in the consciousness of *Ātmā* for one who has seen the distinction.

VIVEKANANDA

IV.24 For the discriminating the perception of the mind as Ātman ceases.

IV.26

तदाहि विवेकनिम्नं कैवल्यप्राग्भारं चित्तम् ॥ २६ ॥

tadā hi viveka-nimnaṃ kaivalya-prāgbhāraṃ cittam

तदा	tadā	then
हि	hi	indeed
विवेक -	viveka-	(towards) discriminatory,
वि - vi-: apart from, particular + √विच् vic: to examine/discern		discerning wisdom; here: distinction: between seer and seeable
निम्नं	nimnaṃ	inclines toward
नि - ni-: in, into + √नम् nam: to bend		
कैवल्य -	kaivalya-	(toward) Transcendent Solitude;
केवल kevala: alone		Final Liberation; Cosmic Freedom; Absoluteness; Independence
प्राग्भारं	prāgbhāraṃ	

प्राक -	prāk-	before; in front	weighted;
भारं	bhāraṃ	load; weight;	gravitating toward;
√भृ bhṛ: to bear		mass (borne)	borne onward

चित्तम्	cittam	energy field called mind
√चित् cit: to perceive; to be bright		in all aspects; mind-field; field of consciousness; consciousness; mind-stuff

ARYA

IV.26 Then the mind, bent towards discriminatory wisdom is weighted on (the side of) the state of absoluteness.

BAILEY

IV.26 The mind then tends toward discrimination and increasing illumination as to the true nature of the one Self.

DVIVEDI

IV.26 Then the mind is bent towards discrimination and is full of *kaivalya*.

FEUERSTEIN

IV.26 Then consciousness, [thus] inclined towards discernment, is borne onwards towards the aloneness [of the power of seeing].

HOUSTON

IV.26 Then *citta*, inclined toward *viveka*-discernment (between *sattva* and *puruṣa*), is borne on towards *Kaivalya*-the aloneness of the power of seeing.

JNANESHVARA

IV.26 Then the mind is inclined towards the highest discrimination, and gravitates towards absolute liberation between seer and seen.

PRABHAVANANDA

IV.26 When the mind is bent on the practice of discrimination, it moves toward liberation.

PUROHIT

IV.26 Intent on discrimination, his mind longs for liberation.

SATCHIDANANDA

IV.26 Then the mind-stuff is inclined toward discrimination and gravitates toward Absoluteness.

SHEARER

IV.26 Then, truly, the mind begins to experience the Self as separate from activity, and is naturally drawn towards Enlightenment.

TAIMNI

IV.26 Then, verily, the mind is inclined toward discrimination and gravitating toward *Kaivalya*.

VIVEKANANDA

IV.25 Then, bent on discriminating, the mind attains the previous state preliminary to kaivalya, isolation.

IV.27

तच्छिद्रेषु प्रत्ययान्तराणि संस्कारेभ्यः ॥ २७ ॥

tac-chidreṣu pratyayāntarāṇi saṃskārebhyaḥ

तद् -	tad-	(of) that
छिद्रेषु √छिद् *chid: to cut*	chidreṣu	[*in*] gap; [*in*] interval; [*in*] between
प्रत्यय - प्रति - *prati-: towards, in direction of* + √इ *i: to go*	pratyaya-	content of mind-field; cognition; cognition principle *immediate arising thought directed to an object—Houston* (here: distracting thoughts)
अन्तराणि	antarāṇi	other
संस्कारेभ्यः सम् - *sam-: together with, completely, perfectly* + √कृ *kṛ: to do*	saṃskārebhyaḥ	[*because of/due to*] saṃskāras; [*from*] past impressions/ subliminal activators

ARYA

IV.27 In the gaps of that mind (when it is not meditating, e.g., a monk wandering for alms) other cogitations and cognitions (continue) because of (previous) saṃskāras.

BAILEY

IV.27 Through force of habit, however, the mind will reflect other mental impressions and perceive objects of sensuous perception.

DVIVEDI

IV.27 In the breaks, there are other thoughts from impressions.

FEUERSTEIN

IV.27 In the intervals of that [involuting consciousness], other [new] presented-ideas [may arise] from the subliminal-activators.

HOUSTON

IV.27 In the intervals of that (*citta*, borne on towards *kaivalya*), other *pratyayas*-thoughts directed toward objects, are due to *sanskāra*-subliminal activators.

JNANESHVARA

IV.27 When there are breaks or breaches in that high discrimination, other impressions arise from the deep unconscious.

PRABHAVANANDA

IV.27 Distractions due to past impressions may arise if the mind relaxes its discrimination, even a little.

PUROHIT

IV.27 Sometimes in Illumination, impressions of the waking mind intervene.

SATCHIDANANDA

IV.27 In between, distracting thoughts may arise due to past impressions.

SHEARER

IV.27 All thoughts that arise to interrupt this discrimination are born of the latent impressions which still exist.

TAIMNI

IV.27 In the intervals arise other *Pratyayas* from the force of *Saṃskāras*.

VIVEKANANDA

IV.26 The thoughts that arise [from time to time] as obstructions to that come from impressions.

IV.28

हानमेषां क्लेशवदुक्तम् ॥ २८ ॥

hānam-eṣāṃ kleśavad uktam

हानम् √हा *hā: to leave*	hānam	cessation; prevention; removal; destruction; ending
एषां	eṣāṃ	[*of*] these; here: old impressions
क्लेशवत् √क्लिश् *kliś: to trouble, to be troubled*	kleśa-vat	[*possessed of*] kleśas/afflictions as in the case of kleśas/primary obstacles/ causes-of-affliction
उक्तम्	uktam	(is) described/explained/said

ARYA

IV.28 The prevention and destruction of these (intervening thoughts) is to be understood like that of the kleśhas (II.10, 11).

BAILEY

IV.28 These reflections are of the nature of hindrances, and the method of their overcoming is the same.

DVIVEDI

IV.28 Their destruction is after the manner of destroying the distractions.

FEUERSTEIN

IV.28 Their cessation [is achieved by the same means] as described for the causes-of-affliction.

HOUSTON

IV.28 The ending of these (*sanskāra* is achieved) as described for the *kleśa*—root causes of pain. (That is, by *pratiprasava*-non-activation).

JNANESHVARA

IV.28 The removal of those interfering thought patterns is by the same means by which the original colorings were removed.

PRABHAVANANDA

IV.28 They may be overcome in the same manner as the obstacles to enlightenment.

PUROHIT

IV.28 They should be destroyed as afflictions are destroyed (II.10-11).

SATCHIDANANDA

IV.28 They can be removed, as in the case of the obstacles explained before. [see Sutras II.1, 2, 10, 26]

SHEARER

IV.28 These are to be destroyed by the same means as were described for the causes of suffering.

TAIMNI

IV.28 Their removal like that of *Kleśas*, as has been described.

VIVEKANANDA

IV.27 Their destruction is in the same manner as that of ignorance, egoity, and so forth, as said before (II.10).

IV.29

प्रसङ्ख्यानेऽप्यकुसीदस्य सर्वथा विवेकख्यातेर्धर्ममेघः समाधिः ॥ २९ ॥

prasaṅkhyāne 'pyakusīdasya sarvathā viveka-khyater dharma-meghaḥ samādhiḥ

प्रसङ्ख्याने — prasaṅkhyāne — [*upon*] entering right knowledge: enlightenment/state of elevation; attainment of highest rewards, [*upon*] the perfection of discrimination; [*in*] the knowledge of the highest discrimination

प्र - pra-: forth, onward +
सम् - sam-: fully, completely, perfectly +
√ख्या khyā: to appear; to be known/named

अपि — api — even

अकुसीदस्य — a-kusīdasya — [*of*] one [*possessed of*] disinterest/ dispassion/detachment/non-self-interest

अ - a-: without + कु ku: deficiency +
√सद् sad: to sit; to apply oneself

सर्वथा — sarvathā — always; completely; totally; in all ways

विवेकख्यातेः — vivekakhyateḥ

- **विवेक -** — viveka- — [*through*] discernment
  वि - vi-: apart from, particular + √विच् vic: to examine/discern
- **ख्यातेः** — khyateḥ — vision; identification
  √ख्या khyā: to be known

→ [*through possession of*] knowledge of discernment/ discriminatory wisdom

धर्ममेघः — dharmameghaḥ

- **धर्म -** — dharma- — virtue; righteousness
  √धृ dhṛ: to hold
- **मेघः** — meghaḥ — cloud
  √मिह् mih: to make water

→ cloud of dharma; cloud of virtue

समाधिः — samādhiḥ — samādhi

सम् - sam-: together with, completely, perfectly + आ - ā-: near to, all around + √धा dhā: to put

ARYA

IV.29 To one who is no (longer) anxious even concerning enlightenment (comes) the dharma-megha samādhi through the thorough knowledge of discriminatory wisdom.

BAILEY

IV.29 The man who develops non-attachment even in his aspiration after illumination and isolated unity, becomes aware, eventually, through practised discrimination, of the overshadowing cloud of spiritual knowledge.

DVIVEDI

IV.29 Even after illumination, there arises, in one who works without attachment, the constant flow of pure discrimination called "the cloud of merit" which is the best *samādhi*.

FEUERSTEIN

IV.29 For the [yogin who is] always non-usurious even in [the state of elevation], [there follows], through the vision of discernment, the enstasy [designated as] 'dharma cloud'.

HOUSTON

IV.29 Of the (*citta*) which always has *viveka-khyāti*-the identification of discernment (between *sattva* and *puruṣa*), is without self-interest even regarding a state of elevation, there is *dharma-megha-samādhi*-absorption in the cloud of *dharma*.

JNANESHVARA

IV.29 When there is no longer any interest even in omniscience, that discrimination allows the samadhi, which brings an abundance of virtues like a rain cloud brings rain.

PRABHAVANANDA

IV.29 He who remains undistracted even when he is in possession of all the psychic powers, achieves, as the result of perfect discrimination, that samadhi which is called "the cloud of virtue."

PUROHIT

IV.29 When the yogi attains final discrimination, renounces even that, he attains the condition called 'Rain-cloud of Divinity'.

SATCHIDANANDA

IV.29 He who, due to his perfect discrimination, is totally disinterested even in the highest rewards remains in the constant discriminative discernment, which is called dharmamegha (cloud of dharma) samadhi.

SHEARER

IV.29 One who has attained complete discrimination between the subtlest level of mind and the Self has no higher knowledge to acquire. This is *dharma megha samādhi*—the state of Unclouded Truth.

TAIMNI

IV.29 In the case of one who is able to maintain a constant state of Vairāgya even towards the most exalted state of enlightenment and to exercise the highest kind of discrimination, follows Dharma-Megha-Samādhi.

VIVEKANANDA

IV.28 Even when arriving at the right discriminating knowledge of the essences, he who gives up the fruits— unto him comes as the result of perfect discrimination, the samadhi called the "cloud of virtue."

IV.30

तत: क्लेशकर्मनिवृत्तिः ॥ ३० ॥

tataḥ kleśa-karma-nivṛttiḥ

ततः	tataḥ	thereby; thence; from that
क्लेश - *√क्लिश् kliś: to trouble, to be troubled*	kleśa-	(of) kleśa: obstruction to samādhi; affliction/misery
कर्म - *√कृ kṛ: to do*	karma-	actions and reactions
निवृत्तिः *नि - ni-: opposed to, downward motion + √वृत् vṛt: to whirl*	nivṛttiḥ	cessation; discontinuance; freedom (from)

ARYA

IV.30 Then the kleŝhas and karmas cease.

BAILEY

IV.30 When this stage is reached then the hindrances and karma are overcome.

DVIVEDI

IV.30 Then (follows) cessation of distractions and action.

FEUERSTEIN

IV.30 Thence [follows] the discontinuation of the causes-of-affliction and of *karman*.

HOUSTON

IV.30 From that, the discontinuation of the *kleśa*-root causes of pain and *karma*.

JNANESHVARA

IV.30 After that dharma-meghah samadhi, the colorings of the kleshas and the karmas are removed.

PRABHAVANANDA

IV.30 Thence come cessation of ignorance, the cause of suffering, and freedom from the power of karma.

PUROHIT

IV.30 Then action and affliction come to an end.

SATCHIDANANDA

IV.30 From that samadhi all afflictions and karmas cease.

SHEARER

IV.30 It destroys the causes of suffering and the bondage of action disappears.

TAIMNI

IV.30 Then follows freedom from *Kleśas* and *Karmas*.

VIVEKANANDA

IV.29 From that comes cessation of pain and works.

IV.31

तदा सर्वावरणमलापेतस्य ज्ञानस्यानन्त्याज्ज्ञेयमल्पम् ॥ ३१ ॥

tadā sarvāvaraṇa-malāpetasya jñānasyānantyāj jñeyam-alpam

तदा	tadā	then
सर्व -	sarva-	(of/from) all
आवरण -	āvaraṇa-	(that which) veils; covers; distorts
आ - ā-: near to, from all sides + √वृ vṛ: to cover		
मल -	mala-	taints; impurities; imperfections
अपेतस्य	apetasya	[*of*] one removed;
अप - apa-: away, away from + √इ i: to go		[*of*] that which has removed
ज्ञानस्य -	jñānasya-	knowledge's; [*of*] knowledge
√ज्ञा jñā: to know		
आनन्त्यात्	ānantyāt	[*because of/due to*] infinity
अ - a-: without, free from + अन्त anta: end + -य -ya: -ness		
ज्ञेयम्	jñeyam	(yet) to be known
√ज्ञा jñā: to know		
अल्पम्	alpam	little

ARYA

IV.31 Then the knowledge, which is (now) free of all veils and impurities, is infinite (and therefore) little (is left yet) to be known.

BAILEY

IV.31 When, through the removal of the hindrances and the purification of all the sheaths, the totality of knowledge becomes available, naught further remains for the man to do.

DVIVEDI

IV.31 Then in consequence of the infinity of knowledge free from all obscuration and impurity, the knowable becomes small.

FEUERSTEIN

IV.31 Then, [when] all coverings of imperfection are removed little [remains] to be known because of the infinity of the [resulting] gnosis.

HOUSTON

IV.31 Then, because of the infinity of knowledge, which has removed the sediment of all coverings, little remains to be known.

JNANESHVARA

IV.31 Then, by the removal of those veils of imperfection, there comes the experience of the infinite, and the realization that there is almost nothing to be known.

PRABHAVANANDA

IV.31 Then the whole universe, with all its objects of sense-knowledge, becomes as nothing in comparison to that infinite knowledge which is free from all obstructions and impurities.

PUROHIT

IV.31 Mind without impurity and impediment, attains Infinite knowledge; what is worth knowing in this world becomes negligible.

SATCHIDANANDA

IV.31 Then all the coverings and impurities of knowledge are removed. Because of the infinity of this knowledge, what remains to be known is almost nothing.

SHEARER

IV.31 Knowledge which has been freed from the veils of impurity is unbounded. Whatever can be known is insignificant in its light.

TAIMNI

IV.31 Then, in consequence of the removal of all obscuration and impurities, that which can be known (through the mind) is but little in comparison with the infinity of knowledge (obtained in Enlightenment).

VIVEKANANDA

IV.30 Then knowledge, bereft of covering and impurities, becoming infinite, the knowable becomes small.

IV.32

ततः कृतार्थानां परिणामक्रमसमाप्तिर्गुणानाम् ॥ ३२ ॥

tataḥ kṛtārthānāṃ pariṇāma-krama-samāptir guṇānām

ततः	tataḥ	then; due to that	
कृतार्थानां	kṛtarthānāṃ		
कृत -	kṛta-	done;	[*possessed of*] those
√कृ *kṛ: to do*		fulfilled	whose purpose
अर्थानां	arthānāṃ	purpose [of]	is fulfilled
√अर्थ् *arth: to intend*			

परिणाम -	pariṇāmā-	(of) transformation; change;
परि - *pari-: all around, in addition to* + √नम् *nam: to bend*		alteration
क्रम -	krama-	(of) sequence; order; process; evolution
√क्रम् *kram: to step/stride*		
समाप्तिः	samāptiḥ	finish; terminate; conclude; end;
सम् - *sam-: completely, fully* + √आप् *āp: to reach*		full completion
गुणानाम्	guṇānām	guṇas'; [*of*] the guṇas
गुण *guṇa: strand*		

ARYA

IV.32 Then the (continuous) order of modification of the guṇas (comes to a) finish.

BAILEY

IV.32 The modifications of the mind stuff (or qualities of matter) through the inherent nature of the three gunas come to an end, for they have served their purpose.

DVIVEDI

IV.32 Then the succession of the transformations of the *guṇas* come to an end, they having fulfilled their end.

FEUERSTEIN

IV.32 Thence [comes about] the termination of the sequences in the transformation of the primary-constituents [whose] purpose is fulfilled.

HOUSTON

IV.32 Due to that, the conclusion of the *karma*-sequential progression of the changes of the *guṇas* whose purpose has been achieved.

JNANESHVARA

IV.32 Also resulting from that dharma-meghah samadhi (IV.29), the three primary elements or gunas (IV.13-IV.14) will have fulfilled their purpose, cease to transform into further transformations, and recede back into their essence.

PRABHAVANANDA

IV.32 Then the sequence of mutations of the gunas comes to an end, for they have fulfilled their purpose.

PUROHIT

IV.32 The procession of Qualities comes to an end; their purpose is fulfilled.

SATCHIDANANDA

IV.32 Then the gunas terminate their sequence of transformations because they have fulfilled their purpose.

SHEARER

IV.32 This *samādhi* completes the transformation of the *gunas* and fulfils the purpose of evolution.

TAIMNI

IV.32 The three *Guṇas*, having fulfilled their object, the process of change (in the *Guṇas*) comes to an end.

VIVEKANANDA

IV.31 Then are finished the successive transformations of the gunas, they having attained their end.

IV.33

क्षणप्रतियोगी परिणामापरान्तनिर्ग्राह्यः क्रमः ॥ ३३ ॥

kṣaṇa-pratiyogī pariṇāmāparānta-nirgrāhyaḥ kramaḥ

क्षण -	kṣaṇa-	moments
√क्षण् kṣan: to break		
प्रतियोगी	pratiyogī	corresponding; correlative; uninterrupted succession
प्रति - prati-: toward, in direction of +		
√युज् yuj: lit.: to yoke; to unite/dissolve; samādhi		
परिणाम -	pariṇāma-	(of) transformations; changes; alterations; modifications
परि - pari-: all around, in addition to + √नम् nam: to bend		
अपर -	apara-	other } (at) final end; termination
अन्त -	anta-	end, terminus } (at) final end; termination
निर्ग्राह्यः	nirgrāhyaḥ	that can be grasped; understood; entirely apprehensible
निर् nir-: free from + √ग्राह् grāh: to grasp		
क्रमः	kramaḥ	sequence; order; process; succession
√क्रम् kram: to step/stride		

ARYA

IV.33 Krama, sequence, (is that state which) corresponding to (each passing) moment, is (finally) grasped at the end of (a series of) modifications.

BAILEY

IV.33 Time,which is the sequence of the modifications of the mind, likewise terminates, giving place to the Eternal Now.

DVIVEDI

IV.33 Succession is that which is known by moments and is cognised at the last modification.

FEUERSTEIN

IV.33 Sequence [means that which is] correlative to the moment [of time], apprehensible at the terminal-point of a [particular] transformation.

HOUSTON

IV.33 The *karma*-sequential progression, correlative to its *kṣana*-moments, is apprehensible at the final end of its changes.

JNANESHVARA

IV.33 The sequencing process of moments and impressions corresponds to the moments of time, and is apprehended at the end point of the sequence.

PRABHAVANANDA

IV.33 This is the sequence of the mutations which take place at every moment, but which are only perceived at the end of a series.

PUROHIT

IV.33 Procession means changes that occur from moment to moment, but seen only when that moment is gone.

SATCHIDANANDA

IV.33 The sequence [referred to above] means an uninterrupted succession of moments which can be recognized at the end of their transformations.

SHEARER

IV.33 Now the process by which evolution unfolds through time is understood.

TAIMNI

IV.33 The process, corresponding to moments which become apprehensible at the final end of transformation (of the *Guṇas*), is *Kramaḥ*.

VIVEKANANDA

IV.32 The changes that exist in relation to moments, and which are perceived at the other end (i.e. at the end of a series), are what is meant by succession.

IV.34 पुरुषार्थशून्यानां गुणानां प्रतिप्रसवः
कैवल्यं स्वरूपप्रतिष्ठा वा चितिशक्तेरिति ॥ ३४ ॥

puruṣārtha-śūnyānāṃ guṇānāṃ prati-prasavaḥ
kāivalyaṃ svarūpa-pratiṣṭhā vā citi-śakter iti

पुरुषार्थ -	puruṣārtha-		
पुरुष -	puruṣa	the Conscious Principle	[*possessed of*] purpose of the Conscious Principle
अर्थ -	artha-	purpose [*of*]	
√अर्थ् arth: to intend			
शून्यानां	śūnyānāṃ	[*of*] those devoid	
√श्वि śvi: to swell			
गुणानां	guṇānāṃ	guṇas'; [*of*] the guṇas	
गुण guṇa: strand			
प्रतिप्रसवः	prati-prasavaḥ	re-absorption; return-to-source; dissolution	
प्रति - prati-: towards, back, in opposition to +			
प्र - pra-: forth, onward + √सू sū: to set in motion			
कैवल्यं	kaivalyaṃ	Final Liberation; Absoluteness; Cosmic Freedom; Independence	
केवल kevala: alone			
स्वरूपप्रतिष्ठा	svarūpapratiṣṭhā		
स्वरूप -	svarūpa-	own form/ nature	established/settled in its own nature
प्रतिष्ठा	pratiṣṭhā	establishment	
प्रति - prati-: towards, in direction of + √स्था sthā: to stand			
वा	vā	or	
चितिशभेः	citiśakteḥ		
चिति -	citi-	awareness	[*possessed of*] (pure) Consciousness Force/ Power of Pure Consciousness
√चित् cit: to perceive/be bright			
शक्तेः	śakteḥ	Power's	
√शक् śak: to be able			

इति **iti** **FINI**

ARYA

IV.34 The dissolution of guṇas (into their original cause) (because they are) no (longer needed) to fulfill any purpose of the Conscious (is called the state of) absoluteness, and (then) the Consciousness Force is established in its own nature.

BAILEY

IV.34 The state of isolated unity becomes possible when the three qualities of matter (the three gunas or potencies of nature) no longer exercise any hold over the Self. The pure spiritual consciousness withdraws into the One.

DVIVEDI

IV.34 This inverse resolution of the *guṇas* void of the motive to act for the *puruśa* is *kaivalya*; or it is the power of the soul centered in itself.

FEUERSTEIN

IV.34 The process-of-involution of the primary-constituents, devoid of purpose for the Self, is [what is called] aloneness [of seeing] or the establishment of the power of awareness in [its] own-form.
In other words, it is absolute.
Finis.

HOUSTON

IV.34 The *pratiprasava*-return-to-source of the *guṇas*, devoid of purpose for *puruṣa*-the self is *kaivalya*, or the abidance in its own essence (*svarūpa*) of *citta-śaki*-the power of awareness (of *puruṣa*-the self / *draṣṭṛ*-the seer).

JNANESHVARA

IV.34 When those primary elements involve, or resolve themselves back into that out of which they emerged, there comes liberation, wherein the power of pure consciousness becomes established in its true nature.

PRABHAVANANDA

IV.34 Since the gunas no longer have any purpose to serve for the Atman, they resolve themselves into Prakriti. This is liberation. The Atman shines forth in its own pristine nature, as pure consciousness.

PUROHIT

IV.34 The dissolution of Qualities in their source,
when nothing remains to be achieved, is liberation;
the revelation of the power of Self, the foundation of the beauty of Self.

SATCHIDANANDA

IV.34 Thus, the supreme state of Independence manifests while the gunas reabsorb themselves into Prakriti, having no more purpose to serve the Purusha. Or, to look from another angle, the power of pure consciousness settles in its own pure nature.

SHEARER

IV.34 The *gunas*, their purpose fulfilled, return to their original state of harmony; and pure unbounded consciousness remains, forever established in its own absolute nature.
This is Enlightenment.

TAIMNI

IV.34 Kaivalya is the state (of Enlightement) following re-mergence of the Guṇas because of their becoming devoid of the object of the Puruṣa. In this state the Puruṣa is established in his Real nature which is pure consciousness.

Finis.

VIVEKANANDA

IV.33 The resolution of the gunas in the inverse order, when they are bereft of any motive of action for the Purusha, is kaivalya (isolation or freedom); or kaivalya is the establishment of the Power of Knowledge in Its own nature.

॥ इति चतुर्थ पादः ॥

iti caturtaḥ pādaḥ

इति	iti	thus; herewith [concludes]
चतुर्थ	caturtaḥ	fourth
पादः	pādaḥ	chapter, part

Thus [Concludes] the Fourth Chapter

॥ इति पातञ्जलयोगसूत्रं समाप्तम् ॥

iti pātañjala-yoga-sūtram samāptam

इति	iti	thus; herewith [concludes]
पातञ्जल -	pātañjala-	Pātañjali's
योगसूत्रं	yoga-sūtram	Yoga-Sūtra
समाप्तम्	samāptam	concludes

Thus Concludes the Yoga-Sūtra of Pātañjali

PART II

THE REALM OF THE YOGA-SŪTRA

What Is Yoga?

Despite many misconceptions, Yoga is a meta-psychological process, not a religion or a system of physical fitness per se. As asserted earlier, Yoga is an ancient system of personal discipline that integrates physical, psychological, and spiritual practices. However, Yoga practices can be integrated into religious observance and can deepen the religious experience of devotees of any religion. The word *Yoga* is synonymous with *samādhi*, the transcendent, superconscious state of being or God realization, referred to by Jesus as "the peace that passeth all understanding."

Philosophically, Yoga presents a hypothesis that this transcendent level of consciousness is available to humans and offers a comprehensive base of theory, ethical interaction, and, most important, technique to help us access it. For the most part Yoga is a practical, not speculative, philosphy. The *Yoga-Sūtra of Patañjali* is the textbook, or technical manual, for the field.

The definition of the word Yoga depends on the context of usage, and, in English, may refer to four possible meanings:

1. A state of transcendent consciousness—samādhi
2. One of the six branches of formal Indian orthodox philosophy that present pathways to this consciousness
3. An ancient system of spiritual disciplines and practices that are said to lead to this state of consciousness
4. A tradition, or school, of Yoga, that perpetuates those practices

Most popular works on Yoga in English maintain that the term Yoga emerges from the Sanskrit root *yuj*. They generally select as their definition: "union; to join, restrain, keep under control, as in yoking." Several scholars, including Swami Veda Bhāratī (formerly Dr. Usharbudh Arya), a Brahmin pandit and Sanskrit professor whose cradle language was Sanskrit, submit that this definition is drawn from the tenth conjugation. Their contention is that while this is correct in itself, it does not reflect the primary focus of Yoga's core texts, including the *Yoga-Sūtra of Patañjali*.

Swami Veda explains that while the yoking aspect has many ancient references, yuj is employed in the *Vedas*, *Upaniṣads*, and the *Yoga-Sūtra* in another context—in several conjugations, the root yuj- or yug- transforms to *samādh-*, as in samādhi, the transcendent, superconscious state of being or God realization. Vyāsa, in his commentary on the *Yoga-Sūtra*, asserts, "Yoga is samādhi." At its etymological core, and particularly in the context of the *Yoga-Sūtra*, the word *Yoga* is a technical term that refers primarily to a transcendent state of consciousness—samādhi—and secondarily to the practices that facilitate this awareness.

Patañjali's very specific definition of yoga is presented at the beginning of his book in Sūtra I.2:

योगश्चित्तवृत्तिनिरोधः

yogaś citta-vṛtti nirodhaḥ
lit.: yoga [is] [the] nirodha [of the] vṛittis [of/in the] citta

योगः	चित्त	वृत्ति	निरोधः
yogaḥ	citta-	vṛtti	nirodhaḥ
Yoga [is]	[of] mind-field	operations	cessation
union [is]	[of] mental	states	dissolution
samādhi [is]	[of] mind-stuff	activities	control
	[of] consciousness	modifications	repression
	[of] energy-field-called-the-mind	fluctuations	suppression
		oscillations	disappearance
		wave-making action	

The sūtra, in Devanagari, the Sanskrit alphabet and grammar,

offers a critical explanation

योगः (yogaḥ) and निरोधः (nirodhaḥ) share an ending, ः

This ending, called *visarga*, creates, in this case, the equivalent of an equal sign: =

Therefore: योगः (yogaḥ) = निरोधः (nirodhaḥ)

[and both = samādhi]

Nirodha is a state of consciousness in itself in which all fluctuations (mental activities), called *vṛittis*, in the energy-field-we-call-the-mind (*citta*) come to stillness: Yoga. The varied word selections made by different translators of this sūtra indicate a wide range of opinion about the nature of this state and how it comes to pass. Because of multiple meanings for each word, the definition of Yoga given by Patañjali can take several forms and be quite fluidic, according to the understanding of the translator.

Two typical translations define Yoga thusly:

A. "Yoga is the suppression of mental operations" (various sources)

B. "Yoga is the dissolution of fluctuations in the mind-field as they are absorbed into their primal origins" (*Arya*)

These definitions contrast two conceptual approaches: a) joining, restraining, controlling, as in yoking, and b) disappearing into samādhi, the transcendent, superconscious state of being or God realization. While both are technically correct, Yoga defined as yoking implies two or more separate things linked together while Yoga defined as a state of transcendent, undifferentiated consciousness suggests a more subtle relationship, perhaps like salt dissolved in water.

These two translations, though quite different, are both correct and will appropriately appeal to people at different stages in their development.

Usharbudh Ayra/Sw. Veda Bhāratī resolves many disputes with this explanation:

> The oral tradition has scant regard for the artificial rules of grammar, but the grammarians themselves admit, as does Patañjali (not in the *Yoga-Sutras* but in the *Mahābhāṣhya*, his work on grammar), that grammarians only acknowledge the usage of words as found in the *Vedas* and among the people. Therefore, one need not concern himself unduly if there appears to be conflict between grammarians and philosophers. Furthermore, since philosophy is being studied here, one needs to accept Vyāsa's statement that the word "Yoga" in the *Yoga-sūtras* means "samādhi."[4]

Later he continues:

> An alternative explanation is that yoga is being taught to the students of Patañjali on two different levels: (1) an experiential level, which cannot be put into formal wording; and (2) a formal system of philosphy with its own terminology. Sometimes the two do not coincide. The formal systematization of the philosophy states that yoga is the control of the modifications of the mind-field and samādhi is the eighth of its limbs (*aṅgas*) and means. Vyāsa, the commentator par excellence, does not wish the student to forget that true follower of yoga must see even beyond these definitions…[5]

---

[4] Arya, Usharbudh. *Yoga-Sūtras of Patañjali with The Exposition of Vyāsa – Vol. 1 – The Samādhi-pāda.* Honesdale, PA: Himalayan International Institute, 1986. p. 74.

[5] Ibid. *Yoga-Sūtras of Patañjali with The Exposition of Vyāsa – Vol. 1 – The Samādhi-pāda.* Honesdale, PA: Himalayan International Institute, 1986. p. 76.

The Inquiry Into Life's Persistent Questions

In the West, the inquiry into reality and social and personal values is called *philosophy* (Gr. *philos*: love [of], *sophia*: wisdom). No school of Western philosophy is over twenty-five hundred years old. In India, philosophy has been a beloved pastime and occupation for at least five thousand years. Every nuance of consideration to be found in Western philosophy was explored to exhaustion in India before Western civilization, as such, appeared. Every school of philosophy in the Euro-cultures has its equivalent in India, but the reverse is not the case. Yoga is a prime example of the difference.

In India the quest for the Real, the heart of philosophy, is called *Darśana*. This is the title given to the orthodox tradition of Indian Philosophy. While Darśana is usually translated as "philosophy," the term is more complex, emerging from the root *dṛṣ*: to see or experience. Darśana might also be translated as "view," "insight," or "experience."

There are six orthodox schools of philosophy, called the *Ṣaḍ Darśana*, forming a body of theory and practice (directed activity). These schools, of which Yoga is a part, fit together as components of a single system. Though not in agreement on every point or mode of approach, each school regards the others' disciplines as intrinsic and necessary elements in a complementary, graduated, and transitioning interrelationship.

Briefly, the Ṣaḍ Darśana are classically presented in the following order:

Nyāya: logic
Vaiśeṣika: natural science
Sāṅkhya: dualistic theory
Yoga: meditation and transcendence
Mīmāṃsa: Vedic interpretation, ritual, and social obligation
Vedānta: unitary theory—culmination of the Vedas

As disciplines, they are often paired:

Nyāya—Vaiśeṣika
Sāṅkhya—Yoga
Mīmāṃsa—Vedānta

One of Yoga's functions in the Ṣaḍ Darśana is to provide a system for inquiry, similar to science in Western philosophy.

Each of the Darśana has an acknowledged founder and a primary core text. Patañjali is not regarded as the ultimate founder of Yoga, but his *Yoga-Sūtra* is a work of such towering authority that all of his predecessors, apart from mythological characters, have been forgotten. This results in Patañjali being accurately referred to as the "father of Yoga," in the [Yoga] era initiated by his *Sūtra*.

All of the sages and *ṛṣis* (sometimes spelled *rishis*), the enlightened seers or sages, who founded or seminally revised a *darśana* field composed the primary core text of the field in the exigical form called *sūtra*.

This brings us to the question:

What Is A *Sūtra*?

The term *sūtra* refers to a traditional Indian pedagogical device. It is a Sanskrit word derived from the root-verb *siv*: to sew, which literally translates into English as "thread." Our English word *suture* is related to it.
A sūtra can be either an excruciatingly brief, terse statement or a complete volume composed of these statements. The intent of both is to present a topic or subject completely but with the utmost succinctness possible. In the form of a very intense phrase, a single sūtra embodies a complete statement that is integral to a series of sūtras. The *Yoga-Sūtra* comprises 196 sūtras that comprehensively address every area of consideration in Yoga.

When sūtra refers to a volume of sūtras it receives the lyrical description: "*a single thread unadorned by a single bead*," reflecting both the distillate quality of each statement and the unbroken continuity in the relationship of the discrete statements. The rigorous simplicity imposed by the sūtra methodology elegantly reveals the essence of the subject under examination. This compression can be so extreme as to take a form closer to a hint or an indication than discourse as ordinarily presented. Translating sūtras is more challenging than translating poetry or jokes. It is not unusual for a sūtra to be so laconic that it is incomprehensible without commentary. These statements combine to form a text that unfolds a complete understanding of a field of inquiry. *Understanding*, in this sense, goes beyond the usual English definition. It is said that just reading the sequence of presentation by the sūtra method promotes a gradual unfoldment into deeper states of consciousness.

No precise equivalents for the sūtra method exist in the Euro-cultures. A sūtra is sometimes also called an aphorism, but this is not altogether accurate. An aphorism is a compact saying that is quite complete and understandable in itself, which not necessarily the case with a sūtra. The sūtras are linked one with another and are not designed to stand alone.

Western scholars contend that the sūtra system evolved prior to written language as a mnemonic device to facilitate memorization of critical texts. Indian scholars, however, assert that in addition to their mnemonic efficiency, sūtras also have an intrinsic existence and power and are discovered by great ṛṣis in the same manner as the sacred syllables known as *mantras*—while the ṛṣi is in samādhi, the enlightened state. Therefore sūtras, both as phrases and complete texts, provide a valid and productive focus for meditation.

Sūtras fall into one of six categories:

adhikara/udesha:	those that state the subject of a text or a portion thereof
sanja:	those that give a definition
paribhasha:	those that give rules for application of other sūtras
vidhi:	those that enjoin an act
iyama:	those that restrict or give injunction against an act
atidesha:	those that present an analogy

These categories apply to all the source texts, which are sūtra-style presentations, of the six schools of Orthodox Indian philosophy.

Who Was Patañjali?

One of the tasty mysteries so often served up by scholars of Indian literary and philosophical history is: how many Patañjalis were there: one, two—or more? Was Patañjali a surname?

Six monumental works in Indian literature are attributed to Patañjali. The best known of these is the *Yoga-Sūtra of Patañjali*. As is usual in these matters, unanimous agreement is unthinkable. However, an army of formidable scholars contends that before undertaking this ultimate description of human psychology and spiritual potential, he wrote the *Mahābhāṣya on the Aṣṭadhyāyī of Pāṇini*. The *Mahābhāṣya* is a set of detailed commentaries clarifying *The Aṣṭadhyāyī of Pāṇini*, the most ancient and comprehensive of all Sanskrit grammars. In the process, Patañjali greatly clarified Sanskrit and, no doubt, cleared the way for his subsequent volume. It is a rare luxury for a scholar to be able to define his language of use at a cultural level before beginning his main work.

In addition to the *Yoga-Sūtra* and the *Mahābhāṣya*, Patañjali (or Patañjalis) has been credited with a number of works, some yet to be translated into Western languages. Among them:

the *Patañjala*, a treatise on alchemy;
the *Adhirā-karika* on the *Sāṅkhya* (one of the six schools of orthodox philosphy);
the *Nidana-Sūtra* on liturgical music;
a volume on metrics;
an exposition on anatomy and medicine;
the *Sri Chidambaśvara Nitya Puja Sūtram*, the rituals and mantras of the Vedic ceremonies conducted at the Nataraja Temple in Cidambaram

Speculation about Patañjali's time period ranges from 150 BCE. to 200 CE., with some authorities confidently placing him around 1000 BCE. or earlier. Widest agreement centers around 200 CE. Various sūtras in the *Mahābhāṣya* provide clues in the debate about when and where this Patañjali lived. Eminent Sanskrit scholar, Sir Ramakrishna Bhandarkar, notes that the Patanjali of the *Mahābhāṣya* makes references in to the city of Pataliputra, and from this infers that he was at least a frequent visitor if not a resident.

While Patañjali is sometimes called "the father of Yoga," he is not the founder of Yoga itself. The most commonly held theory is that he compiled, edited and organized the existent material into a synthesis that was so comprehensive, and expanded by his original contributions, that pre-existent work has been forgotten. Some textual analysts point out that specific sūtras in both volumes attributed to Patañjali were probably later contributions. In the case of the *Yoga-Sūtra*, debate centers around linguistic structures characteristic of different periods. In a sense, the more we endeavor to establish him historically, the more mythical he becomes.

Mythologies surrounding Patañjali abound. He is so intimately associated with the serpent manifestation of Viṣṇu, called Ādiśeṣa or Ananta, that one legend asserts that Patañjali actually was an incarnation of Ādiśeṣa. Other stories relate that when he was born, he fell (*pat*) into the hollow of the hand or the hands in prayer (*añjali*) of Pāṇini, Śiva, or his mother Goṇikā, in the shape of a little snake. Statues and bas-reliefs of Patañjali continue the Ādiśeṣa symbology. He is represented with the upper body of a man, the lower body of a serpent, and with five hoods of Ādiśeṣa spread over him. His incarnation came to a close when he was swallowed by a python—probably one of his disciples. If nothing else, Patañjali's life is a parable of consistency.

The symbology of the serpent is open to a number of interpretations and some confusion. Modern Christian biblical tradition presents the serpent as a snake and holds it forth as a symbol of evil, temptation into desire, and the dark side of Creation. Actually, the Hebrew term in Genesis refers to a small red dragon that figured in later mystic poetry, most notably William Blake's. In most other cultures the serpent is the symbol of wisdom and esoteric lore. Certainly Patañjali and Yoga qualify in these latter respects.

Ādiśeṣa symbolizes manifold functions. He represents the force of gravity in the Hindu cosmology as well as the "coiled" cosmic energy latent in human beings, the *kundalini*, which is called the serpent-power. Kundalini might be said to be the energy latent in matter—a relationship with tremendous potential for release of light—that we know as atomic activity. The statues depicting Patañjali's body configuration may be graphic and emphatic representations of his utter mastery of the kundalini, mastery of his internal physiological processes (and hence, his mind), and mastery of the physical plane as symbolized by gravity. The five hoods of Ādiśeṣa symbolize his mastery of the five senses and their inability to distract him from his spiritual focus. His alternate name, Ananta, means endless or infinite and refers not only to his length, but his quality of consciousness.

Patañjali is occasionally represented in groups of sages and demigods in temple statuary of southern India. He is one of the two sages to whom Śiva specifically manifested himself as Naṭarāja (Lord of the Dance) in His cosmic dance of Creation that spun the universe into motion and maintains its coherence. The Natarāja Temple in Cidambaram, where Lord Śiva is reputed to have revealed Himself as the Cosmic Dancer, has a special bond with Patañjali and he is well represented in statuary in the temple complex.

Whatever his manifestation and whatever the "facts" about his life, Patañjali was one of the most gifted humans ever to grace this planet. The treasures he bestowed on humanity are so profound that it is unlikely that we have more than glimpsed their full measure.

PART III

LINGUISTIC RELATIVITY

OR

WHY SO MANY TRANSLATIONS OF THE SAME BOOK (cont.)

WHAT IS SANSKRIT?

ORIGINS AND DEVELOPMENT

Sanskrit is an utterly unique phenomenon. An ancient classical language, it has a formal phonetic and grammatical record of at least three thousand years. Its organization, complexity, and comprehensiveness supported, enhanced, and perhaps made possible certain masterpieces of genius. We will briefly examine its origins and development.

Languages are generally organized in "trees." The great language families form trunks, and the individual languages and dialects form branches. The Indo-European language tree is one of the largest and most diverse. While a good deal of scholarly controversy swirls around the history of cultural interaction between Central and South Asia, there is little disagreement that the Indo-European languages originated in steppes of Russia and Central Asia. The Indo-European languages are also called Indo-Aryan. Aryan in this case is a cultural technical term that does not designate a specific racial group.

When the Central Asians began their migration out of the steppes, they fanned out over the regions we now call Europe, western Russia, Iran, Afghanistan, Pakistan, and India, establishing substantial influence in a relatively short time (fifteen hundred to two thousand years). One of their most powerful cultural tools was their language. It is now called Indo-European, or Proto-Indo-European.

From Proto-Indo-European evolved eight major language groups, from which most of the modern languages of Europe and many of south and southwest Asia emerged. These eight languages are:

Albanian	Proto-Germanic
Armenian	Proto-Greek
Balto-Slavic	Italic
Celtic	Indo-Iranian

As the Indo-Iranian civilization spread into India, the cultural changes brought about by geographic distances, isolation, and regional characteristics led to dialectical diversity, and the language divided around 1500 B.C.E. Indo-Iranian became Old Farsi (Persian) and Vedic Sanskrit.

The migrators into the Śindhu Valley (now in Pakistan) spoke dialects that became Vedic Sanskrit. It is in this ancient form of Sanskrit that the great Indian scriptures of the *Vedas*, *Upaniṣads*, *Brahmanas* and other works were composed. The Vedic Period (approximately 1500 to 600 B.C.E.) was followed by the Epic Period (600 B.C.E. to C.E. 200), which saw the composition of the *Puraṇas*, the *Mahābhārata*, and the *Ramayana* in the emergent classical Sanskrit. The difference between Vedic and classical Sanskrit is much the same as that between Homeric and Attic Greek or Latin and Italian.

When Europeans discovered Sanskrit (meaning "refined," "elaborated," or "perfected"), some sensed the possibility that a common family of languages existed. An Italian merchant, Filippo Sarsetti (1540–1588), compared Italian with Sanskrit and found that many words with the same meaning were similar in pronunciation.

Sarsetti's observations were followed in 1597 by those of Bonaventura Volcanus, a Flemish scholar who produced a booklet demonstrating startling resemblances between German and Persian.

The evidence continued to mount, and in 1786, pioneer Western linguist Sir William Jones presented to the Royal Asiatic Society in Calcutta the first theory of what he termed the Indo-European language group:

> The Sanskrit language, whatever its antiquity, is of a wonderful structure; more perfect than the Greek, more copious than the Latin, yet bearing to both of them a stronger affinity, both in the roots of verbs and the forms of grammar, than could possibly have been produced by accident; so strong, indeed, that no philologer could examine them all three without believing them to have sprung from some common source, which perhaps, no longer exists. There is a similar reason, though not so forcible, for supposing that both the Gothic and the Celtic had the same origin with the Sanskrit; and the old Persian might be added to the same family.

It has since been established that Sanskrit, Celtic, and Persian do share common roots.

In 1819 Jacob Grimm, who, with his brother, penned the famous fairy tales, established the regularity of sound correspondences in Sanskrit, Greek, and Latin, as well as German, from which English primarily derives. It is known as Grimm's Law. He produced a lengthy table from which this is an excerpt:

Sanskrit	Greek	Latin	English
pita	pater	pater	father
trayas	treis	tres	three
bharami	phero	fero	bear

The Sanskrit that so impressed the Europeans in the late 1700s, had been the sacred language of priests and pandits from antiquity. It was imputed to be of such an exalted, intrinsic spiritual quality that low castes were not allowed to even hear it, let alone learn it, on pain of death. The dialects of the common people were called *Prakrit*, "derived from the fundament" (fundament being one of the definitions of the word Sanskrit), and regarded as common or vulgar.

One of the Prakrits, Pali, was used by Siddārtha Gautama (the Buddha) and became a sacred language in its own right. From the Prakrits emerged most of the regional dialects of modern India, among them Hindi, Marathi, Sindhi, Gujarati, Punjabi, Bihari, and Bengali. Hindi with an admixture of Arabic and Persian vocabulary and written in Persian script is called Urdu. Though the Dravidian dialects of southern India (Kanada, Malayalam, Tamil, Telugu, etc.) are not Indo-European in origin, they have an abundance of Sanskrit words in their vocabularies, and much of their literature is based on Sanskrit models.

It was during the Epic Period that the first alphabets arrived in the Indus Valley of northern India and the great grammarian and linguist Pāṇini made his appearance.

The Sanskrit Alphabet And Grammar

The original Sanskrit alphabet was fully codified in about 700 B.C.E. and is called Brahmi, which means "[writing] of Brahma." It was regarded as a gift to humanity from Brahma, the Creator aspect of the Hindu triune godhead (or trinity). The modern form of Brahmi is called Devanagari (city [language] of the gods). To this day it is used, in various forms, in the multitude of modern Indian languages derived from Sanskrit.

The Devanagari alphabet consists of forty-eight letters: thirty-five consonants and thirteen vowels. These represent every sound in the Sanskrit language. Sanskrit has absolute phonetic consistency: the way a word is written is the way it is spoken and vice versa.

Sanskrit grammar, like Latin and Greek, is highly inflected and complex. It has three genders (masculine, feminine, and neuter); three numbers (singular, dual, and plural); eight cases (nominative, accusative, instrumental, dative, ablative, genitive, locative, and vocative). However, only in the singular of the most common declension does a noun show different forms for each case. Adjectives are inflected to agree with nouns. Verbs are inflected for tense, mode, voice, number, and person in ten conjugations.

An important note: nouns are considered to have their origins in root-verbs.

Sanskrit grammar provides a writer with tools that permit distinctive modes of communication. Sūtras, for example, are composed in a special form that generally eschews verbs. The *Yoga-Sūtra* has fewer than ten. Inflected endings contain the critical nuances. Embodying underlying physical and psychological assumptions of the Vedic civilization, Sanskrit and the sūtra mode permits the transmission of unique cultural concepts and understandings—concepts that do not exist in English.

CROSS-CULTURAL AND TRANS-MILLENNIAL CHALLENGES IN INTERPRETIVE TRANSLATION

As noted earlier, translations of the *Yoga-Sūtra* can vary so greatly that they almost seem like different books. This would answer one part of the question, "Why so many?" Other questions might be, "What is responsible for this variance? What need is there for yet another?"

Clearly Patañjali did not undertake the production of the *Yoga-Sūtra* lightly. One of the greatest minds of all time executed one of the most enormous tasks in history—defining human consciousness and meta-psychology—as a master of one of the most complex and precise languages ever known to man. It is a technical manual written in a technical language designed to provide current, valid direction at all stages of human evolution and understanding. Translation deserves our best efforts and no one person can hope to do it, for reasons that follow.

In modern language theory, a translation is considered equivalent if *relative information value* is sustained between the source language and the target language. This can be more complex than it might appear. Translation of ordinary material from one language to another is a challenging process because precise concept-for-concept and word-for-word equivalents often do not exist, even between modern Western languages. Finally, even when a word-for-word translation is possible, a cultural idiom can add a spin of its own, reducing the idea of literal translation to an amusing figment of the imagination of monolingual people.

Take, for example, a confusion that occurred as the English Bible was being translated into French. As the translators considered the phrase "waters of life," they were initially quite pleased with the literal translation, *eau de vie*. A native speaker reviewing their work pointed out that, while literally correct, in France *eau de vie* refers to an after-dinner drink, a type of fruit brandy. Not what they had had in mind! The translators finally had to settle on *eau vivante* (living waters), which they found approximate and acceptable but far from exact or satisfying. (We will not trace the entomology from English back though Latin to the Greek to the Aramaic original.) The difficulty of moving an apparently "simple" phrase or even a single word from modern English to modern French or modern German is multiplied many times over when taking the Sanskrit of the *Yoga-Sūtra* into English.

As noted earlier, Sanskrit grammar provides a writer with tools that permit distinctive modes of communication facilitating the transmission of unique cultural concepts and understandings. Many of these concepts, and their reflective linguistic structures, do not exist in English. Therefore, some of the more accessible translations have a quality of paraphrasing.

Martin Luther made this commentary on ancient Hebrew: "The words of the Hebrew tongue have a peculiar energy. It is impossible to convey so much so briefly in any other language. To render them intelligibly we must not attempt to give word for word, but only aim at the sense and the idea." His insight would apply equally well to Sanskrit.

Inevitably and unavoidably: *translation is interpretation*! For the following reasons:

1. Any word in any language may have several meanings.
A native speaker or someone with absolute fluency will know all these definitions simultaneously at a subconscious level, whereas a translator will have to make selections that necessarily limit a full transmission of meaning.
Even a brief, apparently simple phrase can present a translator with a considerable challenge.
2. Concept-for-concept and word-for-word equivalents often do not exist between English and Sanskrit. The term *samādhi* is a good example.
3. Underlying subconscious differences and assumptions between modern Western and Indian cultures can affect concept and terminology in subtle (or not so subtle), unnoticed ways.
4. Patañjali probably lived in the Indian culture of approximately 150 B.C.E.—at least 2,150 years ago, although some say much earlier. This culture is nearly as foreign to a modern Indian as it is to a modern American or European.
5. A competent translation of the *Yoga-Sūtra* for meditators requires more than a high level of proficiency in Sanskrit and English and broad familiarity with a profoundly foreign, ancient culture. To authentically and accurately present the *Sūtra*, the translator must have a deep intimacy with Yoga, an experiential authenticity that can come only from practice.
6. Finally, "Sanskrit has seven levels, or grounds, of comprehension, which are accessed according one's level of spiritual development." ~ Sw. Veda Bhāratī [Dr. Usharbudh Arya]

These factors make the *Yoga-Sūtra* a particularly challenging project, presenting the English translator with a dilemma—how to maintain the intentional brevity of the original while fleshing it out so that it becomes comprehensible in a language about as different from Sanskrit as possible.

The elements of language, culture, and Yogic experience render significant distinctions between translations. To quote from an earlier statement, "While I have detailed the difficulties, I don't want to exaggerate them. In fact, the elements that create the apparent discrepancies are actually potential sources of enrichment."

Like the facets of a jewel, they focus and disperse light in different ways.

APPENDIX I

CRITERIA FOR SELECTION: WHY THESE TRANSLATORS?

As mentioned earlier, at least thirty translations of the *Yoga-Sutra* with commentary are available in English. This presents a very practical problem for a compilation. Considerations of page size, format, and readable typeface have limited the number of translations to twelve. Readers would wisely ask, "Why have you selected these translators?"

The intent of this volume is to present a wide range of interpretive approaches. The translators have been selected on the basis of their demonstrated capacity in one or more of the following areas:

Experience in practice
Linguistic proficiency in Sanskrit and English
School of approach
Popularity

Experience in practice: Actual experience in meditation as described by Patañjali is the foremost qualification for a translator in this study. This is also the most challenging to discern. An excessively speculative, pedantic, or highly traditional commentary can a warning signal of a scholar versus a *sadhaka* (one active in a discipline). Practice is the key to Patañjali—experience vs. theory. All of these selected translators show depth of practice or they would not be included!

Proficiency in Sanskrit and English: Proficiency in this sense goes beyond vocabulary and grammar and demonstrates a command of idiom in both languages and an understanding of the underlying cultural assumptions built into, and embodied, in language.

School of approach: Different schools or modes of approach contribute to the variety of insights among translators. The paths represented here are: Sankhya, Vedanta, Theosophical, mystic, academic or scholastic, and eclectic.

Popularity: Many of the translations included here are well read by meditators and while others are quite obscure.

APPENDIX II

BIOGRAPHIES OF THE TRANSLATORS

Pandit Usharbudh Arya, d.Litt./Swami Veda Bhārātī

Dr. Usharbudh Arya (now Swami Veda Bhāratī, since 1992) was born to a distinguished Brahmin family in northern India in the 1930s. His cradle language was Sanskrit and his family lived every aspect of life as a spiritual observance.

At the age of four and a half, he sat for an hour of daily meditation practice with his father. By the age of six and a half, he had memeorized the 4,000 sūtras of Paṇini's Sanskrit grammar. He taught his first class on the *Yoga-Sūtra of Patañjali* at the age of nine. At the age of thirteen, he was examined by senior scholars and found to have unique mastery of the 20,000 mantras of the four Vedas, for each of which he could offer three levels of interpretations known to the traditions. The scholars published articles about him in the Indian press and he was invited to address schools, colleges, universities and crowds of up to 10,000.

For the past sixty years, starting from February, 1947, he has been traveling, lecturing, and teaching world wide on spiritual matters, texts and traditions. He holds Bachelors and Masters degrees from the University of London and a Doctorate in Literature from the University of Utrecht in Holland. He also served as Professor of Sanskrit at the University of Minnesota for many years.

Swami Veda Bhāratī received his yoga-dikśa (initiation into the highest mysteries of meditation) from his Master, Swami Rama of the Himalayas, in February, 1970. He then established the Meditation Center in Minneapolis and now guides numerous meditation groups and centers on all the continents. While he maintains his Western headquarters at the Meditation Center in Minneapolis, he also runs the two Swami Rama ashrams on the banks of the holy river Ganges in Rishikesh at the foothills of the Himalayas.

Swami Veda Bhāratī brings much that is unique to the task of translating Patañjali. If nothing else, his native fluency in Sanskrit places him among a select group of scholars. His familiarity with the traditional schools of Indian philosophy is equally exhaustive, both in breadth of understanding and in detail. Further, his five and a half decades in the West have given him a near-native fluency in English and a functional grasp of its cultural ramifications. His experience in many other cultures of the world give him access to intercultural understanding. Most importantly, while his is undoubtedly the most scholarly of the translations presented in this work, Swami Veda Bhāratī is primarily a meditator of profound commitment, bringing meditational insights and depths to his commentaries in the texts, especially the *Yoga-Sūtras of Patañjali*.

Swami Veda Bhāratī teaches meditation in several languages and has three thousand hours of audio-courses available. For committed meditators in the Yogic traditions, Swami Veda's work is virtually required reading. He has written two volumes on the *Yoga-Sūtra*, exhaustively examining its first two chapters, in twelve hundred pages. He has also written *God*, *Superconscious Meditation*, *Mantra and Meditation*, and *Meditation and the Art of Dying* among many others.

Visit Swami Veda Bhāratī's website: www.swamiveda.org

Alice A. Bailey
1880–1949

Beginning in the 1930s, Alice Bailey produced twenty-five volumes of highly esoteric material. She claimed in her autobiography that she had transcribed twenty books in about thirty years in cooperation with the abbot of a Tibetan Monastery. This was accomplished by a process of telepathic communication of such clarity that she said it was like taking dictation from someone in the room with her (she denied being a medium, insisting she never went into trance or gave over control of her body).

Four of the books in her "opus" were written by Mrs. Bailey, herself. She claimed one of them, *The Light of the Soul*, her *Yoga-Sūtra* contribution, was a formal collaboration with the Tibetan abbot. Mrs. Bailey explained that the Tibetan provided an English translation from Sanskrit and she provided the commentary. She made the following point in her Introductory Remarks: "It should be noted that the translation is not literal, and is not an exact definition of each original Sanskrit term. It is an attempt to put into clear and understandable English, the exact meaning, insofar as it is possible to do so through the medium of that non-elastic and unimaginative tongue."

Alice Bailey's commentary is definitely along Theosophical lines. She classed her work as part of the Theosophical Movement, which she claimed was distinct from the Theosophical Society and its particular forms of orthodoxy.

Her presentation also differs significantly from the orthodox Indian traditions and generates considerable controversy, particularly in regard to her claim of such intimate communication with the Masters. This very controversy, combined with wide readership and a consistently high quality of presentation, argued for the inclusion of this translation—the opinion of other authorities notwithstanding.

Alice Bailey completed her thirty-year life project in November 1949 and departed this world less than a month later. She left behind a legacy of work dedicated to world peace and spiritual unfoldment. In addition to her books, her many lifework projects include founding The Arcane School, which teaches meditation, the Lucis Trust, Lucis Publishing and Triangles. Lucis Trust is a registered Non-Governmental Organization with the United Nations where it maintains an office and works with the United Nations' Temple of Understanding, an interdenominational chapel.

Visit the Lucis Trust website: www.lucistrust.org

M.N. Dvivedi

No biographical data on M.N.Dvivedi could be found. His approach is Theosophical and the Theosophical Society first published his *Yoga Sutras of Patanjali* in 1890. It is probably the first published English translation of the *Sūtras*.

Georg Feuerstein, Ph.D.

Georg Feuerstein, Ph.D., founder-director of Traditional Yoga Studies, is internationally known for his many interpretative studies of the Yoga tradition. Until the beginning of 2004, he served as president and director of the Yoga Research and Education Center, which he founded in 1996.

Since the early 1970s, he has made significant contributions to the East-West dialogue and is particularly concerned with preserving the authentic teachings of Yoga in its various forms. His passion for India's spirituality was awakened on his fourteenth birthday when he was given Paul Brunton's A Search in Secret India and he has followed the yogic path in various forms since that time. For many years, he has been practicing Vajrayana Buddhist Yoga and is associated with the Drikung Kagyu lineage.

Georg has written both academic monographs and also more popular works, and his over thirty books include *The Yoga Tradition*, *The Shambala Encyclopedia of Yoga*, *The Deeper Dimension of Yoga*, and *The Shambala Guide to Yoga*.

From Dr. Feuerstein's website: www.yrec.info/feuerstein.php

Vyaas Houston, M.A.

Vyaas Houston was introduced to Sanskrit in the ashram of Sri Brahmananda Sarasvati (Rammurti S. Mishra, M.D.) in upstate New York. Chanting Sanskrit grammar and mantras comprised a major element of yogic practice with Sarasvati.

In 1987, after teaching Sanskrit and yoga for more than 15 years, he discovered a method for teaching Sanskrit based on the model of *Patañjali's Yoga Sūtras*. His methods were unusually successful in conveying Sanskrit to nearly anyone with a genuine interest. This led him to establish the American Sanskrit Institute in 1989.

Houston's Sanskrit training has provided thousands of people with the opportunity to discover their own unique relationship with Sanskrit. He is the author of many articles, *Sanskrit by Cassette*, and has translated many Sanskrit classics. He is also a musician and has recorded many of the works he has translated.

Visit the American Sanskrit Institute website: www.americansanskrit.com

Swami Jnaneshvara

Swami Jnaneshvara Bharati was born in 1948 in Ohio, USA, spent most of his youth in Florida, and later lived in California, Illinois, Minnesota, Pennsylvania, and Texas. His education includes a BS in Management from Florida State University and an MA in Consciousness Studies, with emphasis in Transpersonal Counseling Psychology from John F. Kennedy University, in California. He worked in advertising, retail store management, counselling and psychiatric social work. He was never married and has no children.

Spontaneously practicing meditation and other yogic practices from early childhood, Swami Jnaneshvara was initiated in meditation by Swami Rama in 1986, ten years to the day prior to Swami Rama leaving the body. This was his first spiritual initiation, as his parents raised him to make his own choices in adult life. Several months after the initiation by Swami Rama, Swami Jnaneshvara met Pandit Usharbudh Arya, through whom supplemental initiation and training were given. He was given novice monastic initiation in 1990, ordained as a Swami of the Himalayan tradition and the order of Shankaracharya in 1993 by Swami Rama, and given one of the highest initiations of direct experience in 1996. Final teachings and instructions were imparted shortly before Swami Rama left the body in November 1996.

Between 1989 and 1994, Swami Jnaneshvara lived and studied in residence at the Meditation Center of Minneapolis, Minnesota and the Himalayan Institute of Honesdale, Pennsylvania. From 1994 to 2001, his residence was Swami Rama's Ashram in Rishikesh, India at the personal invitation of Swami Rama, where he was given advanced practices and initiations. At the direct instruction of Swami Rama, he established an ongoing residential training program in the ashram.

In 1998 and 1999, Swami Jnaneshvara was given training, practices and grace by the venerated sage Naga Swami Hanuman Giri at most honorific initiation in the Shankara tradition, in which a Danda, or staff is bestowed. In 2000, the sage Vratti Baba of Kalimath, Himalayas—a long time friend and spiritual brother of Swami Rama—passed on his initiatory transmissions and legacy at the time of his dropping the body.

While Swami Rama named no single successor of the lineage, Swami Jnaneshvara is one of those whom Swami Rama empowered as a conduit of the teachings of the tradition. Inspired by the goal of providing the ancient wisdom and practices in what Swami Rama has called the "simplest manner possible," Swami Jnaneshvara emphasizes the practical aspects of Yoga, Vedanta, and Tantra in serving others. Following the tradition of Swami Rama, no rituals are performed or promoted, and the practices of contemplation and meditation are purely internal. Nobody is ever asked to be a follower, to change their culture, or to convert from their religion. As taught by Swami Rama, one of his primary tasks, as external teacher is to help others find the teacher within.

Swami Prabhavananda

Swami Prabhavananda's *How to Know God*, written with Christopher Isherwood, is probably the most widely read version of the *Yoga-Sūtra* in the west, certainly in America. A solid, serviceable translation and commentary, it effectively bridges cultural concepts and terms.

Swami Prabhavananda entered *sannyas* (a life dedicated to spiritual practice) through his Master, Swami Brahmananda, in the lineage of Shri Ramakrishna. A prolific translator, author, and collaborator, Prabhavananda was also a senior monk in the Ramakrishna Order of India.

Prabhavananda came to the United States in 1923, eventually founding the Vedanta Society of Southern California in 1929, which grew under his direction to a large collection of dedicated temples and monasteries from Santa Barbara to San Diego.

One of Prabhavananda's unique approaches was to collaborate with skilled writers in English to supplement his skills in Indian languages and facilitate the presentation of his experience and understanding. They helped him create illustrations, analogies, vocabulary, and formats that helped bridge the cultural divide. A striking example of this work is his partnership with Christopher Isherwood in translating the *Bhagavad-Gita*.

In their version of the *Gita*, Prabhavananda and Isherwood rendered many of the verses in poetry and others in prose, creating an original contribution. A noted novelist and journalist, Christopher Isherwood was a disciple of Prabhavananda for over thirty years. His story of the joys and struggles of discipleship, including the work on the *Yoga-Sutra* and *Bhagavad-Gita*, was published in his diary/memoir, *My Guru and His Disciple*.

Prabhavananda's translation and commentary emerge from the Vedanta tradition of Indian philosophy.

Visit the Vedanta Society website: www.vedanta.org/vssc/prabhavananda.html

Shri Purohit Swami

Shri Purohit Swami was one of the first great yogis who came to Europe from India. His books never gained the wide readership they deserve and he has fallen into obscurity.

He is the author of the first autobiography of a yogi ever written: *Autobiography of an Indian Monk*. He collaborated with W.B. Yeats, the famous Irish poet, on an English translation of the principal Upanishads.

Purohit was born in Badnera, Vidarbha, India on October 12, 1882 to a wealthy Maharashtran Brahmin family. His parents gave him the name Shankar Gajannan Purohit. As a child he became proficient in Marathi, English, and Sanskrit. He was well educated, obtaining a B.A. in philosophy at Calcutta University in 1903 and a law degree from Deccan College and Bombay University. As a teenager, he decided to be celibate, but in 1908 he accommodated his parents' wishes and married Godu Bai. After the birth of daughters in 1910 and 1914 and a son in 1915, he resumed his vow of celibacy.

In 1906, Purohit met a young man only four years older than himself named Natekar. Purohit says this meeting "was love at first sight," and Natekar, who later took the monastic name Hamsa Swami, became Purohit's guru.

In 1923 his guru directed him to embark on a mendicant pilgrimage the length and breadth of India. Begging bowl in hand, he passed several years in this way.

In 1930 he went to Europe where he met W.B. Yeats, the great Irish poet, who became a friend and helped arrange for the publication of Purohit's books by leading London publishers. These included *The Autobiography of an Indian Monk* (1932), a translation of Hamsa Swami's *The Holy Mountain* (1934), a translation of the *Bhagavad Gita* (1935), a translation of *The Ten Principal Upanishads* (in collaboration with Yeats, 1937), and a translation of Patanjali's *Aphorisms of Yoga* (1938).

Purohit died in the late 1930s or early 1940s.

From: www.realization.org/page/topics/purohit.htm

Swami Satchidananda
1914–2002

Sri Swamiji was born into a highly spiritual family in South India in 1914. In his youth, he worked in agriculture, mechanics, electronics, and cinematography. At the same time, the richly devotional family atmosphere nurtured his spiritual aspiration.

At the age of twenty-eight, he began his full-time spiritual quest. He studied with some of India's greatest saints and sages, including Sri Ramana Maharshi, Sri Aurobindo, and his own spiritual master, the world-renowned Sri Swami Sivanandaji Maharaj of Rishikesh, Himalayas. He received Sannyas Initiation in 1949 on the banks of the sacred Ganges River.

In the following years, Sri Swamiji served as professor of Hatha and Raja Yoga at the Yoga Vedanta Forest University in Rishikesh and made extensive lecture tours throughout India. In 1953 he was invited to Ceylon (now Sri Lanka). He spent thirteen years serving at the Ashram that he established there and became known and loved throughout the country for his universal, ecumenical outlook.

In 1966, Sri Swamiji made his first global tour, sponsored by an American devotee. The intended two-day visit to New York extended to five months as he was surrounded by hundreds of students, eager for his teachings and guidance. The Integral Yoga Institutes were founded under his direction, and today there are Integral Yoga Institutes and Centers throughout the world. In 1976, he became a US citizen.

Advocating the principle that "Truth Is One, Paths Are Many," Swami Satchidananda dedicated his life to the cause of peace—both individual and universal—and to religious harmony among all people. He sponsored innumerable interfaith symposiums, retreats, and worship services around the world.

The Light Of Truth Universal Shrine (LOTUS), dedicated to the Light of all faiths and to world peace, was opened in 1986 and is located at Satchidananda Ashram—Yogaville in Virginia, USA. Yogaville serves as the international headquarters of the Integral Yoga Institutes and Centers.

Excerpted from: www.yogaville.org

Alistair Shearer

Alistair Shearer did postgraduate work in Sanskrit at the University of Lancaster, after studying literature at Cambridge. He has practiced and taught meditation for many years. He currently divides his time between lecturing and writing on the sacred art of Hinduism and Buddhism, teaching meditation courses, and leading cultural tours to the Indian subcontinent each winter. His latest publications include *The Spirit of Asia* and *Buddha: The Intelligent Heart.*

From the book jacket: *The Yoga Sutras of Patanjali*; Alistair Shearer. Bell Tower Press/Random House

I. K. Taimni

Dr. I. K. Taimni was a well-known member of the Theosophical Society in India, a former member of the Society's General Council, a professor of chemistry at the Allahabad University and a much-admired author of classics like The Science of Yoga, Self-Culture in the Light of Occultism *and* Man, God and the Universe, *among others.*

Originally published in The Theosophist,
February, 1967

The Science of Yoga is another of the popular translations included here, and like *How to Know God*, functions well as an introductory text. The profusion of Sanskrit terms throughout are all well defined. Concepts are explained exhaustively, often with diagrams, reflecting Taimni's academic background.

Taimni's approach is from the more orthodox Theosophical understanding, in contrast to Alice A. Bailey. He wrote several books presenting Theosophy, including *Man, God and the Universe* and *A Way of Self-Discovery.*

Visit: www.questbooks.net

Swami Vivekananda
1863-1902

A wealth of biographical data chronicles Swami Vivekananda's thirty-nine short but exceedingly intense pioneering years from 1863 to 1902. He shares the credit for introducing Yoga to America and England with Paramahansa Yogananda and Swami Rama Tirtha. Vivekananda's adoring biographers describe him as an intelligent, playful, high-spirited boy who grew into a Renaissance Man of India. In his college years, he became inflamed with spiritual longing and this brought him to the feet of Shri Ramakrishna. His initial search was over, but his work had just begun.

Approaching death in August 1886, Shri Ramakrishna commissioned Vivekananda to undertake the care and development of his brother monks and to begin his wider work in the service of humanity. With considerable reluctance Vivekananda did so. Apparently, he never suffered a notable setback and his appearance at the World Parliament of Religions in Chicago in 1893 as representative of India and Hinduism gave him a sudden, enormous thrust into public awareness. His powerfully commanding personal presence, combined with a sharp intellect, wide knowledge of Western thinkers and philosophy, and fine sense of judgment, made him an ideal candidate to break through cultural barriers and introduce Yoga and Vedanta to America and England.

Many people from all strata of society were drawn to him, not a few of them wealthy, well educated and well connected. These students and disciples ensured that his discourses were all taken in shorthand, transcribed, lightly edited, and published. His collected works fill seven volumes. His writing shows an excellent education and deep insight. His illustrations of concepts foreign to Western experience are often quite striking, making them accessible in a practical way.

In his own motherland Vivekananda is regarded as the patriot saint of modern India and an inspirer of her dormant national consciousness. To the Hindus he preached the ideal of a strength-giving and man-making religion. Service to man as the visible manifestation of the Godhead was the special form of worship he advocated for the Indians, devoted as they were to the rituals and myths of their ancient faith. Many political leaders of India have publicly acknowledged their indebtedness to Swami Vivekananda.

Vivekananda's perspective is from the Vedanta.

Visit: www.ramakrishna.org

APPENDIX III

HOW TO PROCURE THESE TRANSLATIONS

All of the translations, except Arya's manuscript and the out-of-print volumes, can be ordered directly online from the publisher, at your bookstore (bring the ISBN), or through Amazon.com.

Yogasutras: Padartha and Bhavartha.
Arya, Pandit Usharbudh, now Swami Veda Bhāratī
This manuscript is not available to the public.
However, Swamiji is a prolific author whose books are available through the Himalyan Institute (www.himalayaninstitute.org) and Motilal Banarsidass (www.mlbd.com).

The Light of The Soul, Its Science and Effect
Alice A. Bailey
ISBN: 0-85330-112-3
Lucis Publishing Co.
www.lucistrust.org
e-mail: newyork@lucistrust.org
120 Wall Street, 24th Floor
New York, NY 10005
USA
Phone: 1 (212) 292-0707
Outside the United States refer to website

The Yoga Sutras of Patanjali
M.N. Dvivedi
Out-of-Print

The Yoga-Sūtra of Patañjali, A New Translation and Commentary
Georg Feuerstein
ISBN: 0-89281-262-1
Inner Traditions International
www.innertraditions.com
e-mail: customerservice@InnerTraditions.com
PO Box 388
Rochester, Vermont 05767-0388
Phone: (800) 246-8648 / (802) 767-3174
Fax: (802) 767-3726

The Yoga Sutra Workbook: The Certainty of Freedom
Vyaas Houston
American Sanskrit Institute
www.americansanskrit.com
email: Sanskrit@sbcglobal.net
980 Ridge Road
Brick, NJ 08724
Phone: (800) 459-4176
Fax: (732) 840-4106 • Local/Overseas: (732) 840-4104

How to Know God: The Yoga Aphorisms of Patanjali
Swami Prabhavanada and Christopher Isherwood
ISBN: 0-87481-041-8
Vedanta Press
www.vedanta.com
e-mail: info@vedanta.com
Vedanta Press & Catalog
1946 Vedanta Pl.
Hollywood, CA 90068
Phone: (800) 816-2242 individuals
Phone: (323) 960-1736 for outside the USA
Phone: (323) 960-1727 if you are a bookstore

Bhagwan Shri Patanjali: Aphorisms of Patanjali
Shri Purohit Swami
Out-of-Print

The Yoga Sutras of Patanjali: Translation and Commentary
Shri Swami Satchidananda
ISBN: 0-932040-38-1
Integral Yoga Publications/Satchidananda Ashram—Yogaville.
www.yogaville.org
e-mail: iyi@yogaville.org
Route 1, Box 1720
Buckingham, VA 23921
Phone: (434) 969-3121
Fax: (434) 969-1303

The Yoga Sutras of Patanjali
Alistair Shearer
ISBN: 0-609-60959-9
Random House, Inc./ Bell Tower, a division of Random House, Inc.
www.randomhouse.com
Random House, Inc.
1745 Broadway
New York, NY 10019
Phone: (212) 782-9000
Alistair Shearer has also written *The Spirit of Asia and Buddha: The Intelligent Heart.*

The Science of Yoga
I.K. Taimni.
ISBN: 0-8356-0023-8
Theosophical Publishing House
www.questbooks.net
e-mail: customerservice@questbooks.net
Orders, inquiries, and correspondence should be addressed to:
Quest Books
Customer Service Department
P.O. Box 270
Wheaton, IL 60189-0270
Phone: (800) 669-9425 (toll-free in USA only)
Fax: 630-665-8791

Raja Yoga
Swami Vivekananda
ISBN: 0-9112-623-X
Ramakrishna-Vivekananda Center
17 East 94th Street
New York, NY 10128
Phone: (212) 534-9445
Fax: (212) 828-1618
www.ramakrishna.org

The Unadorned Thread of Yoga: The Yoga-Sūtras of Patañjali in English
Zambito, Salvatore, ed.
ISBN: 0-9787676-0-8
Yoga-Sūtras Institute
P.O. Box 1375
Poulsbo, WA 98370
Phone: (206) 550-6348
website: www.yogasutras.net

BIBLIOGRAPHY

TRANSLATIONS USED IN *THE UNADORNED THREAD OF YOGA*

Arya, Pandit Usharbudh. *Yogasutras: Padartha and Bhavartha.*
Unpublished manuscript. Minneapolis, MN: Center for Higher Consciousness, 1974.

Bailey, Alice A. *The Light of the Soul, Its Science and Effect.* New York: Lucis Publishing Co., 1955.

Dvivedi, Manilal Nabhubai. *The Yoga Sutras of Patanjali.*
Adyar, Madras: Theosophical Publishing House, 1930.

Feuerstein, Georg. *The Yoga-Sūtra of Patañjali, A New Translation and Commentary.*
Rochester, Vermont: Inner Traditions International, 1989.

Houston, Vyaas. *The Yoga Sutra Workbook: The Certainty of Freedom.*
Warwick, New York: American Sanskrit Institute, 1995.

Jnaneshvara Bharati, Sw. *Yoga Sutras of Patanjali: The 196 Sutras by Patanjali.*
Ft. Walton Beach, FL: Abhyasa Ashram, 2004

Prabhavanada, Swami and Christopher Isherwood. *How to Know God: The Yoga Aphorisms of Patanjali.*
New York: Mentor, 1969.

Purohit, Shree Swami. *The Yoga Aphorisms of Bhagawan Shree Patanjali.*
London: Faber and Faber, 1938.

Satchidanada, Swami. *The Yoga Sutras of Patanjali.* Yogaville, Virginia: Integral Yoga Publications, 1990.

Shearer, Alisair. *The Yoga Sutras of Patanjali.* New York: Random House, 1982.

Taimni, I.K.. *The Science of Yoga.* Wheaton, Illinois: Theosophical Publishing House, 1961.

Vivekananda, Swami.*Raja Yoga.* New York: Ramakrishna-Vivekananda Center, 1955.

OTHER *YOGA-SŪTRA* TRANSLATIONS USED IN REFERENCE

Arya, Pandit Usharbudh. *Yoga-sūtras of Patañjali with the Exposition of Vyāsa; Vol. I Samādhi-pāda.* Honesdale, Pennsylvania: Himalayan International Institute, 1986.

Ballantyne, J.R. and Govind Sastri Devi. *Yoga-sutra of Patanjali.* Calcutta: Susil Gupta, 1960.

Bangali Baba. *The Yogasūtra of Patañjali with the Commentary of Vyāsa.* Delhi: Motilal Banarsidass, 1982.

Codd, Clara. *Introduction to Patanjali's Yoga.* Adyar: Theosophical Publishing House, 1966.

Desikachar, T.K.V. *The Heart of Yoga.* Rochester, Vermont: Inner Traditions International, 1995.

Govindan, Marshall. *Kriya Yoga Sūtras of Patañjali and the Siddhas.* Quebec: Kriya Yoga Publications, 2000.

Hariharananda Aranya, Swami. *Yoga Philosophy of Patanjali.* Albany: State University of New York Press, 1983.

Hewitt, James. *The Complete Yoga Book.* London: Rider, 1983.

Iyengar, B.K.S. *Light on the Yoga Sūtras of Patañjali; Patañjala Yoga Padīpikā.* San Francisco: Aquarian/Thorsons (HarperCollins), 1993.

Johnston, Charles. *The Yoga Sutras of Patanjali.* London: John M. Watkins, 1964.

Judge, William Q. *The Yoga Aphorisms of Patanjali.* Los Angeles: United Lodge of Theosophists, 1920.

Mishra, Ramamurti S. (Shri Brahmananda Sarasvati). *The Textbook of Yoga Psychology.* Monroe, New York: Baba Bhagavandas Publication Trust, 1963.

Prasada, Rama. *The Yoga Sutras of Patanjali with the Commentary of Vyasa and the Gloss of Vachaspati Misha from the Sacred Books of the Hindus, Vol. 4.* Allahbad: Sudhindranath Vasu, 1924.

Rajneesh, Bhagwan Shree. *Yoga: The Alpha and the Omega, Vols. 1-10.* Poona: Rajneesh Foundation, 1977.

Shearer, Alistair. *The Yoga Sutras of Patanjali.* New York: Bell Tower, 1982.

Tola, Fernando and Carmen Dragonetti. *The Yogasutras of Patanjali on the Concentration of the Mind.* Delhi: Motilal Banarsidass, 1987.

Veda Bhāratī, Swāmī. *Yoga-sūtras of Patañjali with the Exposition of Vyāsa; Vol. II, Sādhana-pāda.* Delhi: Motilal Banarsidass, 2001.

Woods, James Houton. *The Yoga System of Patanjali.* Harvard Oriental Series, vol. 17. Cambridge: Harvard University Press, 1914.

Zambito, Salvatore. *ThePath of the Final Liberation.* Yoga-Sutras Institute Press: Poulsbo, Washington, 1999.

ṢAD DARŚANA REFERENCES

Bernard, Theos. *Hindu Philosophy.* New York: Philosophical Library, 1947.

Muller, Max. *The Six Systems of Indian Philosophy.* London: Longmans, Green & Co., 1928.

Rajneesh, Bhagwan Shree. *Vedanta: Seven Steps to Samadhi.* Poona: 1976.

Prabhavanada, Swami with Fredrick Manchester. *The Spiritual Heritage of India.* Hollywood, California: Vedanta Press, 1969.

Radhakrishna, S. and Charles Moore. *A Sourcebook in Indian Philosophy.* Princeton, New Jersey: Princeton University Press, 1973.

Rama, Swami. *Lectures on Yoga.* Honesdale, Pennsylvania: Himalayan International Institute, 1979.

SANSKRIT, LINGUISTICS, SEMITIC AND INDO-EUROPEAN LANGUAGES

Allman, William F. *The Mother Tongue.* "U.S. News and World Report", pages 60-70; Nov. 5, 1991.

Ayalon, Ami. *Language and Change in the Arab Middle East–The Evolution of Modern Political Discourse.* New York, Oxford: Oxford University Press, 1987.

Beeston, A.F.L. *The Arabic Language Today.* London: Hutchinson University Library, 1978 .

Bohm, David. *Wholeness and the Implicit Order.* London, Boston: Ark Books/Routledge, Kegan Paul, 1985.

Kale, M.R. *A Higher Sanskrit Grammar.* Delhi: Motilal Banarsidass, 1977.

Korzybski, Alfred. *Science and Sanity.* Lakeville, Connecticut: International Non-Aristotelian Publishing Co., 1980.

Language in Culture: Conference on the Interrelations of Language and Other Aspects of Culture. (ed. Harry Hoijer). Chicago: University of Chicago Press, 1954.

Macdonell, Arthur A. *A Sanskrit Grammar for Students.* London: Oxford University Press, 1927.

Ross, Philip E. *Hard Words.* "Scientific American", Vol. 264, No. 4, pgs. 138-147; April, 1991.

Russell, Bertrand. Introduction, *Tractus Logico-Philosophicus* by Lugwig Wittgenstein. New York: Harcourt, Brace, 1922.

Sapir, Edward. *Conceptual Categories in Primitive Languages.* Science 74:578, 1931.

Sapir, Edward. Selected Writings in *Language, Culture and Personality.* (ed. David Mandelbaum). Berkeley: University of California Press, 1949.

Shapiro, Michael C. *A Primer of Modern Standard Hindi.* Delhi: Motilal Banarsidass, 1989.

Staal, J.F. (Ed.). *A Reader in the Sanskrit Grammarians.* Cambridge: The MIT Press, 1972.

Whorf, Benjamin L. *Collected Papers on Metalinguistics.* Washington, D.C.: Dept. of State; Foreign Service Institute, 1952.

Wickens, G.M. *Arabic Grammar, A First Workbook.* Cambridge: Cambridge University Press, 1979.

Zograph, G.A. *Languages of South Asia*, vol. 3. (G.L. Campbell, trans.). London: Routledge & Kegan Paul, 1982.

RELATED SOURCES

Arya, Pandit Usharbudh. *God.* Honesdale, Pennsylvania: Himalayan International Institute, 1979.

Ibid. *Mantra and Meditation.* Honesdale, Pennsylvania: Himalayan International Institute, 1979.

Ibid. *Meditation and the Art of Dying*. Honesdale, Pennsylvania: Himalayan International Institute, 1979.

Ibid. *Superconscious Meditation*. Honesdale, Pennsylvania: Himalayan International Institute, 1979.

Bailey Alice A. *The Unfinished Autobiography*. New York: Lucis Publishing Co., 1987.

Isherwood, Christopher. *My Guru and His Disciple*. New York: Farrar, Straus, Giroux, 1980.

Jouveau-Dubreuil, G. *Iconography of Southern India*. Paris: 1937.

Osho. *The Book of Secrets*. 5 Vols. reprinted. NewYork: St. Martins Press, 1997.

Ibid. . *Meditation, The First and Last Freedom*. reprinted. New York: St. Martins Press, 2004.

Prabhavananda, Swami. *The Eternal Companion: The Life and Teachings of SwamiBrahmananda*. Hollywood: Vedanta Press, 1947.

Rama, Swami. *Living with the Himalayan Masters*. Honesdale, Pennsylvania: Himalayan International Institute, 1978.

Ibid. with Rudolph Ballentine, M.D. and Swami Ajaya (Ph.D). *Yoga and Psychotherapy*. Honesdale, Pennsylvania: Himalayan International Institute, 1976.

Rajneesh, Bhagwan Shree. *Glimpses of a Golden Childhood*. Rajneeshpuram, Oregon: Rajneesh Foundation International, 1985.

Ibid. *Meditation: The Art of Ecstasy*. Poona: Rajneesh Foundation, 1976.

Ibid. *The Sound of Running Water*. Poona: Rajneesh Foundation, 1978.

Tejasananda, Swami. *A Short Life of Ramakrishna*. Calcutta: Advaita Ashrama, 1984.